THE WINTER OLYMPICS

The 2002 Winter Olympics Lecture Series was made possible by generous support from the following organizations:

Obert C. and Grace A. Tanner Humanities Center
George S. and Delores Doré Eccles Foundation
The Utah Humanities Council
The Lawrence T. and Janet T. Dee Foundation
The Office of the University of Utah Vice President for Research
The Office of the University of Utah Vice President for Diversity
The University of Utah Office of Undergraduate Studies
    (for David C. Young's visit and associated curricular activities
    as McMurrin Professor)
The University of Utah College of Humanities
The University of Utah Department of History
The University of Utah Gender Studies Program
The University of Utah College of Health
The *Salt Lake Tribune*

THE
WINTER
OLYMPICS

From Chamonix to Salt Lake City

Edited by Larry R. Gerlach

The University of Utah Press

Salt Lake City

The Defiance House Man colophon is a registered trademark of the
University of Utah Press. It is based upon a four-foot-tall, Ancient
Puebloan pictograph (late PIII) near Glen Canyon.

09 08 07 06 05 04
5   4   3   2   1

Library of Congress Cataloging-in-Publication Data

The Winter Olympics : from Chamonix to Salt Lake City / edited by
    Larry R. Gerlach.
      p.   cm.
    ISBN 0-87480-778-6 (hardcover : alk. paper)
    1. Winter Olympics—History.   2. Winter Olympics—Political
aspects.   I. Gerlach, Larry R.
    GV841.5.W55   2004
    769.98—dc22   2003022620

CONTENTS

INTRODUCTION

Larry R. Gerlach

"Here within our grasp lies Utah's hope for future recognition as the nation's most outstanding center for winter sports. Salt Lake City could become a byword in the world, and a source of wealth yet untouched." So wrote Marthinius Strand in February 1937, enthused by the U.S. Olympic ski-jumping team trials held in March 1936 at Ecker Hill in Parley's Canyon just east of Salt Lake City.[1] Strand, who helped inaugurate ski jumping in the Beehive State in 1916, was not thinking of the Olympic Winter Games but of competitive skiing and ski jumping. He was right: Ecker Hill (near what would become the site of the 2002 Olympic ski-jumping venue) and the surrounding mountains were the scene of numerous regional and national ski championships from the early 1930s until the late 1940s, with a brief interruption during World War II.[2] With the expansion of Alpine skiing after the war, Utahns made frequent appearances as Olympic competitors. The 1948 U.S. Olympic ski team—which was composed mostly of Utahns, including Dev Jennings, Jack Reddish, Dick Movitz, Suzy Harris Rytting, and coach Alf Engen—did much to publicize the state's burgeoning ski industry.

I

Notwithstanding speculation in 1928 about the possibility of hosting the 1932 Winter Games,[3] Utahns did not think seriously about hosting the Olympics until 1965. Inspired by Squaw Valley's hosting of the 1960 Winter Olympics, Governor Calvin Rampton formed a seven-man Olympic Committee composed of representatives of the Utah ski industry and old-line merchants. Over the next thirty years a series of bid attempts came to naught. In 1966 Salt Lake was chosen as the U.S. candidate city to vie for the 1972 Games but finished tied for last with Lahti, Finland (seven votes), as the Games went to Sapporo, Japan. Salt Lake subsequently failed to become America's representative in 1967 and again in 1972, when Denver withdrew as host of the 1976 Winter Olympics after voters defeated a referendum authorizing public funding for the Games, which ultimately went to Innsbruck, Austria. Bested again in 1985 (this time by Anchorage, Alaska), in efforts to become the American entry in the 1992 Olympic sweepstakes won by Albertville, France, Salt Lake organizers launched a determined effort to secure the Games. The Utah capital was designated the U.S. entry for the 1998 Games; and a strong finish in 1991 as runner-up to Nagano, Japan, which won by four votes in the fourth round (46–42), ensured that Salt Lake would be the leading candidate for the 2002 Games.

Utah's Olympic quest came to an end on June 15, 1995, when the 104th Session of the International Olympic Committee (IOC) meeting in Budapest, Hungary, voted 55–14 on the first ballot to award the 2002 Winter Games to Salt Lake City. Utahns, whose license plates once boasted and whose ski industry promotions still boast "The Greatest Snow on Earth," would in February 2002 host the Greatest Snow and Ice Show on Earth—the XIXth Olympic Winter Games.[4] The 2002 Olympic Winter Games were destined to be an extravaganza of global proportions, a ritual of cultural communication as well as a commercialized sports and entertainment spectacle. The Winter Games had not always enjoyed such favor or prominence.

The Winter Olympics, dating retroactively to 1924 but not officially part of the Olympic program until 1928, have had an uneasy history. For the first half-century controversies raged continually over whether the commercialism and professionalism in skiing, ice skating, and hockey were compatible with the Olympic ideal of amateurism and even whether winter sports, traditionally restricted geographically to Northern Hemisphere nations, should continue to be part of the Olympic program of international sport. Powerful voices argued against first the addition and then the continuation of the Winter Games. Baron Pierre de Coubertin, founder of the Modern Olympics, was fond of snow and ice sports, viewing them as "among the purest" in their "sporting dignity," but was uneasy about their inclusion in the Olympics, partly because they were essentially confined to Western Europe, Scandinavia, and North America and partly because the commercial nature of skiing was contrary to the Olympics amateur ideal. But the growing popularity of snow and ice sports made their inclusion inevitable. In 1925 the IOC Congress meeting in Prague officially sanctioned the Olympic Winter Games, as they are properly called, and retroactively designated the International Winter Sports Week held in Chamonix, France, in 1924 as the first Winter Olympics.

For the first fifty years, the Winter Games were the source of frequent and bitter controversy. Avery Brundage of the United States, president of the IOC from 1952 to 1972, was an outspoken critic of what he called the "Frostbite Follies" and railed against the inherent commercialism and professionalism of skiing, particularly Alpine skiing, which was fully introduced into the Olympics in 1948. Opposition to the Winter Olympics was so great that the IOC Executive Board in 1964 considered eliminating the Games but eventually voted to continue them only through 1972. Anticipating that Colorado voters in 1972 would reject public funding for the Games, Brundage told the IOC delegates in his farewell address that he hoped "the Winter Olympics receive a decent burial in Denver" and later declared: "This poisonous cancer must be eliminated without further delay."[5] But the growing popularity of snow and ice sports coupled with growing revenue streams from television and corporate sponsors ensured not only continuation of the Games but also expansion of the Winter Olympics program. In 1924 in Chamonix 294 athletes competed in 14 events in 5 sports; in 1972, the year of Brundage's retirement, 1,232 athletes participated in 39 events in 8 sports in Sarajevo; thirty years later, in Salt Lake City, 2,654 participants competed in 78 events in 15 sports.

Controversy aside, hosting the Winter Games has been far more problematic than hosting the Summer Olympics despite involving fewer participants and venues. Winter host cities, typically small mountain resort towns, invariably faced special problems of finance, facilities, transportation, housing, and especially weather. Unlike the Summer Games, Winter venues are mostly outdoors, where wind, temperature, and the amount of snow affect competitions. Until the 1980 the Winter Olympics also suffered from widespread inattention. Press and public alike focused on the Summer Games, which were invariably held in well-known urban areas and featured sports that were both more numerous and more universal than the geographically restricted snow and ice contests. Thus Leni Riefenstahl's famous documentary film of the 1936 Games, *Olympia,* included only the Berlin Summer Games, ignoring the Winter Olympics held six months earlier at Garmisch-Partenkirchen.[6]

No Winter Olympics involved a more difficult labor than the Salt Lake 2002 Games. In addition to the usual logistical preparations and early budgetary concerns, the Salt Lake Organizing Committee (SLOC) faced a public relations and administrative crisis following the disclosure in November 1998 that SLOC executives Tom Welch and Dave Johnson had provided a variety of favors to at least two dozen IOC members, presumably in exchange for support of the committee's 2002 bid attempt. The resultant bid scandal set off a flurry of international criticism and formal investigations by SLOC, the IOC, the United States Olympic Committee, and the U.S. Justice Department. SLOC subsequently underwent administrative restructuring in February 2000 under new chief executive officer Mitt Romney, a Massachusetts businessman, while the IOC expelled six members, accepted four preemptory resignations, and reprimanded nine others.[7]

In July 2000 Welch and Johnson were charged with fifteen felony counts of conspiracy, fraud, and racketeering. A year later U.S. District Court Judge David Sam dismissed the charges as not legally actionable.[8]

Just as the bid scandal began to recede from public memory, terrorist attacks on September 11, 2001, that destroyed the World Trade Center in New York City and damaged the Pentagon outside Washington, D.C., followed by anthrax exposure via the U.S. Postal Service, altered both the philosophical and practical preparations for the Games. Amid widespread concerns about safety and even talk of cancellation, SLOC, assisted by the federal government, undertook the most extensive and costly security preparations in Olympic history. Given the global exposure of the Olympics, officials were also concerned about the possibility of violent protest demonstrations such as those that disrupted the 1999 World Trade Organization meetings in Seattle, Washington. Ultimately, Salt Lake's security more than doubled the security at Atlanta's 1996 Summer Games: the original 5,500-member security force was increased to more than 15,000 military and civilian law enforcement personnel, at a cost of $300 million.

Despite the unusual circumstances and concerns, Salt Lake 2002 was a resounding success. There were no problems of security, transportation, housing, or weather. Salt Lake's was the largest Winter Games in history in terms of the number of events (78), sports (15), and participants (2,654).[9] It was the most diverse Winter Games in terms of both the number of nations (77) and the participation and success of minority athletes. SLOC was also the first local organizing committee to produced a sizable profit, reportedly upward of $100 million. (For a survey of the Salt Lake Games, see Chapter 11.)

II

The Olympic Games, like other sporting events, are not staged simply, or even primarily, for the sake of athletic competition. The ancient Greek Olympics were part of quadrennial religious celebration held in Olympia to honor Zeus, while the modern Games were founded as an athletic festival invested with political and educational purpose. Baron de Coubertin envisioned the Games as a celebration of the mind as well as the body, of the spirit as well as sport, and thus insisted that cultural activities be held in conjunction with the athletic contests.

It was appropriate, therefore, that the University of Utah, site of the Olympic Village as well as the Opening and Closing Ceremonies, should host a scholarly lecture series on the Winter Olympics prior to the staging of the Salt Lake 2002 Games. The lectures, presented from August 2001 to January 2002, provided the campus and the larger community with the views of outstanding scholars on various Winter Olympics issues and activities that greater Salt Lake City would experience in February 2002. After all, every Winter Olympics is both a unique experience and an expression of common issues and historical trends.

The topics assigned were intentionally broad to allow lecturers maximum flexibility in treating fundamental issues. No doubt some readers will regret the absence of certain subjects (say, doping or security), but we hope that all will concur with those that are included. While the lectures focus on the Winter Games, they also speak to matters directly relevant to the Summer Olympiads and the global Olympic Movement. It is fitting that most of the lecturers were from outside the United States, given the international nature of the Olympic Games. It was also appropriate that the lecturers and their presentations represented a variety of academic fields—classics, communication, history, physical education, and sociology—just as the Games themselves embody different sport disciplines. The essays vary in format according to the stylistic preferences of the disciplines. Repetition is inevitable, given the common focus on the Olympics, although overlapping discussions usually offer varying perspectives and analyses.

The Winter Olympics exhibited first and with greater clarity many of the historical and contemporary issues confronting the Olympic Movement, yet scholars have focused on the Summer Olympiads because of their larger size, broader scope, and more widely known sports.[10] The neglect of the Winter Games is stark: compilations of statistical results and commemorative books on individual games are valuable, but there is still no general history and only a handful of scholarly articles on the Winter Olympics.[11] This anthology does not purport to be a formal history, but by offering historical surveys of major themes, we hope that it will serve as a historical introduction to the development of the Winter Olympics and some of the current issues facing the Games.

The chapters of this anthology appear in the order in which the lectures were given, except for the chapter by Roland Renson. His lecture, intended to be the second presentation, was scheduled for September 13, 2001, but the events two days earlier necessitated postponement until January 2002. As a historical overview to provide background for the subsequent lectures, Renson's presentation appears here in its intended sequence. Some essays appear as they were presented as lectures, either as written or in slightly expanded or condensed form; others are modest revisions that are faithful in tone and content to the oral presentations. The final two chapters were not part of the lecture series but provide a postscript to the lectures by exploring aspects of the Salt Lake Winter Olympics.

III

The idea of the Modern Olympics was not an immaculate conception. Pierre de Coubertin, like all aristocratic Frenchmen, had studied the classics (including Pindar) and was especially interested in German archaeological reports on the excavation of Olympia. He also knew about Olympic-type contests in England and the Greek revivalist Games that were the spiritual precursors of the Modern Olympics. Concerned by the militarism of the late nineteenth century, Coubertin envisioned athletic competitions as a means to promote both the physical fitness of young men and international understanding and ultimately peace.

David Young, premier historian of the ancient Olympics, who was also the University of Utah's Sterling M. McMurrin Distinguished Visiting Professor, 2001–2002, inaugurated the Winter Olympics lecture series by discussing "The Roots of the Modern Olympic Games." He suggests some broad historical connections between the ancient and modern Games and examines the specific nineteenth-century antecedents of the Modern Olympics through the contributions of the Greek poet Panagiotis Soustous, the expatriate Greek merchant Evangelis Zappas, Dr. William Penny Brookes of Much Wenlock, England, and, of course, Baron de Coubertin. In so doing, Young sets the stage for the lectures to come by providing a sense of continuity and continuum for the Olympics of Coubertin. Young's metaphoric use of a tree that Coubertin planted at the request of Brookes in the Wenlock Olympic field in 1890 to represent both the roots and the subsequent growth of the modern Games is apposite indeed.

Coubertin participated in and enjoyed winter sports for both sporting and philosophical reasons, but he did not initially envision their inclusion in the Modern Olympics. His reasoning was historical and philosophical. Since snow and ice sports were not part of the ancient Olympics, their inclusion in the modern Games seemed anachronistic. And because for the first quarter of the twentieth century skating and Nordic skiing (i.e., cross-country and ski jumping) were largely confined to Western Europe, Scandinavia, and North America, winter sports did not further the Olympic ideal of widespread geographical inclusion in the Games. Most importantly, Coubertin and his successors feared that the commercialism and professionalism seemingly endemic to skiing and skating would eventually undermine the Olympic core principle of amateurism. Fraught with controversy over amateurism and historically regarded until recently as the unwanted "stepchild" of the Olympics, the Winter Games, always scheduled for February, none-theless have experienced remarkable growth during the past three-quarters of a century. Figure skating, the oldest Winter Olympic sport, was contested for the first time in London in 1908 and again in Antwerp in 1920. In 1924 in Chamonix, France, 16 countries sent 294 athletes to compete in 14 events in 5 sports (designated *post factum* the first Winter Olympics), compared with 2,654 athletes from 77 countries who competed in 78 events in 15 sports during the 2002 Salt Lake Games.

Roland Renson's "The Cool Games: The Winter Olympics, 1924–2002" provides a chronological overview of this sporting epic on snow and ice. His concluding remarks about the "logo-ization" of the Olympics prompt sobering thoughts about the initial idealism of the Games and contempo-rary commercial imperatives. While Renson discusses major issues confronting the Winter Games, the focus of the essay is not on politics, economics, and like matters but on athletes. Renson appreciates that it is the athletes and their athletic performances that first spark our interest in sport and then sustain it. Summer Olympics athletes are more widely and better known than their Winter counterparts, so Renson is careful to give due to the remarkable achievements of those who competed on snow and ice. Com-plementing the more theme-oriented contributions, Renson's essay places the athlete at the forefront of the Winter Olympics story.

If Coubertin was uneasy about winter sports, he was unalterably opposed to women participating in the Olympics. Accepting the prevalent medical beliefs about the physical, physiological, and psychological unsuitability of women for competitive athletics as well as class notions of idealized feminine and ladylike behavior, Coubertin argued that "the Olympic Games must be reserved for men." He refused to alter his stance even after women were officially included in the Olympic program in 1912, contending that com-petitions for women were not "in keeping with my concept of the Olympic Games" and were "impractical, uninteresting, ungainly, and, I do not hesi-tate to add, improper."[12] Coubertin's opposition to female Olympians was so great that his *Mémoires* (1931) contain no mention of women and the Olym-pics. And when women were officially added to the Winter Olympic program in 1928, they competed in only two sports, figure skating and pairs skating.

Despite progress as Olympians, women battled prejudicial attitudes long after Coubertin passed. Utahn Suzy Harris Rytting confronted gender bias as a member of the 1952 U.S. Olympic ski team. Upon arriving in Oslo, Norway, she sought treatment for the flu, whereupon it was discovered that she was two weeks pregnant. Although doctors certified her ability to compete, she was not only dismissed from the team and sent home but also, adding insult to injury, required to return her team jacket.[13] It was not until the 1960s and 1970s that girls and women entered the world of sports en masse, thereby shattering long-held beliefs about female physical capabilities as well as traditional cultural beliefs and gender stereotypes.

Nonetheless, the Salt Lake Games revealed that gender equity is still a work in progress. Traditions die hard: during the competitions the term "ladies'" was used to introduce women's events (e.g., Ladies' Downhill), whereas "men's" not "gentlemen's" designated competition of the opposite sex. And women hockey players, but not men, were required to wear face shields. Women competed in just 37 events (47 percent of the total); and while they competed in the skeleton and two-woman bobsleigh for the first time, they were still excluded from ski jumping, the two-man luge, the four-man bobsled, and the Nordic combined competitions. The future, however, was manifest in two preadolescent girls from Calgary, Alberta, Canada, who walked around the Utah Olympic Park ski-jumping venue with a hand-made sign that read: "We want to jump too."[14]

Local organizing committees continue to have better gender representation than the IOC itself. The SLOC Employee Diversity Report for October 22, 2001, shows that women represented 44.3 percent of all employees, 37 percent of managers, and 22.5 percent of directors and above. There were only 12 women among 123 IOC members in 2002, however, illustrating male dominance at the highest levels of decision-making; and only 2 of the 82 National Olympic Committee nominees for the open IOC slots that year were women, which underscores the point.

Kari Fasting's "The Gendering of the Winter Olympic Games" illustrates the ways in which the Winter Olympic Games, and by extension the Olympic Movement, have been and still are gendered in relation to both the types of events available to women and the number of female athletes and administrators. Fasting's theoretical discussion of gender as a social construct provides an important perspective for the discussion of how women athletes have shaped popular notions about certain sports and their participants, just as her examination of the media portrayal of women athletes contributes to our understanding of the perpetuation of gender stereotypes.

The Olympic Winter Games were not only a late addition to the Olympic program but since their appearance in 1924 have been geographically far more exclusive than the Summer Olympics. Of the nineteen Winter Games to date, twelve (63 percent) have been held in Europe, five in North America (Lake Placid 1932 and 1980, Squaw Valley 1960, Calgary 1988, and Salt Lake 2002) and two in Asia, both in Japan (Sapporo 1972 and Nagano 1998). The two Winter Games canceled by World War II were scheduled for European sites: Garmisch-Partenkirchen, Germany, in 1940 and Cortina d'Ampezzo, Italy, in 1944.

Since the Winter Olympics are usually held in upscale mountain resorts instead of major metropolitan areas like the Summer Games, they face unusual challenges related to transportation, housing and competition facilities, and weather. Salt Lake City was unique in this regard, being by far the largest city ever to host the Winter Games and also being situated in close proximity to ski venues. To aid preparations for the 2002 Games, officials from SLOC, the state of Utah, Salt Lake City, and the University of Utah made frequent visits to Calgary, the Olympic city most comparable to Salt Lake in size and climate as well as the most recent North American host of the Winter Games.

Because Winter Olympics are not staged *in vacuo,* Kevin Wamsley's "Miracles, Modernization, Debt, and Even Disney on Ice and Snow: The North American Contribution to the Olympic Cultural Topography" provides historical background and context for the Salt Lake Games. His comparative survey of the pre-2002 North American Games examines the second-class status accorded the winter festival, the difficulties of hosting with respect to cost and logistics, the unpredictability of weather, and the creation of local and national identities. As Wamsley's essay demonstrates, some of the particulars of the North American Olympics are specific to the individual community, but many considerations are generally applicable to all hosts of the Winter Games.

Amateurism was the cardinal principle that initially undergirded the Modern Olympics. More than a upper-class ploy to create a separate sphere of sporting activity, amateurism was seen by Coubertin and the other aristocrats who founded the Games as essential to realize the ancillary principles of fair play, sportsmanship, and participation for its own sake as essential to honorable athletic competition. As Coubertin feared and his successors experienced, the debate over amateurism raged first and foremost in the Winter Olympics, as ice hockey, skating, and skiing were riddled with commercialism and professionalism. Over the years concerns shifted from the amateur status of athletes to the influence of commercial entities by the 1980s, as evidenced by the ubiquitous television cameras and Coca-Cola logos at Salt Lake 2002. Moreover, Olympic amateurism was challenged by the dictates of democracy, problems of definition, and difficulties of enforceability of Olympic amateur rules.

In "When Amateurism Mattered: Class, Moral Entrepreneurship, and the Winter Olympics," Richard Gruneau examines the emergence of amateurism as a sporting principle, its idealized role and inherent contradictions within the modern Olympic Movement, and how the Winter Olympics hastened its demise as a guiding principle and promoted its current use as a commercial marketing device. IOC president Avery Brundage loathed the

Winter Games for their assault on traditional amateurism principles; his (in)famous expulsion of Austrian skier Karl Schranz the day before the opening of the 1972 Sapporo Olympics was both a case study and a turning point in the amateurism-commercialism struggle. The Games could not withstand the changing socioeconomic realities of society, including the growing commercialization and thus professionalization of sport. Although the Olympics are now unabashedly commercialized and professionalized, they continue to be less self-consciously so than other major sporting events (for example, the exclusion of advertising from venues).

Given the extraordinary sums of money generated by and spent on the Olympics, it is hard to appreciate that until the 1960s the International Olympic Committee faced chronic indebtedness and that the Games themselves had little commercial value. That changed with the onset of satellite television in the 1960s, which in turn created worldwide Olympic exposure and led to the development of strategic sponsorship and marketing programs by the IOC as well as the local organizing committees. The Salt Lake Games were the most expensive in Winter Olympic history. SLOC's $1.3 billion budget, based primarily on corporate sponsorships and $545 million in National Broadcasting Company (NBC) television rights fees, grew to $1.91 billion with additional federal appropriations for security after September 11, 2001.

Stephen R. Wenn's "Television, Corporate Sponsorship, and the Winter Olympics" details the rise of Olympic commercialism from the perspective of the Winter Games and the Olympic Movement generally. Here is the story of the commodification of the Olympics through the IOC's television rights negotiations and contracts with corporate sponsors. As Wenn demonstrates, the IOC's decision to go for the gold, eventually staging separate biennial Games, produced unimagined revenue in addition to unforeseen problems such as conflicts between the IOC and national and local Olympic committees and International Sports Federations over the distribution of funds. Advanced knowledge of guaranteed television revenues also produced heightened competition among a growing number of potential host cities, which in turn encouraged abuses such as those involved in the Salt Lake bid scandal.

Given global television exposure—more than 3 billion people watched the Sydney and Salt Lake Games—the Olympics afford an excellent opportunity to sell a variety of items. Just as corporate advertisers market goods and services, host cities and countries use the Games to promote political ideologies, economic potential, tourism, recreational opportunities, and local culture, including religion. The Utah ski industry, with its numerous resorts and famous powder snow, and tourism, featuring the geologic features of southern Utah, were positioned as the major secular beneficiaries of Salt Lake 2002 promotional efforts. Because approximately 70 percent of Utahns are members of the Church of Jesus Christ of Latter-day Saints (LDS), the church played a major role in planning, subsidizing, and staging the Games. As a result, Salt Lake 2002 was informally dubbed the "Mormon Olympics." While the LDS church maintained a low-profile during the Olympics, the marked success of the Games favorably promoted the state and its dominant religion.

In "Visions and Versions of American Culture at the Winter Games," Mark Dyreson explores how the Winter Olympics have been used as "branding events" to reflect and affect basic American cultural values, to reinforce local and national identities, and to enhance personal and institutional agendas. Although the focus is on the first four Winter Games, from Chamonix in 1924 to Garmisch-Partenkirchen in 1936, the basic concepts are applicable to subsequent Winter Olympics. Indeed, Dyreson notes striking similarities between local issues of concern in the first four Winter Games and Salt Lake 2002.

It is said that in the end everything is political, and this assuredly has been the case with the Olympic Games. They have always been political—by design. The modern Games were created with an avowed political purpose: international understanding leading to world peace, athletes representing countries instead of themselves, awards ceremonies featuring nationalistic symbols (anthems and flags), a bid process pitting cities from various countries against each other, and an administrative structure built on national and international sports organizations, ensuring that politics and nationalism would be conspicuous in the Olympic Movement. Coubertin hoped that such things would promote international brotherhood, whereas the effect has been to accentuate chauvinism and national rivalry.

Jeffrey Segrave's "Toward a Cosmopolitics of the Winter Olympic Games" offers a nontraditional approach to understanding Olympic political issues. After examining the international, national, and domestic politics of the Winter Olympics, he proposes a new way of thinking about the Olympics by placing the politics of the Games in a wider theoretical perspective that explores a still-evolving change in emphasis from the politics of nation-building and ideology to the politics of consumption and commercialism. The Winter Games, he suggests, afford a new way of theorizing politics—a cosmopolitics shaped by globalism and conducive to a new form of cosmopolitanism.

The Olympics are not just a commercialized, professionalized sports entertainment of global proportions. If they were only this, the Games—the Super Bowl of international sport—would not command such respect from both athletes and a worldwide audience. It was Pierre de Coubertin's genius to invest an athletic festival with social, educational, and political purpose—the multifaceted philosophy known as Olympism—and envelop the Games with symbols and slogans, creeds and oaths, rituals and ceremonies that are both cultural signifiers and the cornerstones of tradition.

While rhetoric increasingly clashed with reality and principle eventually gave way to principal, the notion that the Olympics are uniquely about sport and more persists in large measure because of rituals and traditions. The torch relay, the only Olympic activity to occur outside the framework of the Games, is now largely a commercially contrived event. The Salt Lake experience, however, demonstrated that the passage of the flame continues to have a unique ability to generate unbridled enthusiasm and a sense of involvement in communities across the country and an outpouring of deep-felt emotion and support for the Games from within the host city. And while television coverage of the Olympics is episodically geared to viewer preference, a constant feature of broadcasts is the awards ceremony, which enables viewers to accord the athletes respect, even reverence, as they stand on the podium and receive their medals while the national flags of the three medalists are raised and the national anthem of the gold-medal winner is played.

There were novel aspects to these two events in the Salt Lake Winter Games. First, the torch relay became politically important, as the zigzagging of the flame through forty-eight states, with poignant stops in New York City and at the Pentagon, had a profound unifying and inspirational affect on a nation shaken by the terrorist assault of September 11. Second, in a dramatic break with tradition, medals in outdoor events were awarded not after competitions at the venue but collectively each night in downtown Salt Lake City at the $5 million, 20,000-seat Olympic Medals Plaza, where celebrity musical entertainers, highlight videos, and fireworks turned the victory ceremony into three hours of sights, sounds, and partying.

These two most visible and emotion-charged Olympic rituals are the focus of Robert Barney's "Flame and Fanfare: Victory Award Ceremonies and the Olympic Torch Relay." He explores the origin and symbolic importance of the tiered victory podium (which made its initial Olympic appearance in the Lake Placid Winter Games of 1932) and the evolution and dramatic appeal of the torch relay from Pierre de Coubertin's 1912 rhetorical reference to a historic keeping of the Olympic Flame to a carefully orchestrated carrying of a torch ignited at Olympia, Greece, to the site of the current Olympic Games. As public rituals of celebration and community bonding, the victory ceremony and torch relay have significance far beyond the Olympic Games.

Although the Winter Paralympics are distinctly separate from the Winter Olympics, it seemed appropriate, even necessary, to include them in the lecture series for two reasons. First and foremost, both Winter Games are expressions of the highest levels of elite athletic competitions in snow and ice sports. After all, the Greek term *para* means "alongside" or "beside" or "parallel to," so "Paralympics" literally means to accompany the Olympics. The decision to hold the Paralympics at the same site as the Olympics was made in 1988; Sydney 2000 was the first to follow the IOC mandate that the Paralympics should follow directly after the Olympics.[15] Second, the Salt Lake Winter Paralympics marked the first time the Games were held in North America and the first time a single local organizing committee, SLOC, was in charge of both the Olympics and the Paralympics. The Salt Lake Games illustrated the rapid growth of the Paralympic Movement, as 425 athletes from 36 countries competed in 6 categories in 4 sports.[16] They also demonstrated that the Olympics and Paralympics share athletic highs and lows: Steve Cook of Salt Lake City won four silver medals in cross-country skiing, while Thomas Oelsner of Germany was stripped of two gold medals in the same sport because of doping. Finally, the Salt Lake Games revealed the discrepancy between the athletic achievements of the Paralympians and the public's lack of awareness of sport for the physically disabled. While the Paralympics were televised for the first time, coverage was limited to a single hour of tape-delayed highlights each day on cable television. Press coverage, save for the two Salt Lake City dailies, was abbreviated; some newspapers like *USA Today* completely ignored the competitions.

In "The Winter Paralympics: Past, Present, and Future," Gudrun Doll-Tepper surveys the history of the Winter Paralympics as well as the major issues currently confronting the Paralympic Movement. These issues are strikingly similar to those facing the Olympics, which underscores the commonalities between the two elite, worldwide athletic movements. Because the Paralympic Movement is still evolving and its competition is so specialized, Doll-Tepper offers overviews of the history of sport for the disabled (touching upon such topics as events, classifications, doping, gender, equipment, and governing bodies) and provides biographical sketches of important figures in the history of sport for the disabled.

IV

At the conclusion of the Winter Games in 2002, Dick Ebersol, president of NBC Sports, called the Salt Lake Games "far and away the most successful Olympics, summer or winter, in history."[17] Such lavish praise for the Olympics—applicable as well to the Paralympics—was commonplace.

Salt Lake avoided the problems that normally plagued host cities: the logistical arrangements were flawless, the heightened security ubiquitous but unobtrusive, the transportation efficient, the housing ample, the weather picture perfect, and the Games profitable by some $100 million. Although scarred by the pre-Games bid scandal and figure skating and doping scandals during the Games, Salt Lake 2002 also boasted a series of unique features. It was the most diverse Winter Olympics in history in terms of both the number of Southern Hemisphere nations and athletes that competed and the achievements of ethnic minority athletes. The Salt Lake Games took on a special aura as an expression of international peace and solidarity following September 11, 2001, and because of the role of the Church of Jesus Christ of Latter-day Saints before and during the competitions.[18]

The final two essays in this volume, first printed elsewhere, are retrospective reflections on Salt Lake 2002. Lex Hemphill, who before and during the Olympics wrote feature articles on the Games for the *Salt Lake Tribune,* provides a succinct overview of the Salt Lake Olympics.[19]

V

The lecture series upon which this anthology is based was a collective effort. Bob Barney and Kevin Wamsley, former and current directors respectively of the International Centre for Olympic Studies at the University of Western Ontario, provided encouragement and suggestions when the idea of such an undertaking was aborning. Coming up with ideas for projects is easy; organizing and funding a ten-person international lecture series is not. The Lawrence T. and Janet T. Dee Foundation; the George S. and Delores Doré Eccles Foundation; the Utah Humanities Council; the *Salt Lake Tribune;* and the Office of the Vice President for Research, the Office of Undergraduate Studies, the College of Health, the College of Humanities, the Department of History, the Gender Studies Program, and the Obert C. and Grace A. Tanner Humanities Center of the University of Utah provided the financial support required to underwrite the series. Personally and professionally involved in sport for the disabled, John Dunn, then dean of the College of Health, played a major role in planning and hosting the Paralympics lecture.

The Humanities Center provided not only financial support but also essential administrative support; thus its staff warrants a special tribute. Thanks to director Gene Fitzgerald, whose personal and professional support of the series was invaluable; assistant director Holly Campbell, who enthusiastically embraced the project from the beginning and was a perpetual source of inspiration and encouragement; program assistant Rich Tuttle, who handled publicity and media arrangements with aplomb; administrative assistant Emily Heward, then a full-time student, who handled the financial arrangements; and, especially, Lindsey Law, a senior history major who managed to complete graduation requirements while taking care of all the correspondence, travel arrangements, hotel accommodations, and equipment and facilities scheduling with unfailing efficiency and good cheer. To focus one's time and energy on a short-term project is difficult enough; to sustain that commitment over six months is truly remarkable.

Thanks, too, to Lex Hemphill of the *Salt Lake Tribune* for his exemplary coverage of the lecture series as well as for his historical articles that helped educate the community about the Winter Games. My colleague W. Lindsay Adams, a scholar of ancient history with whom I team-taught a summer Olympics workshop for teachers and a course on the history of the Olympics, spearheaded David Young's McMurrin professorship appointment and was a constant source of encouragement and support. Thanks also to another colleague, sport psychologist Keith Henschen, for his support of the lecture series. Finally, special thanks to my wife, Gail, who put up with all that went on for six months and hosted the receptions for the lectures in our home with customary graciousness.

Notes

1. *Utah* (February 1937).

2. For the history of skiing in Utah, see Alexis Kelner, *Skiing in Utah: A History* (Salt Lake City: Alexis Kelner, 1980); and Alan K. Engen and Gregory C. Thompson, *First Tracks: A Century of Skiing in Utah* (Salt Lake City: Gibbs Smith Publisher, 2001).

3. Murray Hulbert, president of the Amateur Athletic Union (AAU), reportedly told H. C. Mortensen, Intermountain delegate to the AAU, that he was "mightily impressed with the natural advantages" of Utah for winter sports (*Salt Lake Tribune,* February 10, 1928). See also Lex Hemphill, *Salt Lake Tribune,* April 14, 2001.

4. Despite the official title, the Olympic Winter Games feature only snow and ice sports, not sports that take place during the winter months, such as basketball, gymnastics, and volleyball.

5. *New York Times,* February 6, 1973.

6. In establishing the Winter Games, the IOC stipulated that they be held the same year as the Summer Games and, if desired by the host organizing committee, be staged in the same country. Winter and Summer Games were held in the same country only three times—in France in 1924, the United States in 1932,

and Germany in 1936. In 1986 the IOC voted to separate the Winter and Summer Games and hold them biennially; the Winter Games launched the new cycle when Lillehammer, Norway, hosted the 1994 Winter Games just two years after they were held in Albertville, France.

7. Expelled were Lamine Keita of Mali, Agustin Arroyo of Ecuador, Sergio Santander Fantini of Chile, Zein El-Abdin Mohammed Ahmed Abdel Gadir of the Sudan, Jean-Claude Ganga of the Republic of Congo, and Paul Wallwork of Samoa. David Sibandze of Swaziland, Charles Mukora of Kenya, Bashir Mohammed Attarabulsi of Libya, and Pirjo Haggman of Finland resigned. Haggman was not implicated in any questionable behavior but resigned because of the involvement of her husband.

8. For context, see Douglas Booth, "Gifts of Corruption?: Ambiguities of Obligation in the Olympic Movement," *Olympika: The International Journal of Olympic Studies* 8 (1999): 43–68.

9. The seventy-eight events, ten more than at Nagano, represented the second largest increase in Olympic history. The largest expansion was in Albertville in 1992, an increase of eleven over Calgary in 1988, from forty-six to fifty-seven.

10. Some 10,651 athletes from 199 countries competed in 300 events in Sydney 2000, compared to 2,654 athletes from 77 countries competing in 78 events in Salt Lake 2002.

11. The following works are the most serviceable sources for information on the Winter Games. John E. Findling and Kimberly D. Pelle (eds.), *Historical Dictionary of the Modern Olympic Movement* (Westport, Conn.: Greenwood Press, 1996), offers succinct surveys of each of the Winter and Summer Olympic Games. The basic statistical record book is David Wallechinsky, *The Complete Book of the Winter Olympics* (Woodstock and New York: Overlook Press, 2001). Ian Buchanan and Bill Mallon, *Historical Dictionary of the Olympic Movement* (2nd ed., Lanham, Md.: Scarecrow Press, 2001), contains brief overviews of the Games as well as commentary on Olympic terminology and personalities.

12. Coubertin, "Women at the Olympics," *Revue Olympique* (July 1912): 109–111, reprinted in W. Lindsay Adams and Larry R. Gerlach, *The Olympic Games: Ancient and Modern* (Boston: Pearson, 2002), pp. 117–118.

13. Suzanne Harris Rytting Papers, Special Collections, Marriott Library, University of Utah.

14. Despite the growing number of ski-jumping contests for women, the IOC continues the ban in the event.

15. The first international competition for disabled athletes, the International Wheelchair Games, was held in England in 1948 at the same time as the London Summer Olympics.

16. Paralympians compete in Alpine Skiing, Nordic Skiing, Ice-Sled Hockey, and Short-Track Racing. They are divided into disability categories: Amputee, Cerebral Palsy, Visually Impaired, Spinal Chord Injuries (wheelchair), and Les Autres (the others). Because of cheating scandals in Sydney, in 2002 the competition for athletes with intellectual disabilities was not held in Salt Lake.

17. *Deseret News,* February 27, 2002.

18. On February 1, 2003, the LDS *Church News* editorialized on the impact of the Olympics: "This month will mark the one-year anniversary of the Salt Lake Winter Olympics—a marvelously successful event that did much for missionary work and the Church's image even though no one did any official proselytizing. . . . This was an example of one type of effective missionary work—teaching through silently living the gospel."

19. Hemphill's essay, reprinted with permission of Greenwood Publishing Group, Inc., Westport, Conn., originally appeared in John E. Findling and Kimberly D. Pelle (eds.), *Historical Dictionary of the Modern Olympic Movement* (2nd ed., Praeger Publishing, 2003).

1

THE ROOTS OF THE MODERN
OLYMPIC GAMES

David C. Young

The last time I was here in Salt Lake City was in 1990. I came to talk about the ancient Games, and the idea to have the modern Games here was still small, still a slim hope, just the seed of an idea. Now look what that has grown into![1] It has branched out into large, magnificent sport facilities all over this region, and around the globe there are athletes training in all kinds of specialties, their minds riveted here. And the whole world will be watching. For years people have asked me, "Today's Olympics are really different from those of ancient Greece, aren't they? Ours are pretty degenerate, right? The ancient ones were a lot better, weren't they?" Not very many years ago, they deplored the greed of modern athletes, "our corrupt money-grubbers" pretending to be amateurs, versus the supposedly pure amateurism of the Greeks.[2] But ancient amateurism proved to be a myth, even a giant hoax concocted by nineteenth-century men merely to justify their own elitist sport with a fictitious ancient precedent. The one thing that the Greeks did *not* have a word for was "amateur athlete." Today amateurism is all but forgotten, a relic of our own past, and nobody mouths that ridiculous nonsense about ancient Greek amateur athletes anymore.[3] Now they tend to deplore other evils, such as the scheduling of events to accommodate prime-time American television or performance-enhancing drugs.

Perhaps those are major changes; but when I think about the differences between ancient and modern Olympics, what strikes me most is the difference in size, the difference in scope: how really big our Games are now compared to the ancient version, and, as we will see, especially how they dwarf their own meager modern beginnings. At IOC Olympiad XXVII, Sydney 2000, 10,651 athletes from 199 countries competed in 300 events. That is big.

The ancient Greek Olympics had only eight wholly distinct athletic events: four running events, three combative events, and the pentathlon, their all-

18

around competition. Fewer than two hundred athletes would have been accepted for those actual competitions. If we add the equestrian events and divide some athletic events into their men's and boys' divisions, we can increase those numbers. But we will still end up with a maximum of fourteen events and three hundred or so competitors at any point in the golden age of Greek athletics, such as the sixth and fifth centuries B.C. Since the ancient program is not well known, I review it here.

The feature event, the one that started it all, was the 200-meter dash, one length of the long ancient stadium.[4] We have the name of every 200-meter victor, every four years, for a thousand years of Olympics. The second event was the 400 meters, two lengths of the ancient track. Those two, the Olympic 200 and 400, are the two that Michael Johnson won in his fabulous, famous, unprecedented double victory in Atlanta in 1996. I was there in the stadium. It was perhaps the most electrifying sporting moment I myself have ever witnessed. But Johnson was not actually the first man ever to win that Olympic combination, as he and everyone else thought. That same combination was won more than a dozen times in antiquity, perhaps more than a score.[5] The only race longer than the 400 in ancient times was simply named the "long one," probably somewhere between one and two miles. Some 250 years after the Olympics began, a fourth and final running event was added. This was called the "armed race," again 400 meters, but runners wore some armor, a helmet and greaves, and carried a shield. They were still otherwise nude, like all Greek athletes in competition. That was it: no more running events, just those four.[6] Though it was rare, adding events to the program is obviously in the authentic tradition of the games, which apparently began with nothing more than that 200-meter dash and added the other events little by little.

The three combative events were wrestling, boxing, and a brutal combination of the two, called the *pancration*. The most renowned athlete of antiquity was Milo, who reigned as Olympic wrestling champion for at least five Olympiads in the sixth century B.C. Ancient boxing had no rounds. The boxers simply hit each other until one of the two could not go on. There were no weight divisions, so obviously all boxers of Olympic class were heavyweights; and the bouts could be brutal, blood-splattering affairs. The third combat event, *pancration,* literally means "all forms of power," that is, "anything goes." This brutal, no-holds-barred event combined boxing, wrestling, kick boxing, and street fighting, with almost no rules at all. In late antiquity, especially, it was a real crowd-pleaser.

The discus event was symbolic of all ancient Greek athletics, distinctively Greek. And no modern man outside of Greece had ever thrown a discus when the Greeks introduced that event to the rest of the world at the first

IOC Olympiad, Athens 1896. They modeled their discus after some that were found in ancient Olympia. There were only three field events in antiquity: the discus, the javelin, and long jump. These events along with special competitions in the 200 meters and in wrestling were part of the five-event all-around competition, the *pentathlon*. No separate winner was recognized in these events: a single overall winner was declared.

Some other features of this program, besides its small size, may seem odd to us. There were no team games and no ball games in the ancient program. Greeks had such activities but saw them as mere "games." They were not part of the Olympics or other athletic festivals. Athletic competition pitted one individual athlete against all the others, each trying to achieve what the others could not. Pindar, foremost among several poets who celebrated the ancient victors, says that the winning athlete is "distinguished among them"; the verb is literally "separated out" from all the others. The catch-phrase "more important to participate than to win" applies well to the modern Games, and losing athletes sometimes express it in all sincerity. But this saying does not apply to the ancient version of the Games at all. On the contrary, there was no second-place prize or recognition; an athlete either won or lost, and to lose was a disgrace.[7]

Archaeology tends to confirm the Olympic starting date that the Greeks gave, 776 B.C. by our calendar. That is before Homer's *Iliad* was composed. Olympics then took place every four years for more than a millennium, well into the latter days of the Roman Empire, about A.D. 400, as antiquity gave way to the early Middle Ages.[8] Apart from warfare and religion, athletics seem to have been the most universal activity in all the city-states of the Greek world. Such things as democracy and Greek tragedy were very much limited to a few special times and places.

The Greeks had scores of other recurring festivals where these same athletic events took place at regular intervals. Some were truly important. But the Games at Olympia were the ultimate in athletic competition; they were in a class of their own. Pindar compares the way they eclipse the others to the way the sun outshines all other stars in the noon-day sky.[9] Above all, the Games were a showcase for human physical excellence, where mortals, as Pindar said, could resemble the gods.[10] In many ways the Olympics passed beyond the athletic events proper to exemplify, even represent, all of ancient Greek civilization at its best.[11] In fact, that is the very reason why they were revived in modern times.

Despite this manifest difference in size and the complexity of their programs, there is, then, one obvious similarity between the ancient and modern Olympics. Our Olympics, just like the ancient Games, attract and exhibit the ultimate in the pursuit of bodily excellence. The ancient and modern

Olympics are the same in that respect and in their essence. Both are the greatest sporting events of their times. But is that enough to justify calling our Games "Olympics"? What does Salt Lake 2002 have to do with antiquity?

Obviously, we must peer into the our own Olympic history. I first review the traditional story of how the Modern Olympics began, as it appeared in all scholarly and official histories until recently and as it is still told in popular books and in the media every four years. In these sources all you ever hear about is a Frenchman named Baron Pierre de Coubertin. For many years Coubertin was idealized, even idolized, as the sole founder of the Modern Olympic Movement.

The standard tale goes like this. In 1892 the French aristocrat Baron Pierre de Coubertin had a happy idea: Why not revive the ancient Olympic Games? In 1894 he held a big meeting in Paris and formed the International Olympic Committee (IOC). In 1896 he organized the very first modern Olympics: Olympiad I, Athens 1896. Americans won almost all the track and field events, but a Greek won the marathon. Coubertin was happy, as were others, and we have enjoyed nice fat Roman numeral Olympiads ever since. Sydney last year was XXVII, the twenty-seventh Olympiad. Because of this unique vision and achievement, the baron passes for something like the saint of the Olympic Games.[12]

There is a tiny bit of truth to this story—but not much. Coubertin played a crucial role, but he was a latecomer to our own Olympic Movement. He bumped into it by chance and was far from the first to propose an Olympic revival or international Olympic Games. The 1896 Athens Olympics were hardly the first Modern Olympics; and, in the end, Coubertin had little to do with organizing them. In fact, "the little French baron," as he is fondly known, did not really have much originality or organizational skill. Coubertin's forte was what we call "PR," public relations. But that very trait was critical to our modern Olympic revival. Without his PR ability and his capacity to convince important sportsmen and politicians, even royalty, to cooperate, there might well be no Sydney 2000 or Salt Lake 2002. To all these people, Coubertin constantly insisted on "all sports, all nations." That became the cornerstone of the modern Games, which extend the Olympic spirit and experience even to the poorest countries on the globe and to all kinds of sports, both summer and winter: a wonderful idea.

Perhaps now, however, we must ask even more pointedly: What has Salt Lake 2002 to do with the Olympic Games of antiquity? Apart from their essence, which we saw was basically the same, the ancient Games were wholly different. The difference in kind between winter sports and the Greek Olympic program is obvious. But our Games are also utterly different from those of the Greeks in other respects. Participants in our Games come from very diverse ethnic backgrounds and hundreds of different countries and speak scores of different languages. The only participants in the ancient Olympics were Greeks, even if they hailed from separately governed, sometimes warring states. And all ancient Greek contestants spoke the same language, mutually intelligible to everyone despite variations in dialect.

While the ancient Olympics recognized only first place, our events have three medalists, and the majority of individual events recognize the first eight places. Modern athletic performances are immediately viewable by virtually everyone on the planet, for the media can beam or report the results almost instantaneously to all corners of the world. The only medium for spreading information in ancient Greece was word of mouth from the several thousand spectators who were actually in the stadium and the eventual availability of a few handwritten reports. Even Coubertin could not have anticipated satellite television; but even in his earliest days newspapers and the telegraph could already spread Olympic news rapidly; telephone and radio were soon to follow. With such great differences from the very inception of our IOC Games in 1896, why would Coubertin call them "Olympics"?

Shortly before the Sydney Games a radio commentator for the British Broadcasting Corporation (BBC) called me, asking questions about how our own Games originated, because, in his words, "What an odd thing to do, to revive the ancient Olympics." I had never thought of it that way. But think about it. The Modern Olympics were not inevitable. Perhaps a vast international modern sport festival was inevitable—but how many people actually watched the few hours of off-prime-time television coverage of the Official Track and Field World Championships earlier this month in Edmonton, Canada? Although they were the legitimate World Championship, they were carried on cable, not network, and the stadium seats were far from full. Compare that with the number of people who watch those events at the Olympics. Track and field sports get very little media attention—unless it is the Olympics; then track and field is supreme, the very focal point of a grand, diverse sporting festival. That same stadium, a huge structure, is overflowing for opening and closing ceremonies as well; thousands of athletes from a few hundred countries march around the track. The stadium seats are full throughout the Games, and hundreds of television cameras send the proceedings to every corner of the world.

The 2001 Goodwill Games just began this very week. They are, in fact, a great international sporting festival, which actually does attract the very best athletes from all over the world. But I had trouble finding any mention of them at all in *USA Today* or any other newspaper that I consulted. Finally, on opening day, *USA Today* carried a story about the Goodwill

Games, but it was just a few inches in one column, in an inconspicuous place on a back page. In vain I watched ESPN (Entertainment and Sports Programming Network) News in hopes of finding out the results of these world-class competitions. By now I need not belabor the immense contrast with the Olympic Games and how strange it is that track and field is king only once in four years, otherwise generally ignored. I hope I have made my point that the Modern Olympics were far from inevitable and that their success, relative to festivals that perhaps *were* inevitable, is scarcely imaginable. How could all that be?

The answer, I am rather sure, is continuity. Not only do the modern and ancient Olympics have the same essence, but they also have the same lineage, the same pedigree, the same source: Greek antiquity. The Modern Olympics are the legitimate lineal descendent of the ancient version. One might even view the modern Games as the inevitable development and maturation of the ancient Olympics, as they, along with history, reach into the twenty-first century. We can never fully grasp how valid it is to call our modern Games "Olympics" until we look beyond Coubertin, even farther back in the history of our Olympic roots. There were, in fact, others besides Coubertin—people even more important, more vital to the realization of the Olympic revival. Although these people have not received the same credit and attention, they are the reason Coubertin named these Games of ours "Olympics."

The noted historian Thomas Carlyle said, "The history of the world is but the biography of great men" (1841). This is especially true in the history of the Modern Olympic Games. Without just a handful of men with great vision, there would be no Modern Olympics, certainly not the authentic and specific version we now know. Foremost on the list to join Coubertin as founders of the modern Olympic revival are two men whose activities I describe here. The first is a Greek poet named Panagiotis Soutsos (1806–1868) and the second an English doctor named William Penny Brookes (1809–1895). They triggered this momentous event, the greatest sporting show on earth.

Olympics: the mere name is magic. The whole world is watching. Never mind the Summer Olympics, Sydney, and track and field. At the Nagano Winter Games four years ago more than 2,000 athletes from 72 countries competed in 68 events. The Winter Games, too, are big. Here in Salt Lake City, the television audience, the Games, and the number of events will be even larger. It just grows and grows.

The modern Olympic Games not only dwarf the ancient Games themselves but also would provoke absolute disbelief and denial in the very men who made it all happen, such as Panagiotis Soutsos and Dr. Brookes. With all their grandeur now, it may be hard for us to believe, but for a half-century or more the idea of reviving the Games, of creating modern Olympics, was treated with so much scorn that it almost never got off the ground. The idea almost died in the cradle many times before it finally succeeded. Throughout most of the nineteenth century almost nobody was interested in the notion of modern Olympics. The whole idea seemed a bizarre anachronism. Olympic Games? Nowadays? Of course not.

Fortunately, there were a tiny few true believers. Brookes, the English doctor, constantly fought apathy and outright opposition. In 1867 he complained: "There are persons who . . . behold the games of ancient Greece as institutions never to be equalled, results never again to be obtained. I . . . am of the opposite opinion."[13] And even before Brookes, the Greek poet Soutsos, too, fought complete apathy and even opposition for decades.

The movement that culminated with Coubertin and Athens 1896 actually began in Athens in the 1830s. A number of modern Olympic Games took place before what we call Olympiad I (Athens 1896). All this earlier Olympic history has come to light just in the past few years, with meticulous detail, in thousands of previously unknown nineteenth-century documents.[14] If we ignore this previous history that authenticates our Olympic Games, we cannot understand Coubertin's role and the 1896 Athens Games—nor all the other Olympiads held thereafter.

It all began with a poem. In 1833 the Greek poet Panagiotis Soutsos began to publish some poems to celebrate the birth of the modern Greek nation, much of which was finally free after winning its War of Independence in 1828. But centuries of Turkish rule had left Greece well behind modern nineteenth-century Europe. Greece had not shared in Western Europe's Renaissance period and Enlightenment. The infrastructure of Greece, its institutions, and its spirit were in a miserable condition when the War of Independence began in 1821. Soutsos felt the heavy burden of ancient Greek glory on his new nation.[15] In his poetry he pointedly asks how Greece can gain the respect of the modern world and live up to its ancient reputation as a great people, a great nation—how it might reestablish the culture and institutions that made ancient Greece great in the eyes of Western culture. While some Greeks wanted to emulate successful contemporary nations such as France and England, Soutsos clearly saw that it was impossible for Greece to catch up quickly with the great nations of the nineteenth century. Rather, he decided, Greece should seek to restore its ancient glory, not count on suddenly jumping to the top of the new world order.

In an 1833 Soutsos poem the ghost of the ancient philosopher Plato looks up from the underworld. He surveys his native land in dismay and addresses the new nation, wondering aloud if he is really looking at Greece:

"Where are your great theaters and marble statues?" he asks. "Where are your Olympic Games?"[16] The Olympics are chosen here to represent the best of ancient Greece, the pinnacle of the Greek achievement. Soutsos held the broad cultural view of what the Games represent. In his next poem the ghost of the famed ancient general and military hero Leonidas calls upon the new Greece to revive the Olympic Games. They will foster friendship, quell discord, he says, and be a means of promoting peaceful relations among otherwise hostile groups.

This idea of restoring antiquity by restoring the Olympic Games took root in the poet's very psyche. Soutsos next took the bold and momentous step of converting his ghosts' poetic idea into a real-life proposal. In 1835 he sent a long and detailed official memo to the government, proposing that Greece revive the ancient Olympic Games as part of its new independence.[17] Greece's young new king, Otto I, installed by the nation's allies, was from Bavaria and still a teenager. Otto agreed to a national festival with contests in industry, agriculture, and ancient Greek athletic games. But nothing happened. In 1842 Soutsos appealed to the king again, this time directly, in print and in public, dedicating his new book to the young monarch and adding: "Let the ancient Olympic Games be revived in Athens." And in 1845 he gave a ringing speech to a crowd of thousands, again urging that the Olympics be revived. Still, nothing happened. Nobody else seemed to care about reviving the Olympics. Yet in a twenty-year campaign Soutsos never gave up; he just kept pushing his revival idea. And finally someone else did care.

Evangelis Zappas (1800–1865), an old war veteran who now lived in Romania, at last answered the lonely call of Soutsos.[18] Zappas liked this Olympic idea. In 1856 he, too, wrote Otto asking that the Olympics be revived. But Zappas said that he himself would pay for it all. After a humble beginning in a Greek village in Albania, Zappas had become one of the richest men in eastern Europe, with vast land holdings and other assets in Romania. He also had stock in the Greek shipping industry. Otto gave Zappas's Olympic proposal to his foreign minister, A. Rangavis, who was strongly opposed to reviving any athletic meetings. He thought athletics were a throwback to ancient, primitive times and, as he rightly observed, were simply not done in the modern world.[19] He suggested to Zappas that agricultural and industrial contests be held instead. After considerable haggling, the two men reached a compromise. In 1858 the first modern Olympiad was announced for Athens in 1859. There would be industrial Olympics and agricultural Olympics, but Zappas would also have his athletic Olympics, a revival of the games of ancient Greece. He had insisted on that and promised cash prizes for the winners.

Suddenly Olympic history took a wonderful, fateful twist. Without this strange, almost incredible turn of events, I doubt that we would be in Salt Lake City planning Olympic Games. A little newspaper clipping is the key that unlocks the door to the entire Olympic mystery: why we call the Games Olympics. In the fall of 1858 Dr. W. P. Brookes in northwestern rural England was reading his local newspaper. A small item about the forthcoming 1859 Greek Olympics caught his eye. It obviously fascinated him, because he clipped it out and pasted it in his scrapbook, where it remains for view this very day.

As a medical doctor in the little village of Much Wenlock, Shropshire, for half a century Brookes carefully kept detailed records of all his many activities in a set of large scrapbooks. Before we review the 1859 Athens Olympics, I must introduce this Englishman. For Brookes is probably the key figure in our Olympic history. He is the link—until recently the missing link—between the Greek National Olympics of Soutsos and Zappas and our International Games begun by Pierre de Coubertin. Now that we have the documents of Brookes, we can follow his work closely and see that our Olympic movement is a single, continuous movement from the first poetic idea of Soutsos in 1833 to the Sydney Games last year and those Winter Games coming here next year.

In 1840 Brookes had formed an organization in his village to encourage farmers and working-class men to improve their minds. The association had an intriguing name: the Much Wenlock Agricultural Reading Society. Brookes collected books and obtained a public reading room for its members. In 1850 he also began to encourage their physical improvement by holding annual athletic contests. He called these "meetings of the Olympian class" of his Reading Society, for he strongly admired the Olympic Games of ancient Greece. These games remained a local, minor event—until Brookes saw that newspaper item about the Soutsos-Zappas Olympic revival in Greece. He then immediately wrote the British ambassador in Athens, Sir Thomas Wyse, wanting to know more about these new Greek Olympics and to get further involved. Brookes himself was now being drawn inextricably into the Greek Olympic revival. First he connected his own local Olympic organization with the new Olympics of Greece. He sent ten pounds sterling as a prize in the Athens distance race. Before the Games, the Greek Olympic organizing committee announced this extra prize, a gift from "the Much Wenlock Olympic Committee in England."[20] Then Brookes changed the name of his 1859 athletic meeting to "The Wenlock Olympic Games,"[21] adding new Greek mottoes, ceremonies, and events. Those first expanded "Wenlock Olympics" actually took place a month before the first National Olympiad in Greece in 1859.

I now return to those Zappas Olympics, held in Athens in 1859, four years before Coubertin was born. Athletes from all over the Greek world, as in ancient times, came to compete. The first Olympic victor of modern times was Demetrios Athanasiou, who won the 200 meters, the classic ancient Olympic footrace. We have the names of all the other victors. But this first modern Olympiad in Athens was no great success. Zappas gave a large sum to excavate and renovate the ancient Athenian stadium—even to restore the seats with marble. But Rangavis refused even to purchase the land on which that stadium lay. So the athletic Games were held in a flat city square, with no seating arrangements.[22] Only the front row of spectators had a clear view of the Games; people behind them pushed toward the front, and a policeman harshly drove them back with his stick. Newspapers complained. In the featured 1,500 meters the leading runner collapsed and later died. As he collapsed, he was passed by Petros Velissariou, from what is now Izmir, Turkey, but then still inhabited by Greeks. Velissariou won the race, Zappas's drachmas, and Brookes's British pounds.

Brookes received the summary results from Wyse and soon enrolled Velissariou as the first "Honorary Member" of the "Much Wenlock Olympic Society," on the same page where Coubertin was enrolled thirty-one years later. Brookes also began to correspond with the Greeks about Olympic Games. He wrote to King Otto and sent a gift to his wife, Queen Amalia. Mr. N. Theocharis, president of the Greek Olympic committee, wrote Brookes that Greece was happy to have "a sister institution of the same name in England"; he also spoke of the "civilizing aims which unite both committees in the same course." So something of an international Olympic movement had already begun.[23]

Bitten by the Olympic bug, Dr. Brookes soon founded countywide Olympics for all the citizens of Shropshire. Here he first had the idea of "movable" Olympics, which go from city to city.[24] The "Shropshire Olympics" were held four times in various cities and drew athletes from all over England. They had a varied modern program, with swimming, shooting, and rowing besides the staple track and field. These Games inspired John Hulley of Liverpool to start annual Olympics there. Hulley's Olympics, too, were serious athletic contests. The 1863 Liverpool Olympics drew more than 12,000 spectators and athletes from all England.[25] In 1865, just as Zappas died in Greece, Brookes and Hulley began to think even bigger: nationwide Olympic Games. Along with E. G. Ravenstein, they formed the National Olympian Association (NOA). Brookes's Olympic movement had advanced from the local to the national level. The aims of the NOA were much like those of our IOC: "To promote moral, intellectual, and physical" excellence. But it, too, focused on athletics. The NOA proposed to hold its National Olympic Games "in rotation in the principal cities . . . of England." For its first Olympiad, the NOA thought big: London in 1866.[26]

The 1866 Olympics were held inside the architectural wonder of the time: the Crystal Palace in London. The program was much like that of early IOC Olympiads; besides track and field, it included such sports as swimming, gymnastics, boxing, wrestling, and fencing. Ten thousand satisfied spectators looked on as a young athlete named W. G. Grace won the high hurdles by twenty yards. They did not know he would later become the most famous cricket player the world has yet known. The Games were a great success, and English newspapers called Brookes "the father of the Olympic movement." Amazingly, just a decade ago our modern Olympic histories still knew nothing of these important Olympic Games, partly because most English people at the time opposed them or ignored them and partly because Coubertin, who knew all about them, later proceeded as if they had never happened.

From the very start, however, the Brookes Olympics were opposed by England's most powerful sportsmen. As soon as the 1866 London Games were announced, in the words of the distinguished English sport historian Peter Lovesey, "[A] shock-wave ran through the running grounds of the capital. The prospect of athletics controlled from anywhere but London was unthinkable. The London contingent mobilized as if the French had landed."[27] The upper-class "gentlemen athletes," as they called themselves, of the London area (mostly Oxford and Cambridge men) quickly created a counter-Olympic organization named "The Amateur Athletic Club" (AAC). This was the first time in history the word "amateur" was used in a name. The AAC managed to hold its own "first annual amateur championship games" immediately, even before the 1866 Olympics could be held. Members of the AAC openly spurned the Olympics; they viewed Brookes and Hulley as provincial outsiders from the North, who, they falsely asserted, allowed "professionals" to compete.

Actually, the NOA explicitly excluded "professional athletes" and disqualified the victor in the 1866 Olympic mile on the grounds that he was a professional.[28] But the NOA and the AAC strongly disagreed on the definition of a "professional." Brookes began his activity as a service to the working class, and he let athletes of any class compete if they qualified. But the AAC was founded in social class elitism. Its rules read that anyone who was "a mechanic, artisan, or labourer" was a "pro," ineligible for amateur contests no matter how innocent he might be of financial gain. This anti-Olympic club was, in fact, the very origin of formal "amateur athletics." Sharp quarrels over the definition of the amateur athlete plagued English athletics for years and later became Coubertin's pretext for the 1894 Paris congress.[29]

The AAC's opposition to the first British Olympics in London in 1866 had little effect on those highly successful Games. Four AAC athletes, in fact, ignored the virtual boycott, and two of them won. The AAC also shunned the next National Olympiad (Birmingham, 1867) but failed to spoil those games. Some good athletes from all around England still came to compete, and the second Olympiad was a moderate success. But the AAC continued to gain control of British sports, as the "mechanics clause" became the national standard. Brookes refused to conform to it. AAC opposition to the third British National Olympic Games in Manchester in 1868 had a ruinous effect. Few first-rate athletes signed up, and Brookes was compelled to move these "National Olympics" to Wellington, a town near Much Wenlock. The next attempt in 1874 shrank to holding the "National" games in Wenlock itself—little more than another version of the games held there since 1859. The British National Olympics had been run aground by the elitists of the amateur movement.

Just then, however, the Olympics got renewed life in Greece. The Greeks had chased King Otto out of their country in 1862. When Zappas died in 1865, his will left an immense sum of money for the revival of the Greek Olympic Games, with permanent facilities to be built in Athens. His will also stated that after four years he was to be exhumed; his head was to be severed from his body and then placed in a new Olympic exhibition building in Athens. But political turmoil kept the Greeks from staging Olympics for a while. The building was not built, and Zappas's head was put on hold. In 1870, however, Otto's replacement as the king, this time a Danish teenager called George I, renewed the Zappas Olympics.

The 1870 Greek Games were a remarkable success. The Olympic committee excavated the ancient stadium in Athens, though it did not rebuild it in white marble as Zappas specified in his will.[30] But even with wooden bleachers, it still made a good site for the 1870 Games, the first stadium of the modern era. Athletes came from all over the Greek-speaking world. The expenses of needy athletes were paid by the organizing committee. A large crowd of 30,000 watched the Games. They included modern gymnastics, as well as the ancient Olympic events in track and field. With perfect order, the athletes contended for Olympic victory, and the winners were crowned, as in ancient times, with an olive wreath. The classic 200-meter dash was won by E. Skordaras of Athens. The wrestling was won by A. Kardamylakis of Crete. We have the names of the first three places in all ten events. The crowd applauded their Olympians as in days of old. It was a true Olympic revival, even a kind of triumph. Greek newspapers now called Zappas "Founder of the Olympics."

The Greek Olympics, too, ran into trouble because of class elitist amateurism, a new import from England. Just after the successful 1870 Greek Olympics, an elitist clique of university professors who were the judges at the 1870 Games, led by the classics professor P. Ioannou, objected that working-class athletes had competed. So they had; even worse, they had won.[31] Skordaras the sprinter was a butcher by trade. And Kardamylakis was an ordinary manual laborer, clearly ineligible by the British AAC rule barring mechanics and laborers. So Ioannou's group formally asked the committee to bar working-class athletes from future Olympiads, to restrict entry to the "more refined classes": namely, their own university students. The Greek officials bowed to this elitist pressure; in the next Olympiad (1875) only students were admitted. There were no entries from the working class. The 1875 Olympics were far inferior to the 1870 Games. The stadium was full of weeds. The number of competitors and spectators was much smaller than in 1870. The upper-class contestants did not take athletics and the Games seriously, and the overall result was so bad that the principal Olympic coach was forced to leave town.

Yet the Olympic Movement itself would not die. It just kept sprouting up again. Brookes now took his turn once more to try to revive his series. He announced new British Olympics for 1877, in Shrewsbury, larger but again not far from Much Wenlock. Then he induced King George of Greece to donate an inscribed cup as a prize for the winner of the pentathlon in those British Olympics. But the indifference and opposition of the AAC still held, and these 1877 British "National" Olympics were a mere shadow of the 1866 Games. Yet instead of giving up, Brookes just decided to think bigger. The result was momentous, the very basis of our own international movement for the revival of the Olympic Games. In 1880 Brookes took the crucial step, a giant step toward our own Games. He formally proposed an international Olympic revival, a cooperative effort based on his British Olympic movement and the Zappas movement in Greece. He gave speeches on that theme and through the Greek ambassador in London, John Gennadius, proposed that international Olympic Games be held in Greece, with athletes of various nations "contending in a generous rivalry with athletes of other nations in the time-consecrated stadium at Athens." That, in fact, is precisely what happened in 1896. But throughout the 1880s Brookes still met only indifference and apathy as he wrote Gennadius time after time, over and over asking that his Olympic proposal be implemented.[32]

So the Brookes call for international Olympics fell on deaf ears in Greece as well as England. The Greek Olympic committee was now controlled by an anti-athletic faction, which refused to hold athletic Olympics of any kind. Instead it spent the money on the opulent building called the Zappeion, which still dominates downtown Athens. When the building was finally completed in 1888, the committee did finally get a relative to bring the head of Zappas from Romania and encased it in the Zappeion. It is still there, right behind a plaque that clearly identifies the spot. And the committee did, in fact, hold agri-industrial Olympics. But no one lifted a finger to carry out the 1888 athletic Olympics, which the committee had announced would take place in the stadium. Since those games were so thoroughly and silently canceled (there was no attempt to prepare the stadium, to enroll any contestants, or officially and openly to cancel them), I conclude that the committee never intended to hold any athletic contests at all.[33]

As Brookes saw so little progress toward his Olympic dream, he turned more and more to writing articles promoting physical education in the English schools, which was his other passion. Several of these articles appeared from 1887 to 1889. At the same time, a young Frenchman, Baron Pierre de Coubertin, also became interested in physical education. Coubertin read the articles by Brookes, endorsed their ideas, and began to quote them. In an 1889 Paris speech, Coubertin announced that he subscribed "to the words spoken twenty years ago by a perceptive speaker at an athletic contest in London." He then quoted from a speech by Brookes at the 1866 London Olympics. This seems rather astonishing: in 1889 the so-called Founder of the Modern Olympics, still in his twenties, had not yet himself written or uttered a word about Olympics. But he was quoting, with no mention of the magic O word, from a speech the Shropshire doctor had delivered at Olympic Games in London almost a quarter of a century earlier.

In 1890 Coubertin wrote to Brookes, asking if he could come to Much Wenlock to exchange ideas about physical education in the schools. Coubertin still had no notion of Olympic Games. But Brookes was aging and ailing. He saw the chance to pass the Olympic torch. When the baron arrived in Wenlock, Brookes staged a special edition of his Wenlock Olympic Games to impress his guest from Paris. Before the Games actually began, he asked Coubertin to plant a tree at the Wenlock Olympic field to commemorate his own visit.

Brookes was a lover of trees. They appear throughout his writings, and the site of his Olympic Games at Wenlock is still ringed with many trees. Some of these trees honored specific people or special occasions and had their own individual entries in a scrapbook where Brookes kept notes on their health and growth. If the occasion was the visit of a guest whom he deemed important to his projects, he asked the guest himself to plant the

tree that honored his own visit. Momentous Olympic moments were especially well represented. As Greece prepared for Zappas Olympiad I in 1859,
Brookes planted a tree in honor of Queen Amalia, who, in her husband's
absence, had signed the official decree that established these Games. When
King George fulfilled a request from Brookes for an inscribed cup as a special prize for the 1877 British National Olympics, Brookes planted a tree in
honor of George and that occasion. His symbol for the Olympic Movement was a tree, which starts from a little seed then starts to grow and
form a sturdy trunk and deeper roots. It gets strong branches with many
leaves, which then produce other branches; and it just keeps growing until
it is gigantic.

The tree-planting ceremony, embodying such Olympic thoughts, was
just a prelude to less symbolic and more practical phases of the strategy
by which Brookes hoped to involve the French baron in his own Olympic Movement. Next came the actual Games themselves; Coubertin was
enthralled by the Wenlock pageantry.[34] And before he left Wenlock,
Brookes filled his ears with the actual history of the Olympic Movement
and of the Olympic Games to that date, both in England and in Greece.
He showed Coubertin a typeset English translation of the victor list from
the 1859 Zappas Olympics and told him about his own national Olympic
Games. Most importantly, he carefully told Coubertin of his own hopes for
future international Olympic Games.

At first Coubertin was unimpressed by Brookes's idea of reviving the
Olympic Games and said so: there was, he wrote, "no need to invoke memories of Greece and to seek encouragement in the past."[35] But he soon
changed his mind; and by 1892 he liked the doctor's Olympic idea so much
that he adopted it as his own and even presented it as his own idea when he
first proposed an Olympic revival at a meeting in Paris in 1892. Meanwhile,
in Greece King George's oldest son, Crown Prince Constantine, had proclaimed a resumption of the Greek series in Athens for that same year and
had started to organize another Zappas Olympiad. But again politics forced
the 1892 Athens Games to be canceled.

Brookes kept corresponding with Gennadius and with Coubertin; but
Coubertin kept him in the dark about his own revival proposal. By 1893
the baron was building a network of his connections in the European royalty and aristocracy and also with influential leaders of the embryonic,
rather elitist amateur sports groups outside of England. He arranged to
hold an International Athletic Congress in Paris in June 1894. The invitations stated that the aim of the congress was to define amateurism, to
resolve the chaos in amateur rules. But by the time the delegates arrived,

Coubertin had renamed it the "Congress for the Revival of the Olympic Games." Notified of Coubertin's proposal by form letter, just before the congress met, Brookes wrote to Coubertin personally wishing him luck in his new Olympic enterprise. He also wrote to the prime minister of Greece, saying: "My friend Pierre de Coubertin, myself, and others are endeavoring to promote international Olympic festivals. I hope your King will patronize such Games."[36]

Coubertin's Paris congress lasted several days. The delegates were wined, dined, and entertained in grand style, including an elaborate fireworks show. The baron soon held the delegates in his hands. No one opposed his plan to form an international Olympic committee to revive the ancient Games. But the delegates did not at first vote for Athens as the site for 1896; they chose London. Coubertin, however, insisted on Athens instead, as Brookes had planned from the start. Since Coubertin declined to connect Brookes in any way to any part of his Olympic activities or even to mention his name, it is not likely that he wanted Athens to oblige Brookes. It is much more probable that Coubertin had a secret agreement with the Greek royal family that Athens would be the first Olympic host.[37] In the midst of the congress, Coubertin received a rather mysterious encouraging telegram from the Greek king. Whatever the case may be, Athens was chosen. And, to his surprise, Demetrios Vikelas was elected the first president of the IOC, preceding Coubertin and all the rest.

Vikelas, a Greek novelist and historian who lived in Paris, was a fascinating man of diverse talents; he even translated Shakespeare into Greek. Although he had never before had a thing to do with athletics, he was the right man for the job. Coubertin suddenly got engaged to be married and lost much of his interest in preparations for the 1896 Games. But Gennadius, who had rebuffed Brookes and his proposal so many times, now wrote a prominent article praising Coubertin and strongly supporting his identical proposal to revive the Games in Athens. He made no mention of Brookes. A professional diplomat and known political opportunist, Gennadius clearly found a French nobleman more worthy of his support than a country doctor. When the Zappas Olympic committee told Vikelas and Coubertin, "No! No money, no cooperation," the ever-ready Prince Constantine offered to chair the organizing committee. Vikelas and Constantine rallied other Greeks behind their efforts.

These pro-Olympic Greeks did almost all the work and fought the anti-Olympic clique in the Greek government. They invoked the memory of Evangelis Zappas as parliament debated whether to hold the 1896 Games, saying that these international Olympics would fulfill the dream of Zappas.

That argument won. As we know, the 1896 Athens Olympics were a great success and inaugurated our own series. Unfortunately, Brookes did not live to see his own Olympic dream fulfilled. He died just a few months before those 1896 Games, joining Soutsos and Zappas in Olympic oblivion, as Coubertin and history forgot all about them. But his dream moves on as reality today, as do the dreams of all these men.

So the Modern Olympics are authentic Olympics. That is why track and field still lies at their core, even though the Olympic program now extends to almost every sport there is, summer and winter. Our games stem from antiquity and at least three founders: Soutsos, Brookes, and Coubertin, each indispensable for the Games' success. That success relied on the originality of Soutsos and his intuitive understanding of how the magic of the ancient Olympics might grip the modern imagination; on the vision, practicality, and tenacity of Brookes to implement that understanding; and on the influential aristocratic contacts and public-relations mastery of Coubertin, sorely needed in the late nineteenth century to carry it all off.

These men believed with their hearts that the Olympics could succeed, could survive. Indeed the Games have survived despite world wars, the Cold War, politics, boycotts, and amateurism—and they keep growing bigger. The ancient Olympics lasted over a thousand years, slowly expanding in their events, competitors, and importance as their world slowly expanded. They were inclusive, not exclusive.[38] Their goal was to bring together in peace the world's best athletes in friendly competition in the pursuit of human excellence. With each of our modern Olympiads, the best athletes from all over our world gather to re-create that original Olympic goal. And it all gets bigger and bigger, as our own world expands more and more rapidly. But that just makes the Brookes's tree image all the more apt. Trees do much the same. I use the oak that Coubertin planted in Wenlock field in 1890 as a specific example. Brookes and Coubertin planted it together as a sapling; it was still small and thin. But each year it has grown, almost exponentially, spreading ever outward, with more and more branches, a thicker trunk, and sturdier and sturdier limbs, taller and taller, till it now towers high above and its wide branches form something like a huge umbrella. Like the Olympics, it just keeps on growing and growing.

On one occasion, Brookes abandoned his Olympic tree metaphor but still focused on natural growth. I close with the very words of Dr. Brookes: "Sow a single seed of a rare plant in the most secluded spot and if the soil and other conditions are favourable . . . , it will grow up and bear another seed, and in time, produce plants sufficient to cover the length and breadth of the land."[39]

When you see the ski jumping up there in Utah Olympic Park, you will know that the "breadth of the land" in his prophetic words was a metaphor for this whole world.

Notes

1. This essay is a slightly modified version of the lecture that I delivered on August 31, 2001, as the first lecture in a series that the University of Utah sponsored in honor of the 2002 Olympics. Since the lecture was delivered several months before the Games took place, it would have conflicted with the essay's argument if I had pretended otherwise for this published version, which, in fact, was written before the Games. Further, in hopes of preserving some of the animation, excitement, and anticipation of that most pleasant evening in Salt Lake City, I have made little attempt to mask the oral origin of most of the sentences. Much of the material here may be found in greater detail, with sources copiously cited, in my book *The Modern Olympics: A Struggle for Revival* (Baltimore: Johns Hopkins University Press, 1996).

2. Such statements are common in print; typical are remarks in Avery Brundage, "Why the Olympic Games?" in *Report of the United States Olympic Committee* (New York: United States Olympic Association, 1948), p. 23 ("The Ancient Olympic Games were strictly amateur"), and throughout such works as Harold A. Harris, *Greek Athletes and Athletics* (London: Hutchinson, 1964) and E. Norman Gardiner, *Greek Athletic Sports and Festivals* (London: Macmillan, 1910).

3. See David C. Young, *The Olympic Myth of Greek Amateur Athletics* (Chicago: Ares Publishers, 1984). Not long after that book appeared, the first United States National Basketball Association (NBA) "Dream Team" won a gold medal in the 1992 Olympics; and since then no classicist has claimed that the Greeks were amateurs.

4. Greeks, of course, did not have the metrical system; but the ancient Olympic stadium was 192.6 meters long. I have rounded that off to 200 to make an equivalent in a modern track program.

5. For the ancient records, how many victories, where, and by whom, see my "First with the Most: Greek Athletic Records and 'Specialization,'" *Nikephoros* 9 (1996): 3–25.

6. There were no hurdles, no marathons (an invention of the 1890s), no relays. Torch races (some perhaps similar to relays) occurred as a kind of intramural sport in some Athenian festivals but were not practiced as serious adult athletic competition at events such as the Olympics.

7. Pindar in two vivid passages describes the loser's humiliated return to his home, taking backroads to avoid the view and taunts of his enemies (*Olympian* 8.67–70, *Pythian* 8.82–87).

8. The Games were terminated by an edict of the Roman emperor that banned all pagan festivals. The precise date, however, and whether the emperor was Theodosius I or Thedosius II is disputed, because the sources are not wholly clear. Some very recent excavations at Olympia suggest that Olympic competition may have extended somewhat longer into the fifth century A.D. than was formerly assumed.

9. Pindar *Olympian* 1.1–6. There were three other very important athletic festivals where the athletes were generally the same ones who competed in the Olympics: the Isthmian, the Pythian, and the Nemean Games. With the Olympics they made up a recognized "Big Four," called the "Circuit," which were more prestigious than any of the scores of other recurring athletic games in ancient Greece. Yet even among the Big Four, the Olympics were unquestionably at the top.

10. Pindar *Nemean* 6.1–7. Sometimes people wrongly claim that the Greeks deified athletic victors. Pindar indeed emphasizes that athletes can resemble the gods; but he vehemently denies that they are or can be gods (*Olympian* 5.24, *Isthmian* 5.14). The distinction he draws is sharp and very clear.

11. There were no contests in art and literature, but the Games still seem to have promoted excellence in these other fields. For example, the noted historian Herodotus chose the Olympic Games as the occasion for the first publication (public reading) of his monumental *Histories*. And sculptors would hope to place their best work at Olympia, in order to display it to a great many people from all over the Greek world.

12. The meetings of all Olympic organizations, the books about the Games, and the hoopla that the media spread every four years are permeated with praise of Coubertin; his heart, buried separately at ancient Olympia at his request, is virtually venerated at International Olympic Academy meetings held there. The Societé Pierre de Coubertin, mainly an organization dedicated to fostering Coubertin's ideas and memory, has a significant global membership and many activities and publications.

13. From the printed version of a June 1867 speech by Brookes in Birmingham in the Brookes Papers.

14. These documents are contained in four collections. The original correspondence between E. Zappas and the Greek government, 1856–1865, is in government archives in Athens. Various documents kept by the Athenian politician S. Dragoumis, who headed the Zappas Olympic Committee during the 1896 IOC Olympiad (to which he was strongly opposed), are in the Gennadius Library, Athens. This collection also contains all the documents of the various phases of the Zappas Olympic committee before Dragoumis presided over it. Coubertin's own file for the 1894 Paris Congress, which created the IOC, contains only about a hundred documents. In 1987 it was still uncatalogued, but photocopies were available by special request at the old IOC Library in downtown Lausanne. It is now catalogued and in the new IOC Library. In 1991 thousands of documents preserved in seven large scrapbooks in which W. P. Brookes meticulously pasted all items in any way related to his Olympic activities (and a few others) lay in an

old trunk in a room in the Cornmarket building, Much Wenlock, Shropshire. I have heard that they have been removed to the IOC Library, Lausanne.

None of these four collections was known to Olympic historical research until the 1980s, when their existence and importance were brought to light. Readers wishing to know more about these materials and my use of them are directed to my book *The Modern Olympics,* pp. 171–175 (with full details).

15. For more than three centuries, from a time before Christopher Columbus discovered America, a conquered Greece was the subject country of a harsh and rapacious Ottoman Empire, with virtually no control over its own affairs and destiny. When Greeks freed themselves from this long and oppressive alien domination, they needed to rebuild their country all over again, seemingly starting "from scratch."

16. "Nekrikos dialogos" (Dialogue of the Dead), *Helios* (The Sun), July 4, 1833.

17. This remarkably long document (in French), actually dating from 1835, was found and published in 1958 (Greek journal *Athena* [1972]: 307–323).

18. Zappas, born to a Greek family in 1800 in Albania, had no schooling. As a very young man he served as a mercenary for the notorious Turkish governor-turned-warlord Ali Pasha. But when the war broke out, he joined the Greek resistance army, serving under the noted Souliot war hero Markos Botzaris. When Greece got its independence, he moved to Romania and began to amass an immense fortune. He felt passionately patriotic about Greece, which he considered his motherland (though he never lived there).

19. There was little that could be called athletics in the first half of the nineteenth century anywhere, except cricket and rowing clubs in England; boxing and wrestling (in various forms) perhaps never fully died out in some cultures.

20. Actually the printed announcement in Greek calls it the "Mud Enlock Olympic Committee"—a forgivable error if one knows the peculiarities of Greek and English script, but it is still amusing.

21. Throughout all his activities, Brookes called both the games of antiquity and his own revivals "Olympian Games" rather than "Olympic Games." Lest that truly insignificant difference mislead or provoke pointless nitpicking, I have usually standardized his "Olympian" to "Olympic." In the *New Webster's Encyclopedic Dictionary* (1994) the entries for the two adjectives are virtually identical.

22. The site, then on the outskirts of the city, is now in downtown Athens, a few blocks north of the Kerameikos. It is now officially named "Plateia Eleftherias" (Freedom Square), but no Athenian calls it anything other than "Koumoundourou" (named after a noted Greek politician of the mid-nineteenth century).

23. These letters, remarkable for their reference to two Olympic committees in international cooperation, are in the Brookes Papers, Scrapbook 4. Further items show some continued mutual interest, however sporadic, on the parts of both the Greeks and Coubertin in the other's Olympic Movement. In the Official Report of the 1875 Athens Olympiad, the Greek Olympic Committee notes the activities of Brookes in holding Olympics in England and remembers

his correspondence and gifts in 1859–1860; in 1877 the Greek king complied with Brookes's request, sending an inscribed cup for the pentathlon victor in what the king himself recognized as "The Modern Olympics of the British."

24. Brookes was the first except for Soutsos, whose 1835 proposal recommended that the revived Olympics be celebrated annually in a four-year rotation among four different cities. "Ambulatory" games, as Coubertin called the movable Olympics, were an integral, even indispensable, feature of Coubertin's Olympic system.

25. For the Liverpool games of 1867 several of the athletes came from France, which marks that event as the first actual international Olympic competition.

26. Young, *The Modern Olympics,* p. 33.

27. *The Official Centenary History of the Amateur Athletic Association* (Enfield, England: Guinness Superlatives, 1979), pp. 18–19.

28. There seem to be no details on the exact nature of the infraction, which soon cost a Mr. C. Nurse, who had won both the mile and the two-mile footraces, his first-place prizes. Thus Jim Thorpe was, in some respects, not the first Olympic victor to be stripped of his honors.

29. Disputes about amateurism remained the bane of the modern Olympics for decades to come, into the lifetimes of most of us. Not, however, all of us: most college freshmen now have never heard of amateurism in either the ancient or the modern Olympics and have no notion what an amateur athlete is. The times have changed quickly. Thirty years ago Avery Brundage was still president of the IOC; and just eighteen years ago America's best hurdlers (Renaldo Nehemiah and Willie Gault) were banned from the 1984 Los Angeles Olympics on the grounds that they were not amateurs.

30. Marble would come later; this is the very place where IOC Olympiad I was held in 1896 and where opening and closing ceremonies (and the marathon finish) will take place in 2004.

31. The need to win always lay at the heart of class elitist amateurism, which was designed to make sure that the upper-class men would win all the contests. If a "gentleman amateur" lost to someone from the working class, he lost not only the prize but also his identity, which was founded on an assumption that he was innately superior to most people.

32. Brookes Papers, Scrapbook 5:52. There are a dozen letters in the Brookes Papers from Gennadius to Brookes, thanking the doctor for his "most recent letter" and the Olympic proposal again but asking him to "be patient," saying that "the time is not ripe," "the Greek government has no money now," and so on— essentially, thanks but no thanks.

33. Some books list athletic Olympics as taking place at this 1888 "Zappas Olympiad" (or date them a year later). Although some people at the time wanted to call them "Olympics," the games that took place in 1889 were sponsored and financed by a private individual, not by the committee or the government. They were held inside a tiny gym, with almost no spectators, and halted in their midst

because the athletes (a few university students) seemed more to run amok than to compete in the events when called (see my book *The Modern Olympics,* p. 64).

34. In our own Olympic ceremonies, the performance of a hymn derives from the Greek Zappas Olympics; but much of the rest—the award ceremonies, the pageantry, the visual displays, parades, and fanfare—derives from the Brookes Wenlock ceremonies. See John J. MacAloon, *This Great Symbol* (Chicago: University of Chicago Press, 1981), p. 149.

35. P. de Coubertin, "Les Jeux Olympiques à Much Wenlock," *La Revue Athlétique* 1 (December 1890): 705–713 (on p. 713 in the original the text reads "pas" where some reprinted versions wrongly have "plus").

36. Young, *The Modern Olympics,* p. 93.

37. Coubertin knew that London was no possibility at all; Charles Herbert, secretary of the AAC (umbrella to all British athletics) and one-third of Coubertin's own sponsoring committee for the 1894 Congress (which speciously focused on amateurism, not Olympics), whose vigorous help would be essential for any games in London, saw nothing "viable" in Coubertin's Olympic plans and seemed actually opposed to having the games at all, anywhere (P. de Coubertin, *Batailles de l'éducation physique: Une campagne de vingt-et-un ans, 1887–1908* [Paris: Librairie de l'Education Physique, 1908], pp. 92–93). Herbert was not at the meeting when the vote on London was taken; apparently he was not in France and may never have attended the Congress.

Even if the delegates did not know, Coubertin knew London was an impossibility. Greece was a wholly different manner. Prince Constantine, frustrated by Greece's failure to hold Olympics in 1892, eagerly signed up as an honorary member of the Congress. Coubertin says that he had asked his archaeologist friend Charles Waldstein, then excavating the ancient stadium at Argos, to "lay the question [the congress and Olympic revival idea] before the Greek royal family." The royal family, in turn, made a trip to Argos—"the first time," Waldstein says, "they had ever visited an excavation outside of Athens" (Young, *The Modern Olympics,* p. 89). Waldstein and Constantine talked several hours that day (exceptional for a member of the royal family). I must stress that I merely conjecture that Coubertin and Greece had a prior agreement on Athens, and the conjecture might prove wrong. Although the evidence is not decisive, it strongly points in that direction.

38. One often hears that Olympic eligibility was restricted to free-born Greeks only; others were barred. Some clarification is needed. Slaves had virtually no individual rights in the ancient world. No slave would even have seriously contemplated Olympic competition, and no owner would have permitted it anyway. Furthermore, Greek-style athletics were not practiced by any peoples except the Greeks, so a dearth of barbarian Olympians is inevitable. Furthermore, there were in fact a few non-Greeks accepted into the competitions. "In all the Olympic stories, there is none about a dispute over this rule" (M. I. Finley and H. W. Pleket, *The Olympic Games: The First Thousand Years* [New York: Viking Press, 1976],

p. 62). Several Romans were in fact Olympic victors, but in the equestrian events only. No Roman would ever have competed in athletics in front of a stadium crowd. One of the last known Olympic victors is reported to have been an Armenian named Varazdat.

39. *Shrewsbury Chronicle,* June 14, 1867 ("Brookes Papers," 4.185, in my book *The Modern Olympics,* p. 39).

2

THE COOL GAMES

The Winter Olympics, 1924–2002

Roland Renson

Sport and trans(s)port have a lot in common. Skis, snowshoes, and skates were developed as cultural artifacts to make transport on snow and ice more efficient and swift (Luther 1926; Mehl 1964; Babelay 1967; Bø 1993; Allen 1996b; Ulmrich 1996; Pfister 2001). This contribution focuses on the typical "modernist" process of changing a means of transport and locomotion into sport and international competition during the twentieth century.

Pierre de Coubertin, the founding father of the Modern Olympic Games, did not favor team games like soccer or ice hockey, but he had a particular interest in individual sports with a military usefulness for men. Coubertin had himself practiced ice-skating in the Bois de Boulogne, which he characterized as "an almost universal exercise, a sport of equilibrium par excellence" (1979: 141). After moving to Switzerland, Coubertin did some skiing and was enthusiastic about that sport. He praised its military usefulness and its health benefit through exercising in the fresh winter mountain air. Although Coubertin was—like his English friends—thrilled by the speed of luges and bobsleighs, he declined them as sports: "They are completely useless." They certainly required some courage, but they had not the least utilitarian application.

The importance of winter sports, in particular skiing, had already been emphasized at the International Olympic Congress of 1905 in Brussels (Comité International Olympique 1905: 255). Coubertin had contemplated the creation of separate Winter Games since 1910, but the Nordic Games, which were the private "playground" of Victor Balck, the great sports and gymnastics promoter of Sweden, stood in the way (Kamper 1964: 22–24; Kruger 1996: 103–105). Coubertin explained: "In addition to the Scandinavian resistance, there was the twofold concern that they could not take place at the same time or in the same place as the Summer Games. It is possible

41

to manufacture artificial ice, but not snow, and even less mountain peaks. Would the Dutch be expected, in 1928, to erect a chain of mountains bought second hand or made specially for the occasion?" (1979: 106).

THE NORDIC GAMES, 1901–1926

The Nordic Games were held for the first time in 1901 and thereafter in 1905, 1909, 1913, 1917, 1922, and 1926. All took place in Stockholm except for 1903, when they were held in Kristiana (Oslo), Norway. Their organization was in the hands of the rather exclusive Swedish Central Association for the Promotion of Idrott ("sport"). This event had a strong nationalistic undertone: through sports the Swedish nation would be unified and "the race strengthened." Moreover, Sweden as a nation and as a site of tourism was to be advertised. It was thus a mixture of nationalistic ideology and commercial marketing. With torches, national folk melodies, and peasants in their picturesque folk costumes and through Skansen's midwinter fest, the Games were an expression of peasant romanticism of the Nordic past ("Gotianism"), nationalism, and royalism (Ljunggren 1996; Jonsson 2001).

The social-democratic press criticized the Nordic Games for being snobbish and too much focused on the upper classes. The banquets and excessive partying were not characteristic of true sportsmen. Those who practiced "real" sports *(idrott)* were the working classes. The skiers from Norrland, the northern part of Sweden, protested that sledders (a typical upper-class diversion) had received better prizes. The Nordic Games were also attacked for not promoting health-related sports but rather replacing these by one-sidedness and sports idiocy. Competitive sports were indeed treated by the working class in a far more serious manner than among the upper classes, who were characterized by a more "nonchalant" attitude toward sports and an unwillingness to exert themselves physically (Ljunggren 1996).

Around the turn of the century it was obvious that Alpine winter sports and Nordic winter sports were moving apart. Nordic skiing was primarily a sport of endurance, and the ski jump combined power and courage, while Alpine skiing was becoming more and more a question of agility (Kruger 1996: 106). Here was a sporting impetus to create a Winter Olympics.

WINTER OLYMPIC PRELUDES: 1908 AND 1920

At the first Olympic congress in Paris in 1894, it was decided to include figure skating in the Olympic program (Coubertin 1979: 107). But Athens, the host of the first Modern Olympic Games, did not have the necessary facilities, so the idea was dropped. The following proposal by Colonel Victor Balck and Captain Henrik Angell (Norway) was accepted at the International Congress of Sport and Physical Education in Brussels in 1905, organized by the IOC: "Let the governments, municipalities, and sport organizations pay special attention to all winter sports and to skiing in particular" (Comité International Olympique 1905: 206). At the IOC session in Budapest on May 24, 1911, the Italian IOC member Count Eugenio Brunetta d'Usseaux proposed to include a winter sports week—skiing in particular—but Colonel Balck, the organizer of both the Nordic Games and the Stockholm Olympics scheduled for 1912, did not want his Nordic Games to be internationalized or moved from 1913 to 1912. So mountaineering was included as a summer sport, but not figure skating as a winter sport (Kamper 1964: 23–24; Kruger 1996). This was thus a clear step backward compared to the 1908 London Games, where figure skating for men, women, and pairs was included in the program. The competitions were held in the Prince's Skating Rink in Knightsbridge (Cook 1909). Ulrich Salchow from Sweden, who won gold, would make a remarkable comeback in Antwerp in 1920, when he finished fourth at the age of forty-two (Verdyck 1920; Kluge 1997: 8).

The Organizing Committee of the Berlin Olympic Games of 1916 decided in November 1913 that skiing and skating would be held in February 1916 on the Feldberg in the Black Forest. The decision on whether to have Winter Olympic Games or not was to be made at the IOC congress in June 1914 in Paris. If a mere six countries were to take part, would these events be called "Olympic"? The German Committee had proposed 50- and 12-kilometer races, a ski jump, and the combination of 12-kilometer and ski jump, as well as figure skating and ice hockey. But in June 1914 Germany launched World War I, and the 1916 Berlin Games never took place (Kamper 1964: 25; Kruger 1996).

Probably the simple fact that the ice rink of the Palais de Glace happened to be there was good enough reason for the organizers of the 1920 Antwerp Games to put figure skating and ice hockey on the program. These events took place on April 24–27, five months before the official opening of the Games. Swedish figure skater Ulrich Salchow, who had been amateur world champion eleven times, only finished fourth; but his young compatriot Gillis Grafstrom won the gold medal. Magda Julin, also from Sweden, won gold in the women's competition. Anti-German feelings were still very high in Belgium at that time, and Julin was forbidden to use the music of "An der schönen blauen Donau" (Blue Danube Waltz), on which she had based her whole training program. American figure skater Theresa Weld was the darling of the Antwerp public, but she had to be content with a third place due to a biased jury. The Canadian ice hockey team, entirely made up of players of the Winnipeg Falcons, won this Olympic premiere by beating the American team. The Canadian players, except for Walter "Wally" Byron, were all Icelandic immigrants; and they had chosen the falcon, the emblem of Iceland, as their crest (Cosentino and Leyshon 1987: 11–17; Renson 1996a: 23–26; 1996b).

The Dutch sports pioneer W. "Pim" Mulier had been an early critic of the proposals of the 1894 Olympic Congress in Paris to create a special prize for mountaineering: "I consider it not a wise decision to give a prize to the one who accomplishes 'the most interesting ascent,' which often means that one tries to reach the most inaccessible top with total disregard for death" (Mulier 1894). During the 12th IOC Session of May 23–27, 1911, Count Brunetta d'Usseaux had discussed the creation of a medal for mountaineering. The question was raised again on June 2, 1921, during the 20th IOC Session in Lausanne. The Committee for Mountaineering, which was led by Dr. Roland Jacot-Guillarmod, proposed the creation of a "prix olympique d'alpinisme." The proposal was accepted unanimously (Lennartz 2001). The IOC also decided on May 26–27, 1921, in Lausanne to take up the question of the winter sports once again. Sweden, Norway, and Finland voted against Olympic winter sports. Nevertheless the conference participants voted in favor of a resolution proposed by Marquis Melchior de Polignac on behalf of the French, the Swiss, and the Canadian Olympic Committees: "The Congress suggests to the International Olympic Committee that in all countries where Olympic Games are held and where it is possible to organize winter sports competitions, such competitions should be put under the patronage of the IOC and arranged in accordance with the rules of the international sports associations concerned" (Mo 1991: 338; see also Kamper 1964: 26).

As the 1924 Games were to be held in Paris, the French Olympic Committee received permission to choose the site of the winter sports week in France. Three towns were candidates: Chamonix in the Alps, Gerardmer in the Vosges, and Luchon-Superbagneres in the Pyrenees. Chamonix, which had already organized the French skiing championships in 1906 and 1908, was chosen. It was also safer in terms of having reliable snow conditions.

CHAMONIX 1924

The Games of the Eighth Olympiad were inaugurated at Chamonix in February 1924. This snowy prelude was a great success from every point of view. Fortunately, the period of thaw was followed (the day before the opening) by a period of intense cold and fine weather. At Chamonix French officials had to overcome hotel shortages. Beds were placed in the corridors, ballrooms, and billiard parlors of hotels, and private people were invited to open their homes. Athletes from sixteen nations took part in the first Winter Olympic Games.

The program consisted of ice hockey, bobsledding, figure skating, skiing, curling, and speed skating for men; women could compete only in figure skating. French warrant officer Camille Mandrillon, surrounded by the national flag bearers, swore the Olympic Oath at the opening of the 1924 Winter Sports Week (*Résultats* 1925; Welch 1996). The 500-meter speed-skating race was the opening event and was won by Charles Jewtraw of the United States, who thereby became the first Winter Olympics gold medalist. Austrian figure skater Herma Planck-Szabo won the first gold medal in women's Winter Olympics. An eleven-year-old Norwegian girl, Sonja Henie, finished last among the eight skaters from six nations. Later, however, she would become one of the most popular and successful female Olympic champions. Gillis Grafstrom again won the men's figure skating. The skating competitions took place outdoors and were thus seriously affected by the weather conditions. A crack athlete was Norwegian cross-country skier Thorleif Haug, who won gold in the 18-kilometer and 50-kilometer races and in the Nordic combined (Kluge 1997: 14–15). Canada and the United States were the finalists in the ice-hockey competition. The match drew a huge crowd; people were watching from roof tops to see the Canadians win 6 to 1. Just after the end of the hockey match, the death of former U.S. president Woodrow Wilson was announced. The Olympic and U.S. flags were lowered to half staff (Welch 1996). The Scandinavians dominated the competition. Norway won four gold, seven silver, and six bronze medals. Finland finished second with four gold, three silver, and three bronze medals.

During the closing ceremony of the 1924 Winter Sports Week in Chamonix, Coubertin presented the Olympic prize for mountaineering to Captain Edward Strutt of Great Britain, representing General Charles Granville Bruce, the leader of the 1922 British Mount Everest Expedition, which had not conquered the summit but had reached the height of 8,320 meters. Gold medals were distributed to all British members of the expedition (Lennartz 2001). Most well known among the team members was George Mallory, who would die on June 8, 1924, together with Sandy Irvine during their attempt to scale the last three- to four-hundred meters of Everest. His mummified body was found on May 1, 1999, during a special search expedition (Hemmleb et al. 1999; Lennartz 1999).

At the closing ceremony of the Winter Sports Week in Chamonix, on February 5, 1924, Coubertin spoke very enthusiastically about their inclusion in the official Olympic program. "I think that many of us would not rest easy if I failed to take this opportunity to express the admiration and gratitude that the efforts made to assure the greatest degree of technical perfection at their first Olympic tournament of Winter Sports inspire in us," said the baron. "Winter sports are among the purest and that is why I was so eager to see them take their place in a definitive way among the Olympic events" (in Muller 2000: 523–524).

Pierre Arnaud and Thierry Terret (1993: 23–116) have nevertheless pointed to the low impact of these first Winter Olympics on winter sports in general: "The Chamonix Games had all in all but minor effects. Winter sports stayed in the years 1924–1930 what they had been before, namely, an opportunity for a few wealthy tourists to spend an altitude vacation in more or less luxury hotels" (Arnaud and Terret 1993: 115). Nonetheless, because the Chamonix competition was an admitted success, representatives from the Norwegian, Swedish, and Finnish ski associations met in Stockholm on June 5, 1924, to send a strong message to the IOC president, asserting that "skiing and other winter sports must not be part of the Olympic Games" (Allen 1996a: 163).

At the 24th IOC session held in Prague on May 27, 1925, the Winter Games were officially included in the Olympic program. Preference would be given to a town in the country of the organizing city of the Summer Games. Should the country not be capable of organizing Winter Games, however, they would be given to a city in another country. Nonetheless, in a letter to the editor of *L'Auto* on January 16, 1925, Coubertin still officially stated that the Chamonix Winter Sports Week "at the occasion of the Eighth Olympiad was not part of the programme, at the express request of the Scandinavians." Three days after the election on May 28 of Henri de Baillet-Latour as the new IOC president, the 8th Olympic Congress entertained a proposal to include retroactively the 1924 Winter Sports Week as the first Winter Olympics (Muller 2000: 525). This proposal was accepted by a vote of 21 to 2 during the 25th IOC Session held in Lisbon on May 3–7, 1926 (Kluge 1999: 54–55). Arnd Kruger (1996: 109–110) has suggested that the Scandinavian countries would probably not have participated had they known in advance that the Chamonix events would become Olympic Winter Games, as these eventually reduced the importance of their own Nordic Games and internationalized the winter sports. Indeed, in 1925 voices were heard in the Nordic countries proposing to limit the size of the Olympic Games program and to discontinue the Winter Games (Jorgensen 1997, 2001).

ST. MORITZ 1928

The 1928 Summer Games were awarded to Amsterdam. The Netherlands had been neutral in the Great War, and its capital city was therefore seen as a politically appropriate place to welcome back the German Olympic team, which had not been invited to the 1920 and 1924 Games. As the Dutch Olympic Committee was unable to stage Winter Games, an agreement was made with the French Olympic Committee to hold them again in Chamonix. This arrangement was strongly criticized by Coubertin, however, and finally the decision was made to stage the Winter Games in St. Moritz in neutral Switzerland. German participation was met with considerable hostility in 1928; the Belgian OC, for instance, protested against the admission of German athletes (*Rapport général* 1928; Phillips 1996: 126–176; Simmons 1996a).

Of the 495 competitors in St. Moritz only 27 (5.4 percent) were women. Curling was dropped from the program; and the 10,000-meter speed skating was canceled because of the poor ice conditions. St. Moritz programmed the first Alpine skiing competitions as a demonstration sport. Norway excelled again by winning seven gold medals. One of them was won by the fifteen-year-old figure skater Sonja Henie, who would repeat this feat at the two following Olympics. Henie thus became the youngest Winter Olympic champion of all time. The Canadian hockey team, composed of University of Toronto students, completely ruled the ice and won its final three games by scores of 11–0, 14–0, and 13–0.

The U.S. team under the leadership of American Olympic Committee president General Douglas MacArthur had been plagued by disputes over the selection process (Simmons 1996a: 230). It gave a weak showing, winning only one gold medal in bobsledding and one in the "skeleton," a one-man sledding event only staged in St. Moritz in 1928 and 1948 before it reappeared in Salt Lake City in 2002. The newly elected IOC president Henri de Baillet-Latour from Belgium declared the second Winter Olympics a success. But serious problems such as defining amateur status and the proposal to sell newsreel rights to the Olympic Games were already looming on the horizon.

Arnd Kruger (1996: 115–117) has noted the "class struggle" in winter sports. The local people in the mountainous areas were often farmers of lower rank; the higher one lived up a mountain, the poorer one was, because of inferior farmland. These "montagnards" were the real skiing experts, however, and often taught the sport to tourists. The amateur status of ski instructors became a hot issue. The obvious social class barriers, which were the implicit *raison d'être* of amateurism, are evident: "those who made money from tourists by teaching them to ski were barred from competition as professionals; those who made money by providing them equipment or lodging were not" (Kruger 1996: 116). Moreover, the commercial value of the winter sports was far more obvious—from the beginning—than in summer sports. Winter Olympics served to advertise and to sell the tourist qualities of a winter resort as "the place to ski."

LAKE PLACID 1932

The little-known village of Lake Placid in the Adirondack forest of New York surprisingly became the venue for the 1932 Winter Games. The Games were brought to Lake Placid almost entirely due to the efforts of one man, Dr. Godfrey Dewey, the vice-president of the highly selective Lake Placid Club. He was the son of Melvil Dewey, founder of the club and originator of the Dewey Decimal Classification system for library holdings. The political backing of New York governor Franklin D. Roosevelt helped to convince the IOC to choose Lake Placid over other candidates such as Lake Tahoe, Yosemite Valley, and Denver. Roosevelt used the opening ceremony and the radio networks, which covered the athletic event, to boost his campaign for the American presidency. Eleanor Roosevelt even took a ride down the newly constructed bobsled run at Mount Van Hoevenberg during the opening ceremony.

The Games were fraught with problems. Avery Brundage, who had just been elected president of the AOC, never had any faith in Dewey's efforts; for example, he objected to the commercial nature of the Winter Games souvenir book, for which the publisher had been permitted to use the Olympic insignia (Allen 1996a). The cutting of about 2,500 trees of the "forever wild" Adirondacks for the construction of the bobsled run caused severe protests from local environmentalists. Moreover, New York was hit by an unusual heat wave in January. Luckily, a winter storm covered the whole area with snow before the opening of the Games on February 4 (Fea 1996a). European speed skaters protested against the newly adopted American "pack style" start, in which athletes skated against each other instead of individually against the clock. The International Skating Union (ISU) accepted the protest and had the races rerun. Nevertheless, the Americans won these races too (Holthausen and Paauw 1992: 95; Fea 1996a).

Lake Placid native Jack Shea, who had taken the Olympic Oath, won the Games' first gold medal, in the 500-meter speed-skating event. He also won the 1,500-meter and would later become mayor of Lake Placid. American skater Irving Jaffee won both the 5,000- and 10,000-meter distance races. Eddie Eagan, who had won the light-heavyweight boxing title at the

1920 Antwerp Games, now won gold again as a member of the U.S. four-man bobsled team. He thus became the only athlete to win gold both in Summer and Winter Games (Kluge 1997: 29). Swedish figure skater Gillis Grafstrom, who had consecutively won gold in 1920, 1924, and 1928, was outclassed by Austrian Karl Schafer. Four years earlier Schafer had partici-pated in the Amsterdam Summer Games as a breaststroke swimmer (Kruse 1995: 57; Kluge 1997: 27). Sonja Henie, the graceful Norwegian figure skater, won her second gold medal at Lake Placid and became the darling of the public. At Lake Placid women's speed skating became an Olympic sport for the first time. The Canadian ice-hockey players were victorious again. Though the final match against the United States ended in a 2–2 tie, they won by a point total. The U.S. team thus won silver; and the German hockey team, whose trip had been paid for by the United States, took bronze (Lattimer 1932; Rubien 1932).

The Games saw an important innovation: the three-tiered medals podium. IOC president Count Henri de Baillet-Latour had first seen the first three athletes stand on a pyramidal dais during the winners' celebration at the Empire Games in Hamilton, Canada, in 1931. He then ordered that this type of dais rather than the traditional platform be used at the Olympic Games; it first appeared at the Lake Placid Winter Games and then that summer in Los Angeles. The podium reversed customary social deferences since the IOC president or his/her representative must look up at the vic-torious athletes instead of bestowing medals from above as before (Barney 1998, 2000; Lennartz 2000b).

The worldwide economic depression and the costs of getting to Lake Placid had reduced participation to 306 athletes (including 32 females) from seventeen nations. John Fea (1996a: 235) has stressed the primary role played by local organizer Godfrey Dewey. His greatest accomplishment had been to convince the State of New York to allocate large funds during a period of depression.

GARMISCH-PARTENKIRCHEN 1936

When the 1936 Olympic Games were awarded to Germany, the German organizers were also eager to host the Winter Olympics. Originally Adolf Hitler and the Nazi Party had been opposed to modern sports and the Olympic Movement. But they eventually changed their views when minister of propaganda Joseph Goebbels and his entourage recognized the political potential of these events to win prestige and credibility for the "new order." The neighboring resorts of Garmisch and Partenkirchen were chosen because they featured all the necessary infrastructure, including ski-jump and bobsled facilities. Moreover, Garmisch and Partenkirchen were situated in Bavaria, where Munich and Nuremberg were strongholds of the National Socialist Party. The two resorts were merged in 1935 to become Garmisch-Partenkirchen. Despite the available infrastructure, a new ski stadium and ice arena were built, as well as cross-country trails, a new ski jump, and a new bobsled run (Ueberhorst 1988; Stauff 1996).

The Games were declared open in a blinding snowstorm by Reichskanzler Adolf Hitler before an enormous crowd. Many teams, including the British, the Canadian, and the French, raised their outstretched arms to the Führer when they marched by. They were presenting the Olympic salute, but the crowd took them for Nazi salutes, which elicited roars of applause (Rurup 1996: 93). The Americans, by contrast, gave only an "eyes-right" and were greeted by no more than a ripple of applause (Hart-Davis 1986: 95). Harold Abrahams, editor of the official report of the British Olympic Association (who wrongly stated that the Americans also gave the Olympic salute), was perplexed when the broadcaster announced: "The British greet the German Führer with the German salute" (Abrahams 1937: 212). Abrahams, who was Jewish, had been the 100-meter gold medalist in Paris 1924 (and featured in the movie *Chariots of Fire*) and supported British participation in the 1936 Olympics. His argument was that the isolation of Germany would not be good for world peace (Hart-Davis 1986: 111). The same interpretation of the German salute appeared in the German official report: "Our Olympic guests did voluntarily what no one dared or wanted to ask them: for the first time, the British and the French offered to their hosts the German salute during an official competition" (Richter 1936: 5).

New competitions appeared. Alpine skiing events were for the first time included in the Winter Olympic Games. Until then the Scandinavian bloc had managed to keep these non-Nordic sport forms out of the program. The Alpine combined, a downhill race and two slalom races, was scheduled for both men and women. Christl Cranz was the first to win the new event for Germany; her compatriot Kathe Grasegger was second (Pfister 1996; Sudholt 1996a, 1996b). One day later, German skier Franz Pfnur won the Alpine combined for men. Also new was the 4 × 10-km Nordic relay, won by the Finnish team. The local folk sport of "Eisschiessen" (a curling variant) and the so-called military ski patrol were added as demonstration sports. The latter was won by an Italian military team.

The Canadian hockey team was involved in two controversies. The first involved the British hockey team, which took to the ice with thirteen players, all but one of them Canadian trained. The Canadians had protested that two members of the British team had not obtained proper transfer papers from the Canadian Amateur Hockey Association (CAHA). The

International Ice Hockey Federation upheld the protest, but Canada eventually waived its complaint. In the end, the Canadians, winners of all former Olympic competitions, were eliminated through their 2–1 loss to Great Britain (Stevens 1985). The second controversy involved the appearance of star player Rudi Ball, who had originally been excluded from the German ice hockey team because he was half-Jewish. He had therefore moved to Italy (to Spain according to Hart-Davis 1986: 96), but he was eventually repatriated to fortify the German team (Kruger 1972: 167; Kluge 1999:108). His selection was heavily criticized both by the Nazis and by Jewish activists, for obvious antithetical reasons (Mandell 1971: 100). During the match between Germany and Canada, feelings ran high, and a riot threatened. First Hermann Goering and then Josef Goebbels took the microphone, begging the spectators to observe the Olympic spirit and to remember that the Canadians were Germany's guests. When the battle on ice ended, the score was Canada 6, Germany 2 (Hart-Davis 1986: 100).

The German Winter Games Organizing Committee, with IOC member Karl Ritter von Halt as its president and Baron Peter Le Fort as its general secretary, was well aware that the organization of the Summer Games would be at risk if any serious political problems arose at Garmisch-Partenkirchen. In light of the boycott movement in the United States and in Europe, they endeavored to remove all signs of anti-Semitic propaganda. To camouflage the gruesome Nazi policy, they did their utmost to create a friendly climate of Alpine "Gemütlichkeit" on the one hand and a perfectly planned program on the other hand (Kruger 1972).

SAPPORO/ST. MORITZ/ GARMISCH-PARTENKIRCHEN 1940

The city of Sapporo, Japan, was awarded the 1940 Winter Games in 1937 after Tokyo had already been given the 1940 Summer Games one year before. After the IOC session of Cairo in 1938, the IOC and the Fédération Internationale de Ski (FIS) had a fierce conflict over the amateur status of ski instructors. As the FIS rejected the IOC's decision to exclude "professionals," the IOC canceled the Alpine ski competition for the 1940 Sapporo Games. Japan, in the meantime, was at war with China; and the Japanese Olympic Committee decided in early 1938 to cancel its hosting of the Summer and Winter Games (Kamper 1964: 70; Bernett 1980).

The executive committee of the IOC on September 3, 1938, meeting in Brussels, awarded the 1940 Winter Games to St. Moritz, which had already demonstrated its organizational capacities in 1928. The Swiss, however, refused to reinstate ski jumping as a demonstration sport, as the IOC had done. The IOC then held a secret vote and took the Games away from St. Moritz and gave them to Garmisch-Partenkirchen, which had staged them only four years earlier. Prior to the meeting, IOC president Henri de Baillet-Latour had confidentially asked the German executive board member of the IOC, Karl Ritter von Halt, whether Garmisch-Partenkirchen could host the Winter Games again. This certainly was a political victory for Nazi Germany but a black page in the biography of Baillet-Latour. The Jewish pogroms had already begun in 1938, and German troops occupied Czechoslovakia from March 1939 onward (Lennartz 2000a). While eighteen nations accepted the invitation to compete at Garmisch-Partenkirchen and Hitler authorized the necessary funding, World War II began with the German invasion of Poland on September 1, 1939, and neither the Winter nor Summer Games took place in 1940 (Constable 1996: 100–119; Scharenberg 1996).

CORTINA D'AMPEZZO 1944

With the exception of Sigfrid Edstrom, who would become Baillet-Latour's successor in 1942, all IOC members in 1937 had supported the continuation of the Winter Games. And in September 1939 the majority of the IOC members voted for Cortina d'Ampezzo, Italy, to host the 1944 Winter Games. But Baillet-Latour decided that no IOC executive meeting or sessions would be held during the war. When the IOC president suddenly died on January 6, 1942, in Brussels, he was replaced by IOC vice-president Sigfrid Edstrom from Sweden (Engelbrecht 1996; Renson 1998). The Cortina d'Ampezzo Games of 1944 were of course never held, but twelve years later the Winter Games of 1956 were awarded to this north Italian ski resort.

ST. MORITZ 1948

St. Moritz, in neutral Switzerland, was the ideal site for postwar Winter Games. Although the Soviet Union did not participate in the 1948 Winter or Summer Olympics, it sent official observers to St. Moritz. Neither Germany nor Japan was invited on the official basis that neither one had a legitimate government, but Italy, Austria, Bulgaria, Hungary, and Romania—all former Nazi allies—sent teams. Protests were raised against team members who had been former Nazis, but only one athlete, an Austrian ski jumper, was not granted a visa by the Swiss government.

Very little peace and goodwill reigned during the Games. Two of the three American bobsleds were obviously sabotaged: bolts were loosened, and the steering mechanism of one sled was almost completely unscrewed.

Two rival American hockey teams appeared in St. Moritz, one authorized by the Amateur Hockey Association (AHA) and the other sanctioned by the Amateur Athletic Union (AAU). The Swiss Organizing Committee decided that the AHA team was qualified to participate, but the AAU team marched with the United States Olympic Committee (USOC) and Avery Brundage in the Opening Ceremony (Simmons 1996b). During the hockey competition, members of the AAU team supported the opposing teams; the AHA team finally finished fourth but was later disqualified by the IOC (Kruse 1995: 73; Kluge 1999: 168–170). There were more troubles: the Canada versus Sweden hockey match ended in a fistfight; speed-skating rules were heavily criticized; a Swiss policeman was accidentally shot by a competitor in the winter pentathlon; the historic Olympic flag of 1920 was stolen, and so was the flag that replaced it (Simmons 1996b: 250).

There were positives as well. Sweden, Norway, and Switzerland won the most medals. Despite all the razzamatazz, the St. Moritz Games added men's and women's downhill and slalom ski races. Gretchen Fraser from the United States took gold in the slalom and became the first non-European to win a skiing event. Skeleton sledding reappeared for the first time since its appearance in 1928, and the winter pentathlon was included as a demonstration sport (Muller 1949; Constable 1996: 121–176). The Games had survived the World War II hiatus.

OSLO 1952

The 1952 Winter Games were awarded to Oslo, Norway, during the IOC session of 1947 in Stockholm, Sweden. Oslo had the famous Holmenkollen ski jump, but it had to construct new facilities for Alpine skiing at Norefjell, five kilometers from Oslo. Snow was so scarce in February 1952, however, that volunteers and soldiers had to move large quantities of snow to the downhill courses. After the 1948 incidents, ice hockey had been removed from the Olympic program, but the dispute between the IOC and the International Ice Hockey Federation (FIHG) was resolved when the Norwegians agreed to build an expensive artificial ice rink. A temporary bobsled run was constructed, built entirely of snow and ice.

Politics loomed large. Anti-German feelings were still high in Norway. Finn Hadt, a Norwegian speed skater, was rejected by the Norwegian Olympic Committee (NOC) because he had collaborated with the Nazis during the war. German IOC member Karl Ritter von Halt, a former Nazi who had been involved in the organization of the 1936 Winter Games, was heavily criticized, but he nevertheless remained a member of the IOC. The West Germans participated in the Oslo Winter Games because the IOC had recognized their National Olympic Committee (NOC), whereas the status of the East German NOC was not resolved yet. The Soviet Union NOC had been recognized, but the Soviet hockey team was denied participation because it had neglected to join the International Ice Hockey Federation (MacDonald and Brown 1996).

For the first time a torch relay was part of a Winter Olympics. A torch run on skis was organized, which brought the Winter Olympic fire lit in the fireplace of ski legend Sondre Nordheim in Morgedal to the Bislett Stadium in Oslo. The last torch bearer was the nineteen-year-old grandson of polar researcher and ski legend Fridtjof Nansen. Thereafter torch relays were part of the Winter Games, a nice example of what Eric Hobsbawm and Terence Ranger (1983) have identified as "invented traditions."

As for the competitions, the Oslo Games added the giant slalom race for both men and women to the program and the 10-kilometer Nordic cross-country race for women, while the Alpine combined for men and women was dropped. Andrea Mead Lawrence of the United States won both the slalom events for women, the first American to win two gold medals. Stein Eriksen from Norway became a local hero by winning gold in the men's giant slalom. Another local hero was speed skater Hjalmar Andersen, who won three gold medals. American figure skater Richard "Dick" Button not only repeated his 1948 victory but also amazed the enthusiastic crowd with a never-before-seen triple jump and double axel. The West Germans made a successful comeback and took gold in the two- and four-man bobsled races (Andersen 1952; Von Mengden 1952).

Canada finished first and the United States second in the hockey competition after a 3–3 draw in the final game. Sweden was third, and Czechoslovakia fourth. Articles in the Soviet press accused the Canadians and the Yankees of conspiracy, which was qualified as a typical example of bourgeois capitalist cheating. The Norwegians had opted for bandy, a Scandinavian variant of ice hockey, as a demonstration sport. Only Finland, Norway, and Sweden competed. The Oslo Organizing Committee was awarded the Olympic Cup for its excellent organizing efforts (MacDonald and Brown 1996).

CORTINA D'AMPEZZO 1956

The northern Italian winter sport resort Cortina d'Ampezzo ("curtain of Ampezzo") was selected for the 1956 Winter Games during the IOC meeting in Rome in 1949. Italian IOC member and avid skier and skater Count Alberto Bona-Cossa, as in 1940, had prepared and defended Cortina's bid against its rivals. With the backing of the Italian National

Olympic Committee (CONI) excellent new facilities were constructed, among them a splendid ice stadium. All the events except for speed skating, held near Lake Niswina, were concentrated near Cortina, which stimulated a joyful atmosphere among the athletes and spectators (Hall 1996).

The Olympic Oath was taken for the first time in the Winter Games by a female athlete, Italian skier Giuliana Chenal-Minuzzo, who later finished third in the downhill race. The Italian national broadcasting company Radio Audizioni Italia (RAI) produced the first live television coverage of the Winter Games (Kruse 1995: 89).

The program was the same as for the Oslo Games except for the addition of the 30-kilometer cross-country ski race and the women's 3 × 5-kilometer relay race. Notably, this was the Soviet Union's first appearance at Winter Games. Soviet athletes entered the Olympic Winter scene "en grandeur," taking home a total of sixteen medals, thus outdoing all other nations by far. Soviet speed skaters won the 500-, 1,500-, and 5,000-meter events, while Soviet women won the 10-kilometer cross-country ski race and the 4 × 10-kilometer cross-country relay race. Moreover, the USSR hockey team captured Olympic gold, leaving the silver and bronze medals to the United States and Canada, respectively. American figure skaters dominated the men's and women's events. Hayes Jenkins won the men's gold, Ronald Robertson silver, and David Jenkins bronze. Tenley Albright won the gold medal in the women's figure skating, and Carol Heiss was second. But the star athlete at Cortina was Austrian skier Anton "Toni" Sailer, who was the first skier to win all three Alpine events—slalom, giant slalom, and downhill.

There were no political problems. In marked contrast to the 1956 Summer Games in Melbourne, the Cortina Winter Games were not plagued by Cold War vicissitudes. The two Germanies competed as a single team.

SQUAW VALLEY 1960

The awarding of the 1960 Winter Olympics to Squaw Valley in California's Sierra Nevada was very much due to one man's enterprise. New York attorney and avid skier Alexander J. Cushing had started a modest ski resort there after he had first fallen in love with the area and then discovered its tourist opportunities. He was shrewd enough to advertise his resort to Avery Brundage and his IOC companions as the ideal spot for "restoring the Olympic Ideal to the Winter Games." Finding the necessary funding for turning this rustic ski resort into an Olympic venue, however, was another game, and Cushing was eventually replaced as chairman of the Squaw Valley Organizing Committee by San Francisco businessman Prentis

Cobb Hale, Jr. (The new committee had the generosity to offer Cushing two free tickets to the Games he had made possible.)

The idea of rustic, intimate Games was soon forgotten when Walt Disney was enlisted as pageant director (Ashwell 1996: 265). Among other things, giant snow creatures made of plaster were erected and a "western night" with a mock gunfight by Hollywood cowboys was staged. IOC president Avery Brundage warned of the "disneyfication" of the Games five days before their opening: "Sport must be amateur or it is not sport at all, but a branch of the entertainment business" (*New York Times*, February 14, 1960).

The Squaw Valley Games featured technological innovations. Artificial indoor and outdoor ice was used for the first time, as were electronic timing and scoring devices. In contrast with these material developments, when warm weather and a lack of snow threatened the Games, Paiute Indians were called in to perform ritual snow dances (Kennedy 1996a: 271). They must have performed extremely well, because a blizzard hit Squaw Valley on the eve of the Games, which forced a brief delay in the opening ceremonies.

The competition, which saw the Soviets win the bulk of the medals followed by the combined German team, produced great performances. American figure skater Carol Heiss took the Olympic oath and also the gold medal in her sport. After the Games she married David Jenkins, who captured gold in the men's figure skating. The female skiing stars were Heidi Biebl from Germany in the downhill race and Yvonne Ruegg from Switzerland in the giant slalom. The American ice hockey players astonished everybody by beating Canada 2–1, then the Soviet Union 3–2, and finally Czechoslovakia 9–4 (Lembke 1960; Rubin 1960); it was the first time the U.S. team had defeated the Soviets.

Two sports made their Olympic debut: the biathlon, which consisted of cross-country skiing and rifle shooting, and women's speed skating, with Lydia Skoblikova from the Soviet Union winning both the 1,500- and 3,000-meter races. The bobsleigh competition, however, which had been on the program of the Winter Games since 1924, was not held. The Organizing Committee had decided not to build a bobsled course because of the high costs involved and presumably because few nations had initially indicated an interest in participating.

There were political developments. Reflecting Cold War concerns, the U.S. State Department refused to issue visas to some of the East German officials and journalists, claiming that they were Communist spies or propagandists (Ashwell 1996: 266). And while South Africa participated in the Winter Olympics for the first time in 1960, it would not do so again until the 1994 Lillehammer Games because of an IOC ban on the apartheid regime (Kruse 1995: 87). On a tragic note, one year after the Squaw Valley Games, on February 15, 1961, a Sabena Boeing 707 coming from New York crashed before landing in Brussels. Among the seventy-two casualties were the seventeen members of the U.S. figure-skating team (Kluge 1999: 307).

INNSBRUCK 1964

Innsbruck, the capital of the Tyrol region of Austria, took the preparations for the IXth Winter Olympics very seriously. Toni Sailer's 1956 sweep of Olympic gold had boosted Austria's fame as a winter sports nation. A ski area was carved out of the mountains, and a new ice stadium was constructed. The athletes were housed, "imprisoned" some said, in the heavily guarded, chain-link–fenced Olympic Village 10 miles from the city (Friedl and Neumann 1967).

For all the detailed planning, things did not go smoothly in Innsbruck. One factor that the organizers could not control was the snow. Because 1964 was one of the mildest winters ever recorded in the Tyrol, snow had to be brought in by trucks from distant sites, hauled up the slopes by wooden sleds, and then delivered in backpacks by 3,000 Austrian soldiers who packed down the runs. Bad luck continued with the accidental deaths of the Australian skier Ross Milne and Polish-born British luger Kazimirez Kay-Skrzypeski during training runs. Critics who argued that luge, introduced for the first time in 1964, was too dangerous be an Olympic sport pointed to Kay-Skrzypeski's death as proof; subsequent serious injuries to two German lugers reinforced their position. Then, after several serious skiing accidents, some argued that the Alpine event should be "split into two separate divisions, one for nations with a skiing tradition and one for non-Alpine countries" (Kennedy 1996a: 272). Finally, during the opening ceremony, Austrian bobsledder Paul Aste, who took the Olympic Oath, must have been inspired by some of the world-peace ideas of the sixties when he deliberately dropped the final word in "for the glory of the sports and the honor of our countries" in the oath and changed it to "the honor of our teams," thereby elevating athlete over nation.

The Games themselves were marked by controversy. Although the political rivalry between the "two Germanies" had worsened since the German Democratic Republic had started to build the infamous dividing wall, a single German team competed in Innsbruck, with "Ode an die Freude" (Ode to Joy) from Ludwig van Beethoven's *Ninth Symphony* as its anthem. The amateur versus professional debate flared up again, however. The U.S. hockey coach complained that his team, which finished fifth, was unfairly matched against European professionals; the Canadian hockey players, who finished fourth after being beaten by the eventual gold-medal-winning Soviets, agreed and boycotted the medals ceremony. The pairs skaters Marika Kilius and Hans-Jurgen Baumler of the united German team were suspected of having signed professional contracts before the Games and returned their silver medals to the IOC in 1966 (the medals were given back to them in 1987) (Kamper and Mallon 1992: 296).

IBM provided computer equipment, which was a major improvement over the time-consuming hand calculation of the competition results (Kennedy 1996a: 273). There were few highlights. Sjoukje Dijkstra from the Netherlands won the very first gold medal in figure skating for her country. The French sisters Christine and Marielle Goitschel finished first and second in the women's slalom then traded positions in the giant slalom (Kluge 1999: 311–360). The most memorable performance came from Soviet speed skater Lydia Skoblikova, who became the first athlete to win four individual gold medals in a single Winter Olympics by sweeping the 500-, 1,000-, 1,500-, and 3,000-meter events. Besides the introduction of luge, for the first time on the Olympic program ski jumping was divided into 70-meter and 90-meter runways.

GRENOBLE 1968

Grenoble marked the beginning of the media era in the Winter Games. After the city was chosen as the 1968 venue, the mayor of Lyon, Albert Michallon, handed over a $25,000 U.S. check to the IOC as first down payment for the television rights (Kluge 1997: 367). "Gigantism" was the term used by IOC president Avery Brundage to describe the capital involved, which according to the official report amounted to a total expenditure of just over 1 billion French francs ($240 million U.S.). Symptomatically, whereas the number of participating athletes did not increase compared to the Innsbruck Games, the size of the press corps increased greatly. They had much to cover, for controversy was the name of these Olympics.

The decentralization of the 1968 Games generated great criticism. Only the skating and ice hockey events were held in Grenoble itself. The other events took place in five distant locations throughout the Dauphine region, which forced the organizers to build three separate Olympic Villages. This decision was certainly not welcomed by those who still believed in the "uniting" spirit of the Games, and the competition venues themselves were criticized.

Political controversy abounded. Much to the dislike of IOC president Brundage, French president Charles de Gaulle and prime minister Georges Pompidou eagerly adopted the Games as a platform to promote French nationalism and Gaullist government policy (Arnaud and Terret 1993: 117–161). Of even greater political significance, however, were some Cold War battles. Although the East German National Olympic Committee had been recognized by the IOC, the North Atlantic Treaty Organization (NATO) forced its members to deny entrance visas to East German delegates. But the French government decided not to block the entrance of an East German Olympic team, thus initiating the beginning of a new era in international sport (Brown and MacDonald 1996: 279).

The modest East German sport debut started with a scandal. After the East German women had scored three of the four fastest times in the women's single luge event, they were disqualified when it was discovered that they had heated the runners of their luges. The IOC's decision to introduce doping control led to the very first tests being done in Grenoble. Only 10 percent of the 86 samples were analyzed; they all proved negative. Sex testing measures, too, were first introduced to the Winter Games at Grenoble. The female downhill world champion of 1966, Erika Schinegger from Austria, was found to be of dubious sexual identity. She decided to become a "he," changed her name from Erika to Erik, and later became a husband (Mogore 1989: 76–78; Kluge 1997: 370).

The major controversy involved commercialism and amateurism. Douglas Brown and Gordon MacDonald (1996: 279) consider Avery Brundage's crusade against commercialism in the Olympic Winter Olympics in Grenoble one of the most memorable and most embarrassing for the Olympic movement. Skiers allowed their images to be used in advertising by the ski industry and received large under-the-table payments for it. For Grenoble, a proposal was made to remove all trademarks from the competitors' skis, but the skiers and manufacturers argued that this would alter the balance of the skis and create technical difficulties for the skiers. A compromise was reached: namely, that the skis would immediately be taken from the athletes after their descent in order to prevent them from displaying their trademarks to the photographers and television. The controversy continued when a photograph appeared in a newspaper showing French super star Jean-Claude Killy exposing his Rossignol ski gloves to the photographer. An irate Brundage refused to participate in the medal ceremonies in the Alpine events of these skiing "sandwichmen." Allen Guttmann wrote in his biography of Brundage, entitled *The Games Must Go On* (1984: 198), that Brundage fought to expose the commercialism of skiers after he had fought in the 1940s to prevent commercial interests from a takeover in ice hockey. He told Dutch IOC member Jonkeer Herman van Karnebeek: "everyone knows both the French and Austrian ski teams are part of their departments of tourism—and that is not sport" (Guttmann 1984: 199).

Controversy attended the competition. Jean-Claude Killy had already won fame for the French skiing tradition during the year preceding the 1968 Games. In Grenoble he duplicated the historical feat of Toni Sailer from Austria by winning three gold medals in the Alpine events: the downhill race, slalom, and giant slalom. His slalom victory was not without dispute. Killy's Austrian rival, Karl Schranz, was disqualified when he missed the twenty-second gate in the course. He complained that he had been hindered by a spectator or an official and was granted a second chance. In this rerun he marked the fastest time of all competitors; but then the jury decided 3 to 2 to maintain his disqualification, which gave Killy his third gold medal (Kluge 1997: 30).

Killy was an *enfant terrible* to Brundage, who saw in him the personification of commercialism in sport. Ironically, Killy would later become the co-president of the Organizing Committee of the 1992 Games of Albertville and an IOC member in 1995.

There were few competitive surprises. The USSR ice hockey team ruled the rink as usual, with the other traditional powers Czechoslovakia and Canada finishing second and third, respectively. U.S. figure skater Peggy Fleming, who had won the world figure skating championships in 1967, easily earned the gold and became the uncontested Olympic Games ice princess of Grenoble.

The Grenoble Games were a turning point where the Winter Olympics reached an unprecedented scale in terms of costs and site dispersion difficulties (Comité d'Organisation 1969; Posey 1996: 110–176). This prompted the IOC to establish a commission to examine the future of the Olympic Winter Games. Brundage especially looked forward to the Sapporo Games of 1972 to come to a final settlement of the contested matters of nationalism and commercialism (Brown and MacDonald 1996: 282).

SAPPORO 1972

Among the venues for the 1972 Winter Olympics, three candidates stood out: Banff (Canada), Salt Lake City (United States), and Sapporo (Japan). It was thought to be too soon after the 1960 Games at Squaw Valley to consider Salt Lake City as an American site. Sapporo saw its chances considerably diminished in April 1966, about one month before the balloting, after a Boeing 727 crashed on a flight from Sapporo to Tokyo, killing 133 passengers and crew. So Banff seemed by far to have the best prospects to win the bid for the 1972 Winter Games. The Games went to Sapporo, however, which had been awarded the Olympic Winter Games of 1940 only to have them canceled because of war (Addkison-Simmons 1996). Sapporo was probably chosen over Banff because Avery Brundage feared a confrontation with Canadian environmentalists. The proposed site was indeed strongly opposed by the Canadian Wildlife Association, which was afraid of an Olympic invasion into the pristine natural areas around Lake Louise.

In February 1971, one year before the Games, the Sapporo Organizing Committee held an international sports week to try out the sport facilities and other accommodations. Everything was carefully planned and meticulously executed, including the provision of female hostesses, offering more than administrative services to their male guests. The hot issue of the professional skiers was raised once more. IOC president Brundage had demanded that ten prominent skiers be excluded because they had been compensated for their participation in a ski camp at Mammoth Mountain, California. At the meeting of the Fédération Internationale de Ski (FIS) in Yugoslavia in 1971, all major European ski countries threatened to boycott the Winter Games if Brundage did not back off from his demand. He eventually did; but then he announced that Olympic athletes, and skiers in particular, would not be allowed to display advertising logos. FIS president Marc Hodler reluctantly agreed that medalists would remove the trademarks from their skis before having their picture taken (Addkison-Simmons 1996: 286–287).

Brundage then became known as the "abominable snowman" when a five-strong accreditation committee decided to disqualify Karl Schranz from Austria, the 1970 world champion in the giant slalom. According to Volker Kluge (1997: 419), he was disqualified not for having his picture taken with his Kneissl skis but for having advertised a coffee brand (Addkison-Simmons 1996: 287). Upon his return to Austria, "the lion of Sankt Anton" was received by chancellor Bruno Kreisky and given the Austrian Order of Merit. Frustrated by continuing controversies, Brundage urged the IOC to eliminate the Winter Olympics after the 1976 Games in Denver, Colorado.

In contrast to all the hassles before the Games, the Sapporo Olympics had a smooth run. In the absence of Karl Schranz, the giant slalom was won by Gustav Thoni from Italy. He won silver in the slalom, and his cousin Roland Thoni won the bronze medal. Gold went to Francisco Fernandez Ochoa from Spain, who won his country's first-ever Winter Olympic medal. Marie-Therese Nadig from Switzerland defeated the favored Annemarie

Pröll from Austria in the downhill race and the giant slalom. Wojciech Fortuna from Poland won the long ski jump, but he would never repeat this "fortuitous" feat again. Galina Kulakova from the USSR finished first in both the 5-kilometer and 10-kilometer cross-country ski races. Ard Schenk from the Netherlands won the 1,000-, 5,000-, and 10,000-meter speed skating. Two U.S. women speed skaters won gold medals: Anne Elizabeth Henning in the 500-meter race and Dianne Mary Holum in the 1,500-meter race. The USSR again very convincingly won ice hockey, with the U.S. team finishing second. For the first time in Olympic history, the Canadians did not compete in hockey, in protest against the professionals on the teams from the Communist countries (Organizing Committee 1973; Ensink 1972; Daniels 1996a: 114–175).

INNSBRUCK 1976

As sport historian John J. Kennedy, Jr., has pointed out, IOC president Avery Brundage had long despised the "Frostbite Follies" for their strong links with professionalism and commercialism as well as their lack of universal appeal (Kennedy 1996b: 289). In his farewell address in 1972, he voiced his desire that "the Winter Olympics receive a decent burial in Denver." He further declared: "This poisonous cancer must be eliminated without further delay" (*New York Times,* February 6, 1973).

Brundage's wish almost came true when in November 1972 Colorado voters rejected a referendum to allocate $5 million in public revenue to fund the 1976 Denver Games. The new IOC president, Michael Morris, Lord Killanin, immediately started his search for a replacement among the cities that had hosted past Winter Games. In 1973 the IOC selected Innsbruck to hold the Games three years later. The so-called Undertaking resulted, as a lesson learned from the Denver debacle. From then on, the IOC required host cities to post a surety bond and sign a contract that guaranteed their obligations as a host city.

Austria saw the awarding of the Olympics as a recompense for the exclusion of its national skiing hero, Karl Schranz, from the 1972 Sapporo Games. Instead of cutting costs by eliminating certain sports from the program, Killanin warned the host city to budget well and to establish tight financial management. Another concern that haunted the organizers of the Innsbruck Games was the threat of terrorism following the massacre at the Munich Games in 1972. After an assault on the Organization of Petroleum Exporting Countries (OPEC) headquarters in Vienna six weeks before the Innsbruck Games, in which three people were killed and eighty taken hostage, exceptional security measures were taken. An army of 5,000 specially trained police and soldiers was assigned to Innsbruck. The Olympic Village, housing 1,650 athletes and officials, looked very much like a fortress, with a two-to-one security-to-athlete ratio. Security costs for the Games were estimated at $1.7 million U.S.

Pregame preparations were excellent, but nature failed to cooperate. Innsbruck had to launch a new "Operation Snowlift." A thousand truckloads of snow were shipped from the Brenner Pass, and soldiers once again hand-packed the ski runs. A welcome heavy snowfall at the opening of the Games freed soldiers from their chores of preparing ski runs, so they switched to guard duties (Kennedy 1996b).

For the first time in Olympic history, at the Opening Ceremony two torches were carried to light dual Olympic flames in honor of the two Olympics in Innsbruck. Franz Klammer took the athletes' oath and would later ski to victory in the downhill race. West German waitress Rosi Mittermaier won the slalom and the downhill (Kluge 1997: 86–88). Soviet cross-country skier Galina Kulakova, who had already captured two medals in Sapporo, now became the first woman to win five gold medals. The East Germans (GDR) won all five bobsled and luge events. The Soviet Union once again led the medal count with twenty-seven medals, thirteen gold. "Ice dance" made its initial appearance on the Olympic skating program and was dominated by Soviet couples, who took the gold and silver medals (*Endbericht* 1976; Valerien 1976; Gerz 1976a, 1976b; Daniels 1996b: 116–176).

Drug busts marred the competition. Kulakova's bronze medal in the 5-km individual race was taken away after she tested positive for ephedrine, a decongestant, leaving her with four Olympic medals. The captain of the Czech hockey team, Frantisek Pospisil, tested positive for codeine in a random drug test after the victory over Poland. The IOC did not expel Pospisil but did banish for life the physician, Otto Trefny, who gave him the drug for the flu. The team also had to forfeit its victory against Poland but still ended second after the USSR, which won its fourth consecutive gold medal.

Mayor Alois Lugger, who had already staged the 1964 Innsbruck Olympics, agreed to make a ceremonial bobsled ride to promote the tourist attractions of his city. He had unbuttoned his trousers to fit more easily in the narrow sled. His triumphant run ended hilariously when his pants fell to his ankles while he was enthusiastically waving to the press and spectators.

LAKE PLACID 1980

Lake Placid, New York, which had hosted the 1932 Olympics, had made unsuccessful bids to be the U.S. host for all Olympic Winter Games since 1956. When the small Adirondack ski resort obtained the Games for the second time, the Lake Placid Olympic Organizing Committee (LPOOC) was formed (Final Report Editorial Committee 1980; Gerz 1980a, 1980b; *Official Results* 1981). Scandals, death, and financial struggles led to a continual reshuffling of the committee members. Only the Reverend Bernard Fell, a Methodist minister, remained a constant in the LPOOC. When the committee was faced with delays in the construction plans and overbudgeting, Peter Spurney, a well-known financial troubleshooter, was called in (Fea 1996b: 295–296).

The LPOOC had to overcome several obstacles. The first obstacle was an environmental one. The Adirondack region was a state park and had been declared to be "forever wild." Moreover, the ski jump was built too close to the historic farm site where the famous abolitionist John Brown still laid "a-mold'ring in his grave." After resolving these problems, the organizers faced financial difficulties. They finally obtained the necessary money for constructing the Olympic Village from the Federal Bureau of Prisons, which would provide the needed $47 million in exchange for the facility's utilization as a federal juvenile prison after the Games (Fea 1996b: 295–296).

Two problems were not overcome. Because very little housing was available in the village of Lake Placid itself, the spectators had to find lodging in far-away hotels and motels. Three two-lane roads were the only access to the village, which created a transportation nightmare. Spectators were stranded at events for hours in the freezing cold. A huge arts festival, which was developed with money from the federal government, did not meet the high expectations because most of the exhibits were in Plattsburg, some 47 miles from Lake Placid.

It was not only cold in Lake Placid; internationally the Cold War also was raging. After the Soviet invasion of Afghanistan in December 1979, U.S. president Jimmy Carter considered a boycott of the 1980 Moscow Summer Games. This did not stop the Soviets from coming to Lake Placid in February. They vowed not to "work counter the spirit of the Olympic Games" (Fea 1996b: 299) and thus acted in line with IOC president Lord Killanin, who hoped to prevent the U.S. boycott of the Moscow Games.

Despite all of these problems, the Lake Placid Games produced outstanding athletic achievements. Ingemar Stenmark from Sweden for the men and Hanni Wenzel from Liechtenstein for the women posted double slalom victories. East Germany's Ulrich Wehling won his third consecutive gold medal in the Nordic combined, and Russian's Irina Rodnina took a third straight gold in pairs figure skating. American speed skater Eric Heiden accomplished what no other athlete had done before (or since) in the Winter Games, capturing five gold medals (one in every speed-skating event) while setting four Olympic records and one world record. The spectacular ice hockey victory of the young American team over the much more experienced Soviet team was generally acclaimed as a symbolic victory of the free world over an aggressive totalitarian regime. President Carter called the players "modern day heroes" (Fea 1996b: 300), probably hoping that their victory would assuage the nation's worries about the American hostages in Iran, the possible boycott of the Moscow Olympics, and the stagnating economic situation.

For the first time since its appearance in the Winter Olympics in 1956, the USSR finished second to another European country—the German Democratic Republic. (Norway won the most medals at Grenoble in 1968.) Although Soviet athletes won more gold, the East Germans won an overall total of twenty-three medals against twenty-two for the USSR (Riordan 1980).

SARAJEVO 1984

There were two main reasons why the IOC awarded the XIVth Winter Olympics to the city of Sarajevo in Yugoslavia and not to Göteborg, Sweden, or Sapporo, Japan. The first reason was that the events would be located in a compact area. The second was that the Olympic influence would move into a nation that, though belonging to the Communist bloc, had always pursued an independent line under its former leader, Josip Broz Tito. Additionally, the Olympics would help tourism in a developing country.

The Yugoslav Organizing Committee, made up of Communists, succeeded in marketing the Winter Olympics with great success and managed ultimately to make a profit. The largest part of a total funding of $100 million U.S. came from the American Broadcasting Corporation (ABC), which bid $91.5 million for the U.S. broadcast rights. Efficient management reduced the original budget of $160 million U.S. to $135 million. The opposite had happened in Lake Placid, where the original budget of less than $100 million had risen to $185 million, thus leaving a large deficit (Dunkelberger 1996: 302–304).

Preparations for the Olympics were impressive. When it was discovered that the Mount Bjelasonica downhill run was 9 meters short (a 800-meter vertical drop is required), a lodge was built on top with both a restaurant and the starting gate on its third floor. Moreover, the preparations greatly improved the general standard of living in Sarajevo. The railway station and airport were expanded, water and sewage systems were improved, and fifteen hotels were either remodeled or newly built (Dunkelberger 1996: 304–305).

The Sarajevo Games were the largest Winter Olympics ever organized. A stunning statistic was the ratio of athletes to journalists: an Olympic Village was built to house 2,200 athletes and delegates, while the village for the press had room for 8,500 journalists!

Whereas former Winter Games had been plagued with a lack of snow, the 1984 Olympics were faced with too much snow and blizzard-like conditions. Races had to be delayed, and the Sarajevo airport even shut down for two days.

After the 11th Olympic Congress of 1981 at Baden-Baden, new IOC president Juan Antonio Samaranch pressed for liberalization of the amateur regulations. Now the international federations were mainly responsible for the decisionmaking in these matters. Nonetheless, the defense of amateurism continued. The Fédération Internationale de Ski maintained its ban on two former "olympionikes," 1980 gold medal skiers Ingemar Stenmark and Hanni Wenzel, for having accepted appearance money. And an agreement was reached that five hockey players from three countries who had competed in the professional National Hockey League (NHL) were withdrawn from Olympic participation (Dunkelberger 1996: 305; Kluge 1997: 565).

The athletic highlight for the local population was when Slovenian skier Jure Franko won the first-ever Yugoslavian Winter Olympic medal, capturing silver in the men's giant slalom. U.S. skiers did unusually well in Alpine events: Billy Johnson, often called "crazy boy" by his teammates, won the gold medal in the downhill race; Debbie Armstrong and Christin Cooper finished first and second, respectively, in the giant slalom; and twins Phil and Steve Mahre won gold and silver in the slalom. Scott Hamilton from the United States won the gold in men's figure skating. Katarina Witt of East Germany made her Olympic debut and won the first of her eventual two gold medals in women's figure skating. Britain's Jane Torvill and Christopher Dean earned unanimous perfect scores in pairs figure skating. Olympic records were set in every women's speed-skating race. The women's 20-kilometer cross-country ski race was added to the program but would be dropped after the 1988 Games (Moravetz 1984; Sarajevo Organizing Committee 1984).

The very successful Sarajevo Winter Olympics had created a friendly and optimistic atmosphere, but this euphoria was only short-lived. Seven years later the country was torn apart in a bitter and cruel civil war. The sites where thousands of enthusiastic spectators had cheered the competitors now held artillery that destroyed former hotels and ski resorts. The bobsled run was turned into a trench for snipers. What once had looked like an Olympic fairy tale had now become a cruel place of blind ethnic terror.

CALGARY 1988

Calgary, Alberta, had made three previous bids to host the Winter Olympics. At the IOC Congress of Baden-Baden in 1981, the Canadian city's fourth bid met with success. The newly formed organizing committee Olympiques Calgary Olympics (OCO) (bilingual in name only) started to prepare a sporting and cultural festival that would affect the whole area (*Rapport officiel* 1988; Galford 1996: 116–184). Citizens were mobilized to contribute to the success of this endeavor by donating time as volunteers and money. After David Leighton (who had been hired as president of OCO at a salary of $100,000 U.S.) resigned, he was replaced by Bill Pratt, former manager of the Calgary Stampede rodeo. Oilman Frank King was named chairman of the committee. Pratt opted for a volunteer labor strategy. Over 9,000 volunteers, working countless hours for OCO, were brought into coordinated action (Wamsley 1996: 310–313).

The Cree Indians were involved in some of the ritual aspects of the Games, and a large exhibition was dedicated to some of their cultural artifacts that had been "removed" to European museums. The Lubicon Cree and their chief, Bernard Ominayak, however, mounted a boycott against the exhibition and against the torch relay because they considered themselves the victims of the oil companies that sponsored these events (Wamsley and Heine 1996a).

Funding was provided by the most lucrative television contract to date for any Olympic Games, Winter or Summer, and by the support of all levels of public and governmental, national, and international corporations. On the Paskapoo slopes west of the city, a US $72 million Olympic Park was constructed. The federal government paid for the design and construction of the ski jumps and the bobsled and luge tracks. Moreover, an athletes' training center and an Olympic Hall of Fame were built on the same site. Seven residence halls at the University of Calgary served as the Olympic Village, requiring students to leave their accommodations in order to house the athletes. The Faculty of Physical Education would benefit greatly from the newly built Olympic facilities once the Games were over.

President Juan Antonio Samaranch, who demanded a "marquis-class" treatment for the IOC members and their families and guests, including being provided a luxury sedan and driver, joined the 60,000 spectators who attended the opening ceremony in the McMahon Stadium (Wamsley 1996: 314). Over 8,000 performers staged a spectacular show of old and newly invented Alberta traditions. Steven Jackson (1998) has characterized the Calgary Olympic opening event as the construction of a "tele-nation," an important site for the analysis of the politics of national identity; and Kevin

Wamsley and Michael Heine (1996b) view the Calgary Olympic experience as the construction of civic identity.

The most unusual aspect of the athletic competitions was that for the first time speed skating was held in an indoor facility and Alpine skiing on artificial snow. Competing in her fourth Olympics, Raisa Smetanina of the Soviet Union won her eighth and ninth cross-country skiing medals. The star athlete in ski jumping was Matti Nykanen from Finland, who won both events. But the inept British ski jumper Michael Edwards, better known as "Eddie the Eagle," who finished last in both events, got an abundant amount of public acclaim as a satirical antihero. Italian super skier Alberto "la Bomba" Tomba and Vreni Schneider from Switzerland won the two slalom events. Tomba did not compete in the new Super Giant Slalom because he had promised his parents not to start in this dangerous event, which combines a downhill race with a giant slalom. Katarina Witt from East Germany won her second consecutive gold medal in figure skating. Dutch speed skater Yvonne van Gennip captured triple gold in the 1,500-, 3,000-, and 5,000-meter events. The USSR won the two-man and four-man bobsled races. The inexperienced four-man Jamaican bobsled team added some interest to the event, but the Jamaicans ended their "cool running" by capsizing in the third turn (Kluge 1997: 87–113). Even on their own holy ground, the Canadian hockey players could not stop the Soviet team, which, as later events would dictate, won its last golden medal in the history of the USSR. Moreover, the Canadians were also beaten by Finland and Sweden, which won silver and bronze, respectively.

Free-style or "hot dog skiing" and short-track skating, which would become official Olympic sports in Lillehammer in 1992, were programmed as demonstration sports. Curling, which had been on the men's program in 1924 and 1932, now made its reappearance as a demonstration sport for men and women; it would become an official Olympic sport ten years later during the Winter Olympics at Nagano in 1998 (Kluge 1999: 611–682, 927).

ALBERTVILLE 1992

Thirteen cities made bids for the 1992 Winter Olympics. Albertville counted on the competition between Barcelona and Paris for the 1992 Summer Games, knowing that IOC president Samaranch wanted these Games for his hometown. If Albertville won, Paris would be virtually "out" and Barcelona "in," because no nation had hosted both the Winter Summer Games since 1936. And that is how it happened: Albertville was chosen during the 91st IOC Session in Lausanne on October 17, 1986; in the longest election in Olympic history, Albertville won on the sixth ballot over Sofia (Bulgaria), 51 to 25.

The Organizing Committee's name was a mission statement in itself: Comité d'Organisation de Jeux Olympiques d'Hiver d'Albertville et de la Savoie (COJO). From the first contacts between politician Michel Barnier and ex–ski champion Jean-Claude Killy, both were motivated for the Olympic bid as a unique opportunity to expand the tourist economy of the Savoie region. Thus the Albertville Games became the most decentralized in Olympic history: ten venues were spread over 650 square miles.

Although the Organizing Committee stated that environmental protection was part of its planning, loud protests were heard against a series of environmental disasters caused by the Games. The worst was the ammonia leak at the La Plagne bobsled and luge run. The track was situated in direct sunlight, and therefore ammonia was brought in to freeze the track (Lellouche 1996: 318–320). The Organizing Committee, however, had opted to "recycle" most of the facilities after the Games. The temporary scaffolding of the Albertville stadium, for instance, was sold to Barcelona for the Summer Games. The widespread international claims of environmental damage that resulted from the Games pressured the IOC to rethink its position on environmental issues. In two years' time, from 1992 to 1994, the IOC went from an organization with no environmental policy to one that declared that environmental protection had become the third dimension of the Olympic movement, alongside sport and culture (Cantelon and Letters 2000).

Several sponsorship "clubs" were created to lure corporations into the Olympic enterprise. There was the Club Coubertin, with the real big fishes such as Crédit Lyonnais, Renault, and nine others. There was also the Club des Quinze, fifteen companies including Club Med, whose resort in Val d'Isère became the skiers' village. It is also worth mentioning that Arthur Andersen Consulting had helped prepare the Albertville bid. The Columbia Broadcasting System (CBS) won the American television rights against its rivals NBC and ABC with a bid of $243 million, $68 million more than NBC and $34 million above the IOC minimum (Lellouche 1996: 320–321; Kluge 1999: 689–693).

The Albertville Games were the first Olympics since the collapse of the Communist states. The former Soviet Union sent a Unified Team, consisting of athletes from Russia, Ukraine, Belarus, Kazakhstan, and Uzbekistan. The team got Adidas sponsorship and used the Olympic flag and the Olympic anthem. The athletes from the former Soviet republics Estonia, Latvia, and Lithuania marched under their own flags for the first time in fifty-six years. East and West Germany, now united, sent a joint team for the first time since the 1964 Innsbruck and Tokyo Games. Yugoslavia had split into Yugoslavia, Croatia, and Slovenia, all participating now as independent nations. Croatia had been admitted into the IOC only twenty days before the Albertville Games.

The XVIth Olympic Winter Games opened with a futuristic mass spectacle. The Olympic Oath was given by the black French figure skater Surya Bonaly. Newly accepted events were short-track speed skating (four events), free-style skiing (two events), and biathlon for women (three events). Free-style ski ballet and aerials, speed skiing, and curling figured as demonstration sports (Organizing Committee 1992).

Athletes from thirty-six countries participated in the Games. The most successful was female cross-country skier Ljubov Egorova, of the Unified Team, who won three gold and two silver medals. Her compatriot, forty-year-old Raisa Smetanina, competing in her fifth Winter Olympics, won gold in the 4 × 5-kilometer cross-country relay. She became the oldest medal winner and the most decorated athlete in the history of the Winter Games with four gold, five silver, and one bronze. Alberto Tomba successfully defended his gold medal in the giant slalom. American Bonnie Blair won the 500- and 1,000-meter speed skating. Sixteen-year-old Toni Nieminen from Finland won gold in the long ski jump and bronze in the short jump (Kluge 1997: 114–118). The Unified Team continued the old-time Soviet tradition by winning the ice hockey competition. Canada, Czechoslovakia, and the United States finished second, third, and fourth, respectively. The reunified German team went home with the most medals: ten gold, ten silver, and six bronze.

Of the 1,808 athletes, 1,318 (73 percent) were men and 490 (27 percent) were women. Most of the women had to take the new "sry gene test," which replaced the former femininity test. In all, 522 doping tests were taken; not a single one was positive.

The closing ceremony brought another bizarre postmodernist spectacle. A Viking ship was featured to announce the Lillehammer Winter Games, which would take place in two years' time. The Games ended with a $52 million U.S. deficit, of which 75 percent was paid by the French government and 25 percent by the Savoie Department.

LILLEHAMMER 1994

When the IOC decided to alternate the Winter and the Summer Games every two years, starting in 1994, the little Norwegian ski resort of Lillehammer took up the challenge of presenting a new bid to compensate for its loss of the 1992 Games. Originally the Lillehammer bid committee promised to hold "compact" Games as a contrast to the widespread venues of the 1992 Games, which had actually been more the Savoie Games rather than the Albertville Games. At the time of the decision taken at the Seoul Summer Games in 1988, the Swedish candidate city of Østersund/Åre lost votes because of an incident in which Sweden accused a Soviet submarine of having violated its territorial waters. Anchorage (Alaska) was eliminated in the second round in part due to its proximity to Calgary. Sofia in Bulgaria was assessed as a big city with unpredictable winter weather. So suddenly the Norwegian city, literally called "Little Hammer," hit the nail on its head with its bid.

The original idea of compact and "low-budget" Games soon had to be given up, however, when the realistic costs of staging the Winter Olympics surpassed the worst-case scenarios. The Norwegian government had to intervene both financially and managerially and created the Lillehammer Olympic Organizing Committee (LOOC). The parliament requested that more venues be dispersed throughout the region. On the occasion of the Lillehammer Games, the Norwegians tried to promote their cultural identity through innovative architecture and top-quality design (Klausen 1999). Such architectural marvels included the "Viking Ship" skating hall in Hamar, whose roof looked like an overturned ship, and the ice hockey hall at Gjøvik, situated in an artificial cave blasted in a solid granite mountain. Prehistoric Norwegian petroglyphs inspired the design of Olympic sport pictograms, which soon became collectors' items (Lillehammer Olympic Organizing Committee 1994, 1995). And since Lillehammer is the only city in the world whose coat of arms bears a skier, during the opening ceremony Stein Gruber made a thrilling ski jump with the Olympic torch to light the flame in the cauldron.

The Lillehammer Winter Olympics qualified as the "first green Olympics." The LOOC wanted to show that a constructive dialogue was possible between environmentalists and Olympic business. After protests from birdwatchers, who feared the disruption of migratory patterns, the Viking Ship building site in Hamar was moved away from the shore of the bird sanctuary. Schoolchildren were called upon to help with the planting of "Olympic forests" and to transplant rare wildflowers from ski or bobsled construction sites. And the most up-to-date energy-saving techniques were used, which lowered energy consumption at Olympic sites by 30 percent (Maloney 1996: 326–329).

Lillehammer also launched the first-ever Olympic humanitarian program. This can be seen as a spiritual marriage between the Norwegian religious tradition of pietism on the one hand and the Olympic ideal of world peace and solidarity on the other. Through the Olympic Aid program, money was raised for the children in war-torn Sarajevo, where the Winter Games had been held ten years before. The Lillehammer Organizing Committee expanded this campaign with relief projects in Beirut, Guatemala, and Eritrea and other African countries.

The athletic competitions ranged from the ridiculous to the sublime. "Koss is the boss": Johann Olav Koss became Norway's national sport hero by winning three speed-skating gold medals in world record time in the 1,500-, 5,000-, and 10,000-meter events. Bonnie Blair from the United States, who had already captured gold medals in two previous Olympics, won gold again in the 500- and 1,000-meter speed-skating races. Her U.S. teammate Dan Jansen finally realized his Olympic dream by winning the 1,000-meter speed-skating race. With a gold medal in the slalom, Swiss skier Vreni Schneider became the first woman to win three gold medals in that event. Female figure skating wallowed in the sordidness of the Kerrigan-Harding incident, which was called "Wounded Knee II" in the Norwegian press. Nancy Kerrigan, U.S. bronze medalist in Albertville, had been clubbed on the knee by an attacker during the U.S. Olympic figure-skating trials one month before the Games. Due to Kerrigan's injury, these trials had been won by Tonya Harding. When the police linked the attack on Kerrigan to Harding and her henchmen, the United States Olympic Committee (USOC) tried to remove Harding from the skating team. This was followed by a lawsuit against the USOC by Harding's lawyers, which postponed any disciplinary action until the Games were over. Ultimately both skating rivals were sent to Lillehammer. Harding failed, probably under the intense media pressure. Kerrigan lost by only a tenth of a point to sixteen-year-old Ukrainian Oksana Baiul in the artistic skating title (Maloney 1996: 331–332; Kluge 1997: 119–121, 1999: 836–837).

Although Russia ended in first position with a total of twenty-three medals (eleven gold, eight silver, and four bronze), the Norwegians did almost as well with a higher total of twenty-six medals (ten gold, eleven silver, and five bronze). There is evidence of home advantage in the Winter Olympics since 1924 onward. It is most significant in the subjectively assessed events. Little or no home advantage, however, was observed in Nordic skiing, bobsled, biathlon, and speed skating (Balmer et al. 2000).

Before the Lillehammer Games, Norwegians did not hold IOC president Samaranch in high esteem. Many thought he was blatantly lobbying for the country's prestigious Nobel Peace Prize, as the Nazis had done for Pierre de Coubertin a long time ago. Samaranch's rhetorical statements and illusory efforts to stop the war in Sarajevo and to end apartheid in South Africa were met with cool suspicion. Once the Games had started in record cold temperatures, however, the Olympic atmosphere became warm and relaxed.

An interesting media analysis by Roel Puijk (1997, 2000) showed that the Lillehammer Games served an integrative function in Norway, where they were broadcast live. But in other countries, especially in the United States, the Games were differently interpreted and contextualized, sometimes even restructured into a more dramatic sequence.

NAGANO 1998

When the Japanese city of Nagano narrowly beat out Salt Lake City (46–42) as the host city of the 1998 Winter Olympics, environmentalists were very concerned that some of the Games-related construction would damage protected mountain forest areas. It took five years of discussion between the FIS and the Nagano Organizing Committee to agree on the length of the downhill race. FIS requested that the start would be at 1,800-meter elevation, whereas the Japanese refused to move it higher than 1,680 meters because of encroachment on a natural park area. Eventually a compromise was reached at 1,765 meters.

The Nagano Games were the largest Winter Olympics ever, with 2,304 athletes and officials from 72 countries participating in 68 events. The official program increased to 7 sport disciplines and 68 events with the addition of curling for men and women, women's ice hockey, and, at Samaranch's request, snowboarding. The two most successful athletes were cross-country skiers: Larissa Lazutina from Russia with three golds, one silver, and one bronze medal and Norwegian Bjorn Daehlie with three golds and one silver medal. Local ski jumper Kazuyoshi Funaki captured gold in the 90-meter ski jump and silver in the 70-meter ski jump. Austrian Alpine skier Hermann Maier won gold in the giant slalom and in the Super G after having survived a disastrous fall in the downhill race. Bart Veldkamp, the only Belgian competitor in Nagano, won bronze in the 5,000-meter speed-skating event. This "newborn" Belgian had won gold for the Netherlands in the 10,000-meter event in 1992, but he had changed nationality in 1995 after a dispute with the Dutch Skating Federation.

Hockey drew the most attention. The U.S. women won gold in the first female ice-hockey competition, with Canada and Finland finishing second and third, respectively. Men's hockey saw the introduction of National Hockey League players. The International Ice Hockey Federation (IIHF) and the National Hockey League (NHL) had reached an agreement in 1995, which now allowed elite-level professionals to play in Nagano. The Czech ice-hockey team, which counted the fewest NHL players in its ranks, won convincingly. The team returned home to Prague in a special governmental plane, where the players were acclaimed by a crowd of 70,000 people (Simon 1998; Kluge 1999: 862–972).

The Games were watched by 1,275,529 ticketed spectators and also televised in more nations and regions than ever before. The total hours of broadcast time increased 55 percent over the Lillehammer Games. Despite the time-zone differences for the American and European markets and the difficulties in scheduling certain events due to bad weather conditions, the cumulative global audience was estimated to equal the 1994 record of 10.7 billion viewers.

IOC president Samaranch declared the Nagano Games the best-organized Winter Olympics in history. They were also a big success as a commercial enterprise. With CBS paying $375 million for the television rights, the total broadcast rights fees skyrocketed to $513,137 million, one-third of the total budget for the Games (Kluge 1999: 851–856). Additionally, the marketing program generated over $300 million U.S. in sponsor revenues, three times as much as Lillehammer and five times the original bid (Nagano Olympic Winter Games 1999).

As an antidote against the Olympic big business, the Japanese intended to organize "Games with a heart" by having children pay only 50 percent of the ticket prices and promoting the Games both as a tribute to the beauty and diversity of nature and as a festival of peace and friendship for all participants and tourists. After the Winter Olympics were over, the Paralympics were staged on the same venues from March 5 to 14 (Kluge 1999: 851–856).

After the Games there were numerous allegations that IOC members were bribed in order to secure their votes for the Nagano bid. When asked to account for the $28 million U.S. spent to make its bid to the IOC, the Nagano Organizing Committee responded that the cash book was lost and it thus could not document these expenditures (Findling 1996: 335–336).

CONCLUSIONS

To summarize this historical overview by pointing out certain distinctive caesurae in the chronological development of the Winter Olympics calls for a periodization based on the IOC presidencies. (John Lucas [1988] adopted a similar approach in his analysis of the transformation of the amateur ideology.) It should be pointed out that no Winter Games were officially held during the IOC presidency of Pierre de Coubertin (1896–1925). The 1924 Winter Sports Week in Chamonix was never recognized as Olympic Winter Games by Coubertin. Only after he had been succeeded by Henri de Baillet-Latour (1925–1942) did this event retroactively become the First Olympic Winter Games.

Baillet-Latour's presidency covered only three Winter Olympics: St. Moritz 1928, Lake Placid 1932, and Garmisch-Partenkirchen 1936. After Sapporo had declined the Games and after they were withdrawn from St. Moritz, Baillet-Latour and the IOC entrusted Garmisch-Partenkirchen with the organization of the 1940 Winter Games despite the annexation of Bohemia and Moravia by the German Reich and despite the gruesome events of the Kristallnacht in 1938. Karl Lennartz (1994: 102) therefore wrote: "By all this, one is tempted to conclude that the staging of the Games at any price was seen as a primary objective, while the defence of general humanitarian principles was pursued with lesser zeal."

Sigfrid Edstrom succeeded Baillet-Latour as de facto IOC president in 1942. He became responsible for reconstructing the postwar Winter Olympics and succeeded in bringing the former Nazi allies Austria, Bulgaria, Hungary, Italy, and Romania back to the Winter Olympics scene in neutral St. Moritz in 1948 and the Federal Republic of Germany to Oslo four years later. Edstrom also engineered the rapprochement with the Soviet Union and its allies, which would participate for the first time during the 1952 Olympic Summer Games in Helsinki.

In previous publications I have labeled Avery Brundage "the old man who would not see" (Renson 1984, 1992). He despised the Winter Olympics. They were in his eyes "Frostbite Follies" with professional athletes of the ice- or snow-businesses as their actors. Brundage stayed in power for a twenty-year period from 1952 until 1972, which coincided with the height of the Cold War. This political rivalry between the East and West was dramatically highlighted each time the Soviet hockey team faced a Western rival on the ice. Except for the Squaw Valley 1960 Olympics, where the U.S. team beat the USSR, the Soviet team won all other finals. The ideological clash between the amateur die-hardism of Brundage on the one hand and the commercial character of the ski circuit on the other hand resulted in the expulsion of Karl Schranz from the Sapporo Winter Olympics in 1972.

In his Olympic memoirs, Lord Killanin (1983) described the start of his IOC presidency as "Progressing from Brundage." Even as one of the vice-presidents under Brundage, he developed a much more pragmatic attitude toward the question of so-called amateurism: "Amateurism varied very much from Federation to Federation. Where equipment was involved, such as horses, yachts, skis, exploitations for commercial purposes are manifest. In the case of skiing there is the added interest of the tourist trade" (Killanin 1983: 80). Together with the two other vice-presidents, Jean de Beaumont of France and Herman van Karnebeek of the Netherlands, he was having meetings with the International Federations in Lausanne, "trying to retain the principles of amateurism but, at the same time, move with the changing times" (1983: 81). This upset Brundage, who realized that he had been short-circuited and that it was too late; professionalism was rapidly gaining momentum. The 1976 Innsbruck Games, where Franz Klammer won the downhill race, symbolized the new Olympic leadership and the radical changes in amateurism.

Killanin surely had his share of troubles on his Olympic pathway from 1972 until 1980. A few months after his election, Denver withdrew from the position of host city for the 1976 Winter Games. He then was confronted with all the technical and political problems connected with the 1976 Montreal Summer Games and the city's flamboyant mayor, Jean Drapeau. Killanin was of the opinion that staging the Games in a tiny place like Lake Placid in 1980 was a mistake, which indeed brought the Olympic movement unhappy publicity (Killanin 1983: 99). But this pipe-smoking pragmatic-conservative always held that the U.S.-led boycott of the 1980 Moscow Summer Games was the most damaging event since the Games had been revived in 1896.

Juan Antonio Samaranch was elected in Moscow on July 16, 1980, and would remain in the Olympic saddle for twenty-one years, the longest IOC presidency ever apart from Coubertin's. Samaranch has many admirers but also lots of fierce enemies because of the commodification and commercial marketing of the Olympic Movement. Bill Mallon stated: "The IOC was once broke, and it was only in the 1980s that it began to achieve financial independence. But all this happened quickly, too quickly for the IOC to adjust" (2000: 25).

Jacques Rogge, future IOC member, who in 1983 was vice-president of the Belgian Olympic and Interfederal Committee, stated at a congress held in Belgium: "Each healthy organism reacts against an aggression by a heightened resistance. The boycott of the Moscow Olympic Games, induced by President Carter, has—as paradoxical as it may sound—increased the power of the IOC and the importance of the Olympic Games" (Rogge 1984: 55). He was referring to the Olympic Congress of 1981 in Baden-Baden in the Federal Republic of Germany, which ushered in "Le nouveau Olympisme à la Samaranch." The Winter Games in Sarajevo 1984 and Calgary 1988 were both peaceful and successful events. The environmental damage caused by the Albertville Games in 1992 raised the awareness of ecological issues. Then in 1994 the tradition established since 1924 that Winter Games preceded the Summer Games was given up with the Lillehammer Games; Winter

Olympics would alternate with the Summer Games every two years. The ecologization or "greening" of the Olympic Movement also had its roots in the Lillehammer experience of 1994.

Winter Olympic Games have often remained in the cold when compared to the attention paid to the Summer Games (Lucas 1980; Guttmann 1992). Nevertheless, the historical itinerary of "The Cool Games" shows— sometimes even more poignantly than the Summer Olympics—how a social and cultural lag has occurred (Ogburn 1922). This gap separates a blurry mythology of so-called Olympism from the economic and political reality of Olympic "logo-ization." While entering the global village, the Olympic movement seems indeed to have become just another corporate entity, selling its logo of the five rings to the highest bidder. Are the terms "Olympic Movement" and "Olympic Family" only euphemisms to obscure the Olympic industry (Lenskyj 2000: 3)? Or do these Olympics still "embody a buoyant faith, a hopeful optimism and a charitable ethic that humanity would be the poorer without" (Baker 2000: 74)?

Should we be yearning for a postmodern Coubertin to bridge this gap or comply with the diagnosis made by the present IOC president, Jacques Rogge: "The Olympic Games are a fact, and a fact is still stronger than a Lord Mayor. Some are fencing with terms like Olympic ideal, Olympic symbol. It is about time to stop attributing to the Olympic movement and the Olympic Games values they do not have. Let us not be naive or romantic. The Olympic Games are nothing more than the greatest sports manifestation in the world. We are not do-gooders. It's more than difficult enough to organize Games, it is more than difficult enough to participate in Games. Let us give up the outmoded hypocritical romantic ideals of our fathers" (Rogge 1984: 58).

Surgeons like Rogge are used to making decisions in terms of priority strategies. Those were obviously his priorities in 1983, eighteen years before being elected to the IOC presidency. But just as the Games and their sociopolitical context are constantly changing, people—even IOC presidents—can change their opinions. During an extensive dialogue in 1996, Rogge declared: "We will have to adjust these sport structures in order to meet the modern needs of athletes, recognize their rights, find alternative ways of financing. Much stricter ethical rules must be established, doping must be fought more vigorously, otherwise we will be completely manipulated by athletes and their managers" (Renson et al. 1996: 12).

It appears to me that what the Olympic Movement needs now—as the Salt Lake City bribery scandal has shown—are ethical reforms to restore its credibility. While the Games have evolved and are now characterized by commodification, ecologization, and logo-ization, their ethical superstructure did not keep up with the pace of change. Here lies their challenge for the twenty-first century.

Note

I would like to thank Robert K. Barney and Kevin B. Wamsley for their assistance and for allowing me to carry on research in the International Centre for Olympic Studies at the University of Western Ontario, London (Ontario).

References

IXes Jeux Olympiques d'hiver Innsbruck 1964: 3me rapport/IX Olympic Winter Games Innsbruck 1964: 3rd report/IX. Olympische Winterspiele Innsbruck 1964: 3. Bericht. 1964. Innsbruck, Austria: Comité d'Organisation des IXe Jeux Olympiques d'Hiver.

"XIII Olympic Winter Games Lake Placid 1980." N.d. In *Encyclopédie mondiale du sport: Les Jeux Olympiques,* vol. 1, pp. i–xx. N.p.: Vaillant.

Abrahams, Harold M. (ed.). 1937. *The Official Report of the XIth Olympiad Berlin 1936.* London: British Olympic Association.

Addkison-Simmons, Donna. 1996. "Sapporo 1972: XIth Olympic Winter Games." In Findling and Pelle (eds.), *Historical Dictionary of the Modern Olympic Movement,* pp. 284–288.

Agence Belge des Grandes Editions. 1949. *Les jeux de la XIVe Olympiade St-Moritz et Londres 1948.* Zurich: Verlagsbuchhandlung Heinzmann.

Allen, E. John B. 1996a. "The 1932 Lake Placid Winter Games: Dewey's Olympics." In Robert K. Barney, Scott G. Martyn, Douglas A. Brown, and Gordon H. MacDonald (eds.), *Olympic Perspectives: Third International Symposium for Olympic Research,* pp. 61–171. London, Ontario, Canada: International Centre for Olympic Studies.

———. 1996b. "The World Wide Diffusion of Skiing to 1940." In Goksøyr, von der Lippe, and Mo (eds.), *Winter Games, Warm Traditions,* pp. 167–181.

Andersen, P. C. 1952. *The Olympic Winter Games Oslo 1952.* Oslo, Norway: Dreyer.

Arnaud, Pierre, and Thierry Terret. 1993. *Le rêve blanc: Olympisme et sports d'hiver en France: Chamonix 1924, Grenoble 1968.* Talence, France: Presses Universitaires de Bordeaux.

Ashwell, Tim. 1996. "Squaw Valley 1960: VIIIth Olympic Winter Games." In Findling and Pelle (eds.), *Historical Dictionary of the Modern Olympic Movement,* pp. 263–269.

Babelay, Jean-Louis. 1967. "Skiing from Its Origins to Our Days." In Jean-Pierre Taillandier and Robert Chastagnol (eds.), *Xth Olympic Winter Games: Grenoble 1968,* p. 197. Paris: Arthaud.

Baker, William J. 2000. *If Christ Came to the Olympics.* Sydney: University of New South Wales Press.

Balmer, N. J., A. M. Nevill, and A. M. Williams. 2000. "Home Advantage in the Winter Olympics (1908–1998)." In Janne Avela, Paavo V. Komi, and Jyrki Komulainen (eds.), *Proceedings of the 5th Annual Congress of the European College of Sport Science*, p. 146. Jyvaskyla, Finland: University of Jyvaskyla.

Barney, Robert K. 1998. "The Great Transformation: Olympic Victory Ceremonies and the Medal Podium." *Olympika: The International Journal of Olympic Studies* 7: 89–112.

———. 2000. "Die Einfuhrung des Podiums." In Karl Lennartz, Walter Borgers, and Andreas Hofer (eds.), *Olympische Siege: Medaillen-Diplome-Ehrenpreise*, pp. 196–204. Berlin: Sportverlag.

Bernett, Hajo. 1980. "Das Scheitern der Olympischen Spiele von 1940." *Stadion: Journal of the History of Sport and Physical Education* 6: 251–290.

Bø, Olav. 1993. *Skiing throughout History*. Oslo: Det Norske Samlaget.

Brown, Douglas, and Gordon MacDonald. 1996. "Grenoble 1968: Xth Olympic Winter Games." In Findling and Pelle (eds.), *Historical Dictionary of the Modern Olympic Movement*, pp. 276–283.

Buytendijk, F. J. J. (ed.). 1929. *Ergebnisse der sportartzlichen Untersuchungen bei den IX. Olympischen Spielen in Amsterdam 1928*, Berlin: Springer.

Cantelon, Hart, and M. Letters. 2000. "The Making of the IOC Environmental Policy as the Third Dimension of the Olympic Movement." *International Review for the Sociology of Sport* 35: 294–308.

Comitato Olimpico Nazionale Italiano. 1956. *VII Giochi Olimpici Invernale/VII Olympic Winter Games, Cortina d'Ampezzo*. Rome: Comitato Olimpico Nazionale Italiano.

Comité d'Organisation/Organizing Committee. 1988. *Rapport officiel des XVes Jeux Olympiques d'hiver: XV Olympic Winter Games: Official Report*. Calgary: XV Olympic Winter Games Organizing Committee.

Comité d'Organisation des Xes Jeux Olympiques d'Hiver. 1969. *Xes Jeux Olympiques d'hiver: Grenoble 1968*. Paris: Arthaud.

Comité International Olympique. 1905. *Congrès international de sport et d'éducation physique*. Brussels: Auxerre.

Congrès International. 1928. *Congrès International d'éducation physique et de sport: Compte rendu*. Amsterdam: D'Olivera.

Constable, George. 1996. *The XI, XII, and XIII Olympiads: Berlin 1936, St. Moritz 1948*. The Olympic Century, vol. 11. Los Angeles: World Sport Research & Publications.

Cook, Theodore A. (ed.). 1909. *The Fourth Olympiad: Being the Official Report of the Olympic Games of 1908*. London: British Olympic Association.

Cosentino, Frank, and Glynn Leyshon. 1987. *Winter Gold: Canada's Winners in the Winter Olympic Games*. Markham, Ontario: Fitzhenry & Whiteside.

Coubertin, Pierre de. 1979. *Olympic Mémoires*. Lausanne: IOC. 1st ed. 1931.

Daniels, George G. 1996a. *The XIX Olympiad: Mexico City 1968; Sapporo 1972*. The Olympic Century, vol. 17. Los Angeles: World Sport Research & Publications.

————. 1996b. *The XX Olympiad: Munich 1972; Innsbruck 1976.* The Olympic Century, vol. 18. Los Angeles: World Sport Research & Publications.

Dunkelberger, Robert. 1996. "Sarajevo 1984: XIVth Olympic Winter Games." In Findling and Pelle (eds.), *Historical Dictionary of the Modern Olympic Movement,* pp. 302–309.

Endbericht [Final Report]: Olympische Winterspiele Innsbruck 1976. 1976. Innsbruck: Innsbruck Organizing Committee.

Engelbrecht, Astrid. 1996. "Cortina d'Ampezzo 1944: Olympic Winter Games (Never Held)." In Findling and Pelle (eds.), *Historical Dictionary of the Modern Olympic Movement,* pp. 246–247.

Ensink, Frans. 1972. *Olympisch Logboek 1972: Sapporo.* Sapporo and Munich: Huisbrand Unie.

Fea, John. 1996a. "Lake Placid 1932: IIId Olympic Winter Games." In Findling and Pelle (eds.), *Historical Dictionary of the Modern Olympic Movement,* pp. 232–236, 295–301.

————. 1996b. "Lake Placid 1980: XIIIth Olympic Winter Games." In Findling and Pelle (eds.), *Historical Dictionary of the Modern Olympic Movement,* pp. 295–301.

Final Report Editorial Committee. 1980. *Final Report; Rapport final/XIII Olympic Winter Games; XIII Jeux Olympiques d'Hiver Lake Placid.* Lake Placid: Ed Lewi Associates/Lake Placid Organizing Committee.

Findling, John E. 1996. "Nagano 1998: XVIIIth Olympic Winter Games." In Findling and Pelle (eds.), *Historical Dictionary of the Modern Olympic Movement,* pp. 335–336.

Findling, John E., and Kimberly D. Pelle (eds.). 1996. *Historical Dictionary of the Modern Olympic Movement.* Westport, Conn.: Greenwood Press.

Friedl, Wolfgang, and Bertl Neumann (eds.). 1967. *Offizieller Bericht der IX. Olympischen Winterspiele Innsbruck 1964.* Vienna: Innsbruck Organizing Committee.

Galford, Ellen. 1996. *The XXIII Olympiad: Los Angeles 1984; Calgary 1988.* The Olympic Century, vol. 21. Los Angeles: World Sport Research & Publications.

Gerz, Alfons. 1976a. *Innsbruck 76.* Zurich: A. Wyss.

————. 1976b. *Innsbruck and Montreal 76.* Munich: Bertelsmann.

————. 1980a. *Lake Placid 80.* Munich: ProSport.

————. 1980b. *Mockba/Lake Placid 80.* Munich: ProSport Verlag für Sport und Kultur.

Goksøyr, Matti, Gerd von der Lippe, and Kristen Mo (eds.). 1996. *Winter Games, Warm Traditions.* Second international International Society for the History of Physical Education and Sport (ISHPES) seminar, Lillehammer, 1994. Lillehammer: Norwegian Society of Sports History.

Guttmann, Allen. 1984. *The Games Must Go On: Avery Brundage and the Olympic Movement.* New York: Columbia University Press.

————. 1992. *The Olympics: A History of the Modern Games.* Urbana: University of Illinois Press.

Hall, Allan W. 1996. "Cortina d'Ampezzo 1956: VIIth Olympic Winter Games." In Findling and Pelle (eds.), *Historical Dictionary of the Modern Olympic Movement,* pp. 258–262.

Hart-Davis, Duff. 1986. *Hitler's Games: The 1936 Olympics.* New York: Harper & Row.

Hemmleb, Jochen, Larry A. Johnson, and Eric R. Simonson (eds.). 1999. *Ghosts of Everest: The Search for Mallory and Irvine.* Seattle: Mountaineers Books.

Hobsbawm, Eric, and Terence O. Ranger. 1983. *The Invention of Tradition.* Cambridge: Cambridge University Press.

Holthausen, Joop, and Ruud Paauw. 1992. *Kroniek van de Olympische Spelen.* Baarn: Tirion.

Jackson, S. J. 1998. "The 49th Paradox: The 1988 Calgary Winter Olympic Games and Canadian Identity as Contested Terrain." In Margaret C. Duncan, Garry Chick, and Alan Aycock (eds.), *Diversions and Divergences in Fields of Play,* pp. 191–208. Greenwich, Conn.: Ablex.

Jonsson, Ake. 2001. *Nordiska Spelen: Historien om sju vinterspel I Stockholm av Olympiskt format 1901 till 1926.* Varnamo: Arena.

Jorgensen, Per. 1997. "From Balck to Nurmi: The Olympic Movement and the Nordic Nations." *International Journal of the History of Sport* 14: 69–99.

———. 2001. "The Nordic Countries and the Olympic Movement 1894–1928." In Arnd Kruger, Angela Teja, and Else Trangbaek (eds.), *Europäische Perskektiven zur Geschichte von Sport, Kultur und Politik,* pp. 59–67. Beitrage und Quellen zu Sport und Gesellschaft 12. Berlin: Tischler.

Kamper, Erich. 1964. *Lexikon der Olympischen Winter Spiele/Encyclopédie des Jeux Olympiques d'hiver/Encyclopaedia of the Olympic Winter Games/De Olympiska Vinterspelen: En uppslagsbok.* Stuttgart: Union Verlag.

Kamper, Erich, and Bill Mallon. 1992. *The Golden Book of the Olympic Games.* Milan: Vallardi.

Kennedy, John J., Jr. 1996a. "Innsbruck 1964: IXth Olympic Winter Games." In Findling and Pelle (eds.), *Historical Dictionary of the Modern Olympic Movement,* pp. 270–275.

———. 1996b. "Innsbruck 1976: XIIth Olympic Winter Games." In Findling and Pelle (eds.), *Historical Dictionary of the Modern Olympic Movement,* pp. 289–294.

Killanin, Lord. 1983. *My Olympic Years.* New York: Morrow.

Klausen, Arne M. (ed.). 1999. *Olympic Games as Performances and Public Event: The Case of the XVII Winter Olympic Games in Norway.* New York: Berghahn Books.

Kluge, Volker. 1997. *100 Olympische Highlights: Wintersport.* Berlin: Sportverlag.

———. 1999. *Olympische Winterspiele: Die Chronik Chamonix 1924–Nagano 1998.* Berlin: Sportverlag.

Knoll, Wilhelm (ed.). 1928. *Die sportortzliche Ergebnisse der II. Olympischen Winterspiele in St. Moritz 1928.* Bern: Paul Haupt.

Kruger, Arnd. 1972. *Die Olympischen Spiele 1936 und die Weltmeinung.* Sportwissenschaftliche Arbeiten 7. Berlin: Bartels & Wernitz.

———. 1996. "The History of the Olympic Winter Games: The Invention of Tradition." In Goksøyr, von der Lippe, and Mo (eds.), *Winter Games, Warm Traditions,* pp. 101–122.

Kruger, Arnd, Angela Teja, and Else Trangbaek (eds.). 2001. *Europäische Perspektiven zur Geschichte von Sport, Kultur und Politik.* Beitrage und Quellen zu Sport und Gesellschaft 12. Berlin: Tischler.

Kruse, Britta, et al. (eds.). 1995. *Kroniek van 100 jaar Olympische Spelen 1896–1996.* Gotersloh: Chronik.

Lattimer, George M. (ed.). 1932. *Official Report: III Olympic Winter Games: Lake Placid 1932.* Lake Placid: Third Olympic Winter Games Committee.

Lellouche, Michele. 1996. "Albertville and Savoie 1992: XVIth Olympic Winter Games." In Findling and Pelle (eds.), *Historical Dictionary of the Modern Olympic Movement,* pp. 318–325.

Lembke, Robert E. 1960. *Die Olympischen Spiele 1960, Rom–Squaw Valley.* Gotersloh: Bertelsmann.

Lennartz, Karl. 1994. "Difficult Times: Baillet-Latour and Germany, 1931–1942." *Olympika: The International Journal of Olympic Studies* 3: 99–105.

———. 1999. "Georges Mallory et l'Everest." *Revue Olympique* 26: 57.

———. 2000a. "Old Borders in Olympism: The Presidency of Baron Henri de Baillet-Latour, the Successor of Baron de Coubertin." In J. Tolleneer and Roland Renson (eds.), *Old Borders, New Borders, No Borders,* pp. 233–240. 11th Conference, ISHPES, Leuven, 1998. Oxford: Meyer & Meyer Sport.

———. 2000b. "Olympische Siege: Medaillen-Diplome-Ehrenpreise." *Forschung-Innovation-Technologie* 2: 18–25.

———. 2001. "Natursportarten in der Olympischen Bewegung." VII. Kongress der ISHPES. Unpublished paper presented in Montpellier, France.

Lenskyj, Helen J. 2000. *Inside the Olympic Industry: Power, Politics and Activism.* Albany: State University of New York Press.

Lillehammer Olympic Organizing Committee. 1994. *The Official Book of the XVII Lillehammer Olympic Games.* Oslo: Lillehammer Olympic Organizing Committee.

———. 1995. *Final Report.* Oslo: Lillehammer Olympic Organizing Committee.

Ljunggren, Jens. 1996. "The Nordic Games, Nationalism, Sports and Cultural Conflicts." In Goksøyr, von der Lippe, and Mo (eds.), *Winter Games, Warm Traditions,* pp. 35–45.

Lucas, John. 1980. *The Modern Olympic Games.* South Brunswick: A. S. Barnes.

———. 1988. "From Coubertin to Samaranch: The Unsettling Transformation of the Olympic Ideology of Athletic Amateurism." *Stadion: International Journal of the History of Sport* 14: 65–84.

Luther, Carl J. 1926. "Geschichte des Schnee- und Eissports." In Gustave A. W. Bogeng (ed.), *Geschichte des Sports aller Volker und Zeiten: Zweiter Band,* pp. 497–556. Leipzig: Seemann.

MacDonald, Gordon, and Douglas Brown. 1996. "Oslo 1952: VIth Olympic Winter Games." In Findling and Pelle (eds.), *Historical Dictionary of the Modern Olympic Movement,* pp. 252–257.

Mallon, Bill. 2000. "The Olympic Bribery Scandal." *Journal of Olympic History* 8: 11–27.

Maloney, Larry. 1996. "Lillehammer 1994: XVIIth Olympic Winter Games." In Findling and Pelle (eds.), *Historical Dictionary of the Modern Olympic Movement,* pp. 326–334.

Mandell, Richard D. 1971. *The Nazi Olympics.* London: Souvenir Press.

Mehl, Erwin. 1964. *Grundriss der Weltgeschichte des Schifahrens (Schigeschichte): I: Von der Steinzeit bis zum Beginn der schigeschichtlichen Neuzeit (1860).* Beiträge zur Lehre und Forschung der Leibeserziehung 10. Schorndorf: K. Hofmann.

Mo, Kristen. 1991. "Norwegian Resistance against the Winter Olympics of the 1920's." In Roland Renson, Manfred Lammer, James Riordan, and Dimitrios Chassiotis (eds.), *The Olympic Games through the Ages: Greek Antiquity and Its Impact on Modern Sport,* pp. 335–343. Athens: Hellenic Sports Research Institute.

Mogore, C. 1989. *La grande histoire du ski.* Chambéry: Agraf.

Moravetz, Bruno. 1984. *Sarajevo '84.* Munich: Verlag für Sport und Kultur.

Mulier, W. 1894. *Atletiek en voetbal.* Haarlem: De Erven Loosjes.

Muller, Norbert (ed.). 2000. *Pierre de Coubertin 1863–1937: Selected Writings.* Lausanne: IOC.

Muller, Otto M. (ed.). 1949. *Les Jeux de la XIVe Olympiade St-Moritz et Londres 1948.* Brussels: Agence Belge des Grandes Editions SPRL.

Nagano Olympic Winter Games. 1999. "Nagano Olympic Winter Games: Marketing Programme Analysis." *Journal of Olympic History* 7: 38–39.

Official Results of the XIII Olympic Winter Games—Lake Placid 1980. 1981. New York: Olympic and Winter Sports Museum.

Ogburn, William F. 1922. *Social Change with Respect to Culture and Original Nature.* New York: B. W. Huebsch.

Organizacioni Komitet. 1984. *XIV zimskih Olimpijskih igara Sarajevo 1984* [Organizing Committee of the XIVth Winter Olympic Games 1984 at Sarajevo]. Sarajevo: Sarajevo Organizing Committee.

Organizing Committee for the XIth Olympic Winter Games. 1973. *The XIth Olympic Winter Games: Sapporo 1972: Official Report.* Sapporo: Sapporo Organizing Committee.

Organizing Committee of the XVI Olympic Winter Games. 1992. *Albertville 92: Back to Nature.* Lausanne: IMS/Studio 6.

Park, Roberta J. 2000. "Cells or Soaring?: Historical Reflections and 'Visions' on the Body, Athletics, and Modern Olympics." *Olympika: The International Journal of Olympic Studies* 9: 1–24.

Pfister, Gertrud. 1996. "Skiing, Gender and Nationalism in Garmisch, 1936." In Goksøyr, von der Lippe, and Mo (eds.), *Winter Games, Warm Traditions,* pp. 250–260.

————. 2001. "Sport, Technology and Society: From Snow Shoes to Racing Skis." *Culture, Sport and Society* 4: 73–98.

Phillips, Ellen. 1996. *The VIII Olympiad: Paris 1924; St. Moritz 1928.* The Olympic Century, vol. 8. Los Angeles: World Sport Research & Publications.

Posey, Carl A. 1996. *The XVIII Olympiad: Tokyo 1964; Grenoble 1968,* The Olympic Century, vol. 16. Los Angeles: World Sport Research & Publications.

Puijk, Roel. 1997. *Global Spotlights on Lillehammer: How the World Viewed Norway during the 1994 Winter Olympics.* Luton, UK: University of Luton Press.

————. 2000. "A Global Media Event?: Coverage of the 1994 Lillehammer Olympic Games." *International Review for the Sociology of Sport* 35: 309–330.

Rapport général du Comité Exécutif des IImes Jeux Olympiques d'hiver et documents officiels divers. 1928. Lausanne: IOC.

Rapport officiel des XVes Jeux Olympiques d'hiver/XV Olympic Winter Games: Official Report. 1988. Calgary: Calgary Olympic Committee.

Renson, Roland. 1984. "De evolutie van de moderne Olympische Spelen." In Herman Van Pelt et al. (eds.), *Macht en onmacht van de Olympische Spelen,* pp. 35–53. Sportacahier 4. Leuven: Acco.

————. 1992. "De Olympische Spelen 1896–1992 in politiek-historisch perspectief." *Politica Cahier* 2: 1–24.

————. 1996a. *The VIIth Olympiad, Antwerp 1920: The Games Reborn.* Antwerp, Belgium: Pandora.

————. 1996b. "Why Winter Sports at the Antwerp Olympic Games 1920?" In Goksøyr, von der Lippe, and Mo (eds.), *Winter Games, Warm Traditions,* pp. 141–153.

————. 1998. "De begrafenis van Henri de Baillet-Latour: Twee verdoken aspecten." *Sportimonium* 18: 53–59.

Renson, Roland, Jacques Rogge, and Bart Vanreusel. 1996. "Sport en ethiek." *Kultuurleven* 63: 5–15.

Résultats des concours des Jeux d'Hiver organisés par le Comité Olympique français. 1925. Paris: Comité Olympique Français.

Richter, Walter (ed.). 1936. *Die Olympischen Spielen 1936 in Berlin und Garmisch-Partenkirchen: Band 1.* Hamburg: Altona-Bahrenfeld.

Riordan, James. 1980. "The USSR and the Olympic Games." *Stadion: Journal of the History of Sport and Physical Education* 6: 291–313.

Rogge, Jacques. 1984. "De Toekomst van de Olympische Spelen." In Herman Van Pelt et al. (eds.), *Macht en onmacht van de Olympische Spelen,* pp. 55–62. Sportacahier 14. Leuven: n.p.

Rubien, Frederick W. (ed.). 1932. *American Olympic Committee Report: Games of the Xth Olympiad, Los Angeles, 30 July–14 August 1932; IIIrd Olympic Winter Games Lake Placid, New York, 4–13 February 1932.* New York: American Olympic Committee.

Rubin, Robert (ed.). 1960. *VIII Olympic Winter Games, Squaw Valley, California, 1960: Final Report.* Sacramento: California Olympic Commission.

Rurup, Reinhard (ed.). 1996. *The Olympic Games and National Socialism.* 2nd ed. Berlin: Stiftung Topographie des Terrors veröffentlich im Argon Verlag.

Sarajevo Organizing Committee. 1984. *Sarajevo '84: Final Report.* Sarajevo: Sarajevo Organizing Committee.

Scharenberg, Swantje. 1996. "Sapporo/St. Moritz/Garmisch-Partenkirchen 1940: Olympic Winter Games (Never Held)." In Findling and Pelle (eds.), *Historical Dictionary of the Modern Olympic Movement,* pp. 242–245.

Simmons, Donald C., Jr. 1996a. "St. Moritz 1928: IId Olympic Winter Games." In Findling and Pelle (eds.), *Historical Dictionary of the Modern Olympic Movement,* pp. 228–231.

———. 1996b. "St. Moritz 1948: Vth Olympic Winter Games." In Findling and Pelle (eds.), *Historical Dictionary of the Modern Olympic Movement,* pp. 248–251.

Simon, S. 1998. *Olympische Winterspiele Nagano '98.* Munich: Sport-Information-Dienst.

Stauff, John W. 1996. "Garmisch-Partenkirchen 1936: IVth Olympic Winter Games." In Findling and Pelle (eds.), *Historical Dictionary of the Modern Olympic Movement,* pp. 237–241.

Stevens, Neil. 1985. "The Big Upset—1936." In Richard Beddoes (ed.), *Winners: A Century of Canadian Sport,* pp. 20–21. Toronto: Grosvenor House.

Sudholt, G. 1996a. "'Das war das Rennen meines Lebens': Christl Cranz, die Olympiasiegerin von 1936, errinnert sich." In G. Sudholt (ed.), *60 Jahre Olympiaort Garmisch-Partenkirchen,* pp. 30–32. Berg am Starnberger See: VGB-Verlagsgesellschaft.

———. 1996b. "'Ich konnte die Strecke heute noch fahren': Silbermedailles-Gewinnerin Kathi Grasegger-Deuschl erzählt von den Olympischen Spielen 1936." In G. Sudholt (ed.), *60 Jahre Olympiaort Garmisch-Partenkirchen,* pp. 33–34. Berg am Starnberger See: VGB-Verlagsgesellschaft.

Taillandier, Jean-Pierre, and Robert Chastagnol. 1967. *Xth Olympic Winter Games, Grenoble 1968.* Paris: Arthaud.

Ueberhorst, Horst. 1988. "Organisation und Verlauf der Olympischen Winterspiele von Garmisch-Partenkirchen 1936." In *The Olympic Movement Past, Present and Future,* pp. 66–79. International Committee for the History of Physical Education and Sport Seminar, Sarajevo, 1988. Sarajevo: Committee of ICOSH Seminar.

Ulmrich, E. 1996. "Facts and Fiction in the History of Skiing." In Goksøyr, von der Lippe, and Mo (eds.), *Winter Games, Warm Traditions,* pp. 192–211.

Valerien, Harry. 1976. *Olympia 1976: Montreal/Innsbruck.* Munich: Sudwest.

Van Wynsberghe, Richard, and Ian Ritchie. 1994. "(Ir)Relevant Rings: The Symbolic Consumption of the Olympic Logo in Postmodern Media Culture." In Robert K. Barney and Klaus V. Meier (eds.), *Critical Reflections on Olympic Ideology: Second International Symposium for Olympic Research,* pp. 124–135. London: University of Western Ontario, International Centre for Olympic Studies.

Verdyck, Alfred. 1920. *Rapport officiel des Jeux de la VIIème Olympiade, Anvers 1920*. N.p.

Von Mengden, Guido. 1952. *Die Olympischen Spiele 1952: Oslo und Helsinki: Das offizielle Standardwerk des nationalen Olympischen Komitees*. Frankfurt/Main: Olympischer Sport-Verlag.

Wamsley, Kevin. 1996. "Calgary 1988: XVth Olympic Winter Games." In Findling and Pelle (eds.), *Historical Dictionary of the Modern Olympic Movement*, pp. 310–317.

Wamsley, Kevin, and Michael K. Heine. 1996a. "'Don't Mess with the Relay—It's Bad Medicine': Aboriginal Culture and the 1988 Winter Olympics." In Robert K. Barney, Scott G. Martyn, Douglas Brown, and Gordon H. Mac-Donald (eds.), *Olympic Perspectives: Third International Symposium for Olympic Research*, pp. 173–178. London: University of Western Ontario, International Centre for Olympic Studies.

———. 1996b. "Tradition, Modernity, and the Construction of Civic Identity: The Calgary Olympics." *Olympika: The International Journal of Olympic Studies* 5: 81–90.

Welch, Paula D. 1996. "Chamonix 1924: Ist Olympic Winter Games." In Findling and Pelle (eds.), *Historical Dictionary of the Modern Olympic Movement*, pp. 223–227.

3

THE GENDERING OF THE
WINTER OLYMPIC GAMES

Kari Fasting

In ancient Greece women were barred from the Olympic Games not only as participants but also as spectators, and any woman caught in Olympia during the Games received the summary judgment of being thrown off a nearby cliff. Women in modern times have sometimes disguised themselves as men in order to be able to compete. Something like this happened 2,500 years ago when in 396 B.C. Kallipateira of Rhodes (the trainer of her son, who was a boxer) disguised herself as a man and went to the Games to watch her son. He won. But when Kallipateira threw her arms around him, her robe came undone, revealing that she was a woman. Because her father and brothers had been Olympic champions, she was spared a one-way trip to the precipice (Levy 1984). This story is an illustration of the gendering of the Olympic Games in ancient times: only men were allowed to compete, only men had access to the stadium, and only men decided upon the consequences if someone broke the rules. But what is the situation today after more than two millennia? Are the Olympic Movement and its Games still gendered?

Before I try to answer these questions, let me explain what is meant by gender. The Canadian sports sociologist Ann Hall notes that some authors in the United States started to use the term "gender," instead of "sex," about twenty-five years ago. According to her, it was "used to designate the psychological, cultural, and social dimensions of maleness and female-ness, whereas sex was used to designate the dichotomous distinctions between females and males based on physiological characteristics that are genetically determined. The distinction, therefore, between sex and gender was meant to differentiate between the biological and the cultural" (Hall 1990: 224). It has been demonstrated, however, that this division and the interaction between sex and gender or between biology and culture are not that clear. We really do not know where biology ends and culture starts. The meaning of biological sex differences may also vary according to the culture. For example, greater physical strength in males tends to be emphasized in Western industrialized countries, in which boys are much more encouraged and motivated to participate in physical activity than are girls. A natural tendency toward greater muscular strength is therefore increased by the cultural importance of physical activity. But in countries where women carry the physical burden, their muscles may be better developed than those of men (Eichler 1980).

Recent research has focused on the process by which this social construction of gender occurs or develops. New terms like "gendering," "gender belief system," and "gender orders" have emerged. There has been an evolution from understanding gender as a variable, focusing on the socialized gender differences, to the understanding of gender as a perspective or perhaps as a result of the process arising from the many relationships within a society.

According to Michael Messner and Donald Sabo (1990: 12), it is important to realize that "the gender order is a dynamic process that is constantly in a state of change." It can also be defined as "a set of power relations, whereby men, as a social group, have more power over women than women have over them: they are socially constructed, not biologically given: and they are not fixed, but rather are subject to historical change and can be transformed" (Hall 1990: 226). Jennifer Hargreaves (1984: 53) has written that "the modern Olympic movement has been imbued with male chauvinism and domination over women." Another sociologist, Nancy Theberge (1991: 385), focuses on women, Olympism, and sport as an issue of control: "Control of athletes, control of practice and control of the very definitions of sport and gender."

Judith Lorber (1994) suggests that a distinction should be made between the various social and individual components of gender. This means that the social construction of gender in individuals reproduces the gendered societal structures; as individuals act out gender norms and expectations in face-to-face interaction, they are constructing gendered systems of dominance and power. An instance of this would be when female athletes' behavior expresses frailty or weakness compared with the strength of male athletes. For example, in figure skating we seldom see a female athlete lift her partner. According to Lorber, individual actions and social institutions may influence each other mutually; nevertheless, "social institutions exist prior to any individual's birth, education, and social patterning" (Lorber 1994: 7). Lorber has integrated different feminist perspectives and offered what she calls a "new" paradigm of gender. She looks upon gender as a social institution, as a social structure that has its origins in the development of human culture, not in biology or procreation. Gender is also a general term encompassing all social relations that separate people into differentiated gendered statuses. It therefore can be seen "as a process of social construction. A system of social stratification, and an institution that structures every aspect of our lives because of its embeddedness in the family, the workplace, and the state, as well as in sexuality, language, and culture" (1990: 5). I would add both sport and the media to this list.

So far one can conclude that gender can be looked upon as process, as stratification, and as structure. As a process, gender creates the social differences that define women and men. We can also use the expression "doing gender" or enacting gender in this connection. As part of a stratification system, gender ranks men above women of the same race and class; and as a structure, gender divides work in the home and workplaces, legitimates those in authority, and organizes sexuality and emotional life. From a structural perspective, gender is the division of people into contrasting and complementary social categories, "boys" and "girls," "men" and "women." In this structural conceptualization, gendering is the process and the gendered social order is the product of social construction.

Sport can be looked upon as a powerful setting for the construction of gender ideology (Willis 1994) and is in itself a very gendered institution, dominated by men and male values and norms. This is also the case for the Olympic Games and for the Olympic Movement as a whole. Major changes, however, have taken place during the last few years. An interesting question is whether these changes have led to or will lead to a change in the gender order not only in sport but in society at large.

Based on this introduction, I start by describing and discussing the gender order in the International Olympic Committee itself and the Olympic Movement. Second, I look at the number of women participating in the Winter Olympic Games and the development of women's events as well as the role of media in the gendering of the Olympic Games. The chapter closes with a discussion of the advocacy work that the IOC has been doing since 1994 in trying to get more women involved in the Olympic Movement.

THE GENDER ORDER OF THE INTERNATIONAL OLYMPIC COMMITTEE AND THE OLYMPIC MOVEMENT

The IOC is a very powerful organization and decides among other things which events or sport disciplines should be included in the Games. In this way it has had and still has an indirect influence on the number of women who can participate in the Games. In addition, the IOC is a self-perpetuating body whose new members are elected by the existing members. The gender, race, and age composition of the current IOC is thus very important in relation to its future member composition. The IOC is heavily gendered, with most members being men. According to Jennifer Hargreaves (1994: 209), since its foundation the IOC has "been an un-democratic, self-regulating and male-dominated institution." In 1894 Baron Pierre de Coubertin, the founder of the modern Olympic Games, chose the members of the first IOC, who helped plan the 1896 Olympic Games. He selected twelve wealthy men who could contribute financially to the activities of the IOC (Davenport 1996). Since then the number of members of the IOC has gradually increased, but it has been and still is very gen-dered. In 1981, when Juan Antonio Samaranch was the president, Pirjo Haggman from Finland and Flor Isava-Foneseca from Venezuela were ap-pointed as the first female IOC members ever. According to Joanna Daven-port (1996), Lord Killanin had tried to select female members but gave up after Tenley Albright, who was a U.S. gold-medal figure skater and secre-tary of the U.S. Olympic Committee, turned down his invitation to join.

Since 1981 a few more women have been appointed members. After the 112th IOC meetings in Moscow in July 2001 the IOC now has 14 female members and 115 men. So 10.8 percent of the IOC members are women. Every time they appoint new members they still appoint more men than women. This also happened in Moscow, where one woman and five men were elected. In 1997 Anita DeFrantz became the first IOC female vice-president. In spite of this, when she ran for the IOC presidency in 2001 she received only 9 of 107 possible votes and was eliminated in the first round.

One normally finds more women in the lower levels of a hierarchical organization. This is not the case for the IOC. In 2000 there were 28 female members of the IOC Commissions and Working Groups, only 11.8 percent of the total of 237 members (IOC 2000); 10 of them were mem-bers of the IOC Women and Sport Working Group. That is a good illustra-tion of the extremely low involvement of women in the IOC system. This pattern mirrors the gender bias in international sport in general, which includes the whole Olympic Movement, the International Sport Federa-tions, and the National Olympic Committees. It seems that what the former director of the IOC, Mme. Monique Berlioux, wrote about twenty years ago still is valid: "National Olympic committees, national or international federations, regional organizations, and organizing committees are all, in practice, run as 'all-male' clubs, in which women are tolerated only in small doses as guests."

The gender composition of the organizing committees of the Olympic Games themselves is also important, of course, indicating the number of women and men who are involved in the preparation for and the arrange-

Table 3.1. Female and Male Participation as Managers,
Administrators, and Volunteers in the Olympic Winter Games
at Lillehammer in 1994

LOOC	Women %	Men %
Administrators	42	58
Managers	14	86
Advisors	33	67
Clerks, secretaries	80	20

ment of the games. Table 3.1 shows the gender representation of the Lille-hammer Olympic Organizing Committee (LOOC).

According to Article 21 of the Norwegian Act on Gender Equality, which deals with representation of both sexes on all official committees, each sex shall be represented by at least 40 percent of the members when a public body appoints or elects committees, governing boards, or councils with four members or more. As table 3.1 shows, this rule was not followed by the LOOC. One of the main reasons for this skewed gender representation was that the committee was not a public body, although it received a lot of money from the Norwegian government. The minister of culture at that time, Ms. Åse Kleveland, commented on this phenomenon in the introductory speech to the Brighton Conference on Women and Sport a few months after the Games: "The arrangement provided a unique opportunity to demonstrate to the whole world what Norwegian gender equality means in practice. From the woman's point of view the success in this respect was not total. After the event it was the key figures from the market-oriented and decision-making male culture who were singled out for the visible accolades" (1994: 8). She noted that men had occupied the leading and high-status positions, while women were very much a supporting army.

As Kleveland said, what is interesting here is how this disproportionate situation could come about in a nation that considers itself to be among the world leaders in the move toward sexual equality. Part of the explanation according to her was that "in a supremely prestigious venture like the Olympic Games, there seems to have been little room for gender concern" (1994: 8); all the key figures in the organization were brought in from private industry. The Olympic Games are primarily a commercial undertaking strongly guided by private enterprise despite their government funding. It is about money. The gender composition of the Lillehammer Organizing Committee could probably have been different if the government had been more active in the recruitment process, as the minister stated in her speech in Brighton (1994: 8–9):

> After the event the government can rightly be criticized for not exploiting the opportunities more forcefully. The government by tying conditions to the recruitment process could have made a much bigger effort to encourage and enable competent women to apply their skills and resources to a project on a grand scale, carrying great prestige and of great national importance. We already look on ourselves as world champions in formalistic equality, and in areas that can be controlled by law. But we have to concede that in practice we still have a long way to go.

One may ask, why is it necessary to have more women involved in the decisionmaking bodies in the Olympic Movement? Why is gender a factor? There are many reasons why it is important to have a better gender balance. For example:

- Women account for more than half the population. Equality in decisionmaking assemblies is therefore a matter of democracy.
- Women and men have different knowledge and expertise. Therefore it is important that the views of both groups be considered.
- Women and men have different values and different interests. Therefore, increased representation of women can lead to new perspectives on many issues.

It is worth mentioning that the United Nations Convention on the Elimination of All Forms of Discrimination against Women (CEDAW) also was a cornerstone in the movement for equality in sport when it was adopted by the United Nations General Assembly in 1979. It has been ratified by 150 states, all of which have undertaken to comply with its provisions. One ultimate goal is to achieve gender balance in international organizations and bodies. This means a 50/50 distribution between the sexes. The International Olympic Committee, which for eighty-seven years had only male members, since 1996 has had the goal of having 20 percent of its membership female by 2005. This is a good example indicating that sport, compared to many other areas in society, has been very slow in promoting gender equality (Flor 1998).

THE PARTICIPATION OF WOMEN IN
THE WINTER OLYMPIC GAMES

In cultures in which sport is important, such as in many Western countries, sports both reflect and create gender identity. Images of ideal masculinity are often constructed and promoted most systematically through competitive sport (Connell 1997), though the same cannot be said about images of ideal femininity. But as Linda Borish (1996: 44) states: "Sport in America expresses and constructs cultural meanings about women. Over time, gender shapes the experiences of women in sport, and certainly the Olympics provides a lens of vision to explore such powerfully gendered messages about sport and the larger culture." The number of female participants and the number of events, particularly events in which women participate, have become important in this perspective.

Before we look at these developments, let us go back to the year 1896, when the first modern Olympic Games took place. This was the only Olympics in which no women participated. According to Hargreaves (1994), however, there is a rumor that there was an "unofficial" female participant. A Greek woman named Melpomene supposedly ran the marathon in protest. Throughout his life Pierre de Coubertin, the father of the modern Games, opposed women's participation (Wilson 1996a). The following quote about the role of women in the Olympics is well known: "In the Olympic Games, as in the contests of former times, their primary role should be to crown the victors" (Boulogne 2000: 24). According to Wolf Lyberg (2000: 47), Coubertin fought for decades against women's participation and declared in his message to the Olympians in 1928: "I am still against the participation of women in the Games. They have been included against my will." It is interesting that women participated in the Games of 1900 in yachting, tennis, and golf; in 1904 they competed only in archery and in 1908 in archery, tennis, and figure skating. These events were included by the local organizing committees but were not formally accepted by the IOC (Wilson 1996a; Pfister 2000).

Both women and men participated in figure skating at the Summer Olympics in 1908. No winter events took place in 1912 and 1916; but in 1920 figure skating for women and men and ice hockey for men were on the program.

In 1912 the IOC made a decision to reassert its authority over the Olympic program. According to Hargreaves (1984), it systematically blocked women's progress and could only be persuaded to allow a few "feminine-appropriate" events to take place outside the official program.

There have always been two possibilities for women who want to participate in sport. They either could try to be integrated and become a part of "men's sports" or could establish their own sport organizations. Historically this has been practiced differently in various countries. Norway, for example, has no tradition of women's sport organizations. This is also true for many other countries. In the United States, for example, the Association for Intercollegiate Athletics for Women was founded in 1971 and existed until the National Collegiate Athletic Association (NCAA) "took over" in the middle of the 1980s. I mention this because one of the first opportunities women had to take part in international sport competitions was in the "Women's World Games" that took place in 1921, 1922, and 1923 in Monte Carlo.

These competitions were organized by the International Women's Sport Federation (FSFI), which was founded in Paris in October 1921. Among the founding mothers of FSFI were representatives from England, Italy, the United States, Czechoslovakia, and France; and a Frenchwoman, Alice Milliat, was behind both the games and the organization (Pfister 2000; Quintillan 2000). According to Gertrud Pfister (2000), the most important activity of FSFI was organizing the Women's Olympic Games, which took place in 1922 in Paris, in 1926 in Gothenburg, in 1930 in Prague, and in 1934 in London. These games documented the need for high-performance female athletics, which found a positive echo among the general public (Pfister 1996). They also proved to be important in the struggle for women's Olympic sport. According to Ghislaine Quintillan (2000: 27), Alice Milliat and her colleagues achieved a dual objective: to overcome Baron Pierre de Coubertin's reluctance to allow women to play a proper part in the Olympic Games and to force the International Amateur Athletics Federation to take women's athletics seriously. FSFI had become an autonomous and powerful body, run by women for women, and a challenge to the Olympic Movement. It was after pressure from the FSFI that the Olympic Games gradually included more and more women's events. The federation was closed down in 1938 and can be said to be the victim of its own success (Quintillan 2000).

In spite of the fact that Coubertin himself did not like the idea of separate Winter Games (Kruger 1996), the IOC decided to arrange separate Winter Olympic Games in 1924 as a trial. These were successful, and it was decided to continue with separate Winter Games. It was surprising to find out that there was resistance toward this from the Nordic countries. They were afraid that Winter Olympics would affect major games that took place in Norway, Finland, and Sweden every winter (Aabø 1993).

Thirteen women, representing 5 percent of the total participants, took part in the first Winter Olympics in 1924. These numbers increased to 788 female athletes in 1998 (36 percent of the participants). Table 3.2 shows women's participation in the Games from 1924 to 2002.

As table 3.2 indicates, women are still underrepresented in the Winter Games compared to men. In the last Winter Olympic Games in Nagano, women accounted for 36 percent of the participants. But there are only a few events now in which women cannot compete, such as ski jumping.

Table 3.2. Women's Participation in
the Olympic Winter Games (IOC 2001)

Year	Sports	Events	%	NOCs	Participants	%
1924	1	2	13	7	13	5
1928	1	2	14	10	26	6
1932	1	2	14	7	21	8
1936	2	3	18	15	80	12
1948	2	5	23	12	77	12
1952	2	6	27	17	109	16
1956	2	7	29	18	132	17
1960	2	11	41	22	143	22
1964	3	13	38	28	200	18
1968	3	13	37	29	211	18
1972	3	13	37	27	206	21
1976	3	14	38	30	231	21
1980	3	14	37	31	233	22
1984	3	15	38	35	274	22
1988	3	18	39	39	313	22
1992	4	25	44	44	488	27
1994	4	27	44	44	523	30
1998	6	31	46	54	788	36
2002	7	37	47			

The largest increase in the number of sports available to women came in 1998, from four sports to six. The largest increase in events occurred from 1988 to 1992, when the number of events for women went from eighteen to twenty-five, an increase of seven events. In 2002 women were able to participate in 47 percent of all events in the Games in Salt Lake City. This development can partly be explained by the IOC decision that all sports seeking inclusion in the program must include women's events (Stivachtis 1998).

Table 3.2 also shows that from 1994 to 1998 the number of female athletes increased dramatically—by 50.7 percent, from 523 to 788. This indicates that both the number of sports and the number of events are important for women's participation. As table 3.2 indicates, more and more countries are represented: a total of fifty-four countries in 1998 (ten more than in 1994). This increase in women athletes in the Olympics probably also reflects the increase in women's participation in sport that has taken place in many countries over the last few years. According to statistics from the IOC's Department of International Cooperation, seventeen National Olympic Committees were represented in Nagano in 1998 by male athletes but no female athletes (Bermuda, Brazil, Chile, Jamaica, Puerto Rico, Trinidad and Tobago, Uruguay, India, Iran, Kyrgyzstan, Mongolia, Belgium, Cyprus, Ireland, Luxembourg, Monaco, and Turkey).

In 1924, 1928, and 1932 figure skating was the only event for women. Alpine skiing was first opened to women in the Olympic program in 1936 (see table 3.3), although the Ski Club of Great Britain had held competitions for female skiers since 1911 in the Swiss Alps (Kruger 1996).

The development of figure skating illustrates how a sport activity is gendered and how this can change over time. In the second half of the nineteenth century the American dance teacher and master of ballet Jackson Haines revolutionized figure skating. He was able to create a way of skating that was admired because of its combination of dance elements and artistic exercises. Figure skating was therefore invented by men for men; in addition, men have invented all the important skating figures (Pfister 2000). When women started to compete in figure skating in the beginning of the twentieth century, "the long skirt and the rules of morality and proper feminine behavior made many figures and jumps impossible, which increased the gender difference in figure skating," as Pfister notes (2000: 22). In the 1920s the difficulty of women's figure skating increased, while at the same time the skaters used more and more elements of dance and glitter and glamour. Sonja Henie became the star and won ten world championships and three Olympics: 1928, 1932, and 1936. According to Pfister (2000), Henie is a perfect example of how feminine ideals in sport as well as in society have changed.

This feminization of figure skating forced the male skaters to distance themselves and to represent masculinity. Male figure skaters reproduced gender difference by jumps and an athletic style. The presentation of masculinity was based on difficult and athletic elements and on the avoidance of "feminine" postures and movements. At the end of the 1970s, however, a "demasculinization" occurred (i.e., a rejection of traditional male signals and symbols, like the rigid posters of the arms and upper body). The male skaters today combine soft, gracious movements, which have been defined as female, with high technical difficulty. As Pfister (2000) notes, this can be interpreted as a "new" masculinity.

In comparing the development of the different events in the Olympics, one will notice that women often have participated for quite a long time in a sport event before it was introduced in the Games. Historically, biological

Table 3.3. Events for Women in the Winter Olympic Games

Year	Sports Events
1924	Single and pairs figure skating
1936	Alpine skiing: downhill and slalom
1948	Combined downhill and slalom
1952	10-km cross-country skiing, Alpine skiing: giant slalom
1956	3 × 5-km cross-country relay
1960	500-m, 1,000-m, 1,500-m, 3,000-m speed skating
1964	5-km cross-country skiing, luge
1976	Ice dancing
1984	20-km cross-country skiing
1988	Alpine skiing: Super G, combined downhill and giant slalom, 5,000-m speed skating
1992	15-km cross-country (hunting start), 30-km cross-country skiing, 7.5-km biathlon, 15-km biathlon, 4 × 7.5-km biathlon relay, freestyle moguls, 500-m short track speed skating and 3000-m relay short track
1998	Curling, ice hockey, and snowboard
2002	Bobsleigh

and medical arguments have been used to deny women access to different sports. Today the medical community has stated that women are actually better suited for participating in ultra-endurance events than men (Bam 1997). In spite of this, the longest distance in cross-country skiing for women is only 30 kilometers (this event was introduced as late as 1992), but men compete in a 50-kilometer race.

On the whole, the medical discourse, with its warnings and prescriptions, has contributed significantly to the marginalization of women in competitive sport (Pfister 1990). Throughout the years various theories on the negative effects of sports on the female body have been presented, but they have been shown to be invalid. The notion that women might lose their ability to bear children, for example, was closely linked to the fear that women could be more "masculine" and as a result turn away from heterosexuality. This also illustrates homophobia, which still exists in the world of sport. Exercises that required strength, daring, and endurance or other traits that men considered "unfeminine" were especially discouraged by the medical profession and branded as potentially dangerous (Pfister 2000). It seems that women have been denied participation in sport on the grounds that women's reproductive systems are vulnerable to injury. The evidence is that there are no medical reasons specific to women that should prevent their participation. This evidence is still often disregarded (Dyer 1982). The female reproductive organs are in many ways more protected inside the body than are men's. And women today can protect the vulnerable parts of their bodies just as male athletes do.

Because men have always had the power in the sport organizations, it is men (with the support of male physicians) who have decided which sports women should participate in. Most of the sports have been developed by and for men and may fit the male body better than the female body. The American sociologist Jay Coackley (1997) wonders what kind of physical skills athletes would need if sports had been shaped by the values and experiences of women instead of men. For example, he writes that "if most sports had been created by and for women the motto for the Olympic Games would not be Citius, Altius, Fortius (faster, higher, stronger); instead it might be 'Balance, Flexibility, and Endurance' or 'Physical Excellence for Health and Humanity'" (1997: 233).

THE MEDIATED IMAGE OF WOMEN IN THE WINTER OLYMPICS

The media and sport are interdependent: sport sells media and the media sell sport (McKay and Rowe 1987; Valgeirsson and Snyder 1986). Figures concerning the global television revenue rights show that the total TV revenue for the Albertville Olympic Games in 1992 was $292 million, which increased to $513 million in Nagano eight years later. The audience increased in the same period from 8 billion to 10.5 billion. Probably due to bad weather and time-zone differences, the number of viewers went down slightly from 1994 to 1998. The 1994 Lillehammer Olympic Games are therefore so far the most watched Olympic Winter Games in history (see table 3.4).

The modern world is greatly influenced by media communication, and most people would agree that the media have the potential to influence societal thoughts and attitudes (Creedon 1994). There are many reasons to believe that the media are active agents in the construction of our meanings and therefore have a large impact on us. Pamela Creedon (1994: 4–5) remarks that "sport is a microcosm of gender values in American culture, and gender values exist at the core of the media system." Media can therefore be said to be a major player in the construction of the ideology of women's sports (Theberge 1991). The media construct and communicate gender values through sports coverage. As Borish (1996: 45) notes: "The huge spectacle of the Olympics reveals the gendered representation of sport and media coverage generally reflects the patriarchal world view of sports

Table 3.4. Television Broadcasts of Winter Olympic Games

	Albertville 1992	Lillehammer 1994	Nagano 1998
Number of Countries Televising	86	120	180
Cumulative Global Audience	8 billion	10.7 billion	10.5 billion
Rights Fees in US$	292 million	353 million	513 million

and the dominance of male sporting activities in the presentation of the Olympics to the public."

Very few studies focus only on the Olympic Games and even fewer on the gender representation of the Winter Olympic Games. Gertrud Pfister (1987) analyzed the large West-German newspaper *Frankfurter Allgemeine Zeitung* and compared reports of female Olympic athletes with female Olympic Games participation between 1952 and 1980. She found an increase in female sport print coverage over time, which corresponded to the growing number of female participants. Pfister concluded that the gender discrimination in relation to representation was diminishing, but that this was not the case for the gender bias in the press, as women's sport was often considered absurd or reported in a sexual context.

Another study examined media treatment of female athletes throughout CBS's 16-day telecast of the 1992 Winter Olympics in Albertville, France (Daddario 1994). The findings revealed that although women were depicted in physically challenging events that defy stereotypical notions of femininity, such as mogul skiing and luge, the sport media reinforced "a masculine sports hegemony through strategies of marginalization" (1994: 275). The television commentators were condescending in their descriptors, which trivialized the achievements of the female athletes. They had a strong tendency to blame female athletes for their failures, while excuses were made for the failures of the male athletes. They also diminished the women by casting them as "little girls." And there was the consensus that female athletes were typically cooperative while the men were typically competitive.

Margaret Carlisle Duncan (1990) examined photographs that accompanied sport stories concerning the 1988 Winter and Summer Olympic Games and the 1984 Summer Games in one Canadian and five American magazines. From a sample of nearly 1,400 pictures, she selected for examination 186 pictures that suggested sexual difference. In the analysis she looked at the content of photographs, including physical appearance, subjects' poses and body positions, expressions, emotional displays, and camera angles.

She further studied the context, which included the visual space, caption, surrounding text, and substance of the article. Her major finding was the continuing association between women's sport and sexuality. Duncan notes that photographs have a powerful capacity to contribute to the construction of ideology: "photographs do not simply create images of women or girls, men or boys; they construct differences between females and males and address viewers as though the differences are natural and real" (1990: 24–25).

Jim Urquhart and Jane Crossman (1999) published an interesting article with the title "The *Globe and Mail* Coverage of the Winter Olympic Games: A Cold Place for Women Athletes." It is a content analysis by gender, controlling for rates of participation, of the Canadian newspaper *Globe and Mail*, covering the sixteen Winter Olympics held between 1924 and 1992. The main conclusions from the study were that "[t]he Winter Olympic coverage by the *Globe and Mail* under-represented women athletes compared to male athletes, used few female journalists, often trivialized female athletes by depicting women in gender-appropriate sports, and placed the sport stories about women's athletic achievements in the latter pages of the sports section" (1999: 197). Figure skating was the only sport where female athletes received more coverage than male athletes in both articles and pictures, and the heroics of female athletes rarely appeared on the front page of the newspaper or the first page of the sports sections.

These results are similar to those of other studies analyzing the presentation of women's sports in the media in general. A common trait that emerges across cultures is the underrepresentation of women's sport. Not only do women's sports get less space and time compared to men's sports, but they are proportionally underrepresented in terms of the number of participants and the number of events. The Amateur Athletic Foundation of Los Angeles, of which Anita DeFrantz is the director, has published reports on television and on newspaper coverage. All reports clearly establish that the media treat women's sport quantitatively differently than men's. The first television studies, published in 1990, showed that only 5 percent of the airtime was devoted to women (Duncan, Messner, and Williams 1990). A follow-up study four years later found a similar result (Wilson 1996b). Stories devoted totally to men's sports received 28.8 times as many column inches as those devoted to women's sports (Duncan, Messner, and Williams 1991). At the same time, statistics show that girls' and women's participation in sport has increased dramatically over the last twenty years.

Another important area is the way in which the female athlete is portrayed in the media. The studies on the Olympic Games are in accordance with other studies from the United States mentioned earlier. The adult women in sport were referred to as "girls," while male athletes of the same age were never called "boys." Female athletes were also called by their first name much more than males were. The studies also found that announcers usually used words suggesting psychological strength and control when describing men's performance. They were much more likely to use words suggesting weakness when discussing female athletes (Wilson 1996b).

Another finding was that "significant differences in the quality of technical production tend to trivialize the women's games, while framing men's games as dramatic spectacles of historic significance" (Duncan, Messner, and Williams 1990: 2). The use of slow motion, instant replays, and on-screen graphics and the provision of verbal statistics were far more pronounced in the coverage of men's games than in the coverage of women's games.

Female athletes who are presented in the media are often sexualized— that is, they are seen as objects of heterosexual desire (Birrell and Theberge 1994; Duncan 1990). Susan Birrell and Nancy Theberge (1994) summarize the different methods of sexualizing female athletes:

- emphasizing physical appearance;
- poses resembling those of soft-core pornography;
- submissive body positions;
- emotional displays; and
- camera angles that look down on women, signaling their inferior position.

As a consequence, sports that traditionally have been defined as feminine (figure skating, swimming, etc.) are also portrayed more effectively and honestly.

Ambivalence—or mixed and contradictory messages—is another theme in describing how women's sport is portrayed in the media. Verbal and visual depictions of sportswomen often seem to combine positive and flattering portrayals with subtly negative suggestions that trivialize or undermine the sports performance (Duncan and Hasbrook 1988). Such an incongruity can also occur when the visual portrayal focuses on female performance yet the narrative description accompanying this visual image focuses on male performance. This happened once to Grete Waitz. When she crossed the New York marathon finish line in victory on the television screen, the commentator's attention focused on who had finished third in the men's race.

The important question is: what does this mean? What kind of consequences does the media coverage of women's sport have—for girls and women in sport and for girls and women in general?

First, the underreporting of women's sport in the media can easily result in the "symbolic annihilation" of the female athlete (Creedon 1994; Birrell and Theberge 1994). It tells us that the female athlete has little, if any, value in this society, particularly in relationship to male athletes. We know that many top-level female athletes have difficulty getting sponsorship. Their looks, not their performances, seem to be more important than for the male elite athletes. A broader and more serious consequence is that underreporting may signal that sport is not for women, which can reduce women's recruitment into sport. In this way the portrayal of women's sports in the media may be looked upon as a barrier to women's involvement, particularly in top-level sport and in sports that traditionally have been looked upon as "masculine."

It is a paradox that while participation in sport can empower women, the media presentation of women's sport may disempower them. Depicting female athletes negatively as is often done can reinforce gender stereotypes where women are looked upon as the "weaker sex," who are powerless. By doing this the sports media reinforce the gender stereotypes in society at large and as such can be looked upon as a strong negative force in changing the gender order in sport itself and in society as a whole. If we are to have a truly democratic society, then women must have the same respect and the same chance to contribute and to succeed as men do.

Theberge (1991) concludes that the myth of female frailty has been replaced by a different version of the ideology of masculine superiority. According to her, gender equality is illusory in the current definition and social organization of sport. As mentioned by Coackley, Theberge notes that "Citius, Altius, Fortius" is a recipe for masculine dominance (1991: 394).

An American article suggests that there are signs that things are perhaps changing (Fink 1998). A strong showing by female athletes in the 1996 Olympics may have provided a bridge leading toward a more accurate and equitable representation of women in sport in the United States. According to Janet Fink, "it appears that a breakthrough of sports has occurred for female athletes in the media. Women athletes, and women who are interested in athletics and exercise, are receiving more attention than ever before" (1998: 40). An extensive study by Susan Tyler Eastman and Andrew Billings (1999: 140), however, showed that this finding can be questioned. They concluded that "despite the claims that the 1996 Summer Games in Atlanta were 'the Olympics of Women,' analysis of the producing network's on-air discourse showed no significant gains in parity for women." A tabulation of over 20,000 names, sports, and associated descriptors in successive Olympics in Lillehammer (1994), Atlanta (1996), and Nagano (1998) was analyzed. The study revealed that the proportions of references of women and men athletes and women's and men's sports stayed at approximately the same imbalanced levels from one Olympics to the next. The conclusion there was that Atlanta was no more a women's Olympics than the prior or succeeding Winter Olympics had been.

I would like to close this discussion by focusing on the fact that men heavily dominate the world of sport journalism. This is also the case at the Winter Olympic Games. At the Games in Nagano in 1998, only 13.3 percent of all accredited journalists were women. Only 47 out of the 220 U.S. journalists (or 21.4 percent) were women. In Nagano only 9.7 percent of the Japanese journalists were women (see table 3.5).

It is reasonable to believe that female and male journalists will differ in their reporting of women's sport, both in relation to the amount of coverage and in relation to the way female athletes are presented. An active policy of employing more female sport journalists will therefore probably also lead to a positive change in the way women's sports are portrayed in media.

THE POLICY WORK OF THE IOC IN PROMOTING WOMEN IN THE OLYMPIC MOVEMENT

During recent years the IOC has systematically worked to promote women in the Olympic Movement in different ways. Taking into account women's marginal positions in the movement, this has surprised many, particularly women in the world of sport. It will also be interesting to see if and how the IOC's work for women and sport will be followed up under the new IOC president and his staff. It all seems to have started in 1994 in Paris, at the IOC Centennial Congress, where key recommendations were adopted to enhance women's participation at all levels and to ensure that— on the basis of the principle of equality of opportunities between men and women—they could play a more significant role in the Olympic Movement (IOC 2000). The outcome of that congress also led to the inclusion in the Olympic Charter of an explicit reference to the promotion of women's advancement in sport. Article 2, paragraph 5, stipulates that "the IOC strongly encourages, by appropriate means, the promotion of women in sport at all levels and in all structures, particularly in the executive bodies of national and international sports organizations with a view to the strict application of the principle of equality between men and women."

The year after that Centennial Congress a Women and Sport Working Group was established to advise the IOC Executive Board on suitable policies to be implemented in this field. It is chaired by vice-president Anita

Table 3.5. Accreditation of Women Journalists by Category:
XVIIIth Olympic Winter Games, 1998, Nagano, Japan

Country	Women	Total	% Women
Australia	5	20	25
Canada	2	41	4.9
China	1	14	7.1
Denmark	3	10	30
Finland	3	36	8.3
France	8	42	19
Germany	20	142	14
Great Britain	2	16	12.5
Hungary	1	7	14.3
Italy	1	35	2.9
Japan	23	236	9.7
Latvia	1	5	20
Liechtenstein	1	2	50
Netherlands	5	28	17.9
New Zealand	1	2	50
Norway	2	49	4
Russian Federation	12	72	16.7
Slovakia	1	11	9
Spain	1	6	16.7
Sweden	6	59	10.2
Switzerland	5	49	10.2
Chinese Taipei	1	1	100
Ukraine	3	7	42.9
United States	47	220	21.4

Note: category E—written press; only countries that sent women journalists are included in the table.

DeFrantz from the United States. In addition to individual members, the working group has representatives from the IOC, the international federations, and the National Olympic Committees as well as representation by athletes. Today the committee consists of fourteen women and seven men.

The IOC has arranged two world conferences on women and sport. The first was in Lausanne in 1996, the second in Paris in 2000. The purpose of these conferences was to assess the progress made on this issue in the sports world, to exchange experiences, and to outline priority initiatives to enhance women's participation in the Olympic Movement (IOC 2000). At both conferences resolutions concerning the future way to involve more women in sports have been adopted. In addition the IOC has established a program of regional seminars for female administrators, coaches, technical officials, and journalists in the national and international sports movement. This program has been in place since 1996.

It is one thing to adopt resolutions; it is something else to implement them in practice. The work that the IOC has done to promote women and sport over the last seven years has been impressive. The committee needs cooperation from the International Sports Federations and the National Olympic Committees, however. It would be interesting to monitor the implementation or the effect of the different initiatives that IOC has taken to promote women and sport. The IOC has not been very successful in appointing women to the organization itself. This may be because the National Olympic Committees and the International Sports Federations probably propose very few women. As noted earlier in this chapter, they still elect mostly men.

In conclusion, one can state that a large improvement has taken place in relation to the number of events for women in the Winter Olympic Games. Nonetheless, female athletes account for only a bit more than one-third of the participants. The fact that women now compete in sports that earlier were allowed only for men may have a positive effect on young girls' and boys' perceptions of femininity and masculinity. The studies on the media-image of female Olympic athletes show that the media may reinforce traditional gender stereotypes through their presentations, but there is no doubt that the media can also do the opposite. They can certainly help to change the gender order of sports since they are active agents in how we see the world.

The center of power in the Olympic Movement is the IOC itself. The figures presented earlier in this chapter show that the IOC and its subcommittees are still very gendered. Studies indicate that changes in the sports organizations themselves are necessary if one wants to recruit more women (Fasting 2000). Emphasizing women's lives, experiences, and values in the further development of sport may be one way. We need studies that focus on the relationship of power, sexuality, and the structure of sports governing bodies and/or how sports organizations construct gender and how gender relations construct the sports organizations. This kind of knowledge is necessary; as women all over the world become more independent, becoming a member of the IOC may not be very attractive unless the committee changes. But in recent years we have experienced the winds of change in the Olympic Movement itself.

References

Aabø, Arnfinn. 1993. *Olympiske Leker 1924–1992 bak resultatene.* Oslo: AL Biblioteksentralen.

Bam, J., et al. 1997. "Could Women Outrun Men in Ultramarathon Races?" *Sport and Exercise* 29: 244–247.

Birrell, Susan, and Nancy Theberge. 1994. "Ideological Control of Women in Sport." In D. Margaret Costa and Sharon Ruth Guthrie (eds.), *Women and Sport: Interdisciplinary Perspectives,* 341–359. Champaign, Ill.: Human Kinetics.

Bø, Olav. 1993. *Skiing throughout History.* Oslo: Samlaget.

Borish, Linda J. 1996. "Women at the Modern Olympic Games: An Interdisciplinary Look at American Culture." *Quest* 48: 43–56.

Boulogne, Yves-Pierre. 2000. "Pierre de Coubertin and Women's Sport." *Olympic Preview* 26: 23–26.

Coackley, Jay. 1997. *Sport in Society: Issues and Controversies.* Boston: McGraw-Hill.

Connell, R. W. 1997. *Gender and Power: Society, the Person and Sexual Politics.* Palo Alto: Stanford University Press.

Creedon, Pamela J. 1994. *Women, Media and Sport: Challenging Gender Values.* Thousand Oaks, Calif.: Sage Publications.

Daddario, Gina. 1994. "Chilly Scenes of the 1992 Winter Games: The Mass Media and the Marginalization of Female Athletes." *Sociology of Sport Journal* 11: 275–288.

Davenport, Joanna. 1996. "Breaking into the Rings: Women in the IOC." *JOPERD (Journal of Physical Education, Recreation and Dance)* 67(5): 26–30.

Duncan, Margaret Carlisle. 1990. "Sports Photographs and Sexual Difference: Images of Women and Men in the 1984 and 1988 Olympic Games." *Sociology of Sport Journal* 7: 22–43.

Duncan, Margaret Carlisle, and C. Hasbrook. 1988. "Denial of Power in Televised Women's Sports." *Sociology of Sport Journal* 5: 1–21.

Duncan, Margaret Carlisle, Michael Messner, and L. Williams. 1990. *Gender Stereotyping in Televised Sport.* Los Angeles: Amateur Athletic Foundation of Los Angeles.

———. 1991. *Coverage of Women's Sports in Four Daily Newspapers.* Los Angeles: Amateur Athletic Foundation of Los Angeles.

Dyer, Kenneth F. 1982. *Catching Up the Men: Women in Sport.* London: Junction Books.

Eastman, Susan Tyler, and Andrew C. Billings. 1999. "Gender Parity in the

Olympics: Hyping Women Athletes, Favoring Men Athletes." *Journal of Sport and Social Issues* 23: 140–170.

Eichler, Margrit. 1980. *The Double Standard: A Feminist Critique of Feminist Social Science*. New York: St. Martin's Press.

Fasting, Kari. 2000. "Women's Role in National and International Sports Governing Bodies." In Barbara L. Drinkwater (ed.), *Women in Sport*, pp. 441–452. Malden, Mass.: Blackwell Sciences, Inc.

Fink, Janet S. 1998. "Female Athletes and the Media: Strides and Stalemates." *JOPERD (Journal of Physical Education, Recreation and Dance)* 69: 37–40.

Flor, Patricia. 1998. "Women and Sport." Unpublished paper presented at the 2nd International World Conference "Women and Sport," Namibia.

Hall, M. Ann. 1990. "How Should we Theorize Gender in the Context of Sport?" In Michael A. Messner and Donald F. Sabo (eds.), *Sport, Men and the Gender Order: Critical Feminist Perspectives*, pp. 223–241. Champaign, Ill.: Human Kinetics.

Hargreaves, Jennifer. 1984. "Women and the Olympic Phenomenon." In Alan Tomlinson and Garry Whannel (eds.), *Five Ring Circus: Money, Power and Politics at the Olympic Games*, pp. 53–70. London: Pluto Press.

———. 1994. *Sporting Females: Critical Issues in the History and Sociology of Women's Sports*. London: Routledge.

Haukeberg, Bjørn Oskar, and Stein Erik Syrstad. 1995. "Der kvinner alltid taper." *Norsk Idrett* 2.

International Olympic Committee (IOC). 2000. "The Promotion of Women in the Olympic Movement, IOC Policy and Initiatives." Document prepared by the Department of International Cooperation, February. Lausanne.

———. 2001. Internet: Women and Sport Facts. September. http://www.olympic.org/ioc/e/news/index_e.html.

Kleveland, Åse. 1994. Paper presented at the First International Conference on Women and Sport: Bringing about Change. Brighton, England, May.

Kruger, Arnd. 1996. "The History of the Olympic Winter Games: The Invention of a Tradition." In Matti Goksøyr, Gerd von der Lippe, and Kristen Mo (eds.), *Winter Games, Warm Traditions*, pp. 101–122. Papers from the 2nd international International Society for the History of Physical Education and Sport (ISHPES) seminar, Lillehammer, 1994. Lillehammer: Norwegian Society of Sport History and International Society for the History of Physical Education and Sport.

Levy, Michael. 1984. "From Stepchild to Heiress: The Story of Women in the Winter Olympics." *Women's Sports* 2: 36–39.

Lopiano, Donna. 1997. "Tomorrow in Women's Sports: Now Is Just the Tip of the Iceberg." Paper presented at the Summit '97. Women's Sport Foundation National Conference, Bloomingdale, Illinois.

Lorber, Judith. 1994. *Paradoxes of Gender*. New Haven, Conn.: Yale University Press.

————. 2000. "Using Gender to Undo Gender: A Feminist Degendering Movement." *Feminist Theory* 1: 79–95.

Lyberg, Wolf. 2000. "Women's Participation in the Olympic Games." *Olympic Preview* (Women and Sport issue) 26: 46–53.

McKay, Jim, and D. Rowe. 1987. "Ideology, the Media, and Australian Sport." *Sociology of Sport Journal* 4: 258–278.

MediaMark Research. 1995. *Sporting Goods Report.* MediaMark Research, Inc.

Messner, Michael, and Donald Sabo. 1990. *Sport, Men and the Gender Order: Critical Feminist Perspectives.* Champaign, Ill.: Human Kinetics.

The Norwegian Act on Gender Equality. Act No. 45 of June 9, 1978, on Gender Equality.

Pfister, Gertrud. 1987. "Women in the Olympics (1952–1980): An Analysis of German Newspapers (Beauty Awards vs. Gold Medals)." Paper presented at the Olympic Movement and Mass Media Conference, Canada.

————. 1990. "The Medical Discourse on Female Physical Culture in Germany in the 19th and Early 20th Centuries." *Journal of Sport History* 17: 183–199.

————. 1996. "The Struggle for Olympia: The Women's World Games and Participation of Women in the Olympic Games." *Journal of the International Council for Health, Physical Education, Recreation, Sport and Dance:* 21–26.

————. 2000. "Women and the Olympic Games: 1900–97." In Barbara L. Drinkwater (ed.), *Women in Sport,* pp. 3–19. Malden, Mass.: Blackwell Sciences, Inc.

————. 2001. "Sport and Gender." Unpublished manuscript.

Pirinen, Riitta. 1997. "Catching Up with Men?: Finnish Newspaper Coverage of Women's Entry into Traditional Male Sports." *International Review for the Sociology of Sport* 32(3): 239–250.

Quintillan, Ghislaine. 2000. "Alice Milliat and the Women's Games." In *Olympic Preview* (Women and Sport issue) 26 (February/March): 27–28.

Salwen, Michael B., and Natalie Wood. 1994. "Depictions of Female Athletes on *Sports Illustrated* Covers, 1957–1989." *Journal of Sport Behavior* 17: 98–107.

Stivachtis, Katia Mascagni. 1998. "Women's Participation in the 18th Olympic Winter Games in Nagano." *Olympic Review* 56: 41.

Theberge, Nancy. 1991. "Women and the Olympic Games: A Consideration of Gender, Sport and Social Change." In F. Landry, M. Landry, and M. Yerles, *Sport—The Third Millennium,* pp. 385–395. Sainte-Foy, Québec: Les Presses de l'Université Laval.

————. 1994. "Toward a Feminist Alternative to Sport as a Male Preserve." In Susan Birrell and Cheryl L. Cole (eds.), *Women, Sport and Culture,* pp. 181–192. Champaign, Ill.: Human Kinetics.

Theberge, Nancy, and Susan Birrell. 1994. "The Sociological Study of Women and Sport." In D. Margaret Costa and Sharon Ruth Guthrie (eds.), *Women and Sport: Interdisciplinary Perspectives,* pp. 323–330. Champaign, Ill.: Human Kinetics.

Tolonene, Kristian. 1998. "VM i Fotball 1998: En oppsummering av seeing på VM-fotballen fra Frankrike." Rapport from NRK Forskningen (NRK research), July.

Urquhart, Jim, and Jane Crossman. 1999. "The *Globe and Mail* Coverage of the Winter Olympic Games: A Cold Place for Women Athletes." *Journal of Sport and Social Issues* 23: 193–202.

Valgeirsson, Gunnar, and Eldon E. Snyder. 1986. "A Cross-Cultural Comparison of Newspaper Sports Sections." *International Review for the Sociology of Sport* 21: 131–140.

Willis, P. 1994. "Women in Sport in Ideology." In Susan Birrell and Cheryl L. Cole (eds.), *Women, Sport and Culture,* pp. 31–45. Champaign, Ill.: Human Kinetics.

Wilson, Wayne. 1996a. "The IOC and the Status of Women in the Olympic Movement: 1972–1996." *Research Quarterly for Exercise and Sport* 67: 183–192.

———. 1996b. "The Portrayal of Women's Sport by the Media." Paper presented at the World Conference on Women and Sport, Lausanne, October 15.

4

MIRACLES, MODERNIZATION, DEBT, AND EVEN DISNEY ON ICE AND SNOW

The North American Contribution to the Olympic Cultural Topography

Kevin B. Wamsley

The Salt Lake City Olympics are the fifth Winter Games to be hosted on North American snow since their modest beginnings in 1924 in Chamonix, France. Visions of skiing, skating, and sledding on crisp, winter days were far removed from the imaginings and narratives about ancient Greek Olympic athletes, adorned by sweat, oil, and symbolic olive leaves conjured up for the inauguration of the modern Olympic Games in 1896. When the Winter Games were first introduced to the Olympic cycle, however, the modern Olympic idea had already been strategically positioned in the minds of many and widely accepted. No nostalgic connections to ancient Greece were necessary.

Considering that Pierre de Coubertin himself and one of his most prominent successors, Avery Brundage, were not enthusiastic about the Winter Games, their historical significance rests on more than a mere complement to the summer festival. Certainly the establishment of Winter Olympic competitions signaled a specific reigning in of "Nordic" sports valued by some internationally influential countries; but the reification of Olympiana within broader sporting and cultural relations was more important. The International Olympic Committee (IOC) had solidified its administrative and ideological influence over international sporting culture in the 1920s. Alternative multisport festivals, including the Women's Olympics, Worker's Olympics, and Nordic Games were all dismantled by the next decade.[1] Coubertin's fears that winter sports were too select, by country, were warranted; but notions that another festival would detract from the Olympic celebrations, originally conceived, proved to be wrong.[2] Indeed, the Winter Olympic Games tightened the IOC's hold on international sport through its association with International Sports Federations and, of course, athletes, by the doubling of public and media exposure offered in multiple host cities.

Coubertin's insistence that the Olympic Games be ambulatory was significant in the legitimizing process that was manifested through organized sport during the twentieth century. The success and popularity of the Olympics only heightened with each new host city. Stratagems that emerged from this ongoing "universalizing" process included bipolar gender relations, class exclusion, and racial divisions, among others.[3] Coubertin's intention in part, he claimed, was to provide opportunities to educate nations about one another.[4] In the first instance, a national and local engagement with the Olympic *idea* and with the sporting and cultural infrastructure of the Coubertinian Games was fundamental. However, an additional legitimizing function obtained in the local interpretation of the Games. Local meanings and identifications, unique by virtue of country, region, or ethnicity, were infused into the experience of the Games by organizers, supporters, and visitors. Such unique engagements at personal or civic levels, whether positive or negative in association, only served to legitimize Coubertin's Olympiana in idea, form, or both. Having two Olympic festivals in a four-year cycle, then, extended the scope of the sports process.[5]

The selection of host cities for the first few Games (Athens, Paris, London, Stockholm) was astutely political to ensure the success of the festival. All locations had noteworthy connections to sport or the current sport leadership. Coubertin sought out "worldly" cities. As a testament to the pervasive influence, indeed the enveloping multimedia presence of the Olympics in the twentieth century, less than one hundred years later, the relationship has been inverted; bid committees now claim that winning the rights to host an Olympic Games is, invariably, announcing the arrival of a "world-class" city.[6] The "chosen" cities must have massive infrastructures in place for the influx of athletes and media personnel, including large airports, hotel complexes, and state of the art athletic facilities. Cities hosting the Winter Olympics have always been significantly different than their Summer counterparts, with unique environmental requirements. In addition to cold weather, the most predominant feature, of course, was immediate access to a mountain of significant slope for Alpine skiing events. Consequently, without exception, all Winter host cities were tourist resorts of some regional, national, or international standing.

The first Olympic foray to North America, St. Louis in 1904, was tenuous at best. Coubertin did not even attend the Games. The Games hosted in North America during the rest of the century, however, both Summer and Winter, are considered to be relatively successful, on the terms of

Olympic organizers and supporters, of course. So much so that the American television market in the last quarter of the twentieth century has ensured the financial stability of the IOC for the foreseeable future.[7] Hosting the Olympic Games has always been challenging for organizers, who are charged with the task of superimposing an institutionalized model on local turf, a process that usually pits boosters against critics, capital development against social concerns. With the exception of Denver, Colorado, where environmentally concerned voters rejected state funding for the 1976 Winter Games, the Olympic boosters have won the day.[8]

The first North American city to host the Winter Games was Lake Placid, New York, in 1932, followed by Squaw Valley, California (1960), Lake Placid (1980), Calgary, Alberta (1988), and Salt Lake City, Utah (2002). Of all issues emerging from the hosting of these Games, without question the most fundamental and contentious across the decades has been financing. Projections for Salt Lake City suggest that $1.5 billion in public money will be doled out.[9] Without question, the most significant changes with direct consequences to host cities occurred under the Samaranch regime. The scope of spectacle has been magnified, to say the least, by millions of dollars in sponsorship emanating from lucrative television contracts and corporate marketing programs. As a result, the celebrations have become more extravagant; but the public debt has not been eliminated. In this era, protests against the Olympics have become more organized and extensive. Unique and compelling issues have emerged for each Winter host city; it goes without saying that all have been bound and influenced by the social, economic, and political particulars of each historic era, both within Olympic culture and beyond to local, national, and international contexts.

As early as 1932, protesters challenged the Olympic Organizing Committee in Lake Placid over the cutting of 2,500 trees in the protected Adirondacks region of New York.[10] The Olympic bobsleigh track was built on this ground, granted by a perpetual easement, with the land reverting back to the state of New York in May 1932.[11] Support in the state assembly for such considerations was abetted by the Organizing Committee's impressive list of honorary and active members, including, among others, Franklin D. Roosevelt, governor of New York; General Douglas MacArthur, past president, American Olympic Committee; Dr. Godfrey Dewey, vice-president, Lake Placid Club; and William J. O'Hare, who served as treasurer of the Winter Games Committee.[12] Lake Placid was awarded the Games in April 1929,[13] withstanding a protest from a California group who argued that the Winter Games should be hosted in the vicinity of the Los Angeles Games of 1932. An influential slate of patrons and associates was crucial to the allocation of public funds in excess of 1 million dollars to build adequate facilities. The outdoor Olympic stadium, where athletes marched in and participated in speed skating and some hockey matches, cost $135,000. The town of North Elba at a cost of $294,000 funded the Olympic arena, an indoor safeguard against bad weather. The controversial bobsled run cost $243,000, running the total expenses for hosting to $1,742,000.00. Low attendance figures produced gate receipts of only $93,415, leaving public costs, financed mainly by the state legislature, of just under 1 million dollars.[14] These costs seem minimal by current standards, but only 364 athletes participated in the Lake Placid games. And these costs were borne by the public purse in spite of the harsh economic climate of the Great Depression during the decade of the 1930s.

Even with the financial shortfall, it was declared that the Games were an investment in the future.[15] The Games proceeded from February 4 to 13, with seventeen nations accepting the invitation of the IOC to attend. Governor Franklin D. Roosevelt opened the Games, citing the usual nostalgic connection to the ancient Games, while invoking a modern sense of athletic honor and an appeal to amateurism:

> It is an evidence of the age of our modern civilization that the Olympics date back nearly 2,800 years, and although in those early days they did not have the Winter Games, we in these later days, through the Winter Games, are trying to carry out the ideals of sport that were instituted in the Olympiads. Throughout the history of these Games, athletes have come to participate in them, seeking no recognition other than the honor received in a simple medal. But that medal has come to typify the very best athlete in all nations in honor as well as health.[16]

Roosevelt's remarks were typical of the sterile political discourse invoked for Olympic ceremonies and congruent with the overall sentiment of American Olympic Association president Avery Brundage's report on the 1932 Games. The tone of Brundage's report for 1932 presaged the tenor of his political activism in ensuring American participation in Berlin in 1936. For Brundage, an ease with the language of officialdom helped to rationalize the complicity of international sport in sustaining forms of oppression and inequality; sport had no place in running the "wrong" sorts of political interference:

> The congregation of many thousands of competitors, athletic leaders and their followers from all over the world, for a fortnight of friendly association in a clean atmosphere of good sportsmanship and good fellowship, cannot help advancing the cause of mankind. Midst the crash of social systems, governments and other man made structures of various kinds,

amateur sport with its shining ideals of friendly courtesy and fair play stands firm and the Olympic torch lights the way to mutual respect and understanding and international good will.[17]

Brundage's politics were not always concealed in ideological ruminations, however. He was relatively consistent in his views on who should participate in the Games.

Athletic feminists, for example, had staved off expulsion from the Games, a threat advanced by IOC president Henri de Baillet-Latour himself, after a gross misunderstanding of the physiological stresses supposedly endured by female participants in the 800-meter race in Amsterdam in 1928. Latour, Brundage, and others had called for the complete removal of women from the Olympics. After much debate and a protest by the American men's athletics team, the IOC voted to continue women's events on the 1932 program.[18] For the IOC and International Federations (IFs) members, who sought to sustain the gender polarities enshrined in the traditional masculinities and femininities celebrated by modern sport, it was the graceful womanhood of figure skaters such as Sonja Henie of Norway that was appropriately represented in the Winter Games. However, female speed skaters and even dog sledders shared the tracks with male counterparts in "unofficial" competitions.

Speed skater Jack Shea, a resident of New York State, won the first medal in Lake Placid and became the first Olympic athlete to mount a podium, now a permanent fixture in the ritual ceremonies of the Games.[19] Shea's Olympic experiences in 1932 became an important point of departure for the recent celebrations in Salt Lake City seventy years later, which involved his grandson. "Pack skating" had been introduced in Lake Placid; but after American victories, including those by Shea, the International Skating Union accepted the protest of the European skaters and forced the races to be adjudicated by time.[20] A resident of Lake Placid, Jack Shea became a local icon, a living connection to Lake Placid's Olympic history.

In American Olympic Committee official reports, environmental concerns and the economic issues of the Depression were seemingly far less significant than the weather. In all Winter Olympic Games, particularly in the first half of the century when the majority of facilities were outdoors, weather was always a major concern. In Lake Placid in 1932 a thaw followed by a heavy snowstorm wreaked havoc upon the bobsled run, and teams of workers had to be called in for major repairs. United States ski-jumping tryouts could not be held in Lake Placid, because there was no snow. The 50-kilometer cross country track had to be remarked, because most of the snow had melted from the course. Velo Saarinen of Finland was the first competitor to arrive at the finish line, with his "face a bloody mass, his shirt and trousers almost torn to shreds."[21]

Such facilities as the Lake Placid bobsleigh track remained temporary, leaving only limited responsibilities in caring for the permanent structures such as the indoor arena for the host town or city. As the Olympic Games grew, in terms of athlete participation and in the scope of facilities considered necessary for hosting a successful Games, post-Olympic costs eventually became a primary concern for organizing committees. Providing an infrastructure superlative to that of the previous Games became as much a part of Olympic competition between host cities, particularly in the symbolic cultural context of the Cold War period, as the prerogative of setting world records became an index of progress for athletes, coaches, and national sport programs. Elaborate, even unique, sport facilities emerged as an expected feature of the Olympic experience, to be invoked as an impressionistic gauge of the host city, organizing committee, and, to the broader audience, the Games themselves. Gauges, impressions, and indices of progress of course could not be invoked until the Games were a "permanent fixture" in the popular imagination. Well before 1960, when the Winter Games returned to North America, the Olympics had firm footing as the most important multisport festival in the world. Unfortunately for host cities, costs continued to escalate.

With the development potential of the post-Games in mind, the bid to host the Squaw Valley Olympics was led by New York attorney Alexander Cushing. With the support of some corporate investors, two U.S. senators, and the governor of California, Cushing attempted to capitalize on the growing fears of IOC president Avery Brundage that the Olympic Games were straying from the original ideals toward commercial development. He promised modest, simple Games, and his bid defeated Innsbruck by two votes on the second ballot. When the costs for developing the site soared, however, the stakes became too high for Cushing, and he was replaced as head of the Organizing Committee.

Building the Olympic facilities (including the Blyth arena, Olympic Village, on-site hospital, press building, upgrades to the ski courses, interstate highway expansion, and airport improvements) drove the costs to $20 million.[22] The state of Nevada shared some costs, as did the U.S. Congress, but most were absorbed by the state of California, whose leaders planned to sell off these holdings after the Games. Television rights infused only $50,000 into the budget.[23] Organizers even canceled the sport of bobsleighing to avoid the costs of building a track.

The Games were opened by Vice-President Richard Nixon. The winner of the 500-meter men's speed-skating event in Oslo in 1952, Ken Henry, lit the cauldron, and the Games announcer drummed out the usual fare: "Let this flame of truth and brotherhood shine brightly through all time, to unite nation to nation and man to man."[24]

Cushing's plans to offer modest, noncommercial Games quickly fell by the wayside as Walt Disney was appointed pageant director and celebrity Art Linkletter provided nightly entertainment in the village. In what Tim Ashwell has called "an artfully created artificial environment,"[25] Disney's giant plaster athlete sculptures towered above the elaborate ceremonies and entertainments, glossing over a U.S. ban on visas for East German journalists,[26] the ever-present two-China issue, and the running tensions between U.S. and Soviet nationalisms.[27] Thomas J. Hamilton, chairman of the Olympic Development program, remarked on the symbolic and practical significance of hosting and performing well in this era: "In this current world of tensions and suspicions, a show of strength in all sports by the United States is needed to further our relationships with the many other nations in the world to whom USA prowess in Olympic competition is a measuring standard of national character."[28] American athletes did not disappoint. The U.S. Olympic Committee called the Games an "unqualified success," praising the "world record breaking performances" and the thrills of close competition, with the gold-medal performance of the U.S. men's hockey team making the "biggest impression."[29] In the end, the Squaw Valley Games were heralded as an Olympic success. However, the $20-million infrastructure—the majority of the cost met by public money—fell into disrepair. Even subsidies for private developers could not sustain the facilities.

Although television rights made little dent in the financial shortfalls of Squaw Valley, the idea of the live broadcast rendered the Olympic ceremonies and pageantry even more significant. Walter Cronkite and the Columbia Broadcasting System (CBS) put names and faces on Cold War actors, usually the stuff of newspaper and magazine columns; live action made for better narrative excitement. Systematic efforts were made to educate the American people on Olympic "ideals." The American Dairy Association published more than a million copies of what was called "The Olympic Story," designed to indoctrinate school children on things Olympic. Over 250 television stations broadcast a series of five-minute films on the Olympics, sponsored by the Dairy Association, during the two years leading up to Squaw Valley. It also produced a 28-minute film entitled *Hold High the Torch*, a documentary on the role of the United States Olympic Committee. The IOC, press, and athletes were treated to dairy bars serving free milk and ice cream throughout the Games.[30] The California Meat Packers provided a hot-dog stand. In addition, United States domestic sponsors provided more than a quarter of a million dollars' worth of footwear and apparel for the Summer and Winter Olympic teams. Wilson Sporting Goods public relations director Marion Miller, a member of the USOC's Supplies and Equipment Committee since 1946, coordinated sponsorship efforts.[31]

The new television audiences of the 1960s had changed the productive capacities of Olympic Games. On-site events were transformed into the precursors of mega-events, and artificial spectacles such as that staged in Squaw Valley were cast more as entertainment for the new, enlarged audiences, dressing the Coubertinian sport infrastructure in new clothes.

The decade of the 1970s was a period of transition for the Olympics, particularly after the departure of the ultra-conservative Avery Brundage as IOC president. The Munich massacre in 1972; the financial disaster of the Montreal Games of 1976; the decline of the rules of amateurism under the leadership of Lord Killanin; and the peak of rivalry between the United States and the Soviet Union had placed the Olympics in a precarious position. There were few cities willing to host an Olympic Games. However, under Killanin's successor, Juan Antonio Samaranch, after the 1980 Games, all things changed.

Twenty years after Squaw Valley, on U.S. soil once again, Cold War politics pulsed through the Winter Games in Lake Placid. From the John F. Kennedy era to the Jimmy Carter era, through competitions over outer space, science, culture, and economy, the symbolic weight of Olympic victory for nations only magnified. Most significant for the United States, beyond the debts and exorbitant costs of facilities, fears of boycott, court injunctions by Taiwan for official status at the Games, and a squashed environmental protest, was the gold-medal victory of the men's hockey team, dubbed the "Miracle on Ice."

Following the 1979 Soviet invasion of Afghanistan, and President Jimmy Carter's threat to boycott the Moscow Olympics of 1980, the Lake Placid Organizing Committee's fears were finally alleviated when the Soviets announced that they would not boycott the Winter Games. Such Cold War tensions, as in previous Olympics since the entry of the Soviets in 1952, permeated the celebration of the Games, the ceremonies, and the response of the American public to United States victories. As in 1960, the Olympic pageantry was Disneyfied once again by that company's Tommy Walker, who coordinated the opening ceremonies.

Capitalizing once again on the IOC's ambivalence toward the commercialization of the Olympics, the Lake Placid organizers promised to deliver unspectacular, simple Games.[32] Environmental concerns raised initially some forty-eight years earlier in Lake Placid came to the fore once again. Commercial developments were not to be undertaken in the Adirondacks region. In the end, although the construction process was delayed somewhat, the

environmental protests were, for the most part, silenced through legislation. The Organizing Committee also came under investigation by the federal government for financial irregularities, in particular the awarding of
construction contracts and the millions of dollars of deficits accrued in the
process. Fundraiser John Wilkins was fired for his transgressions in awarding contracts.[33] The initial, grossly underestimated, budget was projected at
$22 million; the final budget ballooned to $150 million. Television revenues and ticket sales provided only $34 million; the federal and state gov-
ernments granted the rest.[34] In spite of innovative plans for facilities, such
as the conversion of the Olympic Village into a federal prison after the
Games, the city of Lake Placid was left with a $4.3 million deficit and $21.5
million in claims filed by contractors.[35]

During the Games, transportation became a major issue for the Lake
Placid Organizing Committee. Some spectators had to travel hours to reach
the venues because of a housing shortage in the town. Since only the athletes, town residents, and Olympic officials were permitted to drive into
Lake Placid, the majority of spectators had to be bussed in from parking
lots 10 miles away. Bus problems and road conditions during the Games
stranded thousands of spectators at the venues.[36] Infrastructural problems,
however, were quickly overshadowed by events in the Games.

For the White House, where Jimmy Carter remained poised to deal
with the pressing issues of the day, U.S. athletes quickly became national
heroes. Only the victory of the Americans over the Soviet hockey team, on
George Washington's birthday, overshadowed Eric Heiden's brilliant five-
gold-medal speed-skating performances. The value of these victories in distracting attention away from the financial difficulties of the Games was
immeasurable. Robert Paul, Jr., USOC director of communications, cited
the *Sports Illustrated* reading of the hockey gold in his glowing report on
the Games:

> For millions of people, their single, lasting image of the Lake Placid
> Games will be the infectious joy displayed by the U.S. hockey team fol-
> lowing its 4–3 victory over the Soviet Union. It was an Olympian moment,
> the kind the creators of the Games must have had in mind, one that said:
> Here is something bigger than any of you. It was bizarre, it was beautiful.
> Upflung sticks slowly wheeled into the rafters. The American players—
> in pairs rather than in one great glop—hugged and danced and rolled on
> one another.[37]

In addition to the financial insecurities plaguing the Olympics since the
debacle in Montreal in 1976, growing political tensions between the Soviet

Union and the United States brought major boycotts to the Games of 1980 in Moscow and 1984 in Los Angeles. On the one hand, these boycotts were simply enmeshed in broader economic sanctions and political posturing; on the other hand, they signified the eminent status of Olympic sport within international policy. And not having the sport "superpowers" in attendance was bad for Olympic business.

Following the resounding financial success of Peter Ueberroth's Olympic Games in Los Angeles in 1984—and the realization that the Games could turn a substantial profit—cities worked with more fervor to bid for the Olympics. More significantly, new president Juan Antonio Samaranch ushered in an era of commercially determined relationships with multinational corporations, which, in addition to providing a windfall in television broadcast revenues, created new sources of finance for host cities.

Calgary, in 1988, was the first Olympic host city to enjoy the exaggerated base of television revenues. Broadcasters had paid some $20.7 million to televise the Winter Games in Lake Placid in 1980. Slick negotiating tactics by the IOC raised the stakes to $324.9 million for Calgary just eight years later.[38] Of that sum, the American Broadcasting Corporation (ABC) paid $309 million.[39] Indeed the Games of 1988 were expensive, but organizers set aside a "legacy" fund of approximately $40 million to secure the future of Olympic facilities in the city.

Calgary defeated Falun, China, on the second ballot during the 84th IOC session in Baden-Baden in 1981 for the rights to host the XVth Winter Games. Annual home to the internationally renowned Calgary Stampede rodeo since the early part of the twentieth century, the city was well versed in staging sports entertainment; the Olympics, however, were a major event for Calgary. Given the opportunities, more often requirements, of the Olympics to showcase local and national culture for the period leading up to and including the Games, event leaders in cities such as Calgary were forced to consider the idea of local and regional, even national, heritage and the representations of culture that would be positioned for all of the Olympic celebrations. Whose culture would be situated as the Canadian or even western tradition? Calgary had originated as a trading and North West Mounted Police post, growing into a railway town within a regional agricultural and oil development economy. Throughout the twentieth century, the city's inhabitants had embraced a true "western" identity, with cowboys as local symbols and western "hospitality" as the fundamental element of its tourism program. Resorts in the nearby Rocky Mountains had positioned the area as a tourist destination, with outstanding Alpine skiing and even the mountain-climbing opportunities of the known European destinations. An oil boom and prosperous economy had stimulated un-precedented growth in the city, and city leaders wrestled with the often-contradictory images of past and present.

Like the organizers in Lillehammer in 1994, Calgarians became em-broiled in complex processes of identity construction through the bidding procedures and in hosting the Olympics. As part of its long-term economic development, city leaders had to position Calgary as a modern city, with all of the business opportunities of a "world-class" city. The local flavor of western hospitality and friendliness, however, had to be juxtaposed onto new visions of modernity. Training manuals educating Olympic volunteers on how to welcome the world reminded them that, "in spite of its reputa-tion, Calgary is not a cowboy town."[40] Yet the bid committee successfully presented its vision of the modern Calgary in Baden-Baden, using a back-drop of traditional flapjack breakfasts, Stetson hats, and Native dancing provided by Blood chief Lambert Fox and his wife, Yvonne, in traditional dress.[41] In light of such western hospitality and traditions, the bid guaran-teed that the Games would be housed in the most modern facilities.

Once the bid was won, organizers set about ensuring that Calgarians would be excited about hosting the Olympics. They were very successful in generating local enthusiasm; more than 10,000 people volunteered to be a part of the host team in Calgary. In addition, and confirming the city's business development attitude, the Olympics were to announce that Cal-gary had arrived as a "world-class city." This was in spite of a tourism report that cited visitors to the city who claimed that Calgary was a "poor and superficial imitation of the 'true' cities of the world," attempting to be "sophisticated, urbane, and cosmopolitan."[42]

Basic infrastructural requirements such as an international airport and adequate numbers of hotel rooms aside, the costs of building Winter Olympic facilities were enormous. The Calgary Saddledome, modern em-blem of Calgary's western heritage, cost $98 million; the Olympic Oval and Olympic Village facilities, $103 million; ski-jump, bobsleigh, and luge facilities and training centers, $72 million; Nordic Centre, $17 million; alpine facilities, $27 million.[43] The Olympic Programme (TOP) exclusive sponsorship revenues, broadcast revenues, and national sponsorship monies were buffered by more than $500 million in support from the federal, provincial, and city governments. The IOC corporate funding schemes as-sured the financial security of the Olympics, at a time when host cities were reluctant to come forward; yet substantial public funds were still being ex-pended on the elaborate ceremonies, IOC luxuries, and costly facilities. Corporate relationships were being sought for all aspects of the Games, including rituals and ceremonies. The oil and gas company Petro-Canada, for example, sponsored the torch relay. Strategically, corporate colors were red and white, matching the Canadian flag and typical Canadian Olympic uniforms. The cost of the torch relay was $50 million, involving 6,520 participants selected from 6.5 million applicants. The "Share the Flame" torch run, aided by boat, snowmobile, and dogsled, brought increased revenues of $23 million per month to the company.[44]

As the torch made its way across Canada, protests were staged in Kahnawake, Toronto, Edmonton, Lethbridge, and Calgary in support of the Lubicon Cree, a band of Aboriginal Canadians who organized a boycott of the Olympics as part of their political engagement over land claims and long-term suffering at the hands of discriminatory government policies. Oil companies had drilled 400 wells within a 15-mile radius of their community, destroying the traditional hunting grounds of their Lubicon Lake band. In addition to the torch relay, Aboriginals and their supporters protested against the sponsorship of the Games by oil companies, particularly against the "The Spirit Sings" exhibition at the Glenbow Museum in Calgary. The exhibition featured hundreds of artifacts solicited from collections situated around the world that had been stolen or appropriated from North America. Commenting on the direct sponsorship of the exhibit by oil company Shell Canada, Lubicon Chief Bernard Ominayak argued: the "irony of using a display of North American Indian artefacts to attract people to the Winter Olympics being organized by interests who are still actively seeking to destroy Indian people seems painfully obvious."[45]

Aboriginal Canadians had long suffered through discriminatory and assimilative federal policies, leaving desperate social and economic conditions on reserves and for Natives living in mainstream society. Typical media representations depicted Canadian Aboriginals as the romanticized wild savages remembered by colonial tales of the eighteenth and nineteenth centuries. For example, officials wanted to include a Native Canadian history within the ceremonials of the 1976 Olympics but neglected to seek the input of Aboriginals. Hundreds of non-Natives were dressed in "Aboriginal" costumes and adorned with face paint for the closing ceremonies. After Montreal, Native leaders ensured that any future participation or thematic representations in national or international events would have their approval.[46]

Calgary organizers initially forwarded similar ideas, suggesting that an Indian attack and wagon burning should be included in the opening ceremonies in 1988. Organizing Committee president Bill Pratt informed Native leaders that their people should expect to be a major tourist attraction during the Games.[47] Native leaders such as J. Wilton Littlechild, who had observed the farcical ceremony in Montreal, were determined to provide more input to the proceedings. It seemed, though, that organizers could not get beyond stereotypical projections of Aboriginal culture. The Olympic medals displayed a ceremonial Indian headdress with the eagle feathers replaced by winter sports equipment, such as skis and skates. In response to this, specifically, Greg Smith of the Peigan tribe argued that the medal design, while explicitly professing to "show the international community that Indians [were] a part of the games," was a deliberate attempt to downplay Native protests and resistance to the Games.[48]

Although the pre-Games protests were peaceful and nonviolent, the former Los Angeles Games security chief absurdly suggested that the Aboriginal boycott was a security risk of the same magnitude to the Palestinian attack on the Munich Olympics in 1972.[49] Aboriginal protests and any local resistance to the Games were treated with suspicion by the Calgary media, similar to other anti-Olympic resistance movements or criticisms of bids and hosting in other cities, such as in Sydney in 2000 or during Toronto's bids for 1996 and 2008.[50] In popular discourse, the Games were good for city and citizen. Of the Olympics and the similarly scaled urban events to follow in Calgary, Dave Gerlitz argued that Calgarians were easily mobilized: "It's like preaching to the converted when this gets rolling."[51] The autocratic leadership approach of Peter Ueberroth became a benchmark for organizers. President Bill Pratt called it the "let's get it done approach." Under this style, it was understood that firings and personal conflicts were part of the process and necessary for any organizing committee to achieve its goals. Ueberroth himself was brought to Calgary to boost morale among workers prior to the Games.

In the end, the Calgary Olympics were judged to be a tremendous success, capped by Samaranch's praise as the "best Games ever." With such extensive private and public funding, the Organizing Committee was able to bank a legacy fund to ensure the post-Games upkeep of facilities. In the years that followed, however, the Olympic mark remained a prominent feature of the city landscape. Long-term tourist figures did not reach the proportions that are always projected in Olympic bids, but the "Olympic city" projection figured extensively in Calgary's tourist promotion plans. An outcome of the Winter Games successes has been a stream of international sporting and cultural events that Calgary has bid for, won, and hosted in its post-Games era. Frequently, these facilities host national and international events. Further, the prestige of hosting non-Olympic international events has lured civic boosters and corporate sponsors alike—the

World Police/Fire Games in 1997, the Rotary Convention of 30,000 members in 1996, and the recently canceled Ted Turner Goodwill Games scheduled for 2005.

Some of the Calgary Olympic facilities have been well used, while others incur significant maintenance costs with few users. The Olympic Oval at the University of Calgary is arguably the biggest success story of the 1988 Winter Games. It has been marketed as a multiuse facility for elite athletes from around the world and for local residents who wish to speed-skate, play hockey, run, or attend national and international events. The ski jumps and bobsleigh, luge, and skeleton tracks, however, are far less appropriate for public use. Those in favor of sustaining elite performance centers for national-caliber athletes can easily make the case for these facilities. But a Vancouver-Whistler bid for the 2010 Winter Games makes little fiscal or facility sense for Canada.[52] Perhaps one could argue for the construction of facilities in central or eastern Canada; but identical large-scaled Olympic venues located in such proximity would be a waste of public and private money.

Salt Lake City, too, has wrestled and will continue to wrestle with similar issues of competing identities and representations of culture. Unique to Salt Lake has been the media attention in the wake of the IOC bribery scandal and the concerns over safety in light of the attacks on the World Trade Center and Pentagon on September 11, 2001. Although bribery and scandal within the IOC had been extant in Olympic business long before Salt Lake, the city will have to endure its historical association with bribery and graft for the foreseeable future. As in the case of the Games of war-torn Antwerp in 1920 and London in 1948, the Soviet invasion of Hungary in 1956 and Czechoslovakia in 1968, the Mexico and Munich massacres of 1968 and 1972, respectively, and the politically charged Hitler Olympics of 1936, unique stories will emerge about these Games, perhaps in the context of the patriotic responses to the attacks, a rebuilding of American confidence, a valorization of American performances—what the Olympics mean to both host country and participants, what they mean to residents of Salt Lake City. Indeed the ideological and historical legacies will be as captivating as discussions over the residual infrastructural and financial legacies. Provided that people ask critical questions or are permitted to ask critical questions about why the Games are so important, popular, and pervasive or distasteful, overbearing, and expensive, and whose interests are served through them, it will have been a valuable experience. People need to know how and why ice and snow have been historically sculptured as such in North America.

Notes

1. See James Riordan, "The Worker's Olympics," in Alan Tomlinson and Garry Whannel (eds.), *Five Ring Circus: Money Power and Politics at the Olympic Games* (London: Pluto Press, 1984), pp. 98–112; and Bruce Kidd, *The Struggle for Canadian Sport* (Toronto: University of Toronto Press, 1996), pp. 146–183; Kevin B. Wamsley and Guy Schultz, "Rogues and Bedfellows: The IOC and the Incorporation of the FSFI," in Kevin B. Wamsley, Scott G. Martyn, Gordon H. MacDonald, and Robert K. Barney (eds.), *Bridging Three Centuries: Intellectual Crossroads and the Modern Olympic Movement* (London, Ontario: International Centre for Olympic Studies, 2001), pp. 113–118; and Ron Edgeworth, "The Nordic Games and the Origins of the Olympic Winter Games," *Journal of Olympic History* 2, no. 2 (1994): 29–37.

2. See Allen Guttmann, *The Olympics: A History of the Modern Games* (Urbana and Chicago: University of Illinois Press, 1992), p. 41. See also *Pierre de Coubertin 1863–1937: Olympism Selected Writings*, ed. Norbert Mueller (Lausanne: International Olympic Committee, 2000), p. 522.

3. See John Hoberman, *The Olympic Crisis: Sports, Politics and the Moral Order* (New Rochelle, N.Y.: Caratzas, 1986).

4. See Stephan Wasson, "Coubertin's Olympic Quest: His Educational Campaign in America," *Olympika: The International Journal of Olympic Studies* 10 (2001): 59–72.

5. Understanding sport as a social process, as opposed to the essentialist models proposing sport as an entity, is an argument well developed in Eric G. Dunning, Joseph A. Maguire, and Robert E. Pearton (eds.), *The Sports Process: A Comparative and Developmental Approach* (Champaign, Ill.: Human Kinetics Publishers, 1993).

6. See Maurice Roche, *Mega-Events and Modernity: Olympics and Expos in the Growth of Global Culture* (London and New York: Routledge, 2000).

7. See Robert K. Barney, Stephen R. Wenn, and Scott G. Martyn, *Selling the Five Rings: The International Olympic Committee and the Rise of Olympic Commercialism* (Salt Lake City: University of Utah Press, 2002).

8. John J. Kennedy, Jr., "Innsbruck 1976, XIIth Olympic Winter Games," in John E. Findling and Kimberly D. Pelle (eds.), *Historical Dictionary of the Modern Olympic Movement* (Westport, Conn.: Greenwood Press, 1996), p. 289.

9. Associated Press, December 5, 2001, p. S3.

10. John Fea, "Lake Placid 1932," in Findling and Pelle (eds.), *Historical Dictionary of the Modern Olympic Movement*, p. 232.

11. *Report of the American Olympic Committee, 1932* (New York: AOC, 1932), p. 235.

12. Ibid., p. 233.

13. Ibid., p. 235.

14. Ibid.

15. *New York Times*, February 17, 1932, p. 27.

16. *American Olympic Committee Official Report, 1932* (New York: AOC, 1932), p. 235.

17. Ibid., p. 20.

18. See Wamsley and Schultz, "Rogues and Bedfellows: The IOC and the Incorporation of the FSFI."

19. On the history of the podium, see Robert K. Barney, "The Great Transformation: Olympic Victory Ceremonies and the Medal Podium," *Olympika: The International Journal of Olympic Studies* 7 (1998): 89–112.

20. Fea, "Lake Placid 1932," in Findling and Pelle (eds.), *Historical Dictionary of the Modern Olympic Movement*, p. 234.

21. *American Olympic Committee Official Report, 1932*, p. 271.

22. *New York Times,* January 24, 1960, section V, 4:3; *Sports Illustrated,* January 11, 1960, p. 22; and Tim Ashwell, "Squaw Valley 1960," in Findling and Pelle (eds.), *Historical Dictionary of the Modern Olympic Movement*, pp. 263–269.

23. See Barney, Wenn, and Martyn, *Selling the Five Rings.*

24. Harald Lechenperg (ed.), *Olympic Games 1960* (New York: A. S. Barnes, 1960), p. 12.

25. Ashwell, "Squaw Valley 1960," p. 268.

26. *New York Times,* February 11, 1960, 47:3.

27. *New York Times,* February 19, 1960, p. 30; *Sports Illustrated,* March 7, 1960, p. 14.

28. *Quadrennial Report of the United States Olympic Committee* (New York: United States Olympic Association, 1960), p. 53.

29. Ibid., pp. 197–198.

30. Ibid., p. 37.

31. Ibid., p. 38.

32. See John Fea, "Lake Placid 1980," in Findling and Pelle (eds.), *Historical Dictionary of the Modern Olympic Movement*, pp. 295–301.

33. Ibid., p. 297.

34. Barney, Wenn, and Martyn, *Selling the Five Rings;* Fea, "Lake Placid 1980."

35. *New York Times,* October 5, 1980, p. 51.

36. Fea, "Lake Placid 1980," pp. 297–298.

37. United States Olympic Committee, *United States Olympic Book 1980* (Salt Lake City, Utah: Publishers Press, 1980), p. 18.

38. See the full discussion about television negotiations in Barney, Wenn, and Martyn, *Selling the Five Rings.*

39. Scott G. Martyn, "The Struggle for Financial Autonomy: The IOC and the Historical Emergence of Corporate Sponsorship, 1896–2000," Ph.D. dissertation, University of Western Ontario, 2000, p. 230.

40. For a more extensive analysis of the struggle over tradition, heritage, and modernity during the Calgary Games, see Kevin B. Wamsley and Michael K. Heine, "Tradition, Modernity, and the Construction of Civic Identity: The Calgary Olympics," *Olympika: The International Journal of Olympic Studies* 5 (1996): 81–90.

41. K. B. Wamsley and Mike Heine, "'Don't Mess with the Relay—It's Bad Medicine': Aboriginal Culture and the 1988 Winter Olympics," in R. Barney, S. Martyn, D. Brown, and G. MacDonald (eds.), *Olympic Perspectives: Third International Symposium for Olympic Research* (London, Ontario: International Centre for Olympic Studies, 1996), pp. 173–178.

42. Wamsley and Heine, "Tradition, Modernity, and the Construction of Civic Identity," p. 83.

43. See K. B. Wamsley, "Calgary 1988," in Findling and Pelle (eds.), *Historical Dictionary of the Modern Olympic Movement,* pp. 310–317.

44. Ibid.

45. Wamsley and Heine, "'Don't Mess with the Relay,'" p. 174.

46. Janice Forsyth, "Aboriginal Participation in the Montreal Olympic Games," unpublished paper, University of Western Ontario, 2001.

47. Wamsley and Heine, "'Don't Mess with the Relay,'" p. 173.

48. Ibid.

49. Ibid., p. 176.

50. On the issue of local resistance to hosting the Olympics, see Helen Lenskyj, *Inside the Olympic Industry: Power, Politics, and Activism* (New York: State University of New York Press, 2000).

51. Gerlitz was manager of the Calgary Corporate Challenge Games. Wamsley and Heine, "Tradition, Modernity, and the Construction of Civic Identity," pp. 81–83.

52. See Kevin B. Wamsley, "Policy Implications for Hosting the Olympics," *Policy Options* 18, no. 3 (1997): 13–16; Kevin B. Wamsley, "Hosting the Olympic Games in Canada: What Price for World Class?" *Canadian Issues* (Autumn 1999): 14–15.

5

WHEN AMATEURISM MATTERED

Class, Moral Entrepreneurship, and
the Winter Olympics

Richard Gruneau

In this discussion I want to focus on the questions of how and why amateurism emerged as a guiding principle in Western sport. As part of this discussion I highlight some of the deeply rooted contradictions that have always been associated with amateurism and briefly discuss some instances in the history of the Winter Olympics where these contradictions became particularly glaring. Ongoing controversies over amateurism in the Winter Olympics ultimately led the International Olympic Committee to remove the word "amateur" from the Olympic Charter in 1974 and to open the Games fully to professional athletes in the late 1980s. In the hyper-commercialized Olympic Games of the present day, we now take the presence of openly professional athletes for granted. So why bother to pay attention to a concept that no longer has any real presence in international sport? Discussing amateurism in Olympic sport today arguably seems like the intellectual equivalent of closing the barn door after the horse has already gone.

There are two compelling reasons why the history of amateurism should command our attention. First, for more than a century the philosophy of amateurism has been at the center of intense debate about the social value of sport in Western culture. It is a philosophy with diverse origins and has been interpreted in many different ways. These differing interpretations can tell us a great deal about a number of much broader tensions in the development of modern Western cultures. Second, the history of amateurism gives us a useful vantage point from which to analyze and to assess some ongoing paradoxes of the contemporary Olympic Movement, a now blatantly commercial enterprise that successfully mobilizes symbols and memories of lofty noncommercial sporting ideals from the past as a form of "brand" recognition. The claim that the Olympic Games continue to be rooted in a socially valuable moral philosophy is the one thing that differentiates them from other large-scale commercial sporting spectacles. In this sense, faint echoes of amateurism as a social philosophy of sport remain alive within the Olympic Movement; only now the amateur ideal has been emptied of all content, and its symbolic traces are routinely pressed into the service of marketing.

THE EMERGENCE OF AMATEURISM IN WESTERN SPORT

We can best begin to analyze such developments by considering how and why amateurism emerged as a guiding philosophical and organizational principle in modern sport in the first place. Modern organized sport in Western societies has its roots in the late eighteenth and early nineteenth centuries, in a wide range of older local folk games, masculine physical contests of different types, including paramilitary arts of different types (for example, fencing, shooting, boxing), and a diverse array of contests and gaming activities practiced at fairs, picnics, taverns, social clubs, and community outings. Initially, these activities tended to be periodic and were minimally organized, and many activities were more socially oriented than competitive. In other instances, however, competition could be extremely intense, involving significant amounts of both emotional energy and money.

In the United States, especially, a great many of these activities were imbued with an aura of casual commercialism from the outset. The U.S. sport historian Steven Pope has noted, for example, how commercial harness racing drew huge crowds of well-heeled patrons in Long Island early in the nineteenth century.[1] Boat racing, often for prizes that ranged as high as $20,000, was also popular in the United States at this time, along with early circuit professionalism in sports such as "pedestrianism" and boxing.[2] More notable was the development of a vibrant regional saloon culture in the larger cities and towns. This saloon culture catered primarily to male working-class patrons and provided a haven for prizefighting along with other small-scale commercial sporting spectacles such as ratting, dog fights, and cockfights.[3] Even U.S. college sports had commercial connections in the middle of the nineteenth century. During the 1860s Harvard crews competed for cash prizes as high as $500 in Boston Regattas; college track-and-field athletes often engaged in prize-hunting, pitting their prowess against local favorites; and Harvard baseball teams frequently played games against teams of professional players.[4] Baseball was one of the earliest U.S. sports to emerge with ongoing professional leagues.

A number of historians have commented on the pluralistic—some even use the word "democratic"—features of this informal and casually commercial approach to sport.[5] Throughout much of the nineteenth century, saloon keepers, small-time promoters, and sports-facility owners were behind many of the events that grabbed headlines in the sporting magazines that were becoming increasingly popular throughout North America. In some instances, in the first half of the century, these events were even sponsored by members of upper-class sporting clubs that had formed at the time. In this sporting environment, it was not unusual for athletes from privileged family backgrounds to compete in the same competitions with manual laborers and tradesmen.

Somewhat similar patterns of cross-class competition and sponsorship were not uncommon in other Western societies as well, although arguably not to the same extent as in the United States. For example, in Britain, tavern keepers, facility owners, and local promoters also played a key role in the development of open, often commercial, competitions throughout the nineteenth century, and a few trend-setting sporting clubs at mid-century occasionally sponsored competitions where "gentlemen" would compete against working men.[6] In one notable example, Dr. W. P. Brookes, a tireless promoter of sport at the time, was instrumental in organizing "Olympic Games" in his community that featured cash prizes and were open to all competitors. Brookes commented that "such meetings as these bring out free minds, free opinions, free enterprises, free competition for every man in every grade of life. The Olympic Games bring together different classes and make them social and neighborly."[7]

Research on the history of Canadian sports reveals parallel tendencies. Throughout much of the nineteenth century diverse sporting activities were sponsored by tavern owners, facility operators, and local promoters, bringing men from the privileged classes and the working class into similar venues and sometimes into similar competitions. At the same time, following the lead of developments in the United States, organized baseball in Canada grew quickly in rural areas between the 1830s and 1860s, often featuring payment for players' services, prizes, and gate receipts. Organized lacrosse revealed similar commercial tendencies, with skilled Aboriginal players and teams frequently setting a high standard of play. Meanwhile, in the cities, a handful of upper-class recreational sporting clubs occasionally sponsored open competitive sporting contests that brought athletes together from a diversity of social backgrounds: whites and Aboriginals, professionals and manual workers, French and English, British colonials and native-born Canadians.[8] Anticipating the initiative of W. P. Brookes in England—by nearly a decade—a Montreal Olympic Athletic Club was formed in 1842 by 241 leading citizens of the city. This club staged a local "Olympic Games" in Montreal in 1844 that featured open competitions. Archival records note that races were won by "Sergeant McGillvary of the garrison; Tarisonkwan, an Indian; E. Burroughs, a lawyer; and 'Evergreen' Hughes."[9]

The presence of such open competitions in the United States, Britain, and Canada in the first half of the nineteenth century undoubtedly gives substance to the claim that sporting cultures at this time were pluralistic. But it is a gross overstatement to call them "democratic." In all three countries the cultural meanings of sporting events throughout the nineteenth century were tightly framed by the gender, class, and racial prejudices of the time. Even the most "open" sporting competitions were widely understood to be virtually synonymous with demonstrations of masculine vitality and prowess and therefore excluded females without a thought. By the same token, even though "Indians" might occasionally compete against "lawyers," as in the Montreal Olympics of 1844, racial and class prejudices were ingrained in the competitions in significant ways—notably through the common practice of awarding medals and trophies to "gentlemen" and cash prizes to everyone else. From the 1850s through the remainder of the century, these class and racial prejudices in sport began to crystallize into a set of more formal rules of exclusion. The concept of amateurism emerged as a key element in this process.

But where exactly did the idea of amateurism come from? One commonly voiced argument is that the roots of amateurism can be found far back in classical antiquity, notably in Greek sport. The ancient Greeks, the argument runs, initiated competitive athletics "out of a deep, genuine love of sport for sport's sake, and as an appropriate activity for praising their gods."[10] Baron Pierre de Coubertin's creation of the so-called Modern Olympics in 1896 is the event that has played the greatest role in perpetuating this link between amateurism and antiquity. Many of the early leaders in Coubertin's Olympic Movement promoted this argument passionately—the late Avery Brundage, a former IOC president, is an especially notable example.[11]

In recent years, however, historians have substantially challenged the idea that the roots of amateurism lie in Western antiquity.[12] We now know that the ancient Greeks really had no conception of amateur sports. Indeed, in Greek games, gambling, cheating, violence, regional chauvinism, profit-taking, and prejudice were "the norm for most athletic competitions of public note."[13] A more compelling argument is to see amateurism as an "invented tradition," a distinctly modern creation that grew out of a unique and highly complex set of circumstances in Western life during the nineteenth century.[14] Amateurism emerged in the nineteenth century as a unique pastiche of both reactionary and—for the time—progressive ideas. These ideas were connected to two seemingly contradictory impulses: the class-conscious and often racist desire to exclude from sport people who might be defined as social inferiors, and the belief that sport could be an important arena in which to school young men and women in a set of rational and positive cultural values.

LIBERALISM, INDUSTRIAL SOCIETY, AND THE PHILOSOPHY OF AMATEURISM

Both impulses have at least some connection to the ways in which social and economic organization, politics, and cultures in Western nations began to change during the late eighteenth and early nineteenth centuries. An increased confidence in science and human reason, along with the expansion of markets in Europe during the eighteenth century, fueled a widespread reaction to older ideas about the naturalness of social hierarchies and the legitimacy of established religious doctrine. Against the feudal idea of every person having his or her place, more and more people began to argue that human beings had the capacity to rise or fall in social life on the basis of their abilities. Even more notable were the modern liberal ideas that citizens had inalienable civil and political rights; that individual citizens should be treated equally and fairly; and that "the people" in any society had the capacity to govern themselves.

These tendencies were felt acutely in turn of the century Britain, where the close proximity of Jacobinism, post-Enlightenment republicanism, and democratic thinking in France seemed to pose a very real challenge both to older conceptions of aristocratic rule and to the place of the aristocracy as leaders in the definition and maintenance of the national culture. To Britain's conservative Tory establishment, the twin specters of the storming of the Bastille and the terror of the guillotine elevated fears about the dangerous irrationality and power of the masses.[15] Over the next half-century, the advent of new industrial technologies, the enclosures of feudal estates, and the migration of thousands of workers to new industrial cities created additional insecurities for Britain's ruling class. In addition, as the nineteenth century progressed, burgeoning industrial capitalism promised new opportunities for people wanting to raise their social station and contributed to a strengthening middle class. Urban poverty and the popularity of seemingly irrational and rough leisure activities among the new urban masses—such as drinking, gambling, and blood sports—stimulated middle-class movements for social and moral reform. At the same time, the dreary conditions of early industrial work spawned an actively democratic opposition from an increasingly organized working class. All of these developments contributed to a growing sense of crisis throughout the nineteenth century fueled both by upper-class insecurity and by growing middle-class fears of social unrest, social decay, and moral decline.

In this increasingly volatile environment in Britain over the course of the nineteenth century it should not be surprising that upper-class patrons of games and sports became less inclined to sponsor sporting competitions likely to include large crowds of people whom they viewed as their social inferiors and whom they began to fear. Upper-class sportsmen were also less likely to want to compete against such people. In a social environment where the privileged felt secure in their positions, a "well-born" person might well test his prowess in open sporting competition. But an upper-class person's sense of identity and self-worth was not greatly at risk in such sporting competitions, and there was little need to be concerned about the symbolic consequences of losing a contest to a person of lower station. This meant that the emotional stakes for the privileged in such games were likely to be fairly low. A certain amount of casual commercialism could be readily tolerated in the promotion of public amusement, including public displays of masculine prowess. Moreover, occasional instances of cross-class sporting competition offered little threat to the established order.[16]

Things were simply not the same in an increasingly industrial society, with its undercurrents of liberal democratic political idealism, unfettered individualism, social mobility through the market, and accompanying class competition and class tension. The most patrician of the sporting clubs that formed in Britain, Canada, and the United States early in the nineteenth century—especially the aristocratically inclined hunt clubs and yacht clubs—began to act in an increasingly defensive and isolationist manner in the face of these changes. Formed initially as upper-class social and recreational clubs, these patrician enclaves rarely demonstrated great enthusiasm for open sporting competitions. Still, whatever limited interest such clubs may have had in open competitive sport seems to have effectively disappeared by the 1850s. In the latter half of the nineteenth century the most exclusive sports clubs in Britain, Canada, and the United States simply concentrated their energies on providing isolated social and recreational opportunities for the well-born and the rich.

Elsewhere, though, older sporting cultures were adapting in innovative ways to the broader changes that were affecting life in Western societies during the nineteenth century. The team sports that were starting to develop in early nineteenth century British public schools provide one of the most important examples. As Britain became a more entrepreneurial and industrial society, the public schools emerged as a site where the sons of aristocrats, wealthy merchants, and new industrialists began to intermingle. The culture of "gentlemanly" athleticism that emerged within these schools drew on older notions of aristocratic pedigree, privilege, and duty but mixed them with newer bourgeois ideas about the importance of self-help and self-improvement.

The playing field became a vital element in the creation and promotion of this new cultural formation. On the playing field young men were taught that in order to proceed fairly games had to be set apart from the broader rules of social privilege. The goal was to create a new community of peers who recognized and agreed to be bound by higher rules of regulative authority.[17] It was obvious in football, for example, that there could be no fair demonstration of prowess if the son of a bottle merchant was prevented by his lower rank in social life from tackling the son of a lord. At the same time, the old idea that sporting contests were valuable training grounds for virility and courage was subtly integrated with new ideas about self-development and the educative and moral value of games. British schoolboy games dramatized the need to balance the push for self-advancement, and the demonstration of individual prowess, with a responsibility to duty and a commitment to one's peers—precisely the kinds of values that would help to forge and to solidify a powerful new bloc of aristocratic and high-bourgeois class alliances in British society.[18] Unlike the comparatively open commercial culture of the tavern, the new public-school sports culture offered a far more restricted approach to the idea of "equality" in sporting competition. While the culture of the early British public school was evangelistic in its promotion of the virtues of sport, the public-school promotion of sports participation was also closely aligned with the idea that "gentlemen" were distinct from and morally superior to everyone else. Nonetheless, British schoolboy sport was an important vehicle for fostering a self-consciously competitive and achievement-oriented approach to sport within the Victorian upper and middle classes.

This growing emphasis on achievement and prowess in British public-school sport merely extended the trend already established by earlier open competitions, and it was fully consistent with the rapid spread of popular sport imbued with an air of casual commercialism. The ethos of achievement—of sport as a kind of meritocracy—also resonated powerfully with broader struggles for more open, more equal societies in the West. But it was an ethos that was at odds with lingering, yet still powerful, paternalistic sentiments about the naturalness of social distinction based on class, racial, ethnic, and gender lines. The view of sport as an open competitive enterprise also raised new questions about exactly who in society should take responsibility for organizing sport and about the kind of morality that should accompany sport.

In Canada—the case I know best—a new generation of upward-striving, native-born professional and business men took control in the 1870s of the most prominent sports clubs.[19] The directors of these clubs began to see sport as something more than simple upper-class recreation or periodic displays of masculine physical prowess. Instead they came to view sport in a way that reflected key aspects of a British public-school sensibility. Sport was important not only because it promoted masculine strength and vigor but also because it presumably helped to teach good "character." These new directors of sports clubs were themselves often temperance-minded men, Methodist by inclination, with strong conservative values. But their conservatism had little connection to older upper-class sensibilities. Their worldview grew out of the broader culture of business and professional life in Canada at the time—a culture that had come to place great emphasis on organization, regulation, competition, vitality, energy, and the values of self-improvement.

Prominent businessmen and professionals struggled to apply these values to create new forms of sporting organizations in the image of their own cultural ambitions. With that in mind, the most prominent clubs set out to finance and build new sports facilities and to create standardized rules for competition that would allow athletes and teams from across the country to compete with one another. It was not long before a number of these clubs in the largest cities had spun off self-designated "national" organizations designed to promote their sport across Canada by seeking affiliate clubs, publishing national rule books, adjudicating disputes, and organizing sanctioned "national" championships.

Sport historians in the United States have pointed to a similar development of prominent sporting clubs in the latter half of the nineteenth century, along with the proliferation of a great many other clubs that sought to organize sporting activities in small and medium-sized towns. In a fast-changing industrial world many local business groups, churches, unions, and occupational and ethnic associations throughout both Canada and the United States had begun to use sport as way of promoting a sense of membership and identity with the sponsoring community. This lent itself to often intense local rivalries, for example, between civic boosters in adjacent industrial communities, working-class and middle-class club teams, or teams from differing ethnic and religious communities. When a baseball club from a small industrial community played a club from New York or Boston, or, in Montreal, when an Irish working-class lacrosse team challenged a team of clerks and professionals of English origin, the results *mattered* to the communities in question. In other words, by the 1870s athletes were already beginning to act as the symbolic representatives of rival communities in

North America, and this added new incentive to find ways to win. That sometimes meant actively recruiting players from outside the community and paying them, playing a little tougher than the rules allowed, or finding a set of backers to finance a team of community professionals. The successes of sports teams began to be seen as a significant indicator of a community's character and prosperity.[20]

All of this fueled a myriad of disputes: for example, about what was fair and what was not fair in sporting competition; how to control cheating and violence; how gate or prize money should be allocated between competing teams; the kinds of limits, if any, that should be placed on any one team's efforts to recruit good players. Compounding these issues, by the latter third of the nineteenth century, the casual commercialism of earlier years was becoming much more systematic. By the 1870s there was an increasingly clear delineation between work and leisure in Western nations, creating a situation where large groups of people became available for the consumption of commercial entertainment at regular and predictable times. The consolidation of an industrial system based on wage labor and machine production—matched with organized labor's push for nine-hour workdays and holidays on Saturdays—created the conditions necessary for the development of mass audiences. These audiences became new markets to be exploited through the ongoing professionalization of sporting activities. At the same time, the growing demand for sporting equipment in North America was creating an increasingly prominent sporting-goods industry. Industry leaders, such as the Spalding corporation, got into the business of publishing rule books, sponsoring leagues, and seeking alliances with "the leading sports clubs" in various regions.[21]

THE CONTRADICTIONS OF AMATEURISM

The rapid emergence of organized sport as a prominent feature of North American cultural and economic life in the late nineteenth century was not something that everyone viewed as a positive development. For many religious leaders and educated professionals, sport still appeared to be little more than a valueless diversionary spectacle closely connected to idleness, gambling, drink, and violence.[22] Earlier in the century, movements to prevent cruelty to animals, along with those promoting temperance and moral reform in growing industrial cities, had decried the seemingly destructive and irrational features of such popular male working-class recreations as cockfighting, ratting, and prize fighting. With the rapid expansion of cities as specialized sites for commerce and industrial production this moral concern about seemingly irrational and socially destructive uses of leisure became closely linked with economic and political expediency. The drinking, merry-making, and sometimes disorderly recreations popular among working-class men were viewed as activities that disrupted the daily routines of business by encouraging absenteeism, debt, and insubordination. As a result, through-out the nineteenth century, governments in North America made play in the streets illegal, heavily regulated tavern locations and hours, and controlled alcohol consumption at public events. They also often banned sports that they saw as encouraging gambling, cruelty, or irrational violence, and they promoted more seemingly rational forms of recreation in their stead.[23]

The question remained whether sport of any kind should be promoted as a socially desirable, rational, and civilizing activity. The most militant critics of sport in the late nineteenth and early twentieth centuries argued that sport could never be anything other than a socially worthless activity. Sports were not truly "productive" activities, the argument ran. Even worse, not only do sports contribute nothing of value to society, but they distract people from things that are of greater importance. By the early twentieth century this initial resistance to sport was often tacitly linked to a broader type of conservative cultural criticism. Conservative critics typically argued that the thirst among the modern industrial masses for diversionary amuse-ment—and especially through increasingly spectacular entertainments—revealed the spread of dangerously irrational tendencies in Western cultural life. Sport seemingly stood out as a graphic demonstration of such tendencies. Like the Roman circus in antiquity, the argument continued, the spread of modern sport should be understood as an indicator of growing social decay, even barbarism.[24]

Against these views, nineteenth and early twentieth century physical edu-cators, and middle-class proponents of sporting competition, took their leads from new educational theories that stressed the importance of training both the mind and the body. Most notable was John Locke's widely cited reference to "a sound body and a sound mind" in his essay "Some Thoughts Concerning Education." This dictum became a key motto in the "muscular Christian" movement that grew in England throughout the nineteenth cen-tury.[25] Middle-class proponents of sport also championed the perceived virtues of English schoolboy athletics, arguing that rationally organized sport, pursued for its own sake, could indeed be a "civilizing" endeavor. The older argument that sport could develop health and virility among young men—very important for the expansion and defense of empire—was made routinely. But the new nineteenth-century upper- and middle-class evangel-ists for sport typically emphasized other socially desirable values as well: self-reliance, modesty, an appreciation of the importance of fairness, control of one's emotions, and respect for one's adversary. The challenge was to ensure that schools, sporting clubs, and sporting organizations all supported and promoted this rational civilizing agenda in sport and physical education.

Still, many critics remained unconvinced that this civilizing agenda was either possible or desirable if pursued on a broad scale. Certain people in society, the argument ran, were simply not capable of living up to this imagined civilizing agenda. Physical training and gymnastics in schools for military purposes might be appropriate, but the working classes lacked the refinement to appreciate the higher virtues of sports. The masses seemed too tied to rough and irrational recreations; and, more importantly, they seemed to invest the outcomes of sporting competitions with too much significance.

A far better strategy, the argument continued, was to limit the teaching of civilizing sport to young "gentlemen" amateurs—people most likely to approach sport with a strong moral foundation and with a necessary sense of proportion. Here the view of amateurism drew inspiration from the Renaissance image of the leisured gentlemen who excelled effortlessly at a variety of tasks, merging it with aspects of an older aristocratic valorization of physical vitality and the more recent English schoolboy obsession with fair play and sportsmanship. In addition, proponents of this socially exclusive view of competitive sport began to extend the argument to suggest that there were classes of people in society who had definite physical advantages in certain games because of the nature of the work they performed. A mechanic or laborer, for example, could logically be expected to be stronger than a white-collar clerk. Competition between the two was therefore unlikely to create the conditions for fairness necessary to stage socially desirable recreations.

These sentiments circulated and took root in the student-sport culture of Oxford and Cambridge in the 1850s and soon found their way into the official declarations of a growing number of amateur clubs and amateur associations, beginning with a few key clubs in England who restricted their membership to "gentlemen amateurs" and who barred members of the "working classes" from club-sponsored competitions.[26] The first sporting association in England with the word "amateur" in the title was formed in the mid-1860s, and the popularity of social restrictions on sporting competition quickly spread.[27] These restrictions received their most famous formulation in the Henley Regatta's exclusion of mechanics, artisans, and laborers and, eventually, anyone "engaged in any menial duty."[28] Elsewhere, other forms of social exclusion by statute were also added to the definition of amateurism. For example, in Canada in 1873 the Montreal Pedestrian Club defined an amateur as "one who has never competed in any open competition, or for public money, or for admission money, or with professionals for a prize, public money or admission money, nor has ever at any period of his life taught or assisted in the pursuit of athletic exercise as means of liveli-hood or is a labourer or Indian."[29]

In this definition, the class and racially based prejudices are obvious. The problem of losing to imagined social inferiors, or of opening the door to unwelcome cultural values, is solved through a conscious and aggressive strategy of social exclusion. Still, a great many athletes and sports organiz-ers rejected such an exclusive definition of socially valuable "amateur" sport. If sport did have important educative potential, the argument ran, it surely made sense to try to promote it as broadly as possible. With this in mind, many sports organizers from the 1870s through the early twentieth century began to act as self-conscious moral entrepreneurs, aggressively selling their particular vision of positive social values as *a universal stan-dard* for evaluating sport's social worth. The most committed moral entre-preneurs believed that there was no reason why individuals should be formally excluded from participation in amateur sports on the basis of their social origins, as long as they demonstrated complete devotion to the idea of sport as a fair and morally grounded area of cultural life. Indeed, the men who became amateurism's most committed moral entrepreneurs in the early twentieth century were themselves often from humble social origins— including the American Athletic Union's early leader John Sullivan, born of Irish-immigrant parents, and Avery Brundage, the IOC president, who was the son of a stone mason.[30]

In his path-breaking history of the Olympic Games in the nineteenth century, David Young demonstrates clearly how tensions between the socially exclusive view of amateur sports participation and the more evan-gelical view of amateur sport as a broad civilizing force in Western life were clearly evident in Britain as early as the 1850s and 1860s. W. P. Brookes was a notable early champion of the universalist moral entrepreneurial view. "As Christians," he announced, "we should, on moral grounds, endeavor to direct the amusement of the working class." This put Brookes at odds with advocates of class-exclusive amateurism, bringing him into "constant and furious conflict with advocates of class-exclusive amateurism," eventually killing the fledgling British Olympic Movement.[31]

Even those people who were inspired by Brookes's view—including Pierre de Coubertin, years later—were unsure exactly how it would be possible to ensure that a moral agenda could be maintained in universally open sporting competition. The only way to assure this seemed to be to accept the idea that sports participation should be accompanied by a dis-tinctive worldview—a state of mind. From this perspective, amateurism should not be limited to a particular social class; rather, it should be some-thing that *anyone* might aspire to.

Unfortunately, incorporating this abstract goal into any precise organizational definition proved to be virtually impossible. The most popular solution was to define the philosophy of amateurism in negative terms; that is, to define it in terms of what it is not. The seemingly obvious conclusion was to point the finger at the allegedly corrupting powers of money. Like money in the biblical temple, the existence of material rewards seemed to pose the greatest threat to the inherited public-school ideal of playing the game for its own sake. It was argued that money raised the stakes to a point where games lost their intrinsic value and were pursued simply as a means to a financial payoff. Money promotes greed and cheating, the argument ran, and it sustains professionalism. Professionalism, in turn, can be associated with gross ambition, gambling, and moral laxity. Therefore, it seemed that the best way to define amateurism in sport was to juxtapose it to professionalism.

Still, there was simply no magic formula to determine exactly what this meant, leading to a myriad of possible interpretations. For example, amateur purists typically believed that anyone who had ever made any money in sport, say, as a teenaged lifeguard, was a professional and therefore ineligible to compete in sanctioned amateur competitions. Even to have been found to have competed in a competition against someone who had ever earned money for teaching or playing sport was enough to risk excommunication from the amateur church. Others wanted the rule only to apply to money earned directly from sporting exhibitions. Still others believed in the heretical conception that limited forms of compensation were acceptable, as long as a person was not making his sole livelihood from the activity.

From the 1870s through the First World War amateur sports organizers in Western nations spent an enormous amount of time and energy debating these issues and staking out clear positions on them. The stakes were high. At issue was the degree of control that certain individuals, and certain sports organizations, would exercise over the developing world of sport. In these struggles, the major difference between competing individuals and organizations was often little more than where each person or group stood on the amateur question.

COUBERTIN'S OLYMPICS AND THE INTERNATIONAL EXPORT OF AMATEURISM

Seen from the broadest perspective—and distanced from its most aggressively exclusive tendencies—the emergence of amateurism as a guiding principle in sport was an expression of the more widespread attempt by the educated Western middle classes to regulate and to reform the uses and meanings of leisure time among "the people." For example, in Britain and North America by the early years of the twentieth century a clear distinction between the rational use of leisure time and seemingly irrational amusement had become fully institutionalized. Rational recreation was promoted in amateur sports organizations, schools, municipal parks, and libraries. Irrational leisure—typically associated with the older saloon culture, gambling, and "rough" sport—was patrolled by the police.[32] Professional sports still carried the stigma of an earlier attachment to rough leisure, but they increasingly began to occupy a cultural position that seemed to move fluidly between the two poles of rational and irrational recreation. Despite their exclusion from amateur organizations, promoters of professional sport in the early twentieth century did not hesitate to adopt some of the moral entrepreneurs' rhetoric about sport as a character builder. Moreover, in the fast-growing commercial popular culture of the time, most commentators in the commercial media tended not to differentiate between amateur and professional sport stars. Simply stated, commercialism of various types in sport remained a widely accepted part of the cultural landscape among legions of sports fans, and professional sports continued to grow in popularity.

To add to the confusion, even some of the most ardent promoters of amateurism clearly admired the skills of the best athletes in their sport, professional or not. More notably, many of the clubs, teams, and schools that were formally affiliated with the new organizations that developed to promote and to police amateur sport—such as the Amateur Athletic Union (AAU) or the NCAA in the United States—were by no means as ideologically committed to amateurism as the bureaucrats were who ran these organizations. In this environment, many sports clubs simply proclaimed a public commitment to amateurism while quietly accepting professionalism of varying degrees.[33] In addition, as late as the turn of the twentieth century, even the most powerful amateur organizations in North America had yet to consolidate full control over the diverse regions of the United States and Canada.

This was the context in which Pierre de Coubertin—taking up some of the agenda championed earlier by W. P. Brookes—explored the idea of creating the international modern Olympic Games.[34] After the French defeat at the hands of Prussia in 1871 Coubertin had come to the conclusion that the Prussian dedication to physical education had been a factor in his country's defeat. In his search for new models of physical education he became impressed by the English "muscular Christian" movement and by the vitality and dynamism of English public-school sports. British athleticism, he concluded, "constituted a fundamental part of British Imperial Greatness."[35]

Inspired, Coubertin imagined an international sports movement modeled roughly along the lines of late Victorian athleticism. In 1894 he invited an impressive group of foreign scholars, educators, and sports enthusiasts to an international conference on "the principles of amateurism." At the conference Coubertin presented a proposal, in his words, to "revive" the athletic and artistic festival traditions of the ancient Greek Games.[36] Delegates to the conference accepted the proposal enthusiastically, and Coubertin was "authorized to establish an International Olympic Committee (IOC) and to work with it for the revival of the games at Athens in 1896."[37] The delegates also approved the official Olympic motto: "Citius, Altius, Fortius."

While there was a great deal of talk about the philosophy of amateurism in the early years of Coubertin's Olympics, the reality of the fledgling movement was often quite different. Initially, in order to stage the Games at all, significant compromises with commerce and professionalism were made. For example, the 1900 and 1904 Olympic Games in Paris and St. Louis were held in conjunction with international expositions, and the athletic events were literally surrounded by celebrations of commerce. Furthermore, at the insistence of some IOC members, professional fencers were allowed to compete in 1896 and 1900. The Olympic champion cyclists from the United States in 1904 were also paid performers.[38]

Under internal pressure from amateur purists to define the Olympic mandate more clearly, the IOC struck committee after committee to study the meaning of amateurism and to try to define it in practical terms. A parallel series of debates about the precise meaning of amateurism occurred within the major amateur sport organizations in the United States and Canada, with the amateur purists and moral entrepreneurs eventually taking control.[39] The successes of the moral entrepreneurs at the national level—especially in the United States—added momentum to the lobby for a very tough anticommercial position within the IOC. In 1912 the IOC agreed to adopt a definition of amateurism that officially precluded participation by anyone who had ever received any monetary gain at any time for teaching or participating in any kind of sport. In 1925 the amateur rule was modified slightly to allow for greater latitude in interpretation. The 1925 definition read: "An amateur is one who devotes himself to sport for sport's sake without deriving from it, directly or indirectly, the means of existence. A professional is one who derives the means of existence entirely or partly from sport."[40] IOC presidents Sigfrid Edstrom and, later, Avery Brundage became fierce defenders of this "antiprofessional" definition of amateurism as a standard for participation in the Olympics.

The growth of the Olympics as an international movement with self-professed moral overtones gave new life to the amateur code. Ironically, considering the internationalist aspirations of the Olympic Movement, "amateur sport" became closely linked to the burgeoning nationalism of Western industrial societies.[41] This in turn strengthened the influence of National Olympic Committees in their home countries, along with the most prominent amateur associations. But the very successes of the Olympics put new pressures on amateurism, because now the symbolic representational power of modern sport was moved beyond the local realm of small-town rivalries and cross-class or interethnic and interracial conflicts and into the international arena. Winning was something that came to matter more and more to sports fans in the countries that competed in the Games, and this put mounting pressures on National Olympic Committees to field the best possible teams, even if that meant bending the rules of amateurism to the limit.

So, even when the victory of purified amateurism as a standard in international sport seemed virtually complete, the amateur ideal continued to be compromised by a set of deeply rooted contradictions. Amateurism was supposedly connected to a self-consciously educative and civilizing project—the promotion of an imagined culturally superior "state of mind"—but it often simply seemed to operate as an inflexible bureaucratic reflex. Amateurism was supposedly a hymn to fairness and equality, but it preached these virtues through a policy that implicitly favored the wealthy and early on had discriminated in more obvious ways against non-Caucasians and women.[42] Amateur sport, through its association with the Olympics, became closely associated with the goals of internationalism and global fraternity, but it also contributed to the contradictory project of building an imagined national vitality within different nations and to the creation of national programs designed to demonstrate national prowess through sport.

At the same time, the concept of amateurism had to accommodate a philosophical commitment to *both* versatility and specialization. Amateur sport was something to be done as an avocation, but in the Olympics it was also guided by a commitment to the motto "Citius, Altius, Fortius." To take this motto to its logical conclusions implied specialization and professionalization. Finally, amateurism committed itself, ironically, to a non-commercial cultural ideal in a world that was in the process of becoming more and more self-consciously commercial—a world where popular cultural goods, such as music, films, and sports, were in the process of becoming some of the most important and prized commodities of all. Then there was the obvious fact that amateurism was meant to reference a universal code of fairness, but the IOC often seemed to be in the business of negotiating compromises in interpretation in the interests of political expediency. Given these deep contradictions, it is small wonder that the first eighty years of Coubertin's modern Olympics were plagued with controversies centering on amateurism.

SOME CONTROVERSIES SURROUNDING AMATEURISM IN THE WINTER OLYMPICS

The Winter Olympics became particularly visible as a source of such controversies. From the outset, there was considerable dissension within the IOC about the very idea of staging a separate Winter Games. Ice skating had been included in the 1908 Olympics, and ice hockey was added to the 1920 Olympic Games. But Coubertin, and many other members of the IOC, felt that winter sports were insufficiently international—too limited to a handful of northern nations. Opposing this view was a strong Scandinavian lobby within the IOC. Scandinavian members argued that Coubertin's views discriminated against their countries' distinctive sporting heritage, and they fought hard for an opportunity to showcase a broad range of sports involving ice and snow in a separate Winter Olympic Games. With support from British members of the IOC, the Winter Games lobby was eventually successful. And the first Winter Olympic Games were held in Chamonix, France, in 1924.[43]

Interestingly, one of the things that characterized a number of the showcase sports at the Winter Olympics was the extent to which they necessarily relied on commercial operators. Figure skating often took place on rinks provided by local clubs, although certainly not always, but hockey was much more likely to be dependent upon access to commercial ice time.[44] Similarly, Alpine ski racing was completely dependent upon mechanized lifts at ski resorts. After the Second World War, the growing popularity of skiing added a further commercial imperative to the competition. Tourism and ski manufacturing were becoming increasingly important in the economies of several Alpine nations. Not surprisingly, many of the best ski racers in the world grew up in Alpine resort towns, often working as ski instructors after school on weekends from young ages. By the 1930s the Fédération Internationale de Ski (FIS) was pressing the IOC hard for exemptions from amateur prohibitions surrounding the receipt of money for providing skiing instruction. When the IOC refused to bend the interpretation of professionalism to allow this, FIS defied the IOC in 1938 and passed its own independent interpretation of the issue.

A few years later another controversy emerged over the provision of "broken time payments" to athletes to compensate them while attending international competitions.[45] Led by Avery Brundage, the IOC strenuously opposed broken time payments, thereby creating a tense relationship with

FIS and with many of skiing's national sports governing bodies. In the 1960s tensions mounted further over the IOC's objections to skiers endorsing products, culminating in 1968 when Avery Brundage persuaded the IOC to disqualify Austrian ski hero Karl Schranz from the Winter Olympics. Austrians were outraged and gave Schranz a heroes' welcome when he returned home. By this time the ski industry was pouring a significant amount of money into European ski federations, and the FIS had a strong vested interest in defending the right of international associations and their skiers to secure industry endorsements.[46]

The Schranz incident powerfully dramatized the chasm that had grown between the IOC and other international sports governing bodies. Brundage's apparent vendetta against Schranz also revealed the arbitrary nature and hypocrisy of the IOC's selective application of the amateur rules. By the 1960s obvious commercial influences of varying types had found their way into many Olympic sports. At the same time, there was a growing controversy within the Olympics about the presence of fully supported "state-sponsored amateurs" from socialist countries. While technically not professionals according to IOC rules, state-sponsored athletes were often full-time athletes. Critics began to label the situation in state-socialist countries as "shamateurism," and the IOC was routinely castigated for being highly selective and hypocritical in its interpretation of the amateur rule. Indeed, in the highly commercial world of 1960s pop culture, the whole idea of exclusionary definitions of amateurism based on monetary considerations seemed anachronistic and absurd.

Hockey was another sport whose embrace of commerce created problems for the IOC almost from the outset of the Winter Games. In Canada, the birthplace of modern ice hockey, the most prominent hockey associations and teams early in the first decade of the twentieth century began to wage a bitter war over professionalism in the game.[47] By 1914 there was a clear split between openly professional teams and teams affiliated with the newly formed Canadian Amateur Hockey Association (CAHA). Professional hockey soon developed a large following; but amateur teams also remained popular, often drawing gates that rivaled those of some professional teams. It is noteworthy that outside of a handful of teams from private clubs, few amateur teams in Canadian communities were ever models of pristine amateurism—despite the CAHA's best efforts.

Even at their strongest—in the period from just before the First World War to the early 1930s—the moral entrepreneurs who policed amateurism in hockey found it difficult to control the game fully. Amateur teams in many parts of the country (say, in rural Manitoba or Saskatchewan) were not exactly under the microscope of amateur associations whose head offices were in Toronto and Montreal, and there were varying interpretations across the country about the range of economic incentives a team might offer to players yet still fit within the definition of amateurism.[48] On many amateur teams players may not have been paid directly, but team managements collected gate money to cover expenses; they often secured jobs for players, and local businesses were not shy about offering "gifts" to the stars.

Through the 1920s and 1930s amateur teams found themselves in greater competition for good players with growing numbers of semiprofessional and professional teams both in Canada and in the United States. Then, with the deepening of economic depression in the 1930s, the prospect of making even small amounts of money in pro hockey led good players to desert amateur teams in droves. In 1935 the CAHA grudgingly responded to these competitive pressures and by allowing "amateur teams" to offer modest salaries to players and to employ former professional players. This opened the door for the CAHA to begin to negotiate interleague agreements with the National Hockey League (NHL), the pro league that had become the dominant force in Canadian hockey. By the late 1940s the CAHA had become little more than a junior partner to the NHL. "Amateur" hockey among Canada's youth and senior teams was transformed into a feeder system for the pros.[49]

Amateur hockey teams in the United States found themselves faced with similar commercial pressures early in the twentieth century. As in Canada there was growing friction between the moral entrepreneurs (in this case, in the AAU) and commercial rink owners and professional league organizers. With the advent of the Winter Olympics in 1924, the AAU attempted to assume control of the selection of U.S. Olympic hockey teams. In order to do this, the AAU petitioned in 1930 to join the international association that was recognized by the IOC as the governing body responsible for promoting and regulating international amateur hockey—the Ligue Internationale de Hockey sur Glace (LIHG).[50] Once the AAU gained control over the selection of U.S. amateur teams for the Olympics, it expelled a number of teams for professionalism. Several years later these teams formed their own association, the American Hockey Association (AHA), to compete with AAU control. When the AHA was not recognized by the international federation, it simply created its own international body, attracting as members the Canadian and British representatives of the LIHG. Under pressure from the IOC, Britain returned to the LIHG but continued to support the AHA in the 1940s, as did the Canadians, the Swedes, and the Swiss.[51] When the LIHG voted in 1946 that only national *hockey* associations could be members, the AAU lost its status; and the AHA was recognized as the group entitled to select the U.S. Olympic team. The AAU fought the decision at home, enlisting the support of the United States Olympic Committee, and selected a team to represent the United States in the 1948 Winter Olympic Games. But the AHA also selected a team, and both teams arrived in St. Moritz claiming to represent the United States.

This comedy of errors resulted in endless negotiations, threats, and counter-threats, with the result that both teams were initially disqualified by the IOC. The Games Organizing Committee and LIHG officials defied the ban, and the AHA team played. The IOC responded by saying that it would refuse to recognize the results of any games and then softened to a compromise where it was agreed that hockey would continue to be played if games by the AHA team were not counted. But the Organizing Committee and LIHG representatives reneged on their initial agreement to this proposal and made a public announcement that if the AHA team won, its results would be recognized.[52]

The IOC's problems with hockey were painfully obvious. By the mid-1930s the national governing bodies in the major hockey-playing nations had long since retreated from rigidly anticommercial definitions of amateurism. Even the LIHG at large was moving to a more cautious embrace of commerce. The popularity of hockey in the Olympics also made it one of the most profitable sports for Olympic Organizing Committees. The Swiss Olympic organizers' fear of losing this revenue in 1948 played a large role in their support of the AHA. By the late 1940s the CAHA and the AHA were so closely intertwined with professional hockey that there was no longer any significant organizational representation in the sport for a moral entrepreneurial—and antiprofessional—approach to amateurism. For example, Walter Brown, head of the AHA in the late 1940s, was a prominent businessman with investments in hockey and professional basketball—including ownership of the Boston Celtics.[53] In 1952 the IOC grudgingly recognized the inevitable and agreed to settle the dispute between the AHA and the AAU once and for all by endorsing an arms-length committee to select the U.S. Olympic team. The committee's composition was telling: four representatives from the AHA, four from the U.S. Olympic committee (which continued to represent the AAU), and two from the NHL.[54] The amateur purists' long-standing battle to "save" Olympic hockey from commercial influences was effectively over.

CONCLUSION: AMATEURISM, OLYMPISM, AND THE "AESTHETICIZATION" OF SPORT

I want to conclude by suggesting that the most relevant question in the history of amateurism in the Olympics is not "Why did amateurism ultimately collapse in Olympic sport?" Given amateurism's many contradictions, obvious class exclusiveness, and existence in a world where sport was a widely accepted part of commercial popular culture, the more relevant question is "Why was amateurism able to last as long as it did as a guiding principle for the Olympics?" I have not focused directly on this question here, although I have tried to suggest some preliminary points of departure for a more fully developed analysis of why amateurism had such influence as a standard for promoting participation in Western sport. This kind of analysis may be a worthy subject for another essay,[55] but for now it is possible merely to highlight a few of the key points.

The most obvious explanation for the success of amateurism lies in the extent to which the growing popularity of the Olympics elevated the promoters of amateur sport to an international monopoly position. Anyone who wanted to participate in the Olympics was simply forced to follow the amateur line or at least to claim to be following it. The link that developed between Olympic sport and nationalism pushed international sport in a more competitive and commercial direction, much to the chagrin of the defenders of "pure" amateurism. But, at the same time, nationalism strengthened the hand of the moral entrepreneurs by providing increased international interest in the Olympics. After the Second World War, when the contradictions of amateurism appeared to be sharpening to an untenable state, the entry of socialist countries—with their deep aversion to commercialism—into the Olympics gave amateurism another temporary reprieve.

But these historical and structural circumstances only tell part of the story. The philosophy of amateurism was deeply appealing to many people because it suggested that sport could serve a higher cultural purpose beyond mere amusement or crass commerce. Promoting this higher cultural purpose became the ideological core of what we might call "the project of amateurism." This project was itself influenced by a much broader set of social and cultural movements in Western nations from the late eighteenth through the mid-twentieth century. Particularly relevant was the emergent cultural modernism in the eighteenth century that celebrated human creativity and scientific discovery—along with the more general pursuit of individual excellence—in the name of human progress.[56] In this view, the ultimate goal was for human societies to "progress" by developing objective science, universal morality, law, and art, according to their own inner logic. Under the ambit of amateurism sport could make a claim to being a rationally organized and legitimate part of the historical march in the West toward progress through human self-improvement. Seen as a state of mind, rather than a narrow set of rules, amateurism sought to transform lowbrow "uncontrolled" sport into a more regulated and socially worthwhile form of creative physical expression.

The real evocative power of amateurism—and especially Olympian amateurism—did not lie in these modernist elements alone, however. Rather, it lay in the unique way in which traces of cultural modernism were blended with ideas from late Victorian romanticism. Particularly relevant here was the growing widespread interest in late nineteenth century Europe and North America in all things "classical." Coubertin tapped into this interest when he surrounded his imagined festival of international amateur sport with symbols from a so-called premodern "Western" world. His contemporary Olympic Games suggested an imagined continuity between the apparent emergence of Western civilization in classical antiquity and the great heights reached by Western civilization at the turn of the twentieth century. At the same time, the modernist emphasis on reason and universalism in human affairs was both reaffirmed and softened by his attempt to build strong links among sport, art, and poetry.

Once more, there is an intriguing irony about all this: in the push to celebrate sport as a form of rational civilizing culture, the proponents of amateurism in the Olympic Movement chose to reference a host of non-rational images and visceral collective rituals. To paraphrase Walter Benjamin's discussion of the politics of fascism, we might say that Coubertin and his colleagues set out consciously to "aestheticize" late nineteenth and early twentieth century sport.[57] These aesthetics—of classically sculpted male bodies; mythical flames and torches; flags, ritual ceremonies, and mass displays; paintings, sculptures, hymns, and poetry; and public incantations of honor and duty—gave the Olympics a cultural status that no form of sport in Western life ever had in the past.

More importantly, this unique combination of modern rationalist principles and antimodern romanticism made for a powerful and intoxicating cultural brew. In its new aestheticized form, early twentieth century Olympic amateurism had a remarkable capacity to appeal to both political progressives and reactionaries. For progressives, the Olympics clearly seemed to be a positive cultural innovation. The Olympic Games embodied the dream of a new kind of rational internationalism, steeped in universally agreed upon rules for international cultural exchange and within a moral system that emphasized sportsmanship and fairness. As part of this dream, amateur sport was promoted as an activity that the working classes, and people in poor countries, might use to improve themselves. For reactionaries, Olympic romanticism provided a new way to glorify a number of older nonrational cultural themes and values: strength, duty, authenticity, and masculine vitality. The Olympic Games not only provided a framework for the celebration of individual will and prowess; they also dramatized the strength derived from the subordination of will and prowess to higher forms of national or racial purpose.

Against the background of this intriguing combination of cultural influences, the social philosophy of amateurism developed to become a kind of pseudo-religion for its most ardent followers.[58] The Olympics provided a vast socializing mechanism for the ongoing rehearsal of this pseudo-religion. This self-conscious aestheticization of sport within the Olympic Movement did not emerge "naturally" in any way; rather, it was developed by interested intellectuals who took it upon themselves to define and to debate the Olympic philosophy, to write its history, and, in many instances, simply to spread the gospel. Within the circles of international sports governing bodies, and among physical educators and sports people around the world, these intellectuals worked hard to establish the philosophy of amateurism as a new kind of common sense.

Today, while the word "amateurism" is officially gone from the Olympics, the IOC continues to insist that the Olympic Games are committed to higher purposes than mere commercial spectacle. The IOC's new version of common sense is that it is still possible to promote Olympism as a philosophy of life while opening up the Games fully to commercialism. As in the earlier case of amateurism, however, it simply is not very clear exactly what this philosophy of life entails and how the Olympic spectacle actually serves higher social and cultural interests.

It is very difficult to define and agree upon such "higher interests" in any case, and we have seen how the evolution of the apparent universal civilizing mission of amateur sport emerged out of a very clear set of Western, masculine, and class-based moral conceptions. In this sense, there was absolutely nothing inherently universal about them. In addition, I am persuaded by John Hoberman's argument that, despite the IOC's professed commitment to a kind of moral universalism, there has always been an insufficiently strong *ethical* foundation to Coubertin's Olympic creation.[59] The overriding moral imperative has simply been to "have the Games go on," and this has too often forced the IOC and Olympic organizers to make questionable deals with repressive political regimes and simply ignore important moral debates outside of sport.[60] At the same time, the IOC's own moral authority has been tainted by problems of cronyism and scandal over the years, and the IOC today seems to be in the business of accumulating capital rather than in the business of promoting morality. The moral entrepreneurs of the past have given way to the economic entrepreneurs of the present day. Indeed, since the early 1980s, when the IOC began to recognize the value of the Olympics as an exclusive global sports brand, there has arguably been far more attention paid to intellectual property rights within the Olympic Movement than to debates of social and moral purpose. The notable exception is the IOC's decision visibly to defend the "morality" of fair competition by clamping down on the use of performance-enhancing drugs, although even here the drug issue is accompanied by ongoing controversy.

In the face of all this, it is fascinating that the Olympic Games have continued to maintain an image of elevated social and moral purpose beyond that of other large-scale international sporting spectacles. But it is also hard to disagree with John Hoberman's claim that the "moral reputation of the Olympic Movement is one of the public relations phenomena of this century."[61] In the attempt to aestheticize Olympic sport, and to regulate it in the interests of a self-professed moral universalism, Olympic promoters have spun a web of historical illusions. Today these illusions have become a vital part of Olympic marketing. The ongoing aestheticization of Olympic sport—including images and residues of ideas that harken back to the philosophy of amateurism—continues to shape the distinctiveness of the Olympic brand and thereby contributes to the commodity value of Olympic Games. The "public relations phenomenon" that John Hoberman mentions has become an indistinguishable part of the Olympics as a global economic phenomenon.

Notes

1. S. W. Pope, *Patriotic Games: Sporting Traditions in the American Imagination, 1876–1976* (New York: Oxford University Press, 1997), p. 20.

2. Ibid., p. 20.

3. Ibid., pp. 20–21. For a more developed discussion of sport and early saloon culture in the United States, see E. Gorn and W. Goldstein, *A Brief History of American Sports* (New York: Hill and Wang, 1993), pp. 3–46. For a discussion of similar issues and events in Canada, see R. Gruneau and D. Whitson, *Hockey Night in Canada: Sport Identities and Cultural Politics* (Toronto: Garamond Press, 1993), pp. 56–67. A highly detailed case study of this "saloon culture" in Montreal, Canada, can be found in P. DeLottinville, "Joe Beef of Montreal: Working Class Culture and the Tavern, 1869–1889," *Labour/Le Travailleur* 8:9 (1981–1982). Additional materials on sport and saloon culture in Canada can be found in A. Metcalfe, *Canada Learns to Play: The Emergence of Organized Sport, 1807–1904* (Toronto: McClelland and Stewart, 1987).

4. Pope, *Patriotic Games,* pp. 20–21.

5. In Canada, for example, several early sport historians linked the development of sport to the supposedly democratic "frontier spirit" of the late eighteenth and early nineteenth centuries. See M. Howell and N. Howell, *Sports and*

Games in Canadian Life (Toronto: Macmillan, 1969), pp. 54–56; and H. Rox-borough, *One Hundred—Not Out: The Story of Nineteenth Century Canadian Sport* (Toronto: Ryerson Press, 1966). I offer a critique of this position in R. Gruneau, *Class, Sports and Social Development* (Amherst: University of Massachusetts Press, 1983), pp. 93–108.

    6. See E. Dunning and K. Sheard, "The Bifurcation of Ruby Union and Rugby League: A Case Study of Organizational Conflict and Change," *International Review of Sport Sociology*, 11:2 (1976).

    7. D. C. Young, *The Modern Olympics: A Struggle for Revival* (Baltimore: Johns Hopkins University Press, 1996), p. 25.

    8. Metcalfe, *Canada Learns to Play*, pp. 22–26. See also our discussion in Gruneau and Whitson, *Hockey Night in Canada*, pp. 39–43.

    9. Metcalfe, *Canada Learns to Play*, p. 23.

    10. Pope, *Patriotic Games*, p. 18.

    11. See A. Guttmann, *The Games Must Go On: Avery Brundage and the Olympic Movement* (New York: Columbia University Press, 1984), p. 116.

    12. See D. Young, *The Olympic Myth of Greek Amateur Athletics* (Chicago: Ares Publishers, 1984).

    13. Pope, *Patriotic Games*, p. 19.

    14. This idea is discussed in Pope, *Patriotic Games*, pp. 37–40, and was noted earlier by Bruce Kidd, "The Myth of the Ancient Games," in A. Tomlinson and G. Whannel (eds.), *Five Ring Circus: Money, Power, Politics and the Olympic Games* (London: Pluto Press, 1984). A more detailed discussion of relationships between amateurism and "modernity" can be found in R. Gruneau, "The Critique of Sport in Modernity: Theorizing Power, Culture and the Politics of the Body," in E. Dunning, J. Maguire, and R. Pearton (eds.), *The Sports Process* (Champaign, Ill.: Human Kinetics, 1993), pp. 85–93.

    15. E. P. Thompson, *The Making of the English Working Class* (Harmondsworth: Pelican Books, 1968), pp. 441–443.

    16. For more developed discussions of these ideas, see Gruneau, *Class, Sports and Social Development*, pp. 98–103; and Gruneau and Whitson, *Hockey Night in Canada*, pp. 46–77.

    17. E. Dunning, "Industrialization and the Incipient Modernization of Football," *Stadion* 1:1 (1976).

    18. The classic statement on the role of the British public school is R. Wilkinson, *Gentlemanly Power: British Leadership and Public School Tradition* (New York: Oxford University Press, 1964). Also see W. Arnstein, "The Survival of the Victorian Aristocracy," in F. C. Jaher (ed.), *The Rich, the Well-Born and the Powerful* (Urbana: University of Illinois Press, 1973). A more recent and comprehensive treatment can be found in A. Mangan, *Athleticism in the Victorian and Edwardian Public School* (Cambridge: Cambridge University Press, 1981).

    19. For an early statement of this point, see S. F. Wise, "Sport and Class Values in Old Ontario and Quebec," in W. H. Heick and R. Graham (eds.), *His Own Man: Essays in Honour of A. R. M. Lower* (Montreal: McGill–Queen's

University Press, 1974). More recent discussions include Gruneau, *Class, Sports and Social Development;* Metcalfe, *Canada Learns to Play;* and Gruneau and Whitson, *Hockey Night in Canada.*

20. A more developed discussion of the "representational" importance of sport in the late nineteenth century can be found in Gruneau and Whitson, *Hockey Night in Canada,* pp. 67–77.

21. S. Hardy, "'Adopted by All the Leading Clubs': Sporting Goods and the Shaping of Leisure, 1800–1900," in R. Butsch (ed.), *For Fun and Profit: The Transformation of Leisure into Consumption* (Philadelphia: Temple University Press, 1990).

22. David Young argues that an "anti-athletic" stance among the Christian clergy in the West goes back to St. Paul. In addition, he contends that there was a deep-rooted intellectual precedent in Aristotle's *Politics* for not "mixing the physical and the mental," thereby strengthening the Western intellectual's antipathy to sport (*The Modern Olympics,* pp. 188–189, n. 18). However, it is important to distinguish here the differences between Catholicism and Protestantism on matters pertaining to the relationships between body and mind. Protestant movements, for example, were generally more accommodating to the uses of gymnastic exercise in schools. This kind of accommodation was given additional impetus by secular movements in educational philosophy after the Renaissance that claimed to recover classical Greek ideals of balance and harmony. See my discussion in "The Politics and Ideology of Active Living in Historical Perspective," in J. Curtis and S. Russell (eds.), *Physical Activity in Human Experience* (Urbana, Ill.: Human Kinetics Press, 1997), pp. 201–210.

23. There is now a very substantial literature that describes movements for the regulation and reform of leisure and "popular" culture—and popular reactions to these movements—in Western societies in the nineteenth century. Some influential early statements include P. Bailey, *Leisure and Class in Victorian England* (London: Routledge, 1978); Hugh Cunningham, *Leisure in the Industrial Revolution* (New York: St. Martin's Press, 1980); Stuart Hall, "Notes on Deconstructing 'the Popular,'" in R. Samuel (ed.), *People's History and Socialist Theory* (London: Routledge, 1981); R. Rozensweig, *Eight Hours for What We Will: Workers and Leisure in an Industrial City* (London: Cambridge University Press, 1983); E. Yeo and S. Yeo, *Popular Culture and Class Conflict: 1590–1914: Explorations in the History of Labour and Leisure* (Sussex: Harvester, 1981).

24. My discussion here is indebted to Patrick Brantlinger, *Bread and Circuses: Theories of Mass Culture as Social Decay* (Ithaca: Cornell University Press, 1983). See also see Gruneau and Whitson, *Hockey Night in Canada,* pp. 11–30.

25. See my discussion in "The Politics and Ideology of Active Living," pp. 208–210.

26. Young, *The Modern Olympics,* pp. 30–34.

27. Ibid., pp. 32–35.

28. Ibid., p. 193, n. 65.

29. B. Kidd, *The Struggle for Canadian Sport* (Toronto: University of Toronto Press, 1996), pp. 27–28.

30. I am indebted to Steve Hardy for alerting me (in personal correspondence) to this point.

31. Young, *The Modern Olympics,* p. 31.

32. My discussion here draws broadly on ideas found in Bailey, *Leisure and Class in Victorian England;* Hall, "Notes on Deconstructing 'the Popular'"; Cunningham, *Leisure in the Industrial Revolution;* and T. Bennett, "The Politics of 'the Popular' and Popular Culture," in T. Bennett, C. Mercer, and J. Woolacott (eds.), *Popular Culture and Social Relations* (Milton Keynes: Open University Press, 1986).

33. See the discussion of amateurism and Canadian hockey in Gruneau and Whitson, *Hockey Night in Canada,* pp. 56–92.

34. On Coubertin, see J. MacAloon, *This Great Symbol: Pierre de Coubertin and the Origins of the Modern Olympic Games* (Chicago: University of Chicago Press, 1981). MacAloon's work is usefully read in conjunction with the somewhat different interpretation offered by Young, *The Modern Olympics.*

35. A. Senn, *Power, Politics and the Olympic Games* (Urbana, Ill.: Human Kinetics Press, 1999), p. 20.

36. Guttmann, *The Games Must Go On,* pp. 12–13.

37. Ibid., p. 14.

38. Ibid., p. 21.

39. On the amateur professional debate in the United States, see Pope, *Patriotic Games,* pp. 23–45. The Canadian case is well covered in Metcalfe, *Canada Learns to Play,* pp. 99–132.

40. Guttmann, *The Games Must Go On,* p. 55.

41. On relations between nationalism and amateurism, see Pope, *Patriotic Games,* pp. 40–49.

42. John Hoberman makes a compelling case for the argument that the adoption of amateurism, merged with a strong appreciation of masculine vitalism, in the early stages of Coubertin's Olympic "movement," was never very far from a reactionary—indeed racist—vision of "social harmony." See J. Hoberman, *The Olympic Crisis* (New Rochelle, N.Y.: Aristide D. Caratzas, 1986), chapter 2.

43. Guttmann, *The Games Must Go On,* p. 53.

44. Figure skating raised other issues, particularly the extent to which Olympic success almost from the outset paved the way to a professional career. Sonja Henie's success at St. Moritz propelled her into a career as an ice-show performer and film star. Guttmann notes that Avery Brundage always saw her as one of the most graphic symbols of the "materialistic betrayal of Olympic values" (*The Games Must Go On,* p. 58).

45. Guttmann, *The Games Must Go On,* pp. 123, 128–130.

46. On the Schranz case, see Senn, *Power, Politics and the Olympic Games,* pp. 146–147; and Guttmann, *The Games Must Go On,* pp. 119–120.

47. See Gruneau and Whitson, *Hockey Night in Canada*, pp. 72–77.

48. Ibid., pp. 69–72.

49. Ibid., pp. 103–106.

50. Guttmann, *The Games Must Go On*, p. 103.

51. Ibid., p. 104.

52. Ibid., pp. 104–108.

53. Ibid., p. 107.

54. Ibid.

55. Very useful material for this kind of analysis can be found in Hoberman, *The Olympic Crisis*, chapters 1 and 2.

56. My discussion of cultural modernism is indebted to D. Harvey, *The Condition of Postmodernity: An Enquiry into the Origins of Cultural Change* (Oxford: Blackwell, 1989), especially chapters 1 and 2. For a complementary but rather different perspective, see Marshall Berman, *All That's Solid Melts into Air: The Experience of Modernity* (London: Verso, 1983).

57. W. Benjamin, "Art in the Age of Mechanical Reproduction," in *Illuminations,* trans. H. Zohn (London: Fontana, 1970).

58. See Hoberman, *The Olympic Crisis*, pp. 30–31; and Guttmann, *The Games Must Go On*, p. 116.

59. Hoberman, *The Olympic Crisis*, p. 29.

60. Indeed, Hoberman accuses the Olympic Movement of engaging in "amoral universalism" (*The Olympic Crisis*, p. 29).

61. Ibid., p. 29.

6

TELEVISION, CORPORATE SPONSORSHIP, AND THE WINTER OLYMPICS

Stephen R. Wenn

The link between commercialism and the Olympic Games through the sale of Olympic television rights and corporate sponsorship opportunities evokes one of three responses. Critics observe that commercialism promoted an inexorable "commodification" of Olympic tradition. Commodification, states Michael Real, "reduces the value of any act or object to only its monetary exchange value, ignoring historical, artistic, or relational added values."[1] Therefore, the Olympics, charge some academics and journalists, celebrate neither human possibility in terms of athletic performance nor the aims of its founder, Pierre de Coubertin. Rather, the rise of the Olympics as a television spectacle, powered by corporate America, diminished the power of the Olympic message. Historian John Lucas, while still seeing much good in the Olympic Movement, has commented that it is on the "knife edge of catastrophe" in light of the challenge to Olympic ideals posed by the prospect of unarrested commercialism.[2]

Polling firms, however, report that the general public has adopted a more neutral view of recent developments. Sport fans recognize that television networks provide them with the means to follow Olympic events and understand the role played by the money and technical support provided by the IOC's major corporate sponsors. An increasingly commercialized Olympic product did not engender a backlash from the public, if judged by the steadily increasing television audiences.

Finally, Richard Pound, the IOC's marketing guru during the Samaranch years, and his right hand, Michael Payne, the IOC's marketing director, argue that revenue from television and corporate sponsorship has provided the IOC with financial security and empowered the Olympic Movement. Government authorities' dwindling enthusiasm for bankrolling mega-events such as Olympic festivals prompted the IOC's courting of the private sector.

Michael Payne observes that the IOC's marriage with major corporate sponsors facilitated the promotion of the tenets of Olympism on a global level. "There's no way we could afford to send these messages around the world, but the sponsors do it, marrying their message with the message of the Olympic Movement, keeping it alive."[3] In blunt fashion, Pound summarized his view of the relationship between sport and commercialism: "Take away sponsorship and commercialism from sport today and what is left? A large, sophisticated, finely-tuned engine developed over a period of 100 years—with no fuel."[4] Three recent scenarios brought the discussion concerning the Olympic Movement's financial framework and the impact of commercialism on the Olympic Games into sharper focus.

In 1996 the United States Olympic Committee (USOC), the Atlanta Games Organizing Committee (AGOC), and municipal officials sought to capitalize, in a commercial sense, on the Centennial Games. Their competing revenue-generation schemes exasperated IOC officials and buried the city and the Games under "an avalanche of Olympic commercialism." "Municipally-licensed, OCOG (Olympic Games Organizing Committee)-authorized, and USOC-generated billboards, posters, booths, stalls, kiosks, tents, pavilions, roving street hawkers and frenzied vendors smother[ed] residents and Olympic tourists like a horde of locusts," reported Robert Barney.[5] Observers lamented the commercial tawdriness of the Atlanta scene, while Nagano and Sydney organizers furiously scribbled notes about what not to do.

The Salt Lake City scandal, touched off in late 1998 by allegations concerning the conduct of Salt Lake City bid officials and the late René Essomba, an IOC member from Cameroon, also prompted questions concerning the influence of commercialism on the IOC's method of "doing business." An internal review of the conduct of a number of IOC members led to the resignation or expulsion of ten individuals. While the IOC's investigation, and one conducted later by the USOC, centered on the Salt Lake City bid process, questionable conduct on the part of a number of IOC members, National Olympic Committee officials, and bid committee representatives during past bid processes also surfaced.[6]

Added financial security provided by burgeoning television revenue and significant new monies resulting from the IOC's worldwide corporate sponsorship program, TOP (The Olympic Programme, later renamed The Olympic Partners) developed in the 1980s, as well as Peter Ueberroth's model for staging an Olympic festival, altered the bidding environment.[7] An increasing number of communities engaged in the spirited pursuit of host city privileges in the wake of Ueberroth's financially successful 1984 Los Angeles Olympics. A number of bid committees plied IOC members for their votes with vacation opportunities, gifts, and cash. Many resisted, but some attributed a sense of entitlement to their role as IOC members. A period of introspection and analysis in 1999 resulted in the adoption of a reform agenda by the IOC dedicated to enhancing organizational transparency and accountability and improving the level of athlete input in the Olympic decisionmaking process.[8] The IOC's success in this initiative remains a subject of debate among Olympic observers.

The recently contested campaign for the IOC presidency also drew attention to the issue of Olympic commercialism. Canada's Richard Pound, the individual largely responsible for enhancing the IOC's and the Olympic Movement's financial resources in the 1980s and 1990s through the negotiation of television and corporate sponsorship deals, found himself the target of fellow presidential contenders Kim Un-yong (South Korea) and Jacques Rogge (Belgium). Kim and Rogge left little doubt as to their intended target when they expressed concern about the growth of the Games spawned, in part, by steadily increasing Olympic revenues. Pound promised, if elected, to complete a study of the size of the Games and the formula for distributing financial resources to host cities, International Sport Federations (ISFs), National Olympic Committees (NOCs), and athletes. Kim and Rogge, the eventual winner of the presidential election, provided few definitive ideas concerning their plans to temper the ambition of International Sport Federation leaders, many of whom are seeking to enhance, not limit, the profile of their respective sports on the Olympic program. How they planned to thwart the efforts of sport leaders clamoring for an opportunity to have their athletes compete at the Olympic level for the first time was an equally perplexing question without answer.

How and why did the IOC become intertwined with commercial interests, specifically television partners and major corporate sponsors? This chapter examines this question with specific reference to the Olympic Winter Games tradition. Through an analysis of television rights negotiations (primarily U.S.) and corporate sponsorship initiatives in relation to the Olympic Winter Games, I hope that this essay will shed light on the IOC's move from an organization that eschewed any connection to commercial entities to one that now embraces such a relationship. The chapter also demonstrates how commercial revenue served as a source of conflict between the IOC and other Olympic organizations such as the ISFs, NOCs, and Olympic Organizing Committees.

TELEVISION RIGHTS NEGOTIATIONS AND THE OLYMPIC WINTER GAMES

In 1958, after more than two years of consultation with television industry executives from the United States and Europe, IOC president

Avery Brundage proposed the IOC's first formal policy governing the sale of Olympic television rights. His action stemmed from a fiasco in Melbourne that compromised the production of international telecasts of the 1956 Summer Olympics. The Melbourne Olympic Organizing Committee, under the leadership of Wilfrid Kent-Hughes, and representatives of the international television and cinema newsreel industry sparred over Kent-Hughes's demand for remuneration in exchange for access to daily footage for news purposes. Prolonged and fruitless discussions between Melbourne officials and their counterpart negotiators representing the television networks limited the reach of Olympic programming to the domestic market, with the exception of a series of highlight packages aired by a small number of independent stations in the United States. Brundage's effort to generate policy in this area aimed to prevent similar episodes in relation to the upcoming 1960 Winter and Summer Olympic festivals, scheduled for Squaw Valley and Rome, respectively.[9]

Despite his well-known opposition to "commercialized" sport, Brundage believed that the convergence of television and the Olympic Games provided an attractive possibility for the IOC—an opportunity to expand its skeleton staff in Lausanne for better promotion of Olympic ideals throughout the world. Brundage harbored suspicions, however, concerning other possible effects on the Olympic enterprise. "I am not sure that we should ever get into 'business,'" he observed in 1955, "but on the other hand, we should not give millions of dollars away." Brundage surmised that negotiations concerning an acceptable formula for the distribution of the funds posed a possible source of friction between the IOC and Olympic Organizing Committees.[10] The philosophical course that the IOC would follow by forging a relationship with the television industry also left him uneasy.

Brundage's attempt to capitalize on the financial prospects of televised Olympic festivals, while shielding the IOC and the Olympic Movement from the taint of commercialism, is clear from his method of reconfiguring the *Olympic Charter* (Rule 49—Publicity) to encompass the sale of television rights. He ceded responsibility for negotiating the television contracts to the Organizing Committees but placed the distribution of the television revenue accrued from these negotiations under the IOC's jurisdiction. If the Organizing Committees became embroiled in messy negotiations with the television networks, the IOC could remain above the fray, thereby avoiding media criticism, Brundage reasoned.[11] He desired to control the distribution of the money, however, in the process keeping the Organizing Committees (more specifically, their spending of commercial revenue) under his control. Brundage also anticipated approaches from representatives of the International Sport Federations and National Olympic Committees for portions of the newly available revenue. It was a recipe for conflict. The 1960 Organizing Committees had little interest in acceding to his wishes.

Squaw Valley, 1960

The California resort community of Squaw Valley, California, emerged as a surprise victor in the competition to host the 1960 Olympic Winter Games at the IOC's Paris Session in June 1955. A superlative "selling job" by Alexander Cushing, the chief spokesperson for the bid committee, carried the day; however, Brundage also attributed the IOC's decision to fond memories of the Los Angeles experience in 1932 and a measure of sympathy for the United States in light of Detroit's unsuccessful bid for the 1960 Summer Olympics.[12] Rather than celebrating Squaw Valley's success, Brundage stewed over the possibility of a disaster. He considered Squaw Valley unprepared to host an Olympic Winter festival.

Brundage lacked confidence in Cushing's ability to transform "a picnic ground into a high class winter resort."[13] "Even if you get the men and the money required," Brundage wrote Cushing, "it is not going to be a simple matter to provide the facilities and organize the Games properly in four [years'] time."[14] Cushing grew tired of Brundage's skepticism and answered his critic forcefully, but the argument soon ended with Cushing's resignation in 1957 due to a conflict of interest.[15]

Concurrent with Brundage's exploration of the operation of the television industry and the process involved in the negotiations of television rights to sport events, the IOC's chancellor, Otto Mayer, reasserted the IOC's right to distribute television money from the 1960 Olympic festivals.[16] In the late summer of 1955 Brundage had alerted Cushing to the IOC's intent to distribute the television money.[17] Cushing took no notice of the communication. Prentis Hale (president) and Alan Bartholemy (executive director), leaders of the reconstituted Organizing Committee, similarly dismissed Mayer's most recent overture. The IOC could not proffer any legislation to support its initiative. Brundage's modifications to Rule 49 had not been completed; however, in the event that Brundage had finalized that process, Hale and Bartholemy would have contested the claim. The Games had been awarded in June 1955, without any encumbrances of the nature outlined by Mayer. In order to receive state funding for the Games project, Hale and Bartholemy had pledged the receipts from television to the state treasury. They did not accept the IOC's claim on this revenue.[18]

Even Brundage confessed to members of the IOC Executive Board that the IOC had failed to secure the right to allocate the television money at the time when the IOC awarded the Games to Squaw Valley. In August 1955 he observed that "we made no reservation of [the television] rights for the Games of Rome and Squaw Valley [in June], and perhaps we should have done so."[19] This fact, however, did not stop him from trying to convince Squaw Valley organizers that he and Cushing reached such an agreement.[20] Hale and Bartholemy refused to accept Brundage's revisionism. At the IOC's Session in Sofia in September 1957, Brundage abandoned his campaign.[21] This brief skirmish provided an indication of the potential for conflict between the IOC and future Organizing Committees concerning the disposition of television revenue. Brundage's dialogue with Squaw Valley organizers, punctuated by his attempt to rewrite past discussions, and his decision to entrench the IOC's right to distribute television money in the *Olympic Charter* (while at the same time steering clear of direct negotiations with the television networks) neatly summarize his early thoughts on television and the Olympics. He wanted the money afforded by the sale of television rights but feared its effect.

Sapporo, 1972

During the 1960s Brundage's troubles with Organizing Committees concerning television revenue subsided. His decision to claim a modest fixed payment from the 1964 and 1968 Winter and Summer Games Organizing Committees, while granting them control of the remaining television revenue, ameliorated the prospective conflict.[22] Brundage invested significant time, however, trying to appease representatives of the ISFs and NOCs who lobbied for shares of the television revenue that he was uncomfortable placing in their hands. "One should be suspicious of any amateur organization that has money," wrote Brundage in 1965; "the minute this occurs its complexion changes and not for the better."[23] He did not stifle the financial ambitions of representatives of the ISFs such as Berge Phillips of the International Amateur Aquatics Federation (FINA), Roger Coulon of the International Weightlifting Federation (FILA), and Bunny Ahearne of the International Ice Hockey Federation (IIHF) and Giulio Onesti (IOC member from Italy and president of the 1960 Rome Organizing Committee), chief spokesperson for the NOCs. Evolving satellite technology portended live, high-quality transoceanic Olympic telecasts, and Phillips and his colleagues recognized their impact on the future value of Olympic television rights. Brundage's meager handouts were no longer acceptable.[24]

The IOC president reached a settlement with the NOCs and ISFs, while maintaining a method for distributing the television money that favored the Organizing Committees. Brundage defended such an arrangement because the Organizing Committees shouldered the financial burden of staging the Games. In April 1966, after months of negotiations between Lord David Burghley, the Marquess of Exeter (IOC member from Great Britain and president of the International Amateur Athletics Federation [IAAF]), and Onesti, the power brokers on Brundage's handpicked committee that had been assigned the task of devising a new distribution formula, the IOC passed the "Rome Formula." This formula provided roughly 66.6 percent of the television money to the Organizing Committees (Winter and Summer), and 11.1 percent each to the IOC, ISFs, and NOCs.[25]

Even though the ISFs expressed dissatisfaction, it was the 1972 Organizing Committees that devised means to circumvent the new formula. Both the Munich and Sapporo Organizing Committees signed preliminary agreements with U.S. television networks that separated sums for the television rights (divisible according to the Rome Formula) and technical services and equipment (payable directly to the Organizing Committee).[26] IOC officials, according to the text of Rule 49 and the Rome Formula, anticipated subjecting the gross value of each contract to division according to the Rome Formula. Their consternation was palpable.[27] Their counterparts in Sapporo (Organizing Committee secretary-general Tomoo Sato) and Munich (Organizing Committee president Willi Daume) argued that such a policy failed to take into account the expanding cost of telecasting the Olympic Games throughout the world.

Tomoo Sato alerted Ian St. John Lawson-Johnston, Lord Luke, chairman of the IOC's Finance Commission, in September 1969 that Sapporo negotiators, at the request of the U.S. networks, were preparing to hold discussions with the Americans concerning an Olympic television contract.[28] Organizing Committees preferred to deal with the U.S. contract first, because it provided the largest infusion of revenue from television as a result of the competitive nature of the U.S. networks and also established a meaningful negotiating tool to be employed with representatives of television networks in other regions. Within three weeks, Sato advised Luke that the National Broadcasting Company (NBC) had supplied the best offer of the three competing networks ($6,401,000). Sato assured Luke that the rights portion of the contract would be at least $5,000,000. In a follow-up letter, he explained the rationale for the stated terms of the agreement. Japan's national broadcaster, Nippon Hoso Kyokai (NHK), had been retained by the Organizing Committee to provide the necessary broadcast facilities for the international networks. Sato believed that the IOC must share with the Organizing Committee the cost of subsidizing NHK's preparations.[29] The opinion was not shared in Lausanne. Sato assigned the duty of discussing the contract with IOC officials to his Organizing Committee colleague, Shohei Sasaka.

In February 1970 Sasaka caucused with Lord Luke and his fellow members of the IOC Finance Commission. Sasaka's explanation did not appease the members of the Finance Committee, who requested that Sapporo file a complete report on the negotiations in May at the time of the IOC Session in Amsterdam.[30] In the interim, Luke and Sato exchanged correspondence that merely highlighted the determination of each individual to conclude final negotiations on his preferred terms. Sato reported that the deduction for technical services would not exceed $1,000,000, resulting in an improved situation for the IOC.[31] In Amsterdam the Finance Commission pressed Sato to accept the IOC's interpretation of the Rome Formula.[32] Sato's resolve soon dissipated. Following a period of reflection, he abandoned his effort to deduct money from the U.S. television contract for technical services.[33] Willi Daume refused to cower and steadfastly maintained the Munich Organizing Committee's right to deduct $6 million from the $13.5 million U.S. television contract with ABC. In 1971 the IOC conceded this right to Daume in exchange for forgiving a previous loan of $274,000 granted by the Munich Organizing Committee to the IOC and assurance that this approach (the inclusion of a technical services payment) was limited to the U.S. television deal.[34] Daume's success emboldened future Olympic Organizing Committees to challenge the IOC's television policies.

From Innsbruck, 1976, to Calgary, 1988

Negotiations in the major world television markets conducted during the 1970s for the Innsbruck, Lake Placid, and Sarajevo Olympic Winter festivals reflected the fallout from the IOC's management of Daume's initiative. IOC officials, primarily Finance Commission chairman Jean de Beaumont and IOC director Monique Berlioux, squared off repeatedly with Organizing Committee officials who sought to enhance their shares of available television revenue at the expense of the IOC, NOCs, and ISFs.[35] Conflict with the Winter Organizing Committees paralleled similar troubles involving those entrusted with the responsibility to stage the Summer Games. Key issues for debate included the timetable for signing contracts and the amounts of money allocated to the stakeholders.

IOC officials, among them Berlioux, Beaumont, and even Lord Killanin, responded in two ways to the difficulties encountered with the Organizing Committees. First, they understood the need to become more conversant with the methods of the television industry and established a subcommittee of the Finance Commission to handle this task. Killanin believed that the IOC might have to manage the negotiations in the future but could not do so without an enhanced institutional knowledge base.[36] Second, they shelved Brundage's hands-off policy concerning negotiations in order to protect the IOC's financial interests.

Some might argue that the "corporatization" of the International Olympic Committee was a by-product of Samaranch's approach to the "amateur question" and revenue generation (specifically the development of TOP) in the 1980s. However, the IOC's response to this troubled series of negotiations—the formation of the Television Sub-Committee in 1973 to augment the IOC's knowledge of the television industry and the IOC's decision in 1977 to take a place at the negotiating table in the future— defuses this argument.[37] The IOC's first steps toward its current status as a corporate entity preceded Samaranch's arrival in Lausanne on a full-time basis.

Innsbruck, 1976. In June 1973 Innsbruck's mayor, Alois Lugger, pledged the gross television receipts from the contracting U.S. network to the IOC. The Austrians planned to adhere strictly to the IOC's policy concerning distribution of television revenue. Relief turned to anger in Lausanne when Marc Hodler, a member of the Finance Commission and one of the IOC's liaisons with the Innsbruck Organizing Committee, learned that a $10 million contract concluded with ABC during the summer months included a deduction of $2.2 million for technical services. Innsbruck's secretary-general, Karl-Heinz Klee, pressed hard for the deduction. He agreed to Beaumont's request that the fee be reduced to $2 million and provided assurance that the U.S. contract would be the only one devised with a clause for technical services.[38]

Beaumont's timid response is easily explained. His reaction was tempered by the IOC's ongoing troubles with the Montreal Organizing Committee. In May, due to an administrative blunder in Lausanne, the IOC granted Montreal the right to deduct 50 percent of the gross sum of all television contracts for technical services.[39] It was a costly oversight. Some form of concession to Innsbruck was required, and Beaumont considered the $2 million technical services payment palatable. While members of the Finance Commission later sparred with Klee concerning the manner in which

the $8 million should be allocated between the various Olympic organiza-
tions and the Organizing Committee, a compromise arrangement was soon
concluded.[40]

Lake Placid, 1980. Nestled in the Adirondack Mountains of the
eastern United States, the Lake Placid site proved a formidable challenge
for organizers of the 1980 Olympic Winter Games. Desperate for operating
capital, Lake Placid officials negotiated a contract with Roone Arledge and
ABC Sports for $9 million ($3 million payable to the IOC) in advance of
the 1976 Olympic Winter Games, counter to the instructions of the IOC
Executive Board.[41] When news of the tentative ABC/Lake Placid contract
filtered back to New York, NBC and CBS executives angrily claimed, as
they had in the wake of ABC's acquisition of the U.S. rights to the 1976
Montreal Summer Olympics, that they had been shut out of the bidding
process.[42] The IOC believed that interest in the Innsbruck festival might
stimulate better terms in the competitive U.S. sports television market and
deferred granting IOC approval for the contract until it obtained assurance
that ABC's competitors (CBS and NBC) had been granted an opportunity
to bid for the rights.[43]

Even though Lord Killanin became involved in the final negotiations
for the European Broadcasting Union (EBU)/Montreal contract in 1975,
his role was limited. His intervention was intended to bring closure to the
protracted process. Frustration with Lake Placid officials, and NBC and CBS's
lobbying on Capitol Hill for an open, transparent negotiation, prompted
Jean de Beaumont to conduct an auction with representatives of the three
U.S. networks in Paris in May 1976.[44] It was the first time that the IOC
effectively removed the right to negotiate television contracts from an
Organizing Committee and, in part, explains the IOC's move in 1977 to
draft policy empowering the IOC jointly to negotiate all television contracts with future Organizing Committees from 1984 on.

Lake Placid's defiance of the IOC's edict to delay contract negotiations
until the conclusion of the Innsbruck Olympic Winter Games was only one
source of consternation for Beaumont and his colleagues. The tentative
deal with Arledge included some rather shocking provisions from the
IOC's perspective. First, the contract specified that Canada was included in
ABC's telecast territory, forcing a Canadian telecaster to purchase domestic
rights from ABC or refrain from such action, in the process leaving Canadian televiewers with a U.S.-produced telecast. Second, Lake Placid negotiators granted ABC the first million dollars from the sale of television
rights in other television markets and half of each remaining million. Lake
Placid was guaranteed a minimum of $1 million, however, from the sale of

non-U.S. television rights. This form of revenue-sharing agreement—that effectively shut out the IOC, ISFs, and NOCs—was without any precedent in Olympic television negotiations. Claims that ABC required this additional money, in the absence of government support to fulfill its role as host broadcaster, were dismissed.

Following Berlioux's investigation of the initial negotiation with ABC, it was determined that CBS and NBC had been granted an opportunity to bid.[45] Only ABC followed up on its initial site visit in 1974 with a detailed technical proposal; and Lake Placid officials, hungry for operating capital, ran out of patience with NBC and CBS representatives. Within NBC and CBS boardrooms, however, confusion had prevailed in January 1976 when Killanin informed the respective Sports Departments that Lake Placid had been told not to enter into final negotiations until after the conclusion of the Innsbruck Olympic Winter Games.[46] When the IOC reopened discussions with ABC and squeezed Arledge for an additional $1.5 million and the removal of ABC's share of revenue from the sale of television rights in other markets, it appeared that negotiations had concluded.[47] NBC and CBS officials complained to federal politicians that their grievances had not been dealt with by the IOC. Following an approach by Fred B. Rooney, chairman of the Sub-Committee on Transportation and Commerce of the Committee on Interstate and Foreign Commerce, Beaumont opted to appease CBS and NBC's congressional allies and secure more money.[48]

At a meeting of the IOC Finance Commission in Paris, Beaumont received bids from Arledge and his counterparts at NBC and CBS. Arledge was permitted to match the highest competing offer, even though CBS and NBC understood that their bids were secret. It appears that Beaumont was walking a fine line between dealing with the protestations of CBS and NBC (and their congressional friends) and the possibility of a breach of contract suit against Lake Placid from ABC. A flummoxed Arledge agreed to pay $15.5 million (the value of NBC's bid) for the U.S. rights two weeks after the conclusion of the auction in lieu of pursuing the breach of contract suit. Beaumont's final negotiations with Arledge guaranteed the IOC $6.25 million to be distributed to its Olympic partners, a noticeable improvement on the $3 million outlined in the original ABC/Lake Placid agreement.[49]

Although Beaumont's efforts resulted in an increase in Lake Placid's share of U.S. television money from $6 million to $9.25 million, Lake Placid officials seethed at the IOC's conduct. Not only had Beaumont excluded Lake Placid officials from his negotiations with U.S. network officials in Paris, but they also believed that the IOC was grabbing a larger share of the contract than it required. "We mutually agreed . . . ," John Wilkins, one of Lake Placid's key fundraisers, wrote Monique Berlioux, "that while bidding was possible, commercialization of the Olympics was not a desirable goal for the IOC or for the Lake Placid Organizing Committee." Berlioux dismissed his protests and in a charged reply noted that Lake Placid's refusal to adhere to IOC policy forced the IOC's hand.[50]

Stonewalled by Berlioux in their attempt for redress concerning the distribution of the monies from ABC's $15.5 million contract, Lake Placid officials solicited assistance from the United States Olympic Committee. Lake Placid's agreement to this contract hinged on the IOC granting Lake Placid a $1 million interest-free loan and a donation of $1 million. F. Don Miller, USOC executive director, called on the IOC to accept these terms. He alerted Lausanne officials to the Carter administration's discussion of a 30 percent levy on future U.S. Olympic television rights payments due, in part, to the anticipated sale price of the U.S. rights to the Moscow Olympics, between $70 and $100 million. Miller noted that the USOC had made no decision on whether to support the proposal, but he personally favored granting 10 percent of all television revenue to the National Olympic Committee of the host country.[51] Miller's veiled threats did not impress Berlioux, but Beaumont sought compromise. In exchange for the USOC's guarantee of $1.6 million from the sale of television rights in other markets to the IOC and its agreement to abandon lobbying Congress for either the 30 percent tax on the Moscow television rights or its claim for 10 percent of the Lake Placid television revenue, Killanin, on the advice of Beaumont, consented to the proposed loan and donation arrangements.[52]

Sarajevo, 1984, and Calgary, 1988. Discussions on the sale of U.S. television rights to the Sarajevo and Calgary Olympic festivals mark two very significant negotiations in the history of the Winter Olympics. In terms of historical signposts, Sarajevo witnessed the final opportunity for Monique Berlioux to exercise her considerable power in television negotiations, while Calgary provided the stage for the rising star of the IOC's financial and marketing portfolios, Richard Pound.[53] ABC, America's Olympic network during the 1970s and 1980s largely due to the energy, will, and negotiating guile of Roone Arledge, secured U.S. television rights for both festivals; however, Calgary proved to be ABC's last Olympic project. A reported loss of $75 million on the deal and ownership changes dampened ABC's enthusiasm in negotiations during the late 1980s and 1990s. Due to a unique set of market issues and a novel negotiations format, Calgary marked the first and only time that the price for U.S. television rights for the Winter festival exceeded that of the Summer festival held in the same year (Calgary—$309 million, Seoul—$300 million).

Monique Berlioux's profile and authority in Olympic financial matters grew in the 1970s due to her own industriousness and the decisions of Avery Brundage and Lord Killanin to maintain their residences in the United States and Ireland, respectively. When Juan Antonio Samaranch succeeded Killanin in 1980, he elected to establish his principal residence in Lausanne. Samaranch's propensity for micromanaging ran counter to Berlioux's administrative practices and prior sphere of authority.[54] Berlioux, who supported Samaranch's presidential candidacy, was lukewarm about his plan to link the power and mystique of the Olympic rings to a worldwide marketing program as a means of securing additional revenue for the Olympic Movement. Friction and distrust between the two developed, and IOC staff overheard loud arguments on occasion. The primary beneficiary of this soured relationship was Richard Pound.

The U.S. television negotiations for the Sarajevo Olympic Winter Games greatly exercised Monique Berlioux. Sarajevo's point man, Ahmed Karabegovic, resisted the IOC's effort to effect its new policy of joint negotiation. Karabegovic and Berlioux engaged in an extended exchange of correspondence concerning the distribution terms of the $91.5 million contract with ABC that he negotiated in the absence of IOC input and in contravention of existing *Olympic Charter* regulations. Tense meetings between the two followed, with an ultimate resolution reached between Karabegovic and the IOC Executive Board. Berlioux's difficulties prompted action by the IOC on two fronts: the policy of joint negotiation was firmly entrenched in the host city agreements with Calgary and Seoul, host cities for the 1988 Olympic Winter Games and Summer Olympic Games, respectively; and Berlioux assumed control of negotiations with executives from other television markets.[55]

The responsibility for negotiating television contracts for the Calgary Olympic Winter Games fell to Richard Pound, the newly appointed chairman of the Television Rights Negotiation Committee. Pound's ascendance within the IOC's hierarchy was linked with Monique Berlioux's reduced profile in the IOC's revenue-generation operation. Samaranch envisioned Pound as a means of diminishing Berlioux's authority in Lausanne. The Canadian eagerly approached this new portfolio. In conjunction with Calgary organizers, Pound established a "sealed bid" format for negotiations with the U.S. television networks.[56] This approach yielded a bonanza for the Olympic Movement and Calgary officials, as Roone Arledge and ABC paid $309 million for U.S. television rights.

Even though Calgary officials celebrated, the ABC contract had implications for the IOC's future management of television negotiations. First, U.S. executives chafed at the IOC's practice of squeezing the U.S. market for maximum revenue when it was clear that the same thinking did not govern its approach to managing the European market. Pound would have pushed European Broadcasting Union officials, but Samaranch maintained control of negotiations with EBU and refused to give emerging private networks in Europe any opportunity to negotiate. With an uncontested playing field, EBU officials experienced no pressure to pay a premium for Olympic television rights in the 1960s, 1970s, and 1980s. When Samaranch announced the financial terms of EBU's contract for the Calgary rights, the $5.7 million sum left U.S. television executives slack-jawed.[57] American networks had already refused to engage in a "Calgary-like" negotiation process for U.S. rights to the Seoul Olympics, leaving Korean officials, who anticipated a sale price (based on Calgary's success) in excess of $600 million, with NBC's best offer of $300 million.[58]

Enter the United States Olympic Committee

Even more serious for Pound was the reaction of the United States Olympic Committee. While dealing with agitated American television executives concerning the protracted Seoul negotiations, Pound learned of the extent of the USOC's agitation at the disparity between the European and American television contracts. Calgary provided the "call to action" for the USOC. Officials resented the flow of massive amounts of American dollars into the pockets of NOCs around the world, presumably for the enhanced training of competitors for America's Olympians. In the late 1970s the U.S. federal government had granted the USOC exclusive ownership of the Olympic five-ring logo in U.S. territory as part of its Amateur Sports Act. In September 1985 the USOC demanded payment from the U.S. networks for Calgary and Seoul in exchange for selling advertising time to commercial sponsors who planned to use the Olympic rings.[59] ABC executives, already convinced that they would lose $50–60 million on the Calgary project, were frantic. NBC and CBS, the only networks interested in the U.S. rights to the Seoul Olympics, reassessed their negotiating positions. Pound scrambled for a solution.

Pound understood the need to safeguard the U.S. networks' right to sublicense the use of the Olympic rings to commercial advertisers. A three-person committee composed of Pound and fellow IOC members Jim Worrall and Julian Roosevelt found an answer acceptable to all parties. The Calgary and Seoul Olympic Committees and the IOC agreed to share equally in a payment of $15 million to the USOC in order to protect the right of ABC and NBC (the network acquired the U.S. television rights to Seoul for $300 shortly after the USOC's bombshell announcement) to sublicense the use of the Olympic rings to commercial advertisers. The text of the IOC/USOC accord, known as the Broadcast Marketing Agreement, also granted the USOC 10 percent of the U.S. Olympic television contracts for 1992 and beyond.[60] The 1990s were marked by frequent skirmishes between Pound and USOC officials, who sought, both in face-to-face negotiations with Pound and/or Samaranch and through discussions with congressional allies in Washington, to improve the USOC's percentage share of future U.S. Olympic television contracts.[61]

Pound also knew that the only means of alleviating USOC pressure on the IOC was to effect meaningful change in the sums of money obtained from the European Broadcasting Union. He spent a good deal of energy in the late 1980s and early 1990s stressing to Samaranch and Hodler the need to do so. It was a difficult challenge. Samaranch and Hodler dismissed the potential EBU's fledgling competitors (private television networks) to cover an event of the size and broadcast complexity of the Olympics.[62]

The Organizing Committees of the 1992 and 1994 Olympic festivals lacked the ability to press improved terms from EBU because the IOC (specifically Samaranch and Hodler) controlled television negotiations and was no longer tied to a policy of joint negotiation. This change in IOC policy reflected its utter frustration with the Seoul Organizing Committee's television negotiators, who had given Pound and his colleagues many headaches. Samaranch and Hodler stonewalled Pound and representatives of the Albertville, Barcelona, and Lillehammer Organizing Committees. An offer of $300 million for the 1996 Atlanta television rights from Universum Film–AG (UFA), a German network, however, forced EBU's and Samaranch's and Hodler's hands. EBU acquired the European television rights for $250 million. This contract reflected a substantial increase on the $94.5 million paid for European rights to the 1992 Barcelona Olympics.[63] By contrast, the U.S. television rights for Barcelona yielded $401 million, while Atlanta attracted a sale price of $456 million.

Long-Term Television Contracts and the Salt Lake City Connection

"What NBC might lose on the swings (Sydney), it would make up on the roundabouts (Salt Lake City)."[64] This is how the IOC's chief negotiator, Dick Pound, summarized NBC's thinking in its decision to offer the IOC $1.25 billion for the U.S. rights to the Sydney and Salt Lake City Olympic festivals during the summer of 1995. This was not the first multi-

Table 6.1. A Comparison of U.S., European, and
Global Olympic Winter Games TV Revenue
(U.S. Dollars)

Olympic Year and Site	Television Market		
	U.S.	Europe	Global
1960 Squaw Valley	50,000		50,000
1964 Innsbruck	597,326	316,201	936,667
1968 Grenoble	2,000,000	512,822	2,612,822
1972 Sapporo	6,401,000	1,425,669	8,475,269
1976 Innsbruck	10,000,000	1,190,570	11,627,330
1980 Lake Placid	15,500,000	3,855,000	20,725,827
1984 Sarajevo	91,500,000	5,600,000	102,681,750
1988 Calgary	309,000,000	6,900,000	324,896,510
1992 Albertville	243,000,000	20,281,560	291,928,279
1994 Lillehammer	295,000,000	26,103,900	352,745,900
1998 Nagano	375,000,000	72,000,000	512,035,000
2002 Salt Lake City	545,000,000	120,000,000	737,800,000
2006 Turin	613,000,000	135,000,000	832,000,000

Games package granted by the IOC to a television network (Australia's Channel 7 purchased the rights to the Nagano and Sydney festivals for $75 million in early 1995).[65] It was the most important, however, because it acted as a springboard for the "Sunset Project," a series of discussions between Pound and NBC's Dick Ebersol aimed at establishing contract terms for the sale of U.S. television rights for the 2004, 2006, and 2008 Olympic festivals. In turn, these talks resulted in a $2.3 billion deal in late 1995. "We've carved out a love affair with the IOC," Ebersol noted. "In August we got engaged. Now it seemed reasonable," he joked, "to get married and open up a joint checking account."[66] The staggering financial results of Pound's discussions with NBC altered the IOC's approach to television negotiations. The IOC would seek to provide bid committees with firmer financial revenue projections, while also guaranteeing its financial security for the medium term by seeking long-term agreements on other markets. No doubt Salt Lake City organizers breathed a sigh of relief during the crisis of 1999 knowing that their television revenue was secure. It will be for Jacques Rogge, the IOC's new president, to determine if long-term television contracts provide the IOC's best option in the future.

Corporate Sponsorship. On an early December morning in 1982, some four months after Paulo Rossi's goal-scoring prowess and veteran goalkeeper Dino Zoff's solid work sent soccer-mad Italians into the streets in celebration of the nation's World Cup triumph, a package arrived at the IOC's headquarters in Lausanne. The parcel, directed to IOC president Juan Antonio Samaranch by Klaus Jürgen Hempel, managing director of International Sports and Leisure Marketing (ISL), a sports-marketing agency based in Lucerne, Switzerland, was a limited-edition lithograph by Italy's satirical artist Franz Borghese, entitled *The Case against the Bourgeoisie*,[67] Hempel's motivation was clear. He wished to advance the prospect for a relationship between his organization and the IOC, previously discussed in informal fashion by Samaranch and ISL's owner, Horst Dassler. They had considered the development of a worldwide marketing program for the Olympic rings, deemed by ISL to be the "most powerful and visible symbol in the world of sport."[68]

ISL, created in the aftermath of the 1982 World Cup, secured its foothold in the sports marketing domain by attracting the International Football [Soccer] Federation as an exclusive client.[69] Dassler and Hempel eyed the lucrative financial payoff from establishing a similar contract relationship with the IOC. Samaranch, for his part, sought to diminish the Olympic Movement's dependence on one revenue stream—television rights—if major corporate sponsors seeking the advertising cachet of the Olympic rings through exclusive sponsorship rights could be enlisted.[70]

Early in the new year, Samaranch entrusted the Ivory Coast's Louis Guirandou-N'Diaye with the leadership of the newly created New Sources of Finance Commission. His mandate was simple—prepare the ground for the establishment of a working relationship between ISL and the IOC. Guirandou-N'Diaye and his fellow commission members, backed by Samaranch, obtained Executive Board and Session approval in New Delhi in March 1983 for the establishment of a program by ISL, in consultation with the IOC, for the marketing of the five-ring logo (The Olympic Programme—TOP).[71] From a logistical standpoint, an overarching marketing program including all National Olympic Committees negated the arduous task for multinational corporations to negotiate separate agreements with individual NOCs. The Executive Board also argued that such a program could effectively monitor the methods of advertising employed, thereby protecting the Olympic Movement's image and brand.[72] The process seemed so simple to this point.

Dassler and Samaranch did not finalize contractual arrangements until May 28, 1985. The sticking point was the USOC's consent for ISL to market the use of the Olympic rings by TOP sponsors within U.S. territory. As noted above, the USOC, by virtue of terms within the Amateur Sports Act, owned the exclusive rights to the rings in the United States. The USOC assumed correctly that the majority of multinational corporations prepared to commit millions of dollars to Olympic sponsorship were U.S.-based. The adverse financial effect on its domestic sponsorship program as a result of ISL's skimming off potential sponsorship partners for TOP, concluded American Olympic officials, required compensation.[73]

Despite this conclusion, USOC officials still questioned whether the organization should involve itself in TOP at all. Talks between ISL and USOC officials dragged into 1984 with no resolution in sight. The Calgary and Seoul Organizing Committees, with their marketing efforts in the United States on hold, pressed both parties for an agreement. Samaranch grew impatient with the negotiating impasse and the repeated need to revise deadlines established for the conclusion of negotiations. In September 1984 the USOC informed ISL that if the USOC received 30 percent of all TOP revenue, prior to distribution of the monies to the Organizing Committees and NOCs throughout the world, it agreed to grant consent to ISL to sell sponsorship packages complete with the right to use the rings in U.S. territory.[74]

ISL and IOC officials were eager to capitalize on this negotiating opportunity. Samaranch, lacking confidence in Monique Berlioux's ability to "close the deal," replaced her with Richard Pound. USOC participation was critical to the success of the program; however, Pound and his colleagues considered the USOC demand for 30 percent of the gross revenue excessive. USOC officials reconsidered their position. The two sides struck a deal. The USOC was entitled to 15 percent of the gross revenue from the sale of sponsorship packages.[75] Subsequent TOP agreements have yielded 20 percent of the gross revenue for the USOC.

Has the TOP program diversified the IOC's revenue generation operation? When Samaranch moved to Lausanne in 1980, the Olympic Movement depended on television rights sales for over 90 percent of its revenue. Corporate sponsorship, specifically TOP (16.1 percent), in conjunction with local sponsorship initiatives (17.5 percent), now provides over 33 percent of the Olympic Movement's quadrennial income (1997–2000), while the dependency on television has been reduced to 51.2 percent.[76] Tables 6.2 and 6.3 demonstrate, with respect to the Olympic Winter Games Organizing Committees, the steadily increasing revenue available to organizers from TOP and related corporate sponsorship programs such as Lillehammer's Team Birkebeiner and Nagano's Gold initiatives.

Table 6.2. Historical Overview of TOP (1985–2000)

TOP Cycle			
TOP I (1985–1988)	TOP II (1989–1992)	TOP III (1993–1996)	TOP IV (1997–2000)
Sponsors			
Coca-Cola	Coca-Cola	Coca-Cola	Coca-Cola
Kodak	Kodak	Kodak	Kodak
VISA	VISA	VISA	VISA
Time	Time	Time/Sports Illus.	Time/Sports Illus.
Matsushita	Matsushita	Matsushita	Panasonic
Brother	Brother	Xerox	Xerox
Philips	Philips	IBM	IBM
3M	3M	John Hancock	John Hancock
Federal Express	UPS	UPS	UPS
	Bausch & Lomb	Bausch & Lomb	McDonald's
	Mars		Samsung
	Ricoh		
Total Revenue (U.S. dollars)			
$97 Million	$175 Million	$350 Million	>$550 Million
NOC Participation			
154/167 (92%)	169/172 (98%)	197/197 (100%)	199/199 (100%)
Method of Distribution			
Seoul 44%	Barcelona 36%	Atlanta 36%	Sydney 33%
Calgary 20%	Albertville 18%	Lillehammer 14%	Nagano 17%
NOCs 22%	NOCs 20%	NOCs 20%	NOCs 20%
USOC 12%	USOC 18.5%	USOC 20%	USOC 20%
IOC 2%	IOC 7.5%	IOC 10%	IOC 10%

Exclusivity: Protecting the Brand and Managing the Message

The IOC, National Olympic Committees, and local Olympic Organizing Committees have been criticized in the past for their aggressive approaches to preventing the unauthorized use of the five-ring Olympic logo. The Salt Lake City experience has been no different. Does it really matter whether a Utah farmer has the five rings displayed in his corn field?

Table 6.3. Overall Revenue for 1994, 1998, and 2002
Olympic Winter Games

Revenue Source (millions U.S.$)	Organizing Committees		
	Lillehammer	Nagano	Salt Lake City
TV Rights	212	308	545
TOP General	50	70	78
TOP Technical	40	75+	122
OCOG Sponsorship	75	200	550
Licensing	20	14	52
Ticketing	23	91.3	162

On the surface, the degree of vigilance in this matter by the Salt Lake City Organizing Committee appears excessive. Those who find fault with Olympic officials, however, ignore the millions of dollars that domestic and world-wide corporate sponsors are paying for the "advertising connection" to the Olympic rings. In order to maintain the financial strength of this revenue stream, it is imperative that the sponsors receive what they have shelled out the money for—exclusive rights to the use of the Olympic brand. Organizing Committees, needing to meet budgetary demands without the amounts of public money available in the pre–Los Angeles Games era, must maintain healthy partnerships with private-sector sponsors.

Media pundits and some Olympic observers have complained that television networks, especially the U.S. rights holder, possess too much clout concerning the schedule of events. With $3.5 billion invested in the Olympic project between 2000 and 2008, only extreme naiveté would lead one to conclude that NBC should not have some influence in the scheduling of events. In the past, payments provided by the U.S. Olympic television rights holder have dwarfed those contributed by the world's other rights holders; and, to be sure, scheduling concessions were made to the U.S. rights holders. My concern on the television front has less to do with sched-uling issues and more to do with the sometimes unbearable nationalistic overtones of the coverage in the United States and elsewhere. While the networks have a financial responsibility to recoup their expenses by focusing on the athletic performances of "their own," they often sidestep a wonderful opportunity to educate people about the lives of people from other cultures.

While it is in the best interests of Olympic organizations to protect the advertising rights of corporate sponsors, the IOC must protect the tele-vision revenue stream. This protection has come in the form of a comprehensive web monitoring project (as has been employed in recent years at Olympic festivals). Without an aggressive approach on behalf of the sponsors and telecasters, both revenue streams would be adversely affected.

The commercial success of the Olympic Games, however, has spawned a number of problems. First, the unrestrained growth of the Olympic Games in terms of number of sports, events, and athletes poses a significant challenge for Jacques Rogge and his administration. The problem is not as acute for organizers of Winter Olympics as it is for their Summer Olympics counterparts, but the logistical challenge involved in staging an Olympic festival, summer or winter, is immense. In the wake of September 11, 2001, security considerations, always a priority since Munich, assume a heightened profile. A thorough review of the Olympic program is required, with the mandate to shrink its size in order to empower future organizers to stage the Games successfully and to do so with the confidence that athletes and spectators can enjoy the Olympic spectacle in a safe and secure environment.

Second, the wild success of Olympic marketing initiatives contributed to the prostitution of the Olympic city bid process during the Samaranch presidency. The IOC failed to root out members who decided to "cash in" on their status and voting privilege despite indications of such conduct. The Salt Lake City scandal exposed a festering problem and forced the IOC to confront it. The media firestorm of 1999 was not a pleasant experience. "There are some days when you wish you had stayed in bed," observed Richard Pound. "My organization, the International Olympic Committee," he deadpanned, "had almost a whole year of that."[77]

Third, the doping problem preceded the Samaranch presidency and the IOC's marriage with corporate sponsors, but the opportunity for some Olympic athletes to "cash in" on their Olympic success through sponsorship deals (and/or government incentive payments) did nothing to reduce the temptation facing athletes. The World Anti-Doping Agency's challenge in combating the doping problem is severe, but the IOC's will to take on this challenge appears much stronger now than in the past.

Last, IOC's marketing methods became far more sophisticated, but its public relations capabilities did not. The IOC must do a better job of managing its message concerning Olympic marketing. How many people know that the IOC distributes approximately 93 cents of every dollar it receives?[78] While the media are ready to cover the scandals and less likely to spend significant time discussing "feel good" stories, the IOC must better publicize the good work being done by Johann Olav Koss and his Olympic Aid program staff. It should also consider establishing more meaningful linkages between IOC television and corporate sponsorship negotiators and administrators of the Olympic Solidarity program.

In this vein, a move to make public at the earliest moment in the wake of multi-million-dollar contract signings how the IOC plans to spend the money in support of athletes around the world, but especially in developing regions, would be received favorably by the public. Money is available to improve the "competitive" experience of Olympians from developing nations. The IOC is likely to continue the sale of multi-Games television packages, which will enable it to make better plans for long- and medium-term spending initiatives. The will to streamline, enhance, and improve the delivery of expert coaching and state of the art facilities in under-resourced areas is needed. This is perhaps the most important means by which the Olympic Movement can demonstrate that it is, in fact, an international movement, especially for the foreseeable future, when hosting the Games will remain beyond the reach of cities and countries in developing regions.

Notes

1. Michael R. Real, "Is TV Corrupting the Olympics? The (Post) Modern Olympics—Technology and the Commodification of the Olympic Movement," www.rohan.sdsu.edu/ faculty/mreal/OlympicAtl.html (Internet), p. 7.

2. *CBS Sunday Morning* (News Magazine Show), February 8, 1998.

3. Payne quoted in Skip Rozin, "Empowering the Olympic Movement: A Look at the Business Dynamics Behind the Olympics," Special Advertising Section Reprint, *Fortune 500* (Time Inc. USA), p. 7.

4. Pound quoted in *Olympic Marketing Fact File* (Lausanne: IOC, 1998), p. 7.

5. From a chapter entitled "An Epilogue as Prologue: Sydney 2000, The Greatest Games Ever," in Robert K. Barney, Stephen R. Wenn, and Scott G. Martyn, *Selling the Five Rings: The International Olympic Committee and the Rise of Olympic Commercialism* (Salt Lake City: University of Utah Press, 2002), pp. 1–16.

6. Investigative commissions were formulated by the OCOGs of the Sydney and Salt Lake City Games, as well as the USOC, IOC, and U.S. Department of Justice. For Sydney, see *Examiner for SOCOG Report,* T. A. Sheridan, Independent Examiner, March 12, 1999, Archives of the International Centre for Olympic Studies, University of Western Ontario, London, Ontario, Canada (hereafter cited as ICOSA). For USOC, see *Report of the Special Bid Oversight Commission,* March 1, 1999, ICOSA. For the IOC, see *Report of the IOC Ad Hoc Commission to Investigate the Conduct of Certain IOC Members and to Consider Possible Changes to the Procedures for the Allocation of the Games of the Olympiad and Olympic Winter Games,* January 24, 1999; and *Second Report of the IOC Ad Hoc Commission to Investigate the Conduct of Certain IOC Members and to Consider Possible Changes to the Procedures for the Allocation of the Games of the Olympiad and Olympic Winter Games,* March 11, 1999, ICOSA. For Salt Lake City, see *Report to the Board of Trustees,* February 8, 1999, ICOSA.

7. For Ueberroth's story, see Peter Ueberroth with Richard Levin and Amy Quinn, *Made in America: His Own Story* (New York: William Morrow and Company, 1985).

8. For a complete treatment of the IOC reforms, see *IOC 2000 Reforms* (Supplement of the *Olympic Review,* December 1999/January 2000).

9. The Melbourne saga has been tackled by Shane Cahill, "'A Very Hard Crowd to Have Dealings With': International and Australian Television Networks' Resistance to the Demands of the 1956 Melbourne Olympic Games Organizing for a Fee for Television Coverage, 1955–1956," in *On-line Proceedings: 40 Years of Television Conference* (Published by the National Centre for Australian Studies, Monash University, 1996), available from http://www.arts.edu.au/ncas/resources/40years/Cahill.shtml (Internet); and Stephen R. Wenn, "Lights! Camera! Little Action: Television, Avery Brundage and the 1956 Melbourne Olympics," *Sporting Traditions* 10 (November 1993): 38–53.

10. Avery Brundage to Members of the Executive Board, August 3, 1955, *Avery Brundage Collection, 1908–1975* (hereafter cited as *ABC*), Box 114, University of Illinois, Champaign-Urbana. While the original collection is located at this location, I have employed the copy at ICOSA.

11. *Minutes of the 51st Session of the International Olympic Committee,* Cortina, January 24–25, 1956, p. 20, International Olympic Committee Archives, Lausanne, Switzerland (hereafter cited as IOCA). For the text of the revised Rule 49, see *Olympic Charter* (Lausanne: IOC, 1958), pp. 29–30.

12. Avery Brundage to Tug Wilson, August 20, 1955; and Avery Brundage to Albert E. Sigal, November 19, 1955, *ABC* Box 165, ICOSA.

13. Avery Brundage to Cortlandt T. Hill, November 12, 1955, *ABC* Box 165, ICOSA.

14. Avery Brundage to Alexander C. Cushing, September 16, 1955, *ABC* Box 165, ICOSA.

15. Alexander Cushing to Avery Brundage, November 30, 1955, *ABC* Box 165, ICOSA. With respect to his resignation, Allen Guttmann reports that Cushing owned some of the land being developed in preparation for the Squaw Valley Olympic Winter Games. Allen Guttmann, *The Games Must Go On: Avery Brundage and the Olympic Movement* (New York: Columbia University Press, 1984), p. 166.

16. Otto Mayer to Alan E. Bartholemy, June 17, 1957, *ABC* Box 165, ICOSA.

17. According to Mayer, Cushing received a copy of a letter from Brundage to USOC president Tug Wilson dated August 31, 1955, addressing this issue. See Otto Mayer to Avery Brundage, July 31, 1957, *ABC* Box 165, ICOSA. See also Avery Brundage to Alexander Cushing, September 16, 1955, *ABC* Box 165, ICOSA.

18. Alan E. Bartholemy to Otto Mayer, July 10, 1957; and Prentis C. Hale to Avery Brundage, July 9, 1957, *ABC* Box 165, ICOSA.

19. Avery Brundage to Members of the IOC Executive Board, August 3, 1955, *ABC* Box 114, ICOSA.

20. Avery Brundage to the Olympic Winter Games Organizing Committee, August 7, 1957, *ABC* Box 165, ICOSA.

21. *Minutes of the 53rd Session of the International Olympic Committee,* Sofia, September 23–28, 1957, p. 8, IOCA.

22. Stephen R. Wenn, "An Olympian Squabble: The Distribution of Olympic Television Revenue, 1960–1966," *Olympika: The International Journal of Olympic Studies* 3 (1994): 30, 32.

23. Avery Brundage to Ivar Vind (IOC Member, Denmark), September 13, 1965, *ABC* Box 64, ICOSA.

24. Brundage's struggle with the likes of Phillips, Coulon, and Onesti is detailed in Wenn, "An Olympian Squabble: The Distribution of Olympic Television Revenue, 1960–1966."

25. Ibid., pp. 34–40.

26. Herbert Kunze (Secretary General, Munich Organizing Committee) to Avery Brundage, April 11, 1969, *ABC* Box 98, ICOSA; *Minutes of the Meeting of the IOC Finance Commission,* Warsaw, June 4, 6–8, 1969, p. 1, IOCA. For a copy of the contract within these minutes, see "Memorandum of Terms between the Organizing Committee for the XXth Olympiad, Munich 1972 and the American Broadcasting Corporation," Annex #1; and Tomoo Sato to Lord Luke, October 2, 1969; and Tomoo Sato to Lord Luke, October 6, 1969, "Droits de T.V. Sapporo" Binder, IOCA.

27. Lord Luke to Herbert Kunze, November 3, 1969; Lord Luke to Members of the IOC Finance Commission and Monique Berlioux, ca. December 22, 1969, *ABC* Box 98, ICOSA; Lord Luke to Shohei Sasaka (Member, Sapporo Organizing Committee), March 3, 1970, "Droits de T.V. Sapporo" Binder, IOCA; *Minutes of the IOC Executive Board,* Dubrovnik, October 23–27, 1969, p. 10, IOCA; and Marquess of Exeter to Avery Brundage, November 17, 1969, *ABC* Box 55, ICOSA.

28. Tomoo Sato to Lord Luke, September 11, 1969, "Lord Luke TV Rights Munich" Folder, "Lord Luke 1969–1978" Binder, IOCA.

29. Tomoo Sato to Lord Luke, October 2, 1969; and Tomoo Sato to Lord Luke, October 6, 1969, "Droits de T.V. Sapporo" Binder, IOCA.

30. *Minutes of the Meeting of the IOC Finance Commission,* Lausanne, February 20, 1970, p. 4, IOCA. The depths of the Finance Commission's feelings on this issue are implied in the minutes but firmly stated in a follow-up letter sent to Sasaka by Lord Luke. Lord Luke to Shohei Sasaka, March 3, 1970, "Droits de T.V. Sapporo" Binder, IOCA.

31. Lord Luke to Shohei Sasaka, March 3, 1970, "Droits de T.V. Sapporo" Binder, IOCA. This letter was forwarded to Sato by Sasaka upon receipt, and Sato then replied to Luke. See Tomoo Sato to Lord Luke, March 25, 1970, "Droits de T.V. Sapporo" Binder, IOCA.

32. *Minutes of the Meeting of the IOC Finance Commission,* Amsterdam, May 7, 10–11, 1970, pp. 4–5, IOCA.

33. Tomoo Sato to Lord Luke, September 4, 1970, "Droits de T.V. Sapporo" Binder, IOCA.

34. *Minutes of the IOC Finance Commission,* Munich, January 28, 1971, pp. 4–5; and *Minutes of the Meeting of the IOC Executive Board,* Lausanne, March 13–14, 1971, p. 20, IOCA.

35. For separate treatment of these scenarios, see, for Innsbruck, Stephen R. Wenn, "Television Rights Negotiations and the 1976 Montreal Olympics," *Sport History Review* 27 (November 1996): 134 (note 61); for Lake Placid, Stephen R. Wenn, "A Turning Point for IOC Television Policy: U.S. Television Rights Negotiations and the 1980 Lake Placid and Moscow Olympic Festivals," *Journal of Sport History* 25 (Spring 1998): 87–118; for Sarajevo, Stephen R. Wenn, "Conflicting Agendas: Monique Berlioux, Ahmed Karabegovic and U.S. Television Rights Negotiations for the 1984 Sarajevo Olympic Winter Games," in Robert K. Barney, Kevin B. Wamsley, Scott G. Martyn, and Gordon H. MacDonald (eds.), *Global and Cultural Critique: Problematizing the Olympic Games—Fourth International Symposium for Olympic Research* (London, Ontario: University of Western Ontario, 1998), pp. 115–127.

36. Lord Killanin to Jean de Beaumont, Lord Luke, Marc Hodler, Willi Daume, Herman van Karnebeek, and Monique Berlioux, March 6, 1974; and Lord Killanin to Jean de Beaumont, Lord Luke, Marc Hodler, Willi Daume, Herman van Karnebeek, and Willi Daume, April 18, 1974, "N.2 Droits T.V. Dossier General: Innsbruck ABC/UER 1972–1976" Binder, IOCA. The formation of such a subcommittee had been suggested as early as 1966 by Giulio Onesti and his fellow IOC members, who had provided the Executive Board and General Session with preliminary ideas concerning the distribution of television revenue to the IOC, IFs, and NOCs. See "Preliminary Report to the Executive Board of the IOC on Television Policy," *ABC* Box 101, ICOSA. For its mandate, see *Minutes of the Meeting of the Television Sub-Committee,* Lausanne, October 4, 1974, "Composition, Terms of Reference and Powers of the IOC Television Sub-Committee," Annex #2, p. 2, IOCA.

37. *Minutes of the 79th Session of the International Olympic Committee,* Prague, June 15–18, 1977, p. 35, and Annex #33, pp. 98–102.

38. *Minutes of the Meeting of the IOC Finance Commission,* Varna, October 4, 7, 1973, p. 5, IOCA.

39. A number of sources are required in order to understand the series of events resulting in this situation. *Minutes of the Meeting of the IOC Finance Commission,* Paris, June 12, 1973, p. 2, IOCA; *Minutes of the Meeting of the IOC Executive Board,* Lausanne, February 9–11, 1974, p. 4, IOCA; and Lord Killanin to Jean de Beaumont, Lord Luke, Marc Hodler, Willi Daume, Herman van Karnebeek, and Willi Daume, April 18, 1974, "N.2 Droits T.V. Dossier General: Innsbruck ABC/UER 1972–1976" Binder, IOCA.

40. A collection of sources reveals the dialogue between Klee and IOC representatives. *Minutes of the Meeting of the IOC Finance Commission,* Lausanne, February 1, 3, 1973, p. 3, IOCA; *Minutes of the Meeting of the IOC Finance Commission,* Paris, January 28, 1974, pp. 4–5, IOCA; *Minutes of the Meeting of the IOC*

Finance Commission, Varna, October 4, 7, 1973, p. 3, IOCA; Karl-Heinz Klee to Monique Berlioux, January 29, 1974; and Monique Berlioux to Karl-Heinz Klee, February 5, 1974, "N.1 Droits de T.V. Innsbruck: Du 1.2.73" Binder, IOCA; and Alois Lugger to Lord Killanin, October 5, 1973, *Minutes of the Meeting of the IOC Finance Commission,* Varna, October 4, 7, 1973, Annex #5, p. 17, IOCA. The problem stemmed from a lack of communication between the two parties. The IOC had decided that the Rome Formula would be modified with respect to the Innsbruck television money. That is, the money would be distributed in exactly the same fashion as the Munich and Montreal television money (i.e., first, second, third, and each successive million, rather than the Sapporo Winter Games precedent that involved the application of the Rome Formula to the first, second, and third and each successive $200,000). Following further negotiations the two sides settled on using $500,000 in conjunction with the Rome Formula. Therefore, the IOC received the first $500,000, two-thirds of the second $500,000, and one-third of each successive $500,000, while the Organizing Committee received the remaining, and larger, portion (approximately 66.6 percent). The IOC also granted the Innsbruck Organizing Committee an interest-free loan of $1 million.

41. Roone Arledge to the Organizing Committee for the 13th Winter Olympic Games—Lake Placid 1980, February 13, 1976, "Lake Placid '80 TV Rights ABC I" Binder, IOCA.

42. *New York Times,* March 13, 1976, p. 51.

43. Monique Berlioux to Norman L. Hess, March 17, 1975, "Lake Placid 1980/TV-General 1976" Binder, IOCA; and Monique Berlioux to John M. Wilkins, March 8, 1976, "Lake Placid '80 TV Dossier General" Binder, IOCA.

44. *Minutes of the Meeting of the IOC Finance Commission,* Paris, May 25, 1976, p. 4, IOCA; and John M. Wilkins to Monique Berlioux, August 23, 1976, "Lake Placid 1980/TV General 1976" Binder, IOCA.

45. "Report on Visit to Lake Placid, 6th, 7th, 8th of April 1976 (D. Mortureux and M. Berlioux)," May 5, 1976, 4, "Lake Placid '80 TV Dossier General" Binder, IOCA.

46. Lord Killanin to Charles Curran (President, European Broadcasting Union), January 5, 1976, "Lake Placid '80 TV Dossier General" Binder, IOCA.

47. Roone Arledge to Monique Berlioux, May 21, 1976, "Lake Placid '80 TV Rights ABC I" Binder, IOCA.

48. Fred Rooney to Monique Berlioux, May 21, 1976, "Lake Placid '80 TV Dossier General" Binder, IOCA.

49. *Minutes of the Meeting of the IOC Finance Commission,* Paris, May 25, 1976, p. 4, IOCA, "Director's Resume of Meeting Held in Paris, May 1976," "Lake Placid 1980/TV General 1976" Binder, IOCA; Jean de Beaumont and Monique Berlioux to Members of the IOC Finance Commission, June 3, 1976, "Lake Placid '80 TV Dossier General" Binder, IOCA; and Roone Arledge to Jean de Beaumont, June 3, 1976, "Lake Placid '80 TV Rights ABC I" Binder, IOCA.

50. For this exchange, see John M. Wilkins to Monique Berlioux, August 23, 1976; and Monique Berlioux to John M. Wilkins, September 16, 1976, "Lake Placid 1980/TV-General 1976" Binder, IOCA.

51. "Report of Visit to the USA by the IOC Director and Advisers, 6–11 December 1976," *Minutes of the Meeting of the IOC Finance Commission,* Paris, January 5, 1977, Annex #2, pp. 7–9, IOCA; and *New York Times,* November 16, 1976, p. 77.

52. Jean de Beaumont to Lord Killanin, December 15, 1976, *Minutes of the Meeting of the IOC Finance Commission,* Paris, January 5, 1977, Annex #3, pp. 16–17, IOCA; Jean de Beaumont to Julian K. Roosevelt, December 14, 1976, *Minutes of the Meeting of the IOC Finance Commission,* Paris, January 5, 1977, Annex #3, p. 18, IOCA; and *Minutes of the Meeting of the IOC Finance Commission,* Paris, January 5, 1977, p. 3, IOCA.

53. For Berlioux's swan song in the negotiations arena, see Wenn, "Conflicting Agendas: Monique Berlioux, Ahmed Karabegovic and U.S. Television Rights Negotiations for the 1984 Sarajevo Olympic Winter Games," pp. 115–127.

54. For information concerning the Samaranch/Berlioux relationship and Berlioux's resignation, see David Miller, *Olympic Revolution: The Biography of Juan Antonio Samaranch* (London: Pavilion Books, 1992), pp. 33–35; *Minutes of the Meeting of the IOC Executive Board,* Berlin, May 31, June 1–3, 6, 1985, pp. 69–71; and *Minutes of the 90th Session of the International Olympic Committee,* Berlin, June 4–6, 1985, pp. 42–44, IOCA. Berlioux was permitted to provide a statement to the session:

> Rumours. Press reports. My departure from the IOC has been announced. I owe you a full explanation. For many years, I have devoted myself to the service of sport and in particular to the Olympic Movement as an athlete, as an official, as your main assistant, as Director of the IOC. I have held this position for 18 years. Of course, I may occasionally have found myself in disagreement with some of you on particular issues. But this is only normal in an organisation like ours which gathers so many eminent members of such rich and varied character. My only rule of conduct has always been the interests of the Movement and its ideals. As time progressed, differing opinions with the Executive Board have led me—like a journalist evoking a conscience clause—to decide to bring my functions as Director to an end. I will continue however to fulfil my duties until the end of this Session. I should like to thank you for the confidence you have placed in me and for your help which have enabled me to develop an administration that I believe to be efficient and healthy. I shall always be proud of the level it has reached. I shall say no more. A Director has moved on. Long live Olympism as its founder, my fellow countryman Pierre de Coubertin, would have wanted.

55. For a sense of the relationship, and its ultimate result, see Ahmed Karabegovic to Monique Berlioux, January 8, 1980, "Sarajevo TV-General Janvier/

Mai 1980" File; Ahmed Karabegovic to Monique Berlioux, December 11, 1979; Monique Berlioux to Ahmed Karabegovic, December 13, 1979; Monique Berlioux to Ahmed Karabegovic, December 7, 1979, "Sarajevo TV-General 1978–1979" File; Ahmed Karabegovic to Monique Berlioux, January 7, 1980, "Sarajevo TV-General Janvier/Mai 1980" File, IOCA; "Report by the IOC Representatives on Their Visit to Sarajevo Regarding Television Negotiations with the American Broadcasting Companies 21st–24th January 1980," "Sarajevo TV-General Janvier/Mai 1980" File; "Discussion on TV Rights with the Sarajevo OCOG," February 15, 1980, *Minutes of the Meeting of the Finance Commission*, Lake Placid, February 11, 14, 16, 1980, p. 3; Monique Berlioux to CTV Network (Canada), March 28, 1980; and Ahmed Karabegovic to Monique Berlioux, April 2, 1980, "Sarajevo TV-General Janvier/Mai 1980" File, IOCA.

56. Monique Berlioux to Richard Pound, September 16, 1983; Richard Pound to Monique Berlioux, September 19, 1983; Monique Berlioux to Richard Pound, October 3, 1983; and Richard Pound to Monique Berlioux, October 4, 1983, "Calgary 1988 TV-General 1981–1982, Janvier/Octobre 1983" File, IOCA; Richard Pound to Juan Antonio Samaranch, December 29, 1983, "Calgary '88 TV-General Novembre–Decembre 1983" File, IOCA; Richard Pound to Monique Berlioux, January 6, 1984; and, Richard Pound to Arthur Watson, January 9, 1984, "Calgary 1988 TV General 1984" File, IOCA.

57. For Calgary's frustration, see Juan Antonio Samaranch to Frank King, July 11, 1986, "Calgary 1988 TV General 1986" File, IOCA. For Samaranch's position on EBU, this view was provided to me during a discussion with Richard Pound at his Montreal law office on November 26, 1998. For a sample of Pound's written concerns on the low fees paid by EBU, see *Minutes of the Meeting of the IOC Executive Board*, Seoul, April 22–24, 1986, Annex #10, "Report to IOC Executive Board Re: Television Rights," p. 81, IOCA.

58. Ashwini Kumar to Juan Antonio Samaranch, April 8, 1984; Monique Berlioux to Richard Pound, April 17, 1984, "Seoul '88 TV General 1981, 1982, 1983 1984 Jusqu'à Mai 1984" File, IOCA; "IOC/SLOOC Meeting, 5 April 1984"; "Record of Discussion: CBS Presentation Meeting, 6 April 1984"; "Record of Discussion: ABC Presentation Meeting, 6 April 1984"; and "Record of Discussion: NBC Presentation Meeting, 7 April 1984," "RWP/IOC 7398–026 Seoul TV 1988" File, Personal Files of Richard Pound (hereafter cited as PFRP), Montreal, Canada; *Minutes of the Meeting of the IOC Executive Board*, Lisbon, October 15, 18, 1985, p. 53, IOCA; Richard Pound to Park Sei Young, August 2, 1985, "Seoul 1988 TV-General 1985 I" File, IOCA; and Richard W. Pound, *Five Rings over Korea: The Secret Negotiations behind the 1988 Olympic Games in Seoul* (Boston: Little, Brown & Company, 1994), pp. 126–127.

59. Richard Pound to Juan Antonio Samaranch, September 26, 1985, "Seoul 1988 TV-General II" File, IOCA.

60. *Minutes of the Meeting of the IOC Executive Board*, Lausanne, February 11–12, 1986, pp. 5, 7, IOCA; and *Minutes of the Meeting of the IOC Executive Board*, Seoul, April 22–24, 1986, p. 4, IOCA.

61. Stephen R. Wenn, "Riding into the Sunset: Richard Pound, Dick Ebersol, and Long-Term Olympic Television Contracts," in Kevin B. Wamsley, Scott G. Martyn, Gordon H. MacDonald, and Robert K. Barney (eds.), *Bridging Three Centuries: Intellectual Crossroads and the Modern Olympic Movement—Fifth International Symposium for Olympic Research* (London, Ontario: University of Western Ontario, 2000), pp. 38–41. The USOC was involved in crafting "The Olympic Television Broadcasting Act," which was presented to the House of Representatives by Maryland's Tom McMillen in 1990. If passed, the legislation would have empowered the USOC to negotiate future U.S. Olympic television contracts, thereby permitting the American officials to determine the USOC's share of the contract without having to consult the USOC. The IOC's successful effort (largely a result of Richard Pound's constant badgering of Samaranch) to elevate EBU payments for future Olympic festivals, specifically Atlanta, led to the removal of the McMillen bill from Washington's agenda in 1991. In 1996 the USOC tried to push a similar change through the Senate, but an NBC official in Washington alerted the IOC. What infuriated the IOC beyond the USOC's attempt to usurp its intellectual property rights was the fact that the two organizations were (at the same time) engaged in negotiations to elevate the USOC's share of future U.S. television contracts. "Briefing Memorandum: IOC-USOC Meeting, October 8, 1996," "IOC-USOC" File, Personal Computer Files of Richard Pound, Montreal, Canada; and personal communication, Richard Pound to the author, May 12, 1999.

62. *Minutes of the Meeting of the IOC Executive Board,* Lausanne, July 24–26, 1988, pp. 23–25, IOCA.

63. Wenn, "Riding into the Sunset: Richard Pound, Dick Ebersol, and Long-Term Olympic Television Contracts," p. 40.

64. Personal communication from Richard Pound, May 12, 1999.

65. "Marketing Report to the IOC Executive Board, Monaco, 2–4 April 1995," *Minutes of the Meeting of the IOC Executive Board,* April 2–4, 1995, Monaco, Annex #6, p. 71, IOCA.

66. Ebersole quoted in John Slater, "Changing Partners: The Relationship between the Mass Media and the Olympic Games," in Robert K. Barney, Kevin B. Wamsley, Scott G. Martyn, and Gordon H. MacDonald (eds.), *Global and Cultural Critique: Problematizing the Olympic Games—Fourth International Symposium for Olympic Research* (London, Ontario: University of Western Ontario, 1998), p. 60.

67. Klaus Jürgen Hempel to Juan Antonio Samaranch, November 1982, "ISL Marketing" File, IOCA. While the letter was undated, research by Scott Martyn (Faculty of Human Kinetics, University of Windsor) indicates that the letter was written in November but that the letter and package were sent in December. For Samaranch's reply, see Juan Antonio Samaranch to Klaus Jürgen Hempel, December 17, 1982, "ISL Marketing" File, IOCA. I am indebted to Dr. Martyn for his helpful advice on the section of this chapter that deals with the IOC and corporate sponsorship as well as the financial summary of TOP's performance since

1985. For readers interested in detailed treatment of the IOC's corporate sponsorship initiatives, his doctoral dissertation is highly recommended. See Scott G. Martyn, "The Struggle for Financial Autonomy: The IOC and the Historical Emergence of Corporate Sponsorship, 1896–2000," Ph.D. diss., University of Western Ontario, 2000.

68. ISL, *A Presentation to the International Committee* (New Delhi: ISL, 1983), p. 1, IOCA. For the Samaranch/Dassler talks, see Robert K. Barney, Stephen R. Wenn, and Scott G. Martyn, "Family Feud: Olympic Revenue and IOC/ USOC Relations," *Olympika: The International Journal of Olympic Studies* 9 (2000): 62.

69. Klaus Jürgen Hempel to Juan Antonio Samaranch, November 1982, "ISL Marketing" File, IOCA.

70. See *Minutes of the Meeting of the Commission of New Sources of Financing,* September 10, 1988, Seoul, p. 10, IOCA. During Killanin's presidency, the IOC's budget was 98 percent driven by television money. Little had changed during the interim, and particularly worrisome was the fact that in the early 1980s the United States provided over 90 percent of all television revenue.

71. Monique Berlioux to Members of the International Olympic Committee, May 18, 1983, "ISL Marketing" File, IOCA.

72. *Minutes of the Meeting of the Commission of New Sources of Financing,* October 9, 1986, Lausanne, p. 5, IOCA.

73. For details on the "give and take" between the USOC and the IOC, see Barney, Wenn, and Martyn, "Family Feud," pp. 64–67.

74. Don Miller to Jürgen Lenz, September 7, 1984, "ISL Marketing" File, IOCA.

75. Barney, Wenn, and Martyn, "Family Feud," p. 69; Baaron Pittenger (USOC, Secretary General) to Juan Antonio Samaranch, March 5, 1988, "ISL/ TOP II General" File, IOCA; and *Minutes of the Meeting of the Commission of New Sources of Financing,* Seoul, September 10, 1988, p. 2, IOCA.

76. *2000 Marketing Fact File* (Lausanne: International Olympic Committee, 2000), p. 2.9.

77. Richard W. Pound, "What Happens When It Goes Wrong?: Notes on the IOC's Trial under Fire, 1998–1999," in Kevin B. Wamsley, Scott G. Martyn, Gordon H. MacDonald, and Robert K. Barney (eds.), *Bridging Three Centuries: Intellectual Crossroads and the Modern Olympic Movement—Fifth International Symposium for Olympic Research* (London, Ontario: University of Western Ontario, 2000), p. 1.

78. Richard Pound confessed to his frustration on this point during a recent public lecture. Richard Pound, "The Olympic Movement: A Personal Reflection on the Past Twenty-three Years," Laurier Lectures Showcase Lecture, October 1, 2001, Wilfrid Laurier University, Waterloo, Ontario.

7

VISIONS AND VERSIONS OF AMERICAN CULTURE AT THE WINTER GAMES

Mark Dyreson

The modern Olympic Games provide sensational stories for the media. Religious controversies, battles over booze, irregularities in bid processes, overzealous civic boosters, hints of political corruption, backroom deal-making, concerns over security, fears of excessive commercialism, the specter of taxpayer-financed boondoggles, disputes over the environment, ambitious politicians engaged in Olympian self-promotion, small cabals of powerful individuals making secretive decisions—each of these in and of itself is a fascinating topic for the "fourth estate." Stir into the mixture a city in the western United States desperate to acquire the Olympics to boost its reputation, schemes to use the Winter Games to boost a local ski industry, Olympic athletes determined to turn athletic stardom into lucrative careers as celebrities, and culture wars over using the Olympics to market a public image—the dramatic potential grows even richer. When all of these engrossing plot lines are wrapped around a narrative core formed by the intense struggles of nations to assert the superiority of their ways of life through sport, they make for an event that even the least creative journalist in the modern world would have a hard time botching in the never-ending quest to capture the attention of the globe's information consumers.

If these lists immediately make you think of the ballyhoo surrounding Salt Lake City's 2002 production of the Olympics, it also works quite well as a description of American views of the Olympic Games in the 1920s and 1930s. Some of the peculiar twists of the Utah Olympic saga, after historical reflection, turn out to be not as unique as commonly assumed. Other facets of the 2002 Olympic epic have, as many of you perhaps suspect, a distinct peculiarity that can only be understood as a product of Utah's cultures.

Long before the contentious debate surrounding whether or not the 2002 Winter Games are in fact the "Mormon Games,"[1] religious battles broke out over American participation in the Olympics. The earlier religious controversies took various forms. In 1900 at the Paris Olympics the leadership of the American team—then a loose collection of college and club squads rather than an official national team—attempted a Sabbatarian ban on competition inspired by evangelical Protestant fervor. The American team attempted to impose this ban on Sunday Olympic competitions both on its own athletes and on those of the rest of the world. U.S. officials demanded that the French organizers start the Olympics on a Saturday that was the most important political holiday on the French national calendar, Bastille Day, July 14, rather than sully the following Sunday with Olympic events. When the French failed to meet American demands to curb Bastille Day celebrations so that the Olympics could avoid a Sunday start, each of the various clubs and colleges that composed the American team decided for its own athletes whether or not competition on the Christian Sabbath was permissible. This process led to strange results. Some American athletes competed on Sunday, and some did not. A Jewish long-jumper, the best in the world in 1900, was banned by the Christian university he attended from competing in his event. Tempers flared among American athletes over the partial boycott and its impact on letting certain American athletes win while others sat on the sidelines. The French and other Europeans were both scandalized and amused by what they perceived as the astounding American parochialism that sparked the Sabbatarian semiboycott.[2]

American religious controversies would quickly intrude again on the Olympics. A famous photograph from the 1908 London Games of American athlete and divinity student Forest Smithson winning the 110-meter hurdles in world record time while clutching a Bible in his hand as a protest against Sunday competitions has become part of the American Olympic canon. Contemporary newspaper stories about the race made no mention of Smithson's unlikely cargo in the race, a detail that no American journalist would have ignored and a sure sign that the famous photograph was staged—adding an additional twist to Smithson's effort to use the Olympics as a religious platform.[3] In the 1930s the controversial, and very nearly successful, effort of a coalition of American groups to block U.S. participation in the 1936 "Nazi" Olympics was led by Jewish, Catholic, and Lutheran activists who martialed their religious communities to the cause by publicizing Nazi oppression of Jews, Catholics, and Lutherans in Germany.[4]

These incidents indicate that the strife over religion swirling around Salt Lake City in 2002 is not without precedent in American Olympic history. The insertion of religious meaning into Olympic performances in American culture, witnessed in Utah by the oft-repeated tale of Latter-day Saint Alma Richards invoking divine aid to win the gold medal in the high jump in 1912 at Stockholm, is certainly not unique to Mormonism.[5] Interestingly, Sabbatarianism remains a powerful element in the contemporary Utah culture wars that will shape the production of the 2002 Olympics. "Shouldn't the Olympic committee be giving Games vs. the Sabbath some serious thought?" joked Latter-day humorist Robert Kirby in a 1998 column of the *Salt Lake Tribune* that could just as easily have been penned in 1900.[6] What made Kirby's jest particularly pointed is the current Utah dispute over access to golf courses, swimming pools, and other public recreation facilities and the scheduling of baseball leagues, basketball tournaments, and football games on days designated by certain groups for religious rites.[7]

Battles over the consumption of alcohol at Olympian locales also pre-date the "Mormon Olympics." American Olympic efforts in the 1920s and early 1930s, in an era in which prohibition had been constitutionalized in the United States, included campaigns to denounce "demon rum" at Olympic venues. At the Paris Olympics of 1924 the American Olympic Committee (AOC) demanded that the French areas housing U.S. athletes be turned into dry zones—a request that the French found ludicrous. The American Olympic leadership also requested that the French get rid of all the bars in the American zone and remove "all signs advertising spirituous liquors." The *New York Times* justified the AOC actions by announcing that "the committee does not fear that the American contenders will overstep the bounds of training rules, but believes that safety first should be the policy and that temptation should be kept out of sight."[8] Those sentiments seem remarkably similar to the rationale of the Utah Division of Alcohol Bever-age Control's resistance to increased advertising of adult beverages during the Olympic carnival—in spite of constitutional law that would seem to prohibit a state from many of the agency's restrictions on promotions of liquor trade.[9]

The American media made booze and the Olympics into a high-profile story during the prohibition era. Two of the leading sportswriters of the 1920s engaged in a running battle over whether prohibition contributed to American Olympic victories—and to those of another dry nation that fared extremely well in Olympian competition: Finland. Nationally syndicated columnist Grantland Rice, noting that the great Finnish Olympic star Paavo Nurmi was allegedly a teetotaler and that Finland, like the United States, practiced prohibition, argued that resistance to the evils of liquor accounted for both Finnish and American prominence in Olympic sport.[10] Rice's great rival for syndication deals in American newspapers, the *New York Herald Tribune*'s sports editor W. O. McGeehan, scoffed at Rice's dry arguments. McGeehan found it hilarious that Rice believed that prohibition actually kept American or Finnish athletes from drinking. He sarcastically hypothe-sized that prohibition created an environment in which "only the hardy, the mentally alert, and the physically durable can survive" since the quest for illicit libations was such a constant and convoluted battle in both the United States and Finland.[11]

American victory in the 1928 Olympics in Amsterdam led Dr. Ernest H. Cherrington, director of the Department of Education of the Anti-Saloon League of America, to jump into the Olympic liquor debate. He gloated that the United States won more championships than the "representatives of nations handicapped by the liquor traffic" and noted that dry Finland ranked higher than its population warranted.[12] When the 1928 American Olympic team arrived back in New York after the Amsterdam sojourn, drys were horrified to learn that customs authorities had seized large quantities of alcohol from athletes' baggage. They discovered the contraband when one of the Olympians dropped his bags at the pier, shattering its spirituous contents.[13] *The World's Work,* a pro-labor journal noted for its wet ways, pardoned the team by observing that "boys will be boys." The magazine also doubted prohibition's effect on American triumphs, positing that "perhaps Mr. Cherrington has not heard of the bootlegger and 'speakeasy.'"[14]

In 1932, with the repeal of the Eighteenth Amendment on the near horizon, U.S. officials vigorously enforced prohibition at both the Winter Games in Lake Placid and the Summer Olympics in Los Angeles. The chief administrator of the Federal Prohibition Department, Amos W. W. Woodcock, told the press that "possession and transportation of liquor is a violation of the law and there is nothing in the act that would enable the prohibition director to extend immunity to visiting athletes." Woodcock added that "only Congress could extend immunity, and it would be interesting to determine whether Congress could do so legally."[15] An American reporter joked that the "Volsteadian difficulties" of imbibing nations might be overcome by customs agents' making "athletic equipment" an extremely broad category that carried some "quasi-diplomatic privileges."[16] The Associated Press (AP) later reported that the French Olympic team had substituted Cuban cane sugar syrup for wine and that "their trainers think it will give them the same pep as the wines of their native land."[17] Seen from this vantage point, Utah's battles over the sale and consumption of alcohol at the 2002 Winter Games were in fashion in the rest of the United States a mere eight decades ago.

Allegations about crooked civic promoters, political corruption, egocentric boosters, irregular bid processes, secret deals, and wasted tax monies swirled around both American sites for the 1932 Olympics, Lake Placid and Los Angeles. In Los Angeles a gang of real estate developers and avaricious city fathers built the Coliseum and lustily propositioned the IOC for every Olympic Games from 1920 on, until they finally won the bid process for the 1932 Olympics. They coveted the Olympic carnival as the ideal event for promoting the burgeoning "city of angels" to the nation and to the world as a thriving modern metropolis that represented the unbridled vitality of the U.S. economy and the sun-kissed future of American civilization.[18] Similarly, in Lake Placid, a small cabal centered in the Lake Placid Club and ruled with an iron fist by Dr. Godfrey Dewey, son of the inventor of the Dewey Decimal library cataloging system, craved the Winter Games as the perfect gimmick for launching their sleepy Adirondack village into contention as the leading ski resort in the North America.[19] The unrestrained boosterism of Los Angeles power brokers and Lake Placid developers echoes in the current rhetoric about the 2002 Winter Games serving as Utah's "great branding moment," to borrow the corporate-speak of Governor Mike Leavitt.[20] The Great Depression ruined many of the dreams of Los Angeles and Lake Placid Olympic boosters, leaving both Olympic sites with serious financial problems and unrealizable promises of huge profits from the anticipated hordes of Olympic fans. History does not offer encouragement to Utah's taxpayers. It is also highly unlikely that Nike and the host of other corporate partners of the Olympics will deferentially cede Olympic "branding moments" to the "pretty, great state" of Utah.

Still, there is no doubt that the Winter Games can provide "branding moments" for sagacious entities and individuals. New York governor Franklin Delano Roosevelt launched his presidential bid with help from an Olympic Games. He championed the 1932 Lake Placid Winter Games as a public works program that epitomized his plan to employ government and private-sector cooperation to combat the Depression's economic malaise. Roosevelt made the Lake Placid Winter Games into a magnificent wintertime photo opportunity to prepare the groundwork for launching his campaign to win the White House the next November. Then, when red ink swallowed the enterprise, Roosevelt cleverly blamed Godfrey Dewey and his cabal for all of the problems that ensued. Roosevelt's Olympic activism stood in stark contrast to the strategy, or lack thereof, of his opponent in the election of 1932, the incumbent Herbert Hoover. President Hoover claimed that he was far too busy wrestling with real political issues to trifle with invitations to appear at either Lake Placid or Los Angeles. Hoover's decision deprived his campaign of a valuable propaganda opportunity when he sent his vice-president to serve as his stand-in before the world's media at the opening ceremonies of a spectacle beloved by the mass public. Hoover's absence was roundly criticized by the press and seemed to confirm the popular notion that the president was out of touch with the common folk.[21]

What Franklin Roosevelt so shrewdly understood and what Herbert Hoover did not grasp was that American tales about the Olympic Games are, to employ the wonderful image that the anthropologist Clifford Geertz crafted to explain both Balinese cockfights and Shakespearean tragedies, stories that we tell ourselves about ourselves.[22] In American culture Olympic tales have always been primarily political allegories about visions of what the United States and the world are or ought to be. Those who cry that Olympic sport should not be connected to politics are hopelessly naive, thoroughly mendacious, or entirely ignorant of the history of the modern Olympic Games—and, for that matter, the ancient Olympics. Indeed, a headline in a 1998 story in the *Deseret News* captured the fundamentally political essence of American Olympic storytelling in ways that would have warmed Clifford Geertz's heart. "A Chance to Tell Utah's Story," the *Deseret News* blared, "But Which One?"[23]

The modern Olympic Games were explicitly designed to provide opportunities for nations and factions to tell stories about their political visions of the world. Europeans and North Americans constructed the modern Olympic Movement during one of the most fervent period of modern nationalism—the late nineteenth and twentieth centuries.[24] The founders of the Olympics, most especially Baron Pierre de Coubertin, intended the Olympics to lead national revivals in their homelands.[25] The model upon which the French nobleman and his aristocratic cronies built the Olympic formula, the international exposition and world's fair craze of the nineteenth and early twentieth centuries, was essentially a stage designed to promote and highlight national differences in levels of progress, science, technology, quality of life, and other supposed markers of civilization.[26] The veneer of internationalism touting the harmony of all humankind that the baron and his confederates on the International Olympic Committee (IOC) coated the Olympic Movement with was itself one of the attractive political ideologies swirling about the cultural waters in which the founders swam.[27] This internationalist gild was not then, nor is it now, strong enough to move national anthems, national uniforms, national flags, and national medal counts even a slight distance away from the center of the Olympic enterprise.[28]

The Winter Games were born a few decades after their Summer cousins in a similar maelstrom of nationalist politics. Before World War I the Scandinavian nations had pressured the IOC for a set of Winter Games. Ice skating had been on the program in 1908. The Germans planned skiing competitions for the Black Forest in 1916 before those Games became a casualty of the Great War. The chief opponent of adding winter sports to the Olympic program was the United States. Fearing any new innovations that might alter their quest to dominate Olympic national standings, American Olympic officials opposed the idea on the grounds that Nordic nations had special advantages in winter sports. After World War I Great Britain and France called for Winter Games. Ice hockey and skating were on Antwerp's

1920 docket of events. In the aftermath of the war the Scandinavian nations had decided that their own Nordic Games were sufficient and did not rally to support the British and French efforts. IOC president Coubertin also opposed the inclusion of winter sports. In spite of the lack of support from Coubertin and Scandinavia, the IOC agreed to stage an experimental winter sports carnival at Chamonix, a resort town for wealthy Europeans in the French Alps, during the winter of 1924. In order to appease nationalists in Scandinavia the IOC labeled the Chamonix contests a "winter prelude" to the Summer Games rather than admit their desire to officially annex winter sports into the Olympic program. Outside of Scandinavia virtually everyone understood that these new Winter Games were in fact part of the Olympics. The United States remained skeptical of the entire affair but did send a team to this first "experimental" Winter Olympics.[29]

The Winter Games were thus added to American Olympic storylines. The first four celebrations of the Winter Games facilitated the interests of American nationalism in two basic ways. They served as fodder for Americans to make fun of European culture and sport and to promote American sporting practices as fundamentally superior. In a paradoxical twist, they also served as an important adjunct to the Summer Olympics in American calculations in the 1920s and 1930s of national rankings of social fitness. Although the IOC in the 1920s had sought to outlaw national medal counts that identified Olympic victors, the American press enthusiastically endorsed these contests, especially since the United States, with one exception (Berlin 1936), thoroughly dominated the Olympic standings in the interwar years.[30] Those two basic storylines have remained at the heart of American tales about the Winter Games. Sometimes the American media make the Winter Olympics into a Barnum circus filled with delightfully incompetent British ski jumpers, hilariously inept Jamaican bobsledders, and trailer park–dwelling, kneecap-shattering American figure skaters. Sometimes the U.S. media wrap an enormous star-spangled banner around a "miracle on ice." These interpretive patterns were set at the first four Winter Games. Both brands of American Olympic storytelling ultimately served the purpose of defining the United States as an exceptional and superior nation—a tradition that has always been at the center of American culture's interests in the modern Olympic Movement.

A FIRST WINTER "PRELUDE": CHAMONIX, 1924

On January 25, 1924, a small band of Olympic contestants tramped through the streets of the French Alpine village of Chamonix carrying their skates, skis, hockey sticks, and bobsleds to the skating rink for the opening ceremonies. In an all too typical scenario, the U.S. team began the first Winter Games by bickering with their hosts. French organizing officials for the Winter Olympics allowed only two trainers per team in the dressing room with the athletes. The U.S. contingent denounced this policy as "open discrimination against the Americans."[31] U.S. officials also complained bitterly when a British referee was chosen for the United States versus Canada hockey final, perceiving that the official would favor his fellow citizens from the commonwealth over the old rebels against the British Empire. The Americans also groused about the scoring in the ski-jumping competition. The U.S. press did not treat the complainers kindly. The *Atlanta Constitution* sarcastically awarded the American team the Olympic title in "round and lofty denunciation."[32] *Pittsburgh Press* sports editor Ralph Davis admonished that "alibis are never popular" and that the Americans should have "taken their medicine without a whine!"[33]

The Chamonix Games began with a star-spangled moment. On January 27, the opening day of competition, American skater Charles Jewtraw won the 500-meter speed-skating sprint—the first event in the history of the Winter Olympics.[34] Jewtraw's gold medal was the only one that the United States won at Chamonix. The U.S. team garnered two silver medals: Beatrix "Betty" Loughran finished in second place in figure skating, and the American hockey team was runner-up behind Canada. According to the American charts of national standing, constructed in violation of IOC policy, Norway "won" the Winter Games with 134 and ½ points to Finland's 76 and ½, Great Britain's 30, the United States' 29, Sweden's 26, and Austria's 25. "The Norwegians showed splendid form in all the events in which they competed," remarked a *New York Times* reporter. "They were in admirable physical condition and displayed a great efficiency in all branches of Winter Sports, with absolute supremacy in the ski events."[35]

The best American ski performance occurred when Anders Haugen of Minneapolis flew fifty meters in the ski jump, five and two meters farther than the nearest competitors. Haugen finished fourth when his "style" points were added to the distance in the complicated process that (in that era) determined the victor. The American team was dismayed by the scoring of the three-judge panel. But Albert Stenge, the Czech judge (along with a Frenchman and a Norwegian), insisted that Haugen's form and style were poor. "He could not begin to compare with the three Norwegians placed ahead of him. The American threw all style aside and beat all efforts only on distance," asserted Stenge. The judges' explanations failed to appease the Americans. The mayor of Minneapolis was so incensed that he wanted to file a protest. He realized it "would not get us anywhere," but lamented, "it certainly is tough."[36] Ironically, the IOC awarded Haugen the bronze medal in the event in 1979 after an arithmetic error in the scoring was discovered by a Norwegian ski historian.[37]

As the first Games ended and the American team headed home, New York City prepared a rousing welcome for the Olympians. Ticker-tape parades through Manhattan for returning summer Olympians had become an American ritual by the 1920s. Tens of thousands of New Yorkers gathered every four years to welcome their conquering athletic heroes back to U.S. shores.[38] City officials planned to meet the liner on which the winter Olympians crossed the Atlantic at the docks. A ceremonial band would hail the athletes. Then they would march to a public reception hosted by a committee representing Mayor John F. Hylan.[39] The proposed Valentine's Day celebration evaporated, however, because of a lack of public interest and the desire of many of the athletes to hurry on to Saranac Lake, New York, for the national skating championships.[40] The first Winter Games were hardly the sporting mega-event that the Summer Olympics had become in the United States by the 1920s.

A general lack of enthusiasm characterized the American media's as well as the public's responses to the Winter Games. The *New York Times* published an indifferent assessment of the first Winter Games. Norway's and Finland's lead did not surprise the *Times* reviewers. The disappointing showings of Canada, which concentrated too much on hockey, and Sweden did. The United States performed "neither better nor worse than might have reasonably been expected," opined the reporters. "There are great sections of this country where there is no ice or snow and it would be surprising if this nation could develop a team capable of defeating those of the North countries where the children learn to skate and ski at an early age and have opportunities for constant practice that are not available here," remarked the *Times* sports department.[41] More typical of American media responses to the first Winter Games than the *New York Times'* reasonable explanation for the failure of the United States to dominate the international contests was a story entitled "Olympic Games Too European" by Bugs Baker of the *Pittsburgh Press.* Baker joked that the Winter Games were not really sporting contests. "American athletes don't stand a chance in stein-grabbing, toy-making or watch repair," sneered Baker. He managed to slur a wide variety of ethnicities and nationalities in his column, including several European groups as well as Turks, Chinese, Indians, and Zulus. "We might win in baseball and subway jamming, but what are we going to do when we meet the Swiss team in the yodeling contest," Baker smirked. He cheered that the 1932 Olympics were scheduled for Los Angeles and predicted that the U.S. team would best the world in "straphanging, rent collecting and bootlegging."[42]

The American media mainly dismissed the first Winter Olympics as the quaint pastimes of Nordics or antiquated absurdities that did not really test the mettle of modern nations. From those perspectives, the fourth-place finish by the United States did not really matter. The treatment of the first Winter Games as a sideshow foisted on the public by IOC's lovable hucksters set a long-standing pattern in the American press for telling stories about the Winter Olympics. The circus continued four years later, at St. Moritz, Switzerland.

A SECOND WINTER PRELUDE: ST. MORITZ, 1928

As the second installment of the Winter Games approached, knowledgeable observers picked the Scandinavian nations to battle among themselves for the winter sports crown, with Germany as a dark horse. The experts predicted that the Americans might have chances to medal in figure skating, speed skating, and the bobsled races. The United States, following bitter internal fighting between the AOC and the U.S. Hockey Association, failed to send a hockey team to the Winter Games to challenge the heavily favored Canadian squad, which hampered the American team's overall strength.[43] Still, U.S. ski jumper Rolf Monsen, who hurt his knee during a training flight, promised that he would "break both legs" in his quest to bring the United States winter glory.[44]

Once again the U.S. press mainly played the Winter Games for laughs—betraying American views of the winter version of Olympics as an amusing but unimportant spectacle. A front-page story in the *New York Herald Tribune* a few days before the festivities began reported that in light of the heavy betting on the event in Europe authorities had placed the Olympic bobsleds under lock and key in order to foil saboteurs who might be inclined to tamper with the sleds. The story quoted U.S. sledder John Heaton, declaring that "anyone tampering with this baby must pick a Yale lock and know the combination of my safety deposit box." The *Herald Tribune* reporter added that Heaton had nicknamed his bobsled "Hell," while fellow U.S. driver William Fiske dubbed his sled "Satan."[45]

A focus on the sex appeal of the women figure skaters mingled with efforts at comedy in other stories. An AP article revealed that the hemlines of female figure skaters had risen to controversial heights. Beatrix Loughran, the American star, favored a somewhat daring knee-length navy-blue skirt. When asked if she would lower her costume to a more modest length, Loughran laughed: "'I just want to be comfortable.'" Sixteen-year-old gold-medal favorite Sonja Henie of Norway sported a more revealing yellow skirt that ended fully two inches above her knee. France's Andree Joly garnered the most attention in what the AP reporter described only as "an extremely abbreviated" red costume.[46] Cheesecake photographs of Winter Games fans also dotted coverage. The *Pittsburgh Press* ran pictures of English women skiing in extremely short shorts. Queen Elizabeth of Belgium was captured cavorting on ice skates in an outfit that was longer than Andree Joly's but hardly Victorian.[47] Sex appeal, skirt scandals, and skulking gamblers spiced American reporters' efforts to interest the public in the St. Moritz festival.

The Second Winter Games opened on February 11, 1928, in blizzard conditions. In the midst of a blinding snowstorm nine hundred athletes from twenty-five countries filed past President Edmund Schulthess of the Swiss Confederation and an estimated one thousand spectators. Dr. Godfrey Dewey, the ski team manager and a Lake Placid, New York, native who was in Switzerland on a mission to garner the 1932 Winter Games for his hometown,[48] carried the American flag before a crowd that, according to the press, was far more concerned with ogling the female Olympians than with the national banners.[49] Certainly the U.S. reporters present focused their attention on the sex appeal of the female Olympians. They telegraphed reports back to the United States that depicted the opening ceremonies as a fashion show. The American women wore bright and flattering red sweaters. The German women also sported red tops with short white skirts, while the French countered with short white skirts set off by light-blue sweaters. The Austrians wore stunning fur coats; the Scandinavian athletes wore colorful and revealing leggings. A brave Belgian woman slogged through the deep snow in chic low-cut shoes and silk stockings.[50]

The U.S. team managed only a bronze medal in the leading sex-appeal event of the Winter Games, women's figure skating, when Beatrix Loughran finished third.[51] Sonja Henie of Norway won the competition with a stunning performance, leading American Olympic team leader Gustavus Kirby to marvel that "it can be stated without fear of contradiction, that the chances are that the world has never seen a more finished, graceful and dexterous skater."[52] The Norwegian skater became the major star to emerge out of the early Winter Olympics. Henie's gold medal at St. Moritz was the first of three consecutive Winter Games figure-skating competitions she would win, catapulting her to global fame and a long career as a movie star in the United States. Indeed, she became the most successful Olympian of her era to jump to the silver screen, enjoying a longer and more lucrative stay in Hollywood than American sprinter Charley Paddock, who dabbled in silent films in the 1920s, or even than American swimmer Johnny Weissmuller—the cinema's legendary Tarzan.[53]

The American press used much of the rest of the St. Moritz program to construct comic articles about the Winter Games. In hockey, without a U.S.

entry to offer a challenge, the heavily favored Canadians easily rolled to victory over teams that the American press depicted as hilarious bumblers.[54] In the skiing events the Scandinavians, to no one's surprise, trampled the American team. U.S. skier Rolf Monsen, whose name did little to distinguish him from his Nordic rivals and relatives but whose style made the difference clearer, finished sixth in the ski jump while managing to break neither of his legs in the effort.[55] Most of the American press saw the skiing events as amusing trifles of little interest to the U.S. public. The American correspondent for the AP in St. Moritz described one skiing race as a particularly absurd event. A military skiing relay, held on opening day of the Winter Games, pitted national teams of four soldiers against one another in a twenty-mile trek through steep mountain passes. According to the AP reporter, skiers, "drunk with fatigue," dropped like flies in the race. Norway won the race, with the Finns second. U.S. reporters happily noted that the French planned to petition the IOC to ban forever this cruel and unusual spectacle from future Olympic programs.[56]

The American press used the French as the punch-line again in a story about the closing ceremonies at which the medals were awarded to the athletes. According to an AP wire service report the brass band playing national anthems at the awards ceremony—breathless after multiple renditions of the Norwegian, Swedish, and Finnish national tunes and even a few refrains of the "Star-Spangled Banner"—bungled its one shot at France's national hymn. As France's champion pairs figure skaters, "the graceful Andree Joly [and her short skirt] and the stalwart Pierre Brunet," marched forward to receive their gold medals, the band struck up a rendition of the "Marseillaise" that collapsed into "an earbreaking, heartrending cacophony." The disharmonic chords brought gasps and then guffaws from the audience, laughed the AP correspondent. "'Can't you play "The Marseillaise"?'" bellowed Franz Reichel, secretary of the French Olympic Committee, at the bandmaster. "'It has been so long since you won an Olympic event we had forgotten it,'" the bandleader retorted.[57]

Sarcastic jabs at French nationalism did not mean that the American press treated U.S. victories in the same manner. Norwegians and Finns dominated most of the skating races.[58] The exception was the 10,000-meter contest, which produced one of the great nationalistic controversies of the 1928 Olympics. Initial reports declared that Irving Jaffee of New York City had beaten the great Norwegian champion Bernt Evensen to capture the gold medal. Soon after Jaffee and Evensen's heat the ice conditions deteriorated under unseasonably warm temperatures and the official in charge of skating events canceled the 10,000 meters. American officials immediately protested the Swiss referee's decision. An IOC committee in St. Moritz initially sided with the Americans and declared Jaffee the victor. The International Skating Federation overruled the IOC and ordered that the 10,000 meters be reskated. A lingering warm snap over the next few days that melted the Lake Moritz ice made that impossible, especially after the Scandinavian skaters abandoned the Winter Games to compete in an important contest in Oslo. Even the American skating team left for other races. The bureaucratic wrangling combined with the warm snap scuttled Jaffee's apparent victory in the 10,000 meters.[59]

A bitter Gustavus Kirby, the leader of the American squad, told the press that "as far as we are concerned, we consider Jaffee the Olympic champion."[60] Sports editor Ralph Davis of the *Pittsburgh Press* groused that the incident "looked like an attempt to shut this country out of any scoring possibilities" and was probably part of a larger plot by jealous rivals to discriminate against American athletic prowess in the Olympics.[61] The U.S. press assured the nation that popular sentiment was on Jaffee's side. Newspaper stories revealed that the Norwegians had hailed Jaffee as the real champion of the 10,000 meters, that a group of Swiss athletes had paraded under a banner proclaiming Jaffee the deserving winner with a caption reading "Long Live America," that European newspaper correspondents indicated that they would recognize Jaffee as the victor, and that even French IOC members demanded that Jaffee be granted an Olympic championship.[62] In his official report Kirby "strongly" advised the United States Skating Association to make an appeal, as he was "personally of the opinion that it may reverse the one man's decision and Mr. Jaffee be awarded first place in the 10,000 meters." The protests did not change the decision. The race went into the record books officially as no contest.[63]

The U.S. team needed no complaints, protests, or excuses in the bobsledding competitions. On the "Cresta," the St. Moritz bobsled run, the American sledders proved themselves the class of the gathering. Brothers Jennison Heaton and J. R. Heaton, American expatriates living in Paris, finished first and second in the skeleton bobsled race. Their victory was an enormous surprise since they beat England's Earl of Northesk, the longtime record-holder on the Cresta, who had never before lost a race on the track. William Fiske of the United States drove himself and his teammates to victory in the four-man bobsled event. An American team piloted by Jennison Heaton finished second.[64] The AP correspondent on the scene joked that Fiske and Heaton took chances "streaking down the bobsleigh chute that would make a man smoking a cigarette sitting over a powder magazine appear as first rate insurance company risk."[65]

Domination in the bobsled events pushed the American team to a surprising second-place finish in the final tabulations of national rankings from

St. Moritz. The *New York Times* reported that Norway had scored 90 and ½ points to capture the first place honors. The United States finished second with 50 and ½. Following Norway and the United States came Sweden with 40, Finland with 39 and ½, Austria with 22, and Canada with 13 and ½.[66] The AP scored the Winter Games in the same order, with the Americans in second place, while giving slightly different point totals to the teams at the lower end of the standings. Had Jaffee's victory as well as the points for his American teammate who finished sixth in the 10,000 meters been figured into the final total, noted the AP, the U.S. score would have risen to 61 and 2 points, a resounding triumph over the third-place Swedes if still short of the Norwegian mark.[67] The unexpectedly strong American performance was even more startling given the failure of the AOC to field a hockey team—which, although it most likely would not have beaten the powerful Canadians, would in all probability have medaled in the Olympic tournament.[68]

The strong American showing in the Winter Games did not alter the media's vision of ice and snowbound Olympics as an absurd, if strangely entertaining, sideshow. From skaters' costumes to sequestered bobsleds to the many protests launched by the United States and other nations at the Winter Games, American commentators relentlessly skewered the winter carnival. The *Pittsburgh Press*'s Ralph Davis, recovering his sarcastic flair after angrily chastising the IOC for the Jaffee affair, poked at the "black eye" that St. Moritz had received for its warm weather.[69] The American press quoted the leader of the Canadian team, complaining that they had come "to play hockey not water polo."[70] An American AP correspondent joshed that the weather proved the "bitter enemy" of the Winter Games, while St. Moritz's extravagant resort prices for room and board made "cost of living" the "undisputed Olympic champion."[71] The *New York Herald Tribune*'s nationally syndicated columnist W. O. McGeehan jested that "Swiss ice, like the cheese of that country, had holes in it." McGeehan dismissed the entire Winter Games as "one protest after another" and counseled the United States to get rid of the 1932 Winter Games by shipping them north of the border to Canada.[72] Indeed, McGeehan's joke about exporting the Winter Games to Canada began to attract serious attention after AOC leader Gus Kirby admitted that such a deal might not be a bad idea.[73]

THE AMERICAN PRELUDE: LAKE PLACID, 1932

In fact, Montreal, Canada, made a bid for the 1932 Winter Games. So did Oslo, Norway, and seven U.S. sites—Yosemite Valley and Lake Tahoe in California, Duluth and Minneapolis in Minnesota, Denver, Colorado, and Bear Mountain and Lake Placid in New York.[74] Even Salt Lake City promoted itself as a potential host.[75] Sources from inside the winning bid committee in Lake Placid claimed that the competition to garner the prize was so intense that one of the California proposals promised the IOC a $3,000,000 war chest for building facilities. Lake Placid asserted in its winning bid that it had resources "which money cannot buy," including great winter weather, wonderful terrain, more experience in hosting winter sports than any other community in the United States, and an ideal location only twelve hours by train from New York City. The small, obscure Adirondack resort hoped that the Winter Games would propel it to the top of the American winter sports heap.[76]

In the early 1930s the American winter sports heap was a very small drift. Winter sports in the United States were mainly the pastimes of small groups of enthusiasts who lived in the rural frost belt. Scandinavian immigrants and their offspring ruled skiing and skating. A few wealthy New Yorkers who spent long periods idling in winter resorts in Europe dominated bobsledding. In fact, the course that Lake Placid built for the 1932 Winter Games was the first bobsled run in North America. Much of the American spectating public preferred the winter versions of the traditional trinity of American sporting life—basketball, the new intercollegiate football bowls sprouting in warm locales, or rumors from baseball's "hot stove league"— to obscure Winter Games.[77] Dr. Godfrey Dewey, the mastermind of Lake Placid's Olympic campaign, hoped that the Winter Games would change the fundamental "psychological attitude of the general public of the United States toward winter sports" and transform his village in the Adirondacks into the center of a new American passion for skiing, skating, and sledding.[78]

Dewey's dreams would not be realized. The upcoming Los Angeles Summer Olympics commanded the vast majority of the public's attention, while Lake Placid's Olympics failed to make a significant dent in popular consciousness. So obscure were the Winter Games that when the Madison Avenue advertising agency contracted to market the Lake Placid gala to the world asked for permission to advertise in American consulates in Europe and Asia, U.S. State Department officials responded by inquiring as to whether or not the little winter festival had any connection to the real Olympic Games in Los Angeles.[79] Even after assurances from the New York public relations firm that Lake Placid's events were indeed part of the official Olympic program, the State Department forgot to include any mention of the Winter Games in the official invitations it sent to the world's nations to come to the 1932 Olympic Games in Los Angeles.[80]

The federal government's lack of attention to the needs of staging an international event in Lake Placid, standing in marked contrast to the intense interest that federal agencies demonstrated in the Los Angeles summer spectacle, betrayed the general lack of interest in winter sports in American culture. While the Departments of State and Commerce were using the Los Angeles Olympics to construct an ambitious campaign to advertise American culture and sell U.S. products around the world, federal bureaucrats were bungling minor details of the Lake Placid Games.[81] The Office of the Comptroller General, the State Department, and the American Consulate in London became embroiled in a nasty dispute over the request to refund a $10 visa fee to an Englishman who was the coach and father of one of the English figure skaters competing in the Games.[82] The issue of whether visas and passports were required of foreign teams for the Winter Games or whether, as international custom since the 1920 Olympics dictated, Olympic identity cards issued by the IOC were good enough for entry into the United States developed into a battle that the State Department failed to contain, which quickly involved the White House, a New York congressman, and several lobbyists. A joint resolution of Congress eventually legalized the identity cards.[83]

One federal blunder concerned the allegedly mysterious identity of one of the foreign athletes. State Department officials worried that Japan might sneak intelligence agents disguised as members of the Japanese Olympic delegation into Los Angeles or even Lake Placid. Heightened security measures were ordered. When a man showed up at the border crossing in Malone, New York, in February 1932, claiming that he was bound for Lake Placid and in possession of a letter from the Canadian Olympic Committee indicating he was a member of Canada's team, immigration officials briefly detained him for failure to have either a visa or an Olympic identity card. Local border agents in New York allowed the man, identified in their records as a "William Russak," who was a citizen of Poland, to enter the United States. Nervous officials in Washington, however, worried that since Russak had been identified as a native Russian, professed Polish citizenship, and claimed he represented Canada, he might in fact be some sort of impostor. The IOC had not invited Russia to the Olympics since the Revolution had given birth to the Communist regime of the Soviet Union. Suspicious State Department officials cabled Lake Placid to make sure Russak was there with the Polish team as a "bona fide delegate" and not at large in the United States on some unknown, and presumably illicit, mission. When Lake Placid's officials could not locate any Russak on the Polish team's roster, the State Department became increasingly anxious. The mystery was solved when the Lake Placid organizers finally figured out that the man in question was actually William "Shorty" Russick, a longtime resident of Flin Flon, Manitoba, Canada, who took third in the Olympic dog-sled races.[84]

Dewey's campaign to convince the public that Winter Games were not strange arctic customs more at home in circus sideshows or immigrant solstice festivals than among regular American sports was certainly not helped by the inclusion of dog-sled races and curling as demonstration sports at Lake Placid. The old Scottish pastime of curling was not really a threat to unseat basketball as America's winter ritual. Nor did dog-sled racing, in spite of the highly publicized appearance of several mushers who had won Canadian and Alaskan races and even the inclusion of the internationally renowned driver of the dog team who had delivered serum to Nome to fight a diphtheria epidemic in the 1920s, have a chance to blossom into anything more than an exotic curiosity in the U.S. sporting pantheon. The third demonstration offering from the Lake Placid crew, women's speed skating, drew a strong field of Canadian and U.S. athletes who turned in world's record performances at every distance they raced. In spite of those amazing achievements women's speed skating was also not likely to burgeon into the nation's newest sporting craze, since men's speed skating— the one Winter Games event in which the United States consistently medaled in the 1920s and 1930s—drew rather small crowds to its most prestigious American competitions.[85]

To draw real attention to the Winter Games the Lake Placid Club should have pushed the IOC to premiere basketball at its Olympics. Instead, it left that sport for Nazi Germany to debut at the 1936 Summer Olympics in Berlin. Failing to garner basketball, Dewey and his cronies did manage for the first time to marry the Winter Games to the modern advertising industry by hiring a New York City firm to craft a campaign for "merchandising" the Lake Placid Olympics. The publicity agents placed stories in national and international newspapers and magazines; signed American Express as a sponsor to spread Lake Placid posters and booklets around the world; garnered endorsement deals with steamship lines, railroads, and travel agencies; put roadside billboards up all over New York; and endorsed window displays for department and sporting goods stores all over the northeastern United States. They maneuvered for a U.S. postage stamp commemorating the third Olympic Winter Games and hosted a meeting of newspaper publishers to promote coverage. Lake Placid's publicity department negotiated for extensive coverage of the Games in American newsreels and signed radio contracts with both major U.S. broadcasting agencies, the Columbia Broadcasting System (CBS) and the National Broadcasting Company (NBC). Listeners from coast-to-coast could tune in for Olympic coverage. Short-wave broadcasts sent American radio feeds across the Atlantic to Europe. The Lake Placid organizing committee spent about 20 percent of its operating budget ($202,500 out of a $1,045,000 total budget went to publicity, office administration, and travel and entertainment) on generating public interest in the 1932 Winter Games.[86]

While Lake Placid's advertising blitz failed to generate long-term American interest in skiing, skating, sledding, curling, or even dog-sled racing, New York's governor, Franklin Delano Roosevelt, decided that the Games would serve as a great "branding moment" in his quest for the American presidency. Roosevelt cleverly attached his administration to Lake Placid's Olympics and funneled public monies into the project in an effort to make the third Winter Games into a model program of public and private enterprise combining to fight the Great Depression. He promised that the Olympics would bring jobs, tourist dollars, and new vitality to New York's economy. The state provided $500,000 of the $1,045,000 budget for the Lake Placid Olympics.[87] Roosevelt's one defeat in his Olympic campaign occurred when efforts to build the bobsled course on state forest lands brought one of the first environmental clashes in Olympic history. A New York conservation group, the Association for the Protection of the Adirondacks, successfully used the state courts to declare the state's plans to erect a sled run on protected public lands unconstitutional—an ironic portent of the role of the judiciary later in the New Deal.[88] Environmental activists have been nowhere near as successful in disputes along the Wasatch Front as their predecessors were in Lake Placid.

Governor Roosevelt also made sure that he was at the center of the festivities on the frigid February day in Lake Placid when the third Olympic Winter Games began. The parade of nations—seventeen teams in the depression-wracked world made it to the Games[89]—tromped past Roosevelt. The American team dipped the "Stars and Stripes" to New York's head of state. This discredits the treasured but inaccurate American myth that holds that ever since 1908 in London, when the American flag bearer allegedly growled that "this flag dips for no earthly king," the national banner has never been lowered in an Olympian parade.[90] Roosevelt gave a short speech to open the Winter Games and then immediately moved to his next photo opportunity. The governor and Mrs. Roosevelt stayed after the opening ceremonies and watched as Lake Placid native Jack Shea won a gold medal in the first event: the 500-meter speed-skating race. Later that afternoon Eleanor Roosevelt took a wild ride down the bobsled run with the top American driver. That evening the Roosevelts attended an IOC dinner, at which the governor stressed the importance of the Olympics in building international friendships.[91]

International friendship took a backseat to national flag-waving as NBC and CBS broadcast a fortnight's worth of stunning upsets from Lake Placid.

Forty-eight years before a much better known "miracle on ice" at the same site, the United States pulled off an unlikely victory in Lake Placid. The heavily favored Scandinavians dominated skiing, but the United States won all four speed-skating events and both bobsled competitions and finished second to Canada in the hockey tournament to garner a total of six golds, four silvers, and three bronzes to runner-up Norway's three golds, four silvers, and three bronzes. American reporters celebrated the U.S. victory as an astounding upset "because the Norse had been skating and skiing in the frozen North for centuries," while Americans had only recently begun to compete in winter sports.[92] Ignoring as usual IOC protocol, the American media and Lake Placid officials reveled in creating national standings, which crowned the U.S. team as Winter Games champions for the first time. American experts gave the United States 103 points, followed by Norway with 77, Canada with 49, Sweden with 28, and Finland with 25.[93]

In some quarters, even in the United States, the unexpected American victory in Lake Placid was taken with a grain of salt. The Great Depression had made it difficult for other nations to send strong teams to the first American Winter Games. Cynics such as *New York Sun* reporter Edwin B. Dooley noted that the ninety-odd members of the U.S. team totaled only a few more medals than did the handful of Norwegians who ventured to Lake Placid. Dooley's opinion was in part corroborated by one of the intriguing stories about New York's Winter Games. Admiral Robert Byrd actually scouted the Olympics in search of skiers for one of his South Pole expeditions. He was looking for Scandinavian skiers, not Americans. U.S. performances in skiing certainly did not change his mind.[94]

Rancorous debates about American fair play and sportsmanship broke out in speed skating and bobsledding. The use of U.S. rules in speed skating—where competitors raced slowly in large groups for many laps and conserved energy for last-second sprints rather than following the European method of racing two skaters at a time, with the clock deciding the victor—infuriated foreign teams. Irving Jaffee won the 10,000-meter title he had lost to warm weather and bureaucratic wrangling in 1928, but not without a storm of accusations that the American rules let the slower but craftier skater win.[95] American officials also frequently closed the bobsled course after opening practice runs by U.S. teams returned opinions that conditions were too dangerous on the mountain. Foreign teams demanded that they be allowed to practice regardless of the safety issues and accused the Americans of trying to keep competitors from familiarizing themselves with the track in order to guarantee the U.S. bobsledding victories.[96]

The startling U.S. triumph in the "unofficial standings" failed to prevent American reporters from turning the Winter Games into the sports world's leading comic spectacle. "More than a million words already have been telegraphed from here about the games," speculated *New York Herald Tribune* reporter Harry Cross.[97] Many of those words were sarcastic attacks on prohibition-era Lake Placid's pretensions to European winter-resort status, on the uncooperative Adirondack weather, on the notion that international sport contributed to global harmony, and on winter sports in general.[98] The American media frequently treated the Winter Games as a carnival sideshow. Pre-Olympic coverage focused on sleds flying off the bob run and mangling foreign competitors, especially the Germans. Graphic descriptions of fractured skulls, broken bones, and life-threatening injuries filled newspapers. Especially popular were tales of sledders whose previous injuries had kept them out of earlier Winter Games and who ended up in Lake Placid's hospital for the duration of the 1932 competitions.[99] Those stories made Eleanor Roosevelt's thrilling trip down Mount Van Hoevenberg on opening day a remarkably shrewd public relations coup for her husband's campaign.

Other reports poked fun at the gaudy costumes various nations sported on opening day, snickered at the novice Japanese ski jumpers who seemed destined to fatal performances, and kept tabs on the constant bickering among both speed and figure skaters. The mysteries of the Norwegian cult of ski waxing and the oddities of curling provided valuable material for Olympic mirth-makers. So, too, did the constant reports on the insufferable American hosts, on America's insufferable Canadian neighbors, and on America's insufferable foreign rivals. Guffaws about the hemlines of female figure skaters' costumes continued to be a staple.

No one had more fun at the Winter Games' expense than did the venerable sports editor of the *New York Herald Tribune,* W. O. McGeehan, who exiled himself from the comforts of Manhattan to rustic Lake Placid for the Olympics. He savaged all the usual Olympic targets while also flaying Governor Roosevelt's efforts to use the Lake Placid Games as a political stage. From his jab that revenue agents on skis had invaded Lake Placid in search of the alcoholic contraband sequestered in the little kegs tied around St. Bernard guide dogs' necks to his observation that the ancient Greeks had not indulged in ski jumping since they preferred hemlock for suicide in order to keep the body looking good for the funeral, McGeehan missed few opportunities to parody the Winter Games. He made the sled dogs the heroes of Lake Placid's Olympics, noting that they manifested far more "sportsmanship and graciousness" than many of the "human competitors." McGeehan lamented that the poor dogs were not medal eligible even though the canines seemed to best embody the supposed Olympic spirit of festive communal harmony. "But you cannot expect the dogs to grasp the real significance of international sport," he sarcastically concluded.[100] Humans, as McGeehan understood, knew that international sport was primarily about the demonstration of national prowess. The next episode of the Winter Games, scheduled to return to the European Alps at the German resort of Garmisch-Partenkirchen, would underscore that reality.

The final news stories from the Third Winter Games were about red ink. The Olympics left Lake Placid with a deficit of more than $50,000. But if the town's taxpayers greeted that news with something less than enthusiasm, finance committee chairman Willis Wells painted a rosy picture of the Games as a long-term boost for the region's economy. He and his cronies at the Lake Placid Club assured anyone who listened that the Olympics were the town's "branding moment." They were certain the Olympics would make Lake Placid the center of a lucrative American skiing boom.[101] That boom would not appear for several more decades. When it did come, its center was not Lake Placid or the Adirondacks but the new resorts that sprouted in the second half of the twentieth century in the American West, especially those in Colorado—a state that in the 1970s would have the audacity to reject the Winter Games as a frivolous boondoggle.[102]

THE NAZI PRELUDE: GARMISCH-PARTENKIRCHEN, 1936

Germany's use of the 1936 Games as a "branding moment" for National Socialism kept the Olympic Games at the forefront of New York's political frays for the four years following Lake Placid's Olympic season. The American Olympic Movement had historically been centered in New York City. Efforts to boycott the "Nazi Olympics," as they were quickly dubbed in the American press, arose in New York City. The counter-effort to ensure American participation also began there. The boycott very nearly succeeded, but the United States eventually decided to participate in both the Summer and Winter Olympics in 1936.[103] The decision to take part did not diminish the political tensions surrounding the Olympics. Arriving in Germany for the Winter Games, longtime AOC official Gustavus Kirby claimed nearly total ignorance of European politics, going so far as to admit that he did not know what color of shirts the Nazi Party favored. Yet the supposedly nonpolitical Kirby demanded that Hitler keep "Nazi propaganda" out of the Games.[104]

The Nazi regime located the fourth Winter Games in two small villages seemingly sprung to life from a fairy tale in the heart of the Bavarian Alps. The German government spent 3 million marks ($1,200,000) turning the picturesque villages of Garmisch and Partenkirchen into a winter playground as the first exhibit in their "carefully primed" plan to convert the world to adoration for National Socialism. A foreign correspondent in *Time* warned American readers that the Germans hoped that the visiting athletes and tourists might be overwhelmed by hospitality and "would afterward scatter to the world as friendly missionaries for the Third Reich."[105]

Having learned from the United States that the Olympics provided excellent opportunities for marketing national culture, the Germans set about to make certain that the 1936 version of the Olympic Winter and Summer festivals would be dazzling commercials for the "New Germany."[106] As Nazi sports commissar Hans Von Tschammer und Osten put it, in order to make "everyone feel . . . at home" at Garmisch-Partenkirchen, the German government commanded German spectators not to wear military uniforms, hid anti-Semitic newspapers and placards, and ordered the nation to present a hospitable face to the foreigners. In the Bavarian villages around the Olympic site price-gouging was prohibited, and residents were given lessons in English and French to serve foreign visitors better.[107] As an added attraction, American reporters promised potential visitors that—unlike dry Lake Placid in the prohibition year of 1932—tourists would find "unsurpassed beer in every café and restaurant" surrounding Garmisch-Partenkirchen.[108] The facade proved so alluring that the lead *New York Times* reporter covering the fourth Winter Games, Frederick Birchall, declared that "there is probably no tourist here who will not go home averring that Germany is the most peace-loving, unmilitaristic, hospitable and tolerant country in Europe and that all the foreign correspondents stationed here are liars."[109]

The Americans, accustomed to asserting their own versions of nationalism in Olympic forums, realized that they faced a difficult task in defending the Winter Olympic crown they had commandeered in Lake Placid. Without the "home snow" advantage the United States was in trouble.[110] That was especially true since, as *Time*'s athletic expert honestly admitted, "of the 1,000 best skiers of the world, at least 950 are Scandinavians."[111] Most pundits predicted a Norwegian victory and strong showings by the Finns and Swedes. Still, the United States had hopes for bobsledding, hockey, and skating victories.[112]

The fourth Winter Games opened on February 6, 1936, in a fierce snowstorm. A crowd estimated at somewhere between fifty thousand and eighty thousand braved the weather to watch as Hitler, flanked by most of the luminaries of the Third Reich, presided over the opening ceremonies.[113] The Austrians received the most appreciative roar from the crowd.[114] The Americans guaranteed themselves a frosty reception when they botched an "eyes right" greeting—the traditional Olympic salute seemed too near the Nazi salute for American comfort—and refused to dip their flag as they passed by Hitler.[115] Some American competitors at Garmisch-Partenkirchen professed that "they could see little connection between sports and politics" in the Olympic arena.[116] Most members of the American team was more honest. An American skier, Robert Livermore, Jr., found the opening ceremony a poorly executed propaganda statement for the Third Reich. He accused Hitler, whom he and the other skiers referred to as "Mr. Smith" in order "to avoid embarrassment in conversation," of appearing "rather sloppily dressed in an old trench coat over the official brown shirt." Livermore thought that Hitler had failed to provide the kind of magnetic public performance the German leader's reputation promised. Livermore also swore that both the Austrian and Italian teams gave Hitler the fascist rather than the Olympic salute.[117] *Time*'s reporter at the Winter Games described Hitler, his "tiny mustache white with snowflakes," gazing "yearningly at the mountain tops" located just across the German border in Austria.[118]

The United States failed spectacularly in its quest to keep the Winter Games crown. Albion Ross of the *New York Times* characterized the American team's performance as "one disappointment or downright catastrophe after another." With the Americans blundering their way to a fifth-place finish, the Scandinavians garnered "sweet revenge" for their losses in Lake Placid.[119] Norway overwhelmed the competition to take top honors in the myriad of "unofficial" polls. The Norwegians dominated, scoring 121 points to Germany's 57. Sweden finished with 49, Finland 41, the United States 35 and ½, Austria 29 and ½, and Great Britain 25. Only Alan Washbond and Ivan Brown, who "brought home the bacon on the old tin runners" in the two-man bobsled race, managed gold medals for the United States.[120]

In *Scholastic* magazine Jack Lippert explained to American schoolchildren why the United States had failed so miserably in Germany. Bickering and arrogance among the U.S. bobsledders had destroyed most of their medal chances. Lippert disclosed that one American bobsledding pilot had referred to the German course as a "sissy run" he could take "blindfolded while munching on a Limburger cheese sandwich" and then smashed his sled on the first trip down the mountain. American speed skaters suffered from the change to the European style of rules rather than the American style that had prevailed in Lake Placid. Finally, Lippert noted, the Scandinavians had a huge weather advantage over the Americans in training for winter sports. Those factors accounted for the disappointing fifth-place finish for the Americans, reported Lippert to his young readers.[121]

While Lippert broke the bad news of American bungling to the nation's schoolchildren, other U.S. reporters crafted stories out of their traditional winter mixture of nationalism and sensationalism. Once again the Winter Games became a circus of strange events practiced by odd peoples from arctic climates. As in Lake Placid, the spectacle of bobsleds flying off the track and threatening lives and limbs proved a popular topic.[122] Alpine skiing, on the program for the first time, threatened to supplant bobsledding and ski jumping as the Winter Games' most dangerous show. The American press depicted the downhill races as a series of comic calamities.[123] The *New York Times*' Paul Gallico joked that the scene at Garmisch-Partenkirchen looked like a war zone, with injured people on canes, on crutches, and in wheelchairs crowding the village streets. "They were all skiing casualties," he noted with a laugh.[124]

Comedy and national conflict dominated American interpretations of the 1936 Winter Games. A story in *Collier's* magazine hoped that a "Pax Olympica" might result from events at Garmisch-Partenkirchen; but, as usual, international clashes plagued the Winter Games.[125] Speed skaters cried about lack of practice time provided by the German organizers. Figure skaters, particularly the regal three-time champion Sonja Henie, hollered about national bias in judging. Hockey produced perhaps the most intense national rancor. During one match a French player bit a Hungarian opponent. The Americans complained about Italy's rough play and the ploy used by an Italian goalkeeper—he hid the puck in his pants.[126] Everyone complained about the English hockey team, which had upset the favored Canadians to win the gold. Apparently the English team contained two Canadian nationals who were well-known European "non-amateurs." AOC leaders Avery Brundage and Gustavus Kirby fumed over the English tactics. Kirby railed that the Canadians on the English squad were "'crooks not good enough to become honest professionals.'"[127]

In fact, the English were not the only team employing Canadians. American sportswriters pointed out that the U.S. team had one player who had lived in Canada most of his life and starred at Montreal's McGill University. Dan Parker of the *New York Daily Mirror* recalled that in 1924 the U.S. team had four Canadians who "took the oath of American citizenship the night before the boat sailed for Europe."[128] After Italy defeated the United States in a hockey match, John Kieran wrote in his *New York Times* column that he had overheard a subway rider remark that he had not known there were so many Canadians living in Italy.[129]

Paul Gallico wove the themes of nationalism and sensationalism together in his coverage of women's figure skating. He promoted the sex appeal of the women figure skaters. "What lovely legs and bodies those figure-skaters have!" he exclaimed. "And how well those graceful skating costumes show them off!" Gallico rhapsodized that the figure skaters represented the "rhythmic poetry of the human figure in motion." Still, his lustful admiration for their figures did not temper his sarcastic view of their sport. He declared the "school figures" portion of their competitions an absurd bore governed by comical judges who stared as the skaters' tracings on the ice with "all the hawk-like keenness of Sherlock Holmes looking for a footprint." Gallico also asserted that Olympic figure skating contests were "for the most part as completely and joyously crooked and bought and sold as an prize-fight or wrestling championship." He charged that European skating judges were "as fine a set of scamps and vote-peddlers as you ever laid eyes on." No American, claimed Gallico, would ever win an Olympic skating championship since the promoters of European ice carnivals who made enormous profits from promoting skating would never willingly pay the freight for shipping an Olympic heroine from across the Atlantic. He said that at Garmisch-Partenkirchen a European judge had entered the American locker-room on a vote-swapping sortie. The Americans threw the judge out. That decision, according to Gallico, accounted for the poor American showing in figure skating at the fourth Winter Games.[130] Frederick Birchall confirmed Gallico's report and indicated that "sinister rumors" might lead to an "official investigation" of Olympic figure-skating corruption.[131]

The intense nationalism displayed in the Winter Games made the already cynical media even more suspicious of the much ballyhooed Olympic ideal of peaceful internationalism flowing from athletic encounters. *Scholastic*'s Jack Lippert not only detailed the failings of U.S. athletes to American schoolchildren but also warned his young readers to be wary of the common claim that the Olympics contributed to international amity. "There is no evidence that the games serve this purpose, and there is plenty of evidence that they do not," he asserted. Lippert told American youth that the Olympics were marked by constant "quarreling, bickering, and protesting" among the national teams. "At Garmisch the display of bad sportsmanship was worse than ever, and an outstanding offender was our own American Olympic president, Avery Brundage," Lippert averred. "National pride" rather than international understanding was the essence of the Olympics, he concluded.[132]

Many commentators concurred with Lippert's assessment. John Kieran of the *New York Times* related his humorous run-in with a Norwegian living in New York City who demanded more coverage in the American papers of "'Babe Ruth on skis'"—gold-medal ski jumper Birger Ruud.[133] In the *New York Herald Tribune* columnist Richards Vidmer—W. O. McGeehan's successor—suggested that Olympic officials give up their delusions about "amity" and focus instead on the Olympian contribution to "the idea of promoting international enmity." Such a shift, he assured his audience, would make the Olympics "appear to be a howling success." Vidmer sarcastically concluded that "as long as we retain that idea about the

Olympics serving to promote international amity, every time there's a little unpleasantry we're going to shake our heads and lift our eyes with the expression of a prohibitionist watching a debutante down a cocktail." In the final analysis, he asserted, "the only thing anybody cares about anyway is who won."[134]

Vidmer's perspective that winning was the only thing that really mattered reverberated in American media coverage of the fourth Winter Games. Numerous pundits worried that Germany's second-place finish in the winter events signaled that the Third Reich had gotten the message that victory was the best form of propaganda in international sport and that the Germans might challenge American supremacy in the summer Olympics. *Time* reported that the Germans practiced sport with "religious intensity."[135] In an article for *Collier's* Edwin Muller fretted that this religious intensity and the German "form of government would seem to give them a certain advantage over our old-fashioned democracy" in winning tests of prowess in international sport.[136] Muller's worries reflected a growing concern in the 1930s among certain American thinkers that the republican form of government was less efficient than the statist regimes of Europe.

The American defeat at Garmisch-Partenkirchen and the looming fears that the loss symbolized a national decline had some unexpected consequences. One of the leading voices in the fight to boycott the "Nazi Olympics," the Catholic weekly *Commonweal,* concurred in the analysis that the Third Reich had made sport a "national religion." Curiously, *Commonweal* did not renew its call for the United States to pull out of the Berlin Olympics but instead urged Americans to shake off their "feeble fifth"-place finish and to reclaim their position as the leading nation in the twentieth century's burgeoning global sporting culture. "We have an infinitude of athletic material to draw on, a natural athletic and competitive spirit to sustain us, and plenty of cold territory up and down the country to practice in," *Commonweal* cheered. "Perhaps we needed this lesson to start us going," the editors continued. "And if, in the process of coming forward again, the glories in fun and the gains in health of cold-weather games are spread over the total population, as they should be, the 1936 winter Olympics results will turn out not to have been a defeat, after all," they cried. The Catholic weekly looked forward to an American resurgence at the next Winter Games scheduled for Japan in 1940. The *Commonweal* thus transformed itself from a forum for opposing American participation in the 1936 Olympics into a cheerleader for American athletic nationalism.[137]

In other places in the United States in the wake of the American debacle at Garmisch-Partenkirchen, new dreams sprouted about how the nation might increase its medal count in future Olympic Games. No doubt the publishers of *Commonweal* were heartened by the news that broke during the fourth Winter Games that Babe Ruth, recently retired from the New York Yankees, had been named the "commandant" of the American effort to include baseball in the Olympic Games. Ruth was slated to help in the selection of two U.S. teams scheduled to present a baseball demonstration at Berlin's Summer Olympics and to serve as the leading ambassador for baseball's inclusion on the Olympic program.[138] The American plan to make baseball an Olympic sport, a stratagem reminiscent of the more recent use of "dream teams" to maintain U.S. dominion over Olympic basketball, underscored the fact the most Americans concurred with Richards Vidmer's sentiments that at the Olympics "the only thing anybody cares about anyway is who won."[139] Making the American national pastime an Olympic sport would seemingly guarantee future gold medals for the United States. If only Ruth could have managed to persuade the IOC to hold a baseball tournament in the winter at some balmy locale far from the skiers, sledders, and skaters then perhaps the United States might have had a chance to add to its future wins in Winter Games. Interestingly, Olympic baseball, when the sport finally debuted nearly five decades after Ruth and the Americans tried to put it on the official program, has not usually been a boon for the U.S. medal count.

Babe Ruth's Olympic baseball campaign and the stories that Americans told about the first four Winter Games reveal the centrality of nationalism in American understandings of the Olympics. The relentless focus on national standings and medal counts and on national conflicts and controversies underscores that perspective. American chroniclers concentrated on how symbols of national identity appeared in every nook and cranny of the Olympic spectacles, from the opening ceremonies to the athletes' diets and drinking habits. When the U.S. team did well, the nation's storytellers celebrated U.S. victories as evidence for American exceptionalism. Olympic victories in the winter, just as in the summer, signified the superiority of American society. When the U.S. team performed poorly in the Winter Games, as it often did, American storytellers generally dismissed the games as frivolous exercises or bizarre arctic customs.

In general, American reporters framed the Winter Games as an amusing diversion filled with strange events and odd foreigners. The clear message was that winter sports such as skiing, skating, and sledding were not principal elements in American national culture. Norway's "Babe Ruth" might have been a ski jumper, but no American would ever rise to the celebrated status of the "sultan of swat" by strapping boards onto his feet and becoming the "sultan of the skis." In American minds the Winter Games were then, as they are in many ways now, really about the national identities of other nations. That made them fair game for the sarcastic scribblings of American writers who wanted to spread some levity and sell some newspapers during the winter doldrums of the American sporting calendar.

Given those historical realities, the choice to make the Winter Olympics Utah's "branding moment" for the twenty-first century is probably not the wisest strategy for local image-makers to adopt. Even without the bid scandal that landed Salt Lake City's Games in every late-night television comic's storehouse of sure-fire jokes and in the crime sections of the world's newspapers, the Winter Games would still be a major target of opportunity for journalists interested in the curiosities of the world of sport. For a culture hoping to use the 2002 Olympics to prove that it is not peculiar but instead reassuringly mainstream, Hunter S. Thompson's musings on Salt Lake City's "hideous worldwide Karma" from the Olympic imbroglio are probably not a hopeful portent.[140] The tragedies of September 11, 2001, will no doubt shift the media focus away from a circus on skis and skates toward a star-spangled spectacle to some degree.[141] Will it blur the distinctions surrounding American versions of nationalism to the point where no inquiring investigative reporter speculates about whether Utah's true national holiday is the fourth of July or the twenty-fourth of July (Pioneer Day, celebrating the arrival of Mormons in 1847)? That remains to be seen.

Notes

1. The "Mormon Games" label has been applied by a host of local, national, and international media in the years since Salt Lake City won the 2002 bid. John Harrington's "The Mormon Games," *Salt Lake City Weekly,* March 12, 1998, was an early and provocative declaration about Mormon influence in the 2002 Winter Games. By the turn of the century, media around the world had picked up on the label, as England's well-respected *Manchester Guardian* illustrated in a story proclaiming that "the Mormons see the Olympics as an unprecedented opportunity to spread their message" (Duncan Mackay, "Mormons in Dry Run for Olympics," *Manchester Guardian,* February 8, 2001). SLOC leader Mitt Romney, a member of the Church of Jesus Christ of Latter-day Saints, condemned the "Mormon Games" designation as "divisive and demeaning" (Linda Fantin, "Romney Summons Civic Leaders, Pops Champagne to Attack 'LDS Olympics' Charge," *Salt Lake Tribune,* March 17, 2001; Mitt Romney, "Uniting the Community," *Deseret News,* March 18, 2001). In the spring of 2001 the *Salt Lake Tribune* ran a series of major articles on Mormon connections to the Olympics. The stories noted that the "Mormon Games" issue had appeared in a host of print and electronic media, including National Public Radio, the *Seattle Times,* the *Philadelphia Inquirer,* the *Boston Herald,* the *New York Times,* the *Washington Monthly,* the *Winnipeg Free*

Press, the *Sydney Morning Herald,* the *Irish Times,* and *The Economist.* See Christopher Smith and Bob Mims, "SLOC and LDS Church Downplay the Church's Involvement in the Olympics," *Salt Lake Tribune,* March 18, 2001; Linda Fantin, Bob Mims, and Christopher Smith, "From SLOC Leadership to Liquor, Church Has Long Had a Powerful Olympic Voice," *Salt Lake Tribune,* March 18, 2001; "Special Treatment for the Church," *Salt Lake Tribune,* March 18, 2001; "Non-LDS Religious Leaders Cite Minimal Input," *Salt Lake Tribune,* March 18, 2001. Other media in Utah challenged the "Mormon Games" moniker as divisive. See especially Lisa Riley Roche, "Not the 'Mormon Games,'" *Deseret News,* March 16, 2001; Lisa Riley Roche, "Notion of LDS Games Lingers," *Deseret News,* March 17, 2001. Indeed, the *Salt Lake Tribune*'s March 18, 2001, series on the "Mormon Olympics" sparked a major "Credibility Roundtable" sponsored and published by the newspaper about bias in media coverage of religion in Utah. See "Are Utah's Religions Covered Fairly?" *Salt Lake Tribune,* April 29, 2001. The contentious debates within Utah about the "Mormon Olympics" or "Mo-lympics" designation continue to generate national attention. See Kenneth L. Woodward, "A Mormon Moment," and Ana Figueroa, "Salt Lake's Big Jump," *Newsweek,* September 10, 2001, 44–53. As the *Newsweek* story broke, SLOC president Romney continued to decry the "Mormon Olympics" designation, while SLOC public relations officials schemed to "put an end" to "Mormon Olympics" stories. Linda Fantin, "'Mormon Games' Annoys Romney," *Salt Lake Tribune,* August 30, 2001. One sign that the label does capture certain realities about Utah's presentation of the Olympic extravaganza is that even the *Deseret News,* owned and operated by the Church of Jesus Christ of Latter-day Saints, has speculated that the Olympics have generated a widening split over a series of cultural and religious issues between Mormons and non-Mormons within Utah. Carrie A. Moore, "Will Games Help Unite or Widen Split over Faith?" *Deseret News,* February 9, 2001.

2. Caspar Whitney, "The Way of the Sportsman," *Outing* 36 (July 1900): 423–424; Caspar Whitney, "The Sportsman's View-Point: Mug Hunters and Disregarded Agreements at Paris Games," *Outing* 36 (August 1900): 566–567; Caspar Whitney, "The Sportsman's View-Point: Broken Faith at the Paris Games," *Outing* 36 (September 1900): 678–679; George Orton, "The Paris Athletic Games," *Outing* 36 (September 1900): 690–692; "Yankee Athletes Barred," *New York Times,* July 16, 1900, p. 5; "Americans Win at Paris," *Chicago Tribune,* July 16, 1900, p. 8; "Seven More Victories," *Chicago Tribune,* July 17, 1900, p. 9. For an overview of the efforts to impose American culture on the Paris Games, see Mark Dyreson, *Making the American Team: Sport, Culture, and the Olympic Experience* (Urbana: University of Illinois Press, 1998), pp. 53–72.

3. Dyreson, *Making the American Team,* p. 147.

4. Richard Mandell, *The Nazi Olympics* (New York: Macmillan, 1971); Allen Guttmann, *The Games Must Go On: Avery Brundage and the Olympic Movement* (New York: Columbia University Press, 1984).

5. Lee Benson and Doug Robinson, *Trials and Triumphs: Mormons in the Olympic Games* (Salt Lake City: Deseret Book, 1992), p. 5.

6. Robert Kirby, "Why Not Close State Roads on the Sabbath?" *Salt Lake Tribune,* April 16, 1998.

7. "Golf, Swim on Sunday?" *Salt Lake Tribune,* January 7, 1994; "The Mayor Shanks One in Provo," *Salt Lake Tribune,* January 10, 1994; "No Golf on Sunday?" *Salt Lake Tribune,* March 10, 1994; "Provo Mayor Again Makes Waves by Closing City Pool on Sunday," *Salt Lake Tribune,* July 14, 1994; "Into the Drink with This Decision," *Salt Lake Tribune,* July 17, 1994; "Non-Mormon Clergy in Utah Want Pool Open Sundays," *Salt Lake Tribune,* April 27, 1995; Robert Kirby, "Close Pool on Sunday?" *Salt Lake Tribune,* June 28, 1995; Robert Kirby, "Provo Pool Controversy to Make More Waves," *Salt Lake Tribune,* June 30, 1995; Peter Scarlett, "Non-LDS Faiths in Utah County Grow in Small Steps," *Salt Lake Tribune,* July 5, 1997; Paul Rolly and JoAnn Jacobsen-Wells, "Sometimes on Sunday," *Salt Lake Tribune,* September 19, 1997; Phil Miller, "Provo Candidates Awash in Pool Politics," *Salt Lake Tribune,* October 4, 1997; "Y. in Trouble If NCAA Allows Sunday Play," *Salt Lake Tribune,* April 20, 1998; Patrick Kinahan, "Sunday Play an Old Problem for BYU," *Salt Lake Tribune,* April 21, 1998; Kurt Kragthorpe, "NCAA's Decision Tempers BYU's Cougar Classic Victory Celebration," *Salt Lake Tribune,* April 23, 1998; Joe Baird, "NCAA to Play on Sunday But Y. Won't," *Salt Lake Tribune,* April 23, 1998; "Never on Sunday," *Salt Lake Tribune,* April 24, 1998. Apparently, the NCAA is in the process of reconsidering the policy. See Michael C. Lewis, "NCAA Board Changes Mind on BYU Rule," *Salt Lake Tribune,* August 12, 1998; Dan Harris, "Mayor Wants to Ban Monday Night Baseball," *Salt Lake Tribune,* March 27, 1998; "Monday Night Baseball," *Salt Lake Tribune,* April 1, 1998; "Never on Sunday," *Salt Lake Tribune,* April 14, 1998; Edward McDonough, "Utah Mayors Are Acting Tyrannically," *Salt Lake Tribune,* May 3, 1998.

8. "Wants Dry Village for Olympic Teams," *New York Times,* June 28, 1924. See also "Olympic Contenders Show to Form in Paris," *Norfolk Journal and Guide,* July 5, 1924.

9. Norma Wagner, "Groups: Ban Beer Sponsors in Olympics," *Salt Lake Tribune,* February 25, 1998; Steven Oberbeck, "Come 2002, This Bud's for Utah," *Salt Lake Tribune,* March 11, 1998; Pat Capson Brown, "Ban Ads for Sake of 'Future Beer Drinkers,'" *Salt Lake Tribune,* March 15, 1998; Marci Von Savoye, "BYU Student: Drop Beer as Olympic Sponsor," *Salt Lake Tribune,* March 25, 1998; Mike Gorrell, "Groups Talk Olympics, Beer," *Salt Lake Tribune,* April 14, 1998; Joan O'Brien, "Utah Booze Fight: Health Crusade or a Holy One?" *Salt Lake Tribune,* May 3, 1998; Tom Barberi, "Some People Never Learn," *Salt Lake Tribune,* July 7, 1997; Joy Baltezore, "Thirsty for a Booze Debate?" *Salt Lake Tribune,* December 7, 1997; Kirsten Stewart, "SLOC Still Ponders Big Questions: Drink Up?" *Salt Lake Tribune,* August 15, 2000; Mark Eddington, "Can Provo Swallow Suds Sale?: Beer Poses Tough Choice Ice Events in 2002," *Salt Lake Tribune,* September 16, 2000; Linda Fantin, "Romney Calls for Dry Medals Plaza," *Salt Lake Tribune,* September 28, 2000; Rebecca Walsh, "Beer Will Flow at the Gallivan during Games," *Salt Lake Tribune,* March 21, 2001; Tom Barberi

and Laurie J. Wilson, "State Moves Quickly to Stamp Out Growing Alcohol Scourge," *Salt Lake Tribune,* April 1, 2001; Christopher Smart, "Hits & Misses," *Salt Lake City Weekly,* June 21, 2001; Phil Sahm, "A Liquor Loophole for 2002," *Salt Lake Tribune,* June 25, 2001.

10. Grantland Rice, "The Sportlight," *New York Herald Tribune,* July 17, 1924, p. 12.

11. W. O. McGeehan, "Down the Line," *New York Herald Tribune,* July 19, 1924, p. 10.

12. "Dry Hails Olympic Victory," *New York Times,* August 13, 1928, p. 23.

13. "Walker Welcomes Olympic Athletes," *New York Times,* August 23, 1928, p. 23.

14. "Americans at Amsterdam," *World's Work* 56 (October 1928): 584–585.

15. "Law Is Law, Says U.S. Dry Chief, as He Bars Beer and Wine in Diet of Olympic Invaders," *New York Times,* April 22, 1932, p. 25.

16. Duncan Aikman, "Making Games Alibi-Proof," *New York Times Magazine,* June 19, 1932, p. 19.

17. "French Olympic Team to Get Sugar in Place of Wines," *New York Times,* April 13, 1932, p. 15.

18. Steve Riess, "Power without Authority: Los Angeles' Elites and the Construction of the Coliseum," *Journal of Sport History* 8 (Spring 1981): 50–65. See also Mark Dyreson, "Marketing National Identity: The Olympic Games of 1932 and American Culture," *Olympika: The International Journal of Olympic Studies* 4 (1995): 23–48; David Welky, "Viking Girls, Mermaids, and Little Brown Men: U.S. Journalism and the 1932 Olympics," *Journal of Sport History* 24 (Spring 1997): 24–49.

19. E. John B. Allen, "The 1932 Lake Placid Winter Games: Dewey's Olympics," *Olympic Perspectives: Third International Symposium for Olympic Research* (October 1996): 161–171.

20. Thomas Burr, "Leavitt Urges State Leaders to Market Utah during the Games," *Salt Lake Tribune,* September 10, 2001.

21. Dyreson, "Marketing National Identity," pp. 27–31.

22. Clifford Geertz, "Notes on a Balinese Cockfight," in *The Interpretation of Cultures* (New York: Basic Books, 1973), p. 448.

23. Lisa Riley Roche, "A Chance to Tell Utah's Story: But Which One?" *Deseret News,* March 8, 1998.

24. Allen Guttmann makes this argument with great force in *Games and Empires: Modern Sports and Cultural Imperialism* (New York: Columbia University Press, 1994), pp. 120–138.

25. For good surveys of the nationalism embedded in the Olympic Movement, see John MacAloon, *This Great Symbol: Pierre de Coubertin and the Origins of the Modern Olympic Games* (Chicago: University of Chicago Press, 1981); David C. Young, *The Modern Olympics: A Struggle for Revival* (Baltimore: Johns Hopkins University Press, 1996); Allen Guttmann, *The Olympics: A History of the Modern Games* (Urbana: University of Illinois Press, 1992); and Alfred E. Senn,

Power, Politics, and the Olympic Games (Champaign, Ill.: Human Kinetics, 1999). Excellent studies of the nationalism and sport that deal with certain aspects of the Olympic experience include Douglas Booth, *The Race Game: Sport and Politics in South Africa* (London: Frank Cass, 1998); Mike Cronin, *Sport and Nationalism in Ireland: Gaelic Games, Soccer and Irish Identity since 1884* (Dublin: Four Courts, 1999); John Nauright, *Sport, Culture, and Identities in South Africa* (London: Leicester University Press, 1997); S. W. Pope, *Patriotic Games: Sporting Traditions in the American Imagination, 1876–1926* (New York: Oxford University Press, 1997); Andrew Morris, "'I Can Compete'! China in the Olympic Games," *Journal of Sport History* 26 (Fall 1999): 545–566; and Cesar Torres, "Mass Sport through Education or Elite Olympic Sport? Jose Benjamin Zubiaur's Dilemma and Argentina's Olympic Sports Legacy," *Olympika: The International Journal of Olympic Studies* 7 (1998): 61–88.

26. For a provocative (and jargon-laden) reading of these connections, see Maurice Roche, *Mega-Events and Modernity: Olympics and Expos in the Growth of Global Culture* (London: Routledge, 2000).

27. For an interesting history of the Olympic Movement's location in the history of internationalist enterprises, see John Hoberman, "Toward a Theory of Olympic Internationalism," *Journal of Sport History* 22 (Spring 1995): 1–37.

28. My definitions of nationalism are heavily influenced by Benedict Anderson, *Imagined Communities: Reflections on the Origin and Spread of Nationalism,* rev. ed. (London: Verso, 1991). For an enlightening treatment of the linguistic power of sport in national cultures, see William J. Morgan's "Sport and the Making of National Identities: A Moral View," *Journal of the Philosophy of Sport* 24 (1997): 1–20.

29. J. P. Abramson, "First Winter Olympics in 1924 Unrecognized for 15 Months," *New York Herald Tribune,* February 2, 1936, sec. III, p. 3; E. John B. Allen, "'We Showed the World the Nordic Way,' Skiing, Norwegians, and the Winter Olympic Games in the 1920s," in Kay Schaffer and Sidonie Smith (eds.), *The Olympics at the Millennium: Power Politics and the Olympic Games* (New Brunswick, N.J.: Rutgers University Press, 2000), pp. 72–88; Guttmann, *The Olympics,* pp. 41–42; Senn, *Power, Politics, and the Olympic Games,* pp. 39–41. John Allen's argument that the creation of the Winter Games in the 1920s was more divisive than generally understood in Scandinavia, with some factions claiming the "Nordic Olympics" were the best site for winter sports while other groups supported the incorporation of winter sports in the Olympic program, is generally confirmed by Scandinavian scholars. See, for instance, Per Jørgensen, "From Balck to Nurmi: The Olympic Movement and the Nordic Nations," in Henrik Meinander and J. A. Mangan (eds.), *The Nordic World: Sport in Society* (London: Frank Cass, 1998), pp. 69–99.

30. In the early 1920s the United States demanded that the IOC create an official Olympic system for determining national standings, since the Americans charged that other countries were constructing point-systems in an effort to minimize the margins of American victory. The IOC pointedly refused to endorse

any such system designed to rank nations and provide such a blatant, as Allen Guttmann notes, "invitation to chauvinism" (Guttmann, *The Olympics*, p. 43). See also Senn, *Power, Politics, and the Olympic Games*, pp. 41–42.

31. "Olympic Opening Dubious," *Pittsburgh Press*, January 25, 1924, p. 32.

32. "American and Canadian Hockey Teams Play Today," *Atlanta Constitution*, February 3, 1924, sporting section C, p. 1.

33. Ralph Davis, "Sport Chat," *Pittsburgh Press*, February 6, 1924, p. 26.

34. "Jewtraw Triumphs in 500 Meter Race," *Pittsburgh Press*, January 26, 1924, p. 13; "Finns Lead the Nations in 1st Day of Olympics," *Atlanta Constitution*, January 27, 1924, p. 3B. Jewtraw remembered bowing his head and thinking, "for my country and God, I'll do my best." Sixty years later, when he was speaking with Olympic chronicler William Oscar Johnson, tears came to Jewtraw's eyes when he recalled the playing of the "Star Spangled Banner" at the victory ceremony. "The whole American team rushed out on the ice. They hugged me like I was a beautiful girl," reminisced the Olympic champion. "My teammates threw me in the air. The loudspeakers were booming out in French, 'Charlie Jewtraw of the U.S. of A. wins the first race in the first Winter Games!'" (William Oscar Johnson, "As It Was in the Beginning," *Sports Illustrated*, December 26, 1983–January 2, 1984, p. 105).

35. "Norway Wins Title in Olympic Games," *New York Times*, February 5, 1924, p. 18; "Strength on Skis Wins for Norway," *New York Times*, February 7, 1924, p. 12. See also "Finns Lead the Nations in 1st Day of Olympics," p. 3B; "Finns Carry Off First Honors in Skating Games," *Atlanta Constitution*, January 28, 1924; "U.S. Team Drops to 4th Place in Olympic Race," *Atlanta Constitution*, February 1, 1924, p. 15.

36. "Norwegians Triumph in Olympic Ski Jumping Contest," *Pittsburgh Press*, February 2, 1924, p. 9; "Norway Wins Title in Olympic Games," p. 18.

37. In 1974 Norwegian skiing historian Toralf Stromstad, who won a silver medal in the 1924 Nordic combined, found an arithmetic error in the scoring of the 90-meter ski jump. Norwegian-born Anders Haugen had actually placed third, making him the only American to ever achieve a medal-winning performance in Olympic ski jumping. Haugen, at age eighty-three, received his long overdue bronze medal in 1974, in a ceremony at Oslo, Norway. David Wallechinsky, *The Complete Book of the Winter Olympics* (Woodstock, N.Y.: Overlook, 2001), p. 290.

38. Dyreson, *Making the American Team;* Mark Dyreson, "Selling American Civilization: The Olympic Games of 1920 and American Culture," *Olympika: The International Journal of Olympic Studies* 8 (1999): 1–41.

39. "City to Welcome Skaters," *New York Times*, February 8, 1924, p. 15.

40. "U.S. Olympic Stars Back from France," *New York Times*, February 14, 1924, p. 12.

41. "Comment on Current Events in Sports: Olympic Games," *New York Times*, February 4, 1924, p. 25.

42. Bugs Baker, "Olympic Games Too European," *Pittsburgh Press*, February 6, 1924, p. 28.

43. "Canadian Six Put in Olympic Final," *New York Times,* February 9, 1928, p. 21; "Olympics to Open at St. Moritz Today," *New York Times,* February 11, 1928, p. 12; "Scandinavians Are Favorites at St. Moritz," *New York Herald Tribune,* February 9, 1928, p. 25; "Olympics of 1928 Open To-day with Winter Sports Program," *New York Herald Tribune,* February 11, 1928, p. 14.

44. "Farrell Ties 1924 Olympic Time for '500' at St. Moritz," *New York Herald Tribune,* February 8, 1928, p. 20.

45. "Olympic Sleds Guarded to Foil Gambling Coup," *New York Herald Tribune,* February 10, 1928, p. 1.

46. "U.S. Bobsleds 1st and 3rd in St. Moritz Derby," *New York Herald Tribune,* February 10, 1928, p. 21.

47. "Skiing in Abbreviated Costumes" and high-society photos of Miss Berry Scott Lloyd of London skiing and Queen Elizabeth of Belgium skating at St. Moritz, *Pittsburgh Press,* February 19, 1928, photogravure section, pp. 1 and 7.

48. E. John B. Allen, *From Skisport to Skiing: One Hundred Years of an American Sport, 1840–1940* (Amherst: University of Massachusetts Press, 1993), p. 92.

49. "900 Athletes Open Olympics in Storm," *New York Times,* February 12, 1928, sec. 10, pp. 1 and 6.

50. "Olympic Games Started," *Pittsburgh Press,* February 11, 1928, sec. 1, p. 11; "Ninth Olympiad Gets Underway in a Snowstorm," *Pittsburgh Press,* February 12, 1928, sporting section, p. 6; "Blinding Snow Features 1928 Olympics Start," *New York Herald Tribune,* February 12, 1928, sec. IV, pp. 1 and 6; "900 Athletes Open Olympics in Storm," pp. 1 and 6; "U.S. Skaters Race in Olympics Today," *New York Times,* February 13, 1928, p. 24.

51. "U.S. Girl Is 3rd in Figure Skating Event," *New York Herald Tribune,* February 19, 1928, sec. IV, p. 1; "U.S. Places Third in Figure Skating," *New York Times,* February 19, 1928, sec. 10, p. 1.

52. Gustavus T. Kirby, "Report of Gustavus T. Kirby," in *Report of the American Olympic Committee: Ninth Olympic Games, Amsterdam, 1928; Second Olympic Winter Sports, St. Moritz, 1928* (New York: American Olympic Committee, 1928), pp. 339–342.

53. Wallechinsky, *The Complete Book of the Winter Olympics,* pp. 53–54; Bud Greenspan, *Frozen in Time: The Greatest Moments at the Winter Olympics* (Santa Monica, Calif.: General Publishing Group, 1997), pp. 19–20.

54. "Canada Easily Wins Olympic Hockey Title," *New York Herald Tribune,* February 20, 1928, p. 14.

55. Kirby, "Report of Gustavus T. Kirby," and Dr. Godfrey Dewey, "Report of Manager, Ski Team," in *Report of the American Olympic Committee,* pp. 342, 344–349.

56. "Skiers Collapse in Military Ski Race through Alps Passes," *New York Herald Tribune,* February 13, 1928, p. 16.

57. "Marseillaise Too Much for St. Moritz Band, Leader Blames Sparsity of French Victories," *New York Times,* February 21, 1928, p. 21.

58. "Chicago Skater Ties for Third in Olympic Skating," *Pittsburgh Press,* February 13, 1928, sec. 1, p. 27; "Norwegian Skaters Win 6 of 12 Places in Two Olympic Races," *New York Herald Tribune,* February 14, 1928, p. 26.

59. "Olympic Protest Is Filed," *Pittsburgh Press,* February 14, 1928, sec. 1, p. 27; "Irving Jaffee Captures Olympic 10,000-Meter Skating Title on Protest of U.S. Officials," *New York Herald Tribune,* February 15, 1928, p. 22; "Olympic Skaters to Leave," *Pittsburgh Press,* February 15, 1928, sec. 1, p. 29; "Jaffee's Olympic Victory Ruled Out as Race Is Ordered Re-Run," *New York Herald Tribune,* February 16, 1928, p. 20.

60. "Olympic Program Resumed," *Pittsburgh Press,* February 16, 1928, sec. 1, p. 35.

61. Ralph Davis, "Ralph Davis Says," *Pittsburgh Press,* February 16, 1928, sec. 1, p. 32.

62. "Jaffee's Olympic Victory Ruled Out as Race Is Ordered Re-Run," p. 20; "Olympic Program Resumed," p. 35; "Miss Loughran Starts Olympic Skating, But Thaw Causes Halt," *New York Herald Tribune,* February 17, 1928, p. 21; "John Heaton Gives U.S. First Official Olympic Title, Winning Skeleton Bobsleigh Race," *New York Herald Tribune,* February 18, 1928, p. 14.

63. Kirby, "Report of Gustavus T. Kirby," pp. 339–342.

64. "John Heaton Gives U.S. First Official Olympic Title, Winning Skeleton Bobsleigh Race," p. 14; "Norway Takes Premier Honor, Sweden Third," *New York Herald Tribune,* February 20, 1928, p. 15; Kirby, "Report of Gustavus T. Kirby," p. 342.

65. "U.S. Takes Second as Olympics Close," *New York Times,* February 20, 1928, p. 13.

66. Ibid.

67. The AP had Finland at 39 and Canada at 112. "Norway Takes Premier Honor, Sweden Third," *New York Herald Tribune,* February 20, 1928, p. 15.

68. Richard E. Danielson, "Why the Olympic Games and How?" *Sportsman* 4 (July 1928): 21.

69. Davis, "Ralph Davis Says," p. 32.

70. "Miss Loughran Starts Olympic Skating, But Thaw Causes Halt," p. 21.

71. "Norway Takes Premier Honor, Sweden Third," p. 15.

72. W. O. McGeehan, "Down the Line," *New York Herald Tribune,* February 18, 1928, p. 15.

73. "U.S. May Yield Winter Sports to Canada in '32," *New York Herald Tribune,* February 15, 1928, p. 22.

74. George M. Lattimer (compiler), *Official Report: III Olympic Winter Games, Lake Placid, 1932* (Lake Placid, N.Y.: III Winter Olympic Games Committee, 1932), pp. 47–48.

75. Lex Hemphill, "Salt Lake City's Olympic Hopes Born Long Before the '60s Bid," *Salt Lake Tribune,* April 14, 2001.

76. Lattimer, *Official Report: III Olympic Winter Games,* pp. 43–52.

77. Allen, *From Skisport to Skiing;* William J. Baker, *Sports in the Western World,* rev. ed. (Urbana: University of Illinois Press, 1988).

78. Lattimer, *Official Report: III Olympic Winter Games,* pp. 137–138.

79. Letter from E. Morrill Cody, James F. Newcomb & Company, Inc., to Henry L. Stimson, U.S. Secretary of State, September 10, 1930; Letter to James F. Newcomb & Company, Inc., from William R. Castle, Jr., Assistant Secretary of State, U.S. Department of State, October 2, 1930; Letter from E. Morrill Cody, James F. Newcomb & Company, Inc., to Henry L. Stimson, U.S. Secretary of State, October 3, 1930, State Department Records Division, Record Group 59, National Archives and Record Administration II, College Park, Maryland (hereafter referred to as NARA II).

80. Memorandum from Harry H. Bundy, Assistant Secretary of State, U.S. Department of State, to American Diplomatic Officers, September 15, 1931, State Department Records Division, Record Group 59, NARA II.

81. Letter from Robert J. Phillips, Liaison Officer, U.S. Department of Commerce, Bureau of Foreign and Domestic Commerce, to Wilbur J. Carr, Assistant Secretary of State, U.S. Department of State, April 10, 1930; Letter from Robert J. Phillips, Liaison Officer, Bureau of Foreign and Domestic Commerce, U.S. Department of Commerce, to Wilbur J. Carr, Assistant Secretary of State, U.S. Department of State, March 28, 1930; Questionnaire No. 302, "Sports," Department of Commerce, Bureau of Foreign and Domestic Affairs, from Eric T. King, Chief, Specialties Division, Approved by the Questionnaire Committee on March 25, 1930, James W. Furness, Acting Chairman, State Department Records Division, Record Group 59, NARA II.

82. Memorandum from Albert Halstead, American Consul General to Great Britain, to Henry L. Stimson, U.S. Secretary of State, January 11, 1932; Letter from Wilbur J. Carr, Assistant Secretary, U.S. Department of State, to Albert Halstead, American Consul General to England, September 23, 1932; Letter from Herbert C. Hengstler, Chief of the Division of Foreign Service Administration, U.S. Department of State, to E. C. Paarman, Third Olympic Winter Games Committee, September 23, 1932; Memorandum from Nathaniel P. Davis, American Consul to England, to the U.S. Secretary of State [Henry L. Stimson], October 8, 1932; Memorandum from A. Dana Hodgdon, Chief of the Visa Division, U.S. Department of State, to the Division of Foreign Service Administration, U.S. Department of State, October 26, 1932, State Department Records Division, Record Group 59, NARA II.

83. Memorandum from Division of International Conferences and Protocol, U.S. Department of State, to Wilbur J. Carr, Assistant Secretary of State, U.S. Department of State, December 30, 1930; Memorandum from MVB, Division of International Conferences and Protocol, U.S. Department of State, to Richard Southgate, Division of International Conferences and Protocol, U.S. Department of State, January 2, 1931; Letter from Wilbur J. Carr, Assistant Secretary, U.S. Department of State, to Ernest Gamache, Secretary of the III Olympic Winter Games Committee, June 16, 1931; Letter from Godfrey Dewey,

President of the III Olympic Winter Games Committee, to Bertrand H. Snell, U.S. Representative from New York, July 20, 1931; Letter from Bertrand H. Snell, U.S. Representative from New York, to Wilbur J. Carr, Assistant Secretary, U.S. Department of State, July 20, 1931; Telegram from Bertrand H. Snell, U.S. Representative from New York, to Wilbur J. Carr, Assistant Secretary, U.S. Department of State, July 31, 1931; Memorandum for the Files, U.S. State Department, August 27, 1931; Memorandum from the Division of International Conferences and Protocol, U.S. Department of State, to Richard Southgate, U.S. Department of State, September 8, 1931; Memorandum from William R. Castle, Jr., Undersecretary, U.S. Department of State, to President Herbert Hoover, October 1, 1931; Memorandum from William R. Castle, Jr., Undersecretary, U.S. Department of State, to Wilbur J. Carr, Assistant Secretary, U.S. Department of State, October 31, 1931; Joint Resolution 72 of the 72nd U.S. Congress in U.S. State Department Files, December 19, 1931; Telegram from the Henry L. Stimson, U.S. Secretary of State to American Diplomatic and Consular Officers, December 21, 1931, State Department Records Division, Record Group 59, NARA II.

84. Internal Memorandum for file from G.T., Visa Division, U.S. Department of State, February 2, 1932; Letter from A. Dana Hodgdon, Chief of the Visa Division, U.S. Department of State, to Doctor Godfrey Dewey, President of the III Olympic Winter Games Committee, February 15, 1932; Letter from Godfrey Dewey, President of the III Olympic Winter Games Committee, to A. Dana Hodgdon, Chief of the Visa Division, U.S. Department of State, February 26, 1932; Memorandum from the U.S. Secretary of State [Henry L. Stimson] to the U.S. Secretary of Labor, March 2, 1932; Letter from A. Dana Hodgdon, Chief of the Visa Division, U.S. Department of State, to Doctor Godfrey Dewey, President of the III Olympic Winter Games Committee, April 5, 1932; Letter from Godfrey Dewey, President of the III Olympic Winter Games Committee, to A. Dana Hodgdon, Chief of the Visa Division, U.S. Department of State, April 13, 1932; Letter from W. W. Husband, Second Assistant Secretary of Labor, U.S. Department of Labor, to the U.S. Secretary of State [Henry L. Stimson], March 16, 1932, State Department Records Division, Record Group 59, NARA II.

85. Lattimer, *Official Report: III Olympic Winter Games,* pp. 251–262; *General Rules and Program, III Winter Olympic Games, Lake Placid,* 1932 (Lake Placid, N.Y.: III Winter Olympic Winter Games Committee, 1931); and "Daily Program, Feb. 4–15 Summaries, III Winter Olympic Winter Games," in State Department Records Division, Record Group 59, NARA II.

86. Lattimer, *Official Report: III Olympic Winter Games,* pp. 87, 93–108; "Two National Radio Chains to Give Details of Winter Olympic Contests at Lake Placid," *New York Times,* January 12, 1932, p. 31.

87. Lattimer, *Official Report: III Olympic Winter Games,* pp. 67, 90.

88. Ibid., pp. 157–165.

89. Austria, Belgium, Canada, Czechoslovakia, Finland, France, Germany, Great Britain, Hungary, Italy, Japan, Norway, Poland, Romania, Sweden, Switzerland, and the United States competed in Lake Placid. Ibid., pp. 173–178.

90. Dyreson, *Making the American Team,* pp. 136–137, 160–161.

91. "Roosevelt Invokes an 'Olympic Peace,'" *New York Times,* February 5, 1932, p. 21; "Count Baillet-Latour Says Harmony Rules among Nations at Winter Games," *New York Times,* February 12, 1932, p. 27; Lattimer, *Official Report: III Olympic Winter Games,* pp. 167–180.

92. Harry Cross, "United States Wins Winter Olympics with 88 Points to Norway's 77," *New York Herald Tribune,* February 14, 1932, sec. III, pp. 1 and 3.

93. Arthur J. Daley, "Fiske's Team Wins Olympic Bob Title," *New York Times,* February 16, 1932, p. 25; "Snap-Shots from the Winter Olympics," *Literary Digest* 112 (February 27, 1932): 48–49; Lattimer, *Official Report: III Olympic Winter Games,* pp. 264–269; "Daily Program, Feb. 4–15 Summaries, III Winter Olympic Winter Games," p. 20.

94. "Byrd, Hunting Skiers, Becomes Bobsledder," *New York Herald Tribune,* February 10, 1932, p. 20.

95. Harry Cross, "10,000-Meter Speed-Skating Trials in Olympic Games Rules 'No Races' after Long Dispute," *New York Herald Tribune,* February 6, 1932, p. 17; Harry Cross, "4 U.S. Skaters among 8 Qualifiers for 10,000-Meter Final," *New York Herald Tribune,* February 7, 1932, sec. III, pp. 1 and 3.

96. Harry Cross, "Four Injured as German Bobsled Ends Mile a Minute Dash with 50-Foot Fall," *New York Herald Tribune,* February 1, 1932, p. 17; Harry Cross, "Olympic Bob Run Slowed by Layer of Snow after Seven Foreign Teams Complain," *New York Herald Tribune,* February 2, 1932, p. 24; Harry Cross, "500 See Four Germans Injured as Sleigh Plunges 75 Feet Off Lake Placid Run into Rocks," *New York Herald Tribune,* February 3, 1924, p. 20; "The Bobsledders," *New York Herald Tribune,* February 4, 1932, p. 16.

97. Harry Cross, "Fiske Leads in Olympic Bobsledding as Drivers Refuse to Race Last 2 Heats on Slow Course," *New York Herald Tribune,* February 15, 1932, p. 18.

98. The weather was so bad—a lack of early snow combined with severe blizzards and then unseasonably warm rain during the Games that led to delays in several events—that the Lake Placid Club's official report felt compelled to defend itself by noting that they had to "contend with the most unusual weather conditions in Adirondack history." They supported their claim with an official bulletin from the New York state weather bureau that the winter of 1931–1932 was the strangest climatic year on record. Lattimer, *Official Report: III Olympic Winter Games,* p. 70.

99. Cross, "Four Injured as German Bobsled Ends Mile a Minute Dash with 50-Foot Fall," p. 17; Cross, "Olympic Bob Run Slowed by Layer of Snow after Seven Foreign Teams Complain," p. 24; Cross, "500 See Four Germans Injured as Sleigh Plunges 75 Feet Off Lake Placid Run into Rocks," p. 20; "The Bobsledders," p. 16.

100. W. O. McGeehan, "Down the Line," *New York Herald Tribune,* February 3, 1924, p. 22; February 4, 1932, p. 22; February 5, 1932, p. 18; February 6, 1932, p. 18; February 7, 1932, sec. III, p. 2; February 8, 1932, p. 18; February 9,

1932, p. 22; February 10, 1932, p. 22; February 11, 1932, p. 26; February 12, 1932, p. 18.; February 14, 1932, sec. III, p. 4.

101. "Winter Olympics Drew $96,000; Lake Placid Deficit $52,468," *New York Times*, February 17, 1932, p. 27.

102. Allen, *From Skisport to Skiing*.

103. Guttmann, *The Olympics*, pp. 51–71; Senn, *Power, Politics, and the Olympic Games*, pp. 49–63; Mandell, *The Nazi Olympics*.

104. "German Officials Warned by Kirby," *New York Times*, February 2, 1936, sec. 5, p. 3.

105. "Games at Garmisch," *Time* 27 (February 17, 1936): 37–42.

106. The success of the United States in 1932 in promoting American culture to the world's media through the Olympics paved the way for the production of the "Nazi Olympics" in 1936. Dyreson, "Marketing National Identity," pp. 23–48.

107. "OLYMPICS: Germany Plays Host for Fourth Winter Games," *News-Week* 7 (February 8, 1936): 24–25; "Games at Garmisch," pp. 37–42; "Premiere in a Snow Storm," *Literary Digest* 121 (February 5, 1936): 37–38.

108. Al Laney, "Ice Olympics to Set Record for Attendance," *New York Herald Tribune*, February 2, 1936, sec. III, p. 3.

109. "OLYMPICS: With Winter Sports Wind Up a Norwegian Triumph," *News-Week* 7 (February 22, 1936): 33.

110. Abramson, "First Winter Olympics in 1924 Unrecognized for 15 Months," sec. III, p. 3; "1932 U.S. Team Led in Winter Sports," *New York Times*, February 2, 1936, sec. 5, p. 3.

111. "Games at Garmisch," pp. 37–42.

112. "OLYMPICS: Germany Plays Host," pp. 24–25.

113. "Games at Garmisch," pp. 37–42.

114. "Premiere in a Snow Storm," pp. 37–38.

115. "80,000 See Hitler Launch Olympics for 28 Nations," *New York Herald Tribune*, February 7, 1936, pp. 1 and 18; Frederick T. Birchall, "Hitler Opens the Winter Olympics; U.S. Defeats Germany in Hockey," *New York Times*, February 7, 1936, pp. 1 and 22; "Games at Garmisch," pp. 37–38.

116. "Winter Olympics on Deck," *Literary Digest* 120 (December 14, 1935): 39.

117. Robert Livermore, Jr., "Notes on Olympic Skiing: 1936," *Atlantic Monthly* 157 (May 1936): 620–621.

118. "Games at Garmisch," pp. 37–42.

119. Albion Ross, "Canada Beats U.S. at Hockey, Ruud Wins Ski Jump," *New York Times*, February 17, 1936, p. 23.

120. "Olympic Wind-Up," *Literary Digest* 121 (February 22, 1936): 37.

121. Jack Lippert, "The Winter Olympics," *Scholastic* (February 29, 1931): 22.

122. "Bobsledding May Be Called Off as Result of Practice Mishaps," *New York Herald Tribune*, February 7, 1936, p. 18.

123. Dwight Shepler, "The Winter Olympic Games at Garmisch-Partenkirchen," *Sportsman* 19 (March 1936): 21–23, 70–71.

124. Paul Gallico, *Farewell to Sport* (New York: Knopf, 1938), p. 327.

125. Edwin Muller, "Coming Down the Mountain," *Collier's* 97 (February 1, 1936): 24, 33.

126. "OLYMPICS: With Winter Sports Wind Up a Norwegian Triumph," p. 33.

127. Harry Cross, "Canadian Berths on British Six Hit by Kirby on Arrival Home," *New York Herald Tribune,* February 18, 1936, p. 25.

128. "Hockey Blast and 'Caesar's' Wife," *Literary Digest* 121 (February 29, 1936): 38.

129. John Kieran, "Sports of the Times," *New York Times,* February 13, 1936, p. 31.

130. Gallico, *Farewell to Sport,* pp. 236, 331–333.

131. Frederick T. Birchall, "Military Display Marks Visit of Hitler and Aides to Games," *New York Times,* February 14, 1936, p. 13.

132. Lippert, "The Winter Olympics," p. 22.

133. John Kieran, "Sports of the Times," *New York Times,* February 16, 1936, sec. 5, p. 2.

134. Richards Vidmer, "Down in Front," *New York Herald Tribune,* February 14, 1936, p. 22.

135. "Games at Garmisch," pp. 37–42.

136. Muller, "Coming Down the Mountain," pp. 24, 33; "Games at Garmisch (Cont'd)," *Time* 27 (February 29, 1936): 32–34.

137. "The Olympics," *Commonweal* 23 (February 28, 1936): 480.

138. "Ruth in Olympic Post," *New York Times,* February 9, 1936, sec. 5, p. 8.

139. Vidmer, "Down in Front," p. 22.

140. Hunter S. Thompson, "'Hey, Rube': Olympic Disaster in Utah," *ESPN. Com,* June 25, 2001. Available from http://espn.go.com/page2/s/thompson/010625.html (Internet). For a brief outline of the cultural clashes emerging within Utah regarding the 2002 Winter Games, see Mark Dyreson, "Olympic Games and Historical Imagination: Notes from the Faultline of Tradition and Modernity," *Olympika: The International Journal of Olympic Studies* 7 (1998): 25–42.

141. Linda Fantin, "Sober 2002 Games May Befit a Far More Serious World," *Salt Lake Tribune,* October 14, 2001.

8

TOWARD A COSMOPOLITICS OF
THE WINTER OLYMPIC GAMES

Jeffrey O. Segrave

At the risk of sounding distinctly like Lewis Carroll's Mad Hatter let me initiate my analysis of the politics of the Winter Olympic Games by touching on a proposition that is perhaps now moribund but has nonetheless exercised a remarkably persistent hold over the public imagination at the same time that it has occupied a hallowed place in the dominant discourse of sport: namely, the notion that sport is essentially nonpolitical or above politics, that there is a categorical distinction between politics and sport. For Pieure de Coubertin, the founder of the Olympic Movement, there was no such distinction. The rhetoric of sport as antipolitics was ushered in by the cataclysmic political upheavals of the first half of the twentieth century and the betrayal of post-Enlightenment rationality, the result of which was the migration of sport from the category of the political to the category of the cultural and in the United States to the category of the economic (MacAloon 1991). The apolitical sanctity of sport was further promulgated by subsequent leaders of the Olympic Movement, most notably IOC president Avery Brundage, as a way of bolstering a sagging Anglo-Saxon hegemony of sport with its attendant class distinctions and favored moral assumptions.

Once viewed as a secondary annex, a mere prelude to the Summer Games, and mythologized and romanticized as belonging to a realm of bucolic, idealized simplicity, a world of snowy landscapes and isolated Alpine villages, the Winter Olympics have appeared even more immune from *Realpolitik*. Winter sport athletes are invariably portrayed as characters in a fairy tale or figures in a Currier and Ives lithograph, not actors in a highly politicized and globalized entertainment spectacle. Of equal interest is the specific lack of formal, academic treatment given to the politics of the Winter Games. Historically, in fact, journalistic sources, official reports, and other materials gleaned from the likes of programs, bulletins, newsletters, and media guides, and not academic sources, have for the most part provided the most detailed accounts of daily events, ceremonies, performances, and even political issues and developments. The general dearth of scholarship on the politics of the Winter Olympic Games, as well as the fact that treatises on the politics of the Summer Games have largely focused on negotiations between formal political agencies, attests to the once dominant conviction that real politics was about class, about "left" and "right," and that not even a politics of culture, let alone a politics of sport, was central to a true understanding of the epistemology of power.

Throughout the humanities and social sciences, however, culture and symbolism, language and ritual, have become recognized as politically constituted and constitutive, irrespective of their relations to the struggle for resources. As Gerrit Gong (1984) writes, "the politics of culture have been too long overlooked and underestimated" (p. 244); "different ideologies, vying with each other in a struggle for power, have once again made cultural standards and norms an issue of confrontation" (p. 246). Once the materialist paradigm is rejected, then the political significance of sport is revealed and the Olympic Games are exposed for what they truly are—a globalized cultural performance that accrues enormous political and economic capital.

Focusing on the resolution of conflict and disagreement as the stimulus for political activity, the emphasis within traditional definitions of politics has typically fallen on the actions of formal political institutions and focused on what has often been termed "high" politics involving political parties, national and international governmental institutions, and recognized pressure groups. In keeping with contemporary thinking, however, I want to define politics more broadly, recognizing that the defining characteristic of political activity is the use and control of resources, tangible and intangible, at all levels of social and cultural life. In this view, political power not only resides in the formal actions of governments but is in fact woven into the very fabric of everyday life. Therefore, I argue with Adrian Leftwich (1984) that politics lies at the core of "*all* collective social activity, formal and informal, public and private, in *all* human groups, institutions and societies, not just some of them, and it always has" (p. 63). On this account I can expand my analysis to include the moments of international diplomacy that have touched on the Winter Olympics as well as to address the Games as a performative and public mega-event constituted by a powerful amalgam of local, regional, national, and global cultures and forces. In other words, only by embracing a politics of culture can the full political salience of the Winter Games be appropriately acknowledged.

I have two primary purposes in this chapter. First, I want to classify and categorize the politics of the Winter Olympics, to pull together into one place selective examples of the political incidents that have surrounded the

Games since their formal inception in 1924. Second, however, I want to place my overview of the politics of the Games in a broader theoretical perspective, one that recognizes a shift in emphasis from the politics of nation-building and ideology to the politics of consumption and commercialism. Of particular relevance here is the fact that the Winter Olympics were from the beginning negotiated out of the nation-building ambitions of North American and Western European countries as well as out of the dreams of organizing committees and visionary individuals who saw in winter sports enormous economic and commercial capital. Superimposed on both localist and nationalist agendas is the seemingly inexorable development of globalization, in the contours of which lay the debate about the hegemony of Eurocentric conceptions of sport modeled most obviously in the Winter Olympic Games program. In the end, I would like to suggest that the Winter Olympics stand on the cusp of a new neo-modern era, one precipitated by the implosion of the Communist states in Eastern Europe and one that embraces a new way of theorizing politics, a cosmopolitics at once shaped by the forces of globalism and yet conducive to a new form of cosmopolitanism (Cheah and Robbins 1998).

THE POLITICS OF THE WINTER OLYMPIC GAMES

If, as Karl Marx once remarked, historical events tend to occur twice, once as tragedy and subsequently as farce, then there is certainly something farcical about the Winter Olympics. The turmoil surrounding Salt Lake City's bid for the 2002 Winter Games is nothing new; overenthusiastic pampering of IOC members by bid committees has long been a feature of both Summer and Winter Games, and yet another manifestation of the inherently political nature of the Games (Johnson and Verschoth 1986).

While the Winter Games may well have been cursed less than the Summer Games by the excesses of nationalism, gigantism, terrorism, and political boycotts, the winter festival has not been without ongoing political incidents and tensions. Environmental mismanagement, expressions of Cold War politics as well as the residual fall-out from the demise of the state socialist regimes in Europe, fractious relations between the IOC and its most affluent and influential member, the USOC, as well as the ever emerging revelations about the patronage of IOC members are just a few of the issues that constitute the panoply of Winter Olympics Games politics. The difference between the politics of the Summer Games and the politics of the Winter Games remains largely a matter of degree and not kind—the Winter Games appear less political because the Summer Games seem so political. Nevertheless, because of limitations of geography and their abiding association with the dedicated winter sports industry and because of their overt bias toward the already dominant nations—the results of which constitute what Barrie Houlihan (1994) describes as the second wave of Western cultural imperialism—the Winter Games are particularly revealing as a conduit for theorizing the political evolution of the Olympics over the course of the twentieth century. Before turning to my theoretical position, however, let me first classify the politics of the Winter Games into four interlocking categories: namely, international, national, local, and domestic politics.

International Politics

Spared many of the egregious excesses of a twentieth-century geopolitics that has threatened the very existence of the Olympic Movement, including most obviously devastating boycotts, the politics of apartheid, and invasive terrorist activity, the Winter Olympics have nonetheless routinely reflected and refracted and in fact contributed to the construction of the ongoing political exigencies that have beset the world at large. Numerous international tensions have spilled over into the Olympic winter arena, including post–World War II resentments, the war in Bosnia, and Israeli/Palestinian, North/South Korean, and Iraqi/U.S. relations. It seems inconceivable that Islamic/American tensions will not also impinge on the Salt Lake City Games; and just as Juan Antonio Samaranch once flew to Sarajevo to seek suspension of the Balkan conflict prior to the games in Lillehammer, so also Jacques Rogge flew to Washington to request a truce in the Afghan conflict on the eve of the 2002 Games. But like the Summer Games the Winter Games might best be remembered as a crucial site in the conduct and transmogrification of Cold War politics.

Predicated on the divisions of Germany and China into two mutually hostile factions, the ideological and economic enmity between the Soviet Union and the United States, as well as the worldwide process of decolonization, the Cold War threatened to submerge the entire Olympic edifice at the same time as it heightened public interest in the Games themselves. Against the backdrop of a divided world and under the increasingly sophisticated and attentive eye of the television camera, winter athletes like their summer counterparts served as ideological shock troops engaged in symbolic confrontations of seemingly epic proportions. Reflective of the paranoid disposition of the Western European and North American powers toward the ascendance of state socialism and despite the establishment of separate Olympic Committees as early as 1952; in Cortina D'Ampezzo (1956), Squaw Valley (1960), and Innsbruck (1964) East and West Germany competed as one nation. It was not until the Sapporo Games of 1972 that East Germany achieved the ultimate objective of competing as an autonomous state within the Olympic forum. The specifically diplomatic contours of the German situation erupted in 1960, when the IOC threatened to remove the Games from Squaw Valley if the United States, seeking to monitor travel to and from socialist countries, refused to accept duly recognized and accredited competitors from the socialist states of Europe.

Matters of formal diplomatic relations also problematized the IOC's ongoing political negotiations with both nationalist and Communist China. Confronted by tectonic historical developments and shifting global allegiances, and operating within the context of its own traditions and politicized power blocs, the IOC finally felt the full brunt of its own deliberations on the eve of the Lake Placid Olympics when the Taiwanese delegation was denied access to the Olympic Village because Taiwan had not officially accepted the conditions by which the IOC had formally negotiated its participation. The politics of Asia, as the most recent award of the 2008 Summer Olympics to Beijing verifies, has remained a permanent feature of the Olympic political landscape.

But at the very core of Cold War politics lay the scepter of the rivalry between the Soviet Union and the United States and the blatant use of sport by both sides as a form of surrogate warfare in the service of foreign diplomatic missions and trade delegations. And just as the Czech/USSR hockey matches of the 1960s and early 1970s reflected the internal politics of the Warsaw Pact countries, so also a plethora of athletic confrontations—crystallized most memorably in the 1980 Lake Placid hockey game between the two superpowers—personified and defined the portentous struggle between communism and capitalism as both the Soviet Union and the United States sought to expand their markets as well as their ideological and political sovereignty. Nearly trampled in the diplomatic aftermath of the Soviet invasion of Afghanistan, the 1980 Lake Placid Games survived the delicate negotiations between Washington and Moscow that ultimately resulted in the reciprocal boycotts of the Moscow and Los Angeles Summer Games. Not only a site for the escalation of the Cold War, the Winter Games also served as the initial site in its attenuation. The dissolution of the state socialist systems in Eastern Europe during 1989 resulted in a patchwork quilt of national Winter Games participation that reflected the transient dynamics of a Europe in transition. The Albertville Games of 1992, the first Games of the "New World Order," featured a unified German team that marched together for the first time since 1964, a Unified Team that comprised a loose confederacy of Russia, Ukraine, Byelorussia, Kazakhstan, and Uzbekistan; a restructured Yugoslavia represented by the flags of Yugoslavia, Croatia, and Slovenia; and teams from the newly independent states of Latvia, Estonia, and Lithuania. By the 1998 Games in Nagano even the Unified Team had dissolved.

Another significant aspect of international politics in the Winter Olympic Games is the problematic participation of Third World and emergent nations. On the one hand, the Olympic arena offers nations representation on the transnational bodies of sport, access to diplomatic channels, a conduit to corporate sponsorship, and acknowledgment and visibility within the nexus of global politics. On the other hand, participation has often presumed what amounts to capitulation to the hegemonic forms and practices of Western standards and the demise or marginalization of indigenous folk games and sport forms. Houlihan (1994: 204) in fact argues that the IOC has never sought to define sport development as anything other than the reinforcement of Western traditions and forms. As a result, the Winter Olympics have invariably been subject to criticism as being a public reaffirmation of the myths of Western civilization because of the esoteric nature and hegemonic forms of winter sports, because geography and climate impose limitations on participation and success as well as on hosting opportunities and because the Winter Games reaffirm and reinforce the ongoing political influence of the already powerful nations of the West and their allies on the international organs of transnational sport and in the world at large. In the worst-case scenario, the price for nations and athletes seeking identity and recognition in sports that are invariably counter to their own cultural expressions is humiliation, ridicule, and stereotyping.

As Helen Lenskyj (2000) has also pointed out, it was no coincidence that the vast majority of the IOC members alleged to have acted improperly during the Salt Lake City bid scandal were from Africa, Asia, and South America, and culture, geography, and race were often patronizingly and stereotypically used to rationalize and excuse inappropriate conduct. In other words, despite the presence of Third World athletes, including Argentines and Mexicans as well as more recently Africans and Jamaicans, the Winter Games have remained to a great extent "a genuine affair of the North" (Kramer-Mandeau 1996: 155).

While the Winter Games, since their inception in 1924, have been a party to evolving global political developments, it has been during the last two decades in particular that the Games have borne witness to the most radical shift in the conduct of world politics. The breakdown of the entire social, political, and economic systems of Eastern Europe not only has led to the demise of the Communist Party as a hegemonic power but also has facilitated the ascendance of the liberal market society. Olympic leadership, as Samaranch's tenure has demonstrated, especially with regard to the Salt Lake City scandal, relies now as heavily on diplomatic negotiations with the corporate/media complex as with governments and world leaders. The victory of liberal market society has occurred not only in the former Communist societies of Central and Eastern Europe but also within the larger historical context of a burgeoning reclamation of modernization, democratization, and universalism throughout the world. As J. C. Alexander (1994: 184–185) argues, because "the recent revivals of market and democracy have occurred on a world wide scale" and because "notions of commonality and institutional convergence have re-emerged . . . we are witnessing the rebirth of a fourth post War version of mythopeic thought: Neo-modernism."

Neo-modernist arguments in favor of universalism have also brought with them a renewed advocacy of cosmopolitanism, not the privileged cosmopolitanism with its "luxurious free-floating view from above" but "actually existing" cosmopolitanisms whose normative power and ideological power acknowledge the actual historical and geographical contexts from which they emerged (Robbins 1998: 1). This is the cosmopolitanism that represents the best expression and the best hope for the future of the Olympic Movement.

National Politics

As has been clear throughout the course of the twentieth century and most especially of late as communities aspire to national self-determination in the wake of the collapse of communism, the Winter Olympics remain tied to one of the most clearly discernible features of national politics, the process of nation-building itself, a process in particular evidence in the genesis of the Winter Games.

Although winter sports were already well established in Europe in the early decades of the twentieth century, the incorporation of winter sports into the Olympic Movement was in part the result of protracted negotiations that took the form of a variety of contested ruminations about the role of winter sports in identifying, formulating, and communicating a sense of national consciousness, particularly among the countries of Northern Europe (Goksøyr, von der Lippe, and Mo 1996). Initial Scandinavian opposition to the idea of a separate Winter Games was prompted in large measure by the fear that a Winter Olympics would threaten the already well-regarded Nordic Games and the particularistic national interests they served. Despite the ongoing antipathy between Sweden and Norway and a regional politics typified as much by confrontation as by cooperation, apathy as much as intransigence, the tradition of winter sports in Northern Europe nonetheless honored and consolidated a mutual sense of Scandinavianism with its nostalgic Nordist heritage and its idealized style of peasant folk culture.

Few European nationals had greater atavistic and mythological associations with winter sports than the Scandinavians.

In the end, though, with the dissolution of the Nordische Spiele in 1926 and the establishment of a dedicated Winter Olympic Games program, winter sports gave up much of their specifically Scandinavian mythos in favor of the more formalized bureaucratic version of modern competitive sport. Only the subsequent political battle for control of the Olympic program between Nordic and Alpine events remained as a reminder of Idraet (sport) and the specifically Scandinavian cultural ideology that winter sports had once embodied.

Manipulating the Winter Olympics for the purposes of developing a sense of national identity was also salient for those countries emerging in the aftermath of two world wars. From the use of drugs—"nationalism out of a needle" as one Olympic official put it—to elaborate and often self-serving point-scoring systems, from the subornation of judging (especially in ice dancing and figure skating) on the basis of national and ideological affiliation to the organization of fine arts festivals, nations manipulated the Winter Games for the purposes of distinct nationalist agendas. In both the USSR and the German Democratic Republic performance in winter sports was a significant part of a larger program of sport production dedicated to formulating and proselytizing particular forms of national socialism.

The politics of the Winter Games, however, have taken on a new complexity with regard to participation by nations emerging from the process of decolonization. Unlike sporting traditions exported by the imperial powers, often as part of the planned global dissemination of European standards of civilization and as a way of intentionally undermining indigenous sports, winter sport participation has for the most part been self-imposed, often the result of individual initiative and ingenuity. Whether as a form of self-denigration, cultural dependence, or the perpetuation of a colonial mentality or as a source of national pride and a moment of genuine national self-determination, an increasing number of decolonized nations are embracing the discultural sports of the Winter Games as a forum for obtaining international acknowledgment. The price for acknowledgment, though, is accommodation to the hegemony of the tradition of Western sports or in the case of Kenya's first Winter Games athlete, cross-country skier Philip Boit, manipulation as a marketing ploy in the global ambitions of Nike. Furthermore, while the Winter Games testify to an elite athleticism that is no longer so heavily dependent on a racial hierarchy, the bodies of winter are still predominantly white and the popular appeal of "dark bodies" is often predicated on exoticism and novelty rather than performance and acceptance. In other words, as much as the Winter Olympics continue to blur racial boundaries they still preserve normative, Western standards and identities that stymie the development of coherent and authentic national cultures (Schaffer and Smith 2000).

In keeping with other analyses of the politics of sport, we can also argue that the Winter Olympics have commonly and in some cases notoriously been drafted into service as a vehicle for constructing and projecting an image of the state and its political and ideological priorities. In discussing the linkage between sport and political ideology, John Hoberman (1993) points out that in both fascist and Communist regimes sport heroes and athletic occasions were celebrated as political assets, as part of the propaganda machinery to demonstrate the superiority of a particular political system and way of life. In Nazi Germany the Winter Olympics at Garmisch-Partenkirchen served as a powerful political statement on behalf of a resurgent Germany, a further step in the stabilization and popularization of the Nazi ideology (Cohen 1996; Mandell 1971). Specifically set in Bavaria, the home of the National Socialist Party, the games of Garmisch-Partenkirchen celebrated Nazism in the form of contrived mass pageantry that cloaked the Games in the legitimizing robes of classical Olympic antiquity at the same time as it proclaimed the majesty of the *Volk*. The political significance of the Garmisch-Partenkirchen Games, heralded as the greatest sports festival the world had ever witnessed, lay in their appropriation of Olympic internationalism for distinctly nationalist purposes, as a mechanism for consolidating fascism in Germany and in Europe and as a carefully managed cultural performance whose success empowered and emboldened Nazi leaders to further their political objectives both at home and abroad.

Nor can it be said that the German Games were an aberration in the political history of the Winter Games. Numerous other host countries have since sought to use the Winter Games to harmonize national image and international intention with Olympic protocol through the use of prescribed and created symbols and rituals (Klausen 1999).

In the post–World War II Communist regimes of the Soviet Union and its satellites, Winter Olympic performances were habitually used to advertise the supremacy of a doctrinaire Marxist-Leninism. Even Americans, despite their lack of a tradition of state-sponsored sport, have embraced the notion that achievement in the Olympic arena is evidence of a superior culture, and Winter Olympic success routinely engenders euphoric nationalist sentiments—most notably in the case of the 1980 hockey team. While, as Hoberman (1993: 24) notes, "the ultimate basis for this identification may well be irrational, planning to create it is not." Consequently, whether the result of state policy or private enterprise, the product of ideology or foreign policy, or the consequence of a carefully orchestrated system of federally sponsored drug application, spectacular athletic performances have routinely become the medium for collective national representation. In a scene that has in one form or another repeated itself around the world, over 130,000 Czechs welcomed their victorious hockey team home to Prague after the 1998 Nagano Games: "Thanks to you," proclaimed Premier Joseph Tovosky, "billions of people now know what is the Czech Republic. Also thanks to you, there's a good mood in the country and people have even discovered patriotism inside themselves" (Druzin 1998). In such cases, the Winter Games offer yet another grandiose arena in which, as S. W. Pope (1997: 40) puts it, nations can "invent and popularize symbols of their sporting and political culture by linking athletic success to national mythology."

Like athletic performances, hosting opportunities also become the pretext for nationalistic fervor. Forever striving to be awarded the accolade of "the best Games ever," countries are judged not only by their athletic prowess but also by their organizational acumen. Seeking to host a Winter Games invariably borders on an obsession and is often viewed by a region's corporate and political elite as the Holy Grail of world recognition. Speaking in exactly the sort of hyperbolic terms that now typify the announcement of Olympic stewardship, H. Koenig (1983: 148) wrote: "The IOC's selection of Sarajevo is the greatest publicity coup this nation has brought off since its inception." Embraced as an opportunity to boost tourism, to encourage the winter ski trade, and to foster economic expansion and revitalization, Olympic hospitality also becomes a part of the machinery of political socialization and furthering distinct national agendas.

Norway's prime minister specifically used the success of Norwegian athletes at the Lillehammer Games as a metaphor to promote his country's ambitions within the context of the larger capitalist realities of a newly configured Europe, the projection of a contemporary and innovative Norway rather than a nostalgic and cliché-ridden one (Hoberman 1993). In Japan the Nagano Games were eagerly embraced as an antidote to a sluggish Japanese economy, the Asian currency crisis, and the resignation of Japan's foreign minister amid the turmoil of a bribery scandal. In larger symbolic terms, Sarajevo became an opportunity for redemption, expiation for Yugoslavia's role in the onset of World War I; Nagano, a form of apologia, atonement for Japan's contribution to the devastation of World War II.

But nowhere are the historical particularities of nationalism crystallized more than in the opening and closing ceremonies of the games. Increasingly elaborate, compelling, and expensive techno-productions operate as powerful paradigms for presenting ideological versions of national identity and national priorities, classic examples of what Michael Billig (1995: 44) calls "hot nationalism." Whether in the form of Olav Bjaaland's idea of a ski relay from historical Morgedal to the Bislett Stadium, Midori Ito clad in traditional kimono lighting the flame in Nagano, the reenactment of the Calgary Stampede, or Kristin and Hakon, the mascots for the Lillehammer Games, the rituals, performances, figures, and symbols of the Olympic ceremonial are profoundly political. Through the manipulation of nostalgia, memory, and imagination—what Homi Bhabha (1994: 145) calls "the scraps, patches, and rags of daily life"—the opening ceremonies depict a community as a historically specific form of consciousness. Moreover, as anthropologists have clearly demonstrated, the presentation of a culture through the Olympic ceremonial is not a cohesive manifesto but rather the result of contested negotiations, different voices, and distinctive inflections seeking legitimization and hegemonic privilege within a culture. Roel Puijk (2000), for example, has shown how the presentation of Norwegian culture and national identity during the opening ceremonies of the Lillehammer Games was actually the result of protracted struggles, conflicts, and discussions among a wide variety of actors, including organizing committees, corporate interests, media representatives, and activists, each choosing among and seeking to find acceptance for a variety of elements deemed typically Norwegian.

Furthermore, if, as John MacAloon (1991) has contended, the Olympic Games are one of the most salient forms made available to the transnational community for formulating and proselytizing a particular national identity, especially in relation to other global national identities, then once again the nations of the West are advantaged in their historical and geographically derived domination of the Winter Olympics forum. This domination continues to privilege a historically well established and recognized Eurocentric way of life—and way of sport—within a universal organization that is located at the nexus of global politics.

Moreover, one of the most powerful mechanisms by which nations and national politics are constituted is through the modern mass media. Whatever else the Olympics have become, they have certainly become what Daniel Dayan and Elihu Katz (1992: 9) call a media event, flamboyant and continuous broadcasts that "integrate societies in a collective heartbeat and evoke a renewal of loyalty to the society and its legitimate authority." As globally televised mega-events, the Winter Olympics, like the Summer Games, produce and reproduce contested ideological themes and political messages through a highly sophisticated arsenal of micro-electronic technology that targets national audiences in selective and tailored ways. In Calgary, for example, as M. McNeill (1996: 119) has shown, Canadian television manufactured an Olympic extravaganza that recreated "the hegemonic consolidation of consent to popular views about sport and nationhood" and specially packaged hockey as an "indigenous product" for national consumption.

Even the same event can be framed differently within different political contexts. In France the defeat of Bjorn Daehlie and the Norwegian cross-country team at the hands of Italy was located at the vortex of European regional characteristics; in Norway the loss was rationalized in "personal" rather than national terms; and in Italy the victory was positioned between the metonymic images of northern and southern Italy (Puijk 2000). Foreign policy can also be woven into the fabric of Olympic sports discourse (Riggs, Eastman, and Golobic 1993). In each case, though, the media transforms the living room into what Puijk (2000: 310) calls "an extended public place." Through typically conventionalized although always negotiated and transacted presentations of athletic performances, cultural exhibitions, Olympic ceremonials, and even advertisements, Olympic spectators are continually subject to interpellation, especially as nationals, and exposed to a vast array of demonologized stereotypes by which they can characterize themselves as well as their others. In the end, it is, as T. B. Farrell (1987: 64) notes, out of the "intersection of commercial media contrivance and actual competitive performance" that the specifically political content of the Olympics arises.

Nor, of course, are audiences merely passive receptacles. Nationalism and national identities are never linear, stable, and predictable but rather convoluted, complex, and random. Looking at the Olympics from a personal interpretive order, R. E. Rinehart (1998) suggests that nationalism is actually best construed as nationalisms; and, arguing against the historical certainty of nationalism, Bhabha (1994: 140) claims that the nation is actually "an obscure and ubiquitous form of living the *locality* of a culture" and nationness "a form of social and textual affiliation." If such be the case, then spectacles like the Winter Olympics must be located at the very heart of the political project, because every four years they offer a semiotic and discursive platform for the invention and management of traditions—myths, narratives, rituals, deixis—whereby national identities are created as if they were eternal features of the political landscape, nationalities as what Billig (1995: 29) calls "invented permanencies."

But while the Winter Olympics often serve as the quintessential, even if contested, expression of nationalism, they also now exist in a new geopolitical climate that threatens the autonomy and dominion of the nation-state itself. Attacked from below by the forces of localism, the nation-state is also under attack from above by the forces of globalization. The emergence of a world economy, the transnationalization of military command structures and alliances, the global diffusion of technology, and the rise of global hybrid cultures as a result of modern mass migration, consumerism, and mass communications have all served to undermine the stability of the nation-state as a viable economic unit, as a bounded culture territory, and as a political sovereign realm. The Winter Olympic Games, like modern sport in general, operate as a powerful factor in the globalization process. The incorporation of National Hockey League players into the 1998 Winter Games, the increasing dependence of Winter Olympic teams (especially European and Japanese ice hockey teams) on dual nationals and "borderless athletes" (Chiba, Ebihara, and Morino 2001: 203), and the burgeoning migration of athletic labor into a wide variety of winter sports are all significant features of the global sportization process and all contribute to the ongoing problematization and even gradual denouement of the nation-state as an institution and nationalism as a form of consciousness (Maguire 1999).

Although it is by no means clear what the alternative to nationalism is at this point, and because contemporary critics of nationalism see it as a historically situated form of consciousness and even as a privative ethnic identity that masquerades as universalism, cosmopolitanism is clearly a viable option as an ideal political project precisely because it embodies the sort of genuine universalism Coubertin envisioned for the Olympics in the first place, a cosmopolitanism grounded in a sympathetic, charitable relationship between nationals. Whatever reservations there may be about contemporary forms of transnationalism, organizations like the Olympic Movement provide the material conditions for a newly emergent cosmpolitanism that can serve as promissory of some egress from the xenophobias and excesses of nationalism, tribalism, and identity politics that wrought havoc throughout the twentieth century.

Local Politics

While the Winter Olympics have developed into one of the most visible and charismatic spectacles in what Maurice Roche (2000: 3) calls "a dense eco-system and social calendar of public cultural events," the Games are nonetheless located in place and time. They are, to borrow a phrase from Roland Robertson (1995), "glocal" in the sense that they are both global events in world society and local as hallmark events that have profound implications and consequences for a particular community; they are, as J. Longman (1998: C1), puts it, both "extravagantly international and stirringly local."

As a local mega-event the Games of Lillehammer have been characterized as "the most expensive staging and most complex and spectacular event in Norwegian history" (Klausen 1999: 2). From a political perspective, hosting the Winter Olympics requires a mobilization of ever-expanding coalitions of local, regional, national, and international sectors of life, including

corporate, industrial, governmental, sports, religious, activist, arts, entertainment, and volunteer interests. Located at the nexus of a vast interlocking bureaucracy of corporate, political, and Olympic organizations, local
organizing committees are themselves constituted by a dazzling array of
politicized bodies that seek to provide the organizational, symbolic, and
material infrastructure requisite to hosting what now entails close to a million on-site spectators as well as a guesstimated global audience of close to
2 billion. In Sarajevo a 79-member organizing committee supervised the
work of numerous commissions and boards, including an executive committee that coordinated the work of 13 working committees and commissions
and a Coordinating Committee of Experts that oversaw 164 substantial
projects (Niketic 1984).

Initiated by local political, civic, and business elites, the Winter Games
promise to serve and legitimize the influx of government and corporate
capital, validate massive construction projects, promote economic gains,
offer global publicity, and hence endow upon a region a lasting beneficial
legacy. Staging a successful Winter Olympics can also politically translate
into efforts to secure the award of the more prestigious Summer Games.
Branko Mikulic, president of the organizing committee for the Sarajevo
Games, declared in his report to the IOC that Yugoslavia "was willing to
organize Olympic Games in the future too." In 1984, in a letter to the IOC,
Belgrade announced its preliminary candidature to organize "one of the
Summer Olympic Games in the future" (quoted in Niketic 1984: 22).

Given that the Winter Olympics are routinely held in rural, often remote
and sparsely populated locales, the Games have inevitably been plagued by
all sorts of parochial problems. An acute shortage of accommodations hampered both the 1924 Chamonix and 1980 Lake Placid Games. In Lake Placid
the limited housing in the village allowed private owners to rent their homes
for prices as high as $60,000 for the duration of the festival. Transportation
problems also compromised the Lake Placid Games, as Canadian charter
buses were specially commissioned to alleviate the logistical logjam. Site
geography has also been problematic. The 1968 Grenoble Games were
actually held at three different villages, and even the scaled-down Games in
Albertville proved to be the most decentralized Games in history; ten venues
were spread out over 650 square miles of the Savoie. The weather has also
confounded Olympic organizers. While a late December blizzard threatened
the Albertville Games, rain, unexpected warmth, and a general dearth of
snow have jeopardized numerous other Games. Three thousand Austrian
army personnel transported 20,000 cubic meters of snow to the Innsbruck
venues in 1964, causing the 1976 Innsbruck bid committee members to quip

that "if we could hold the games without snow in 1964, we can hold them with snow in 1976" (Kirsch 1973: 35).

But issues that may once have been benignly consigned to the category of the politics of organization have now become the cause for a politics of resistance. Moments of resistance and protest have emerged as a result of the ever-escalating size and scope of the Winter Games and a growing critique of the Games as a consumerist product that legitimizes and rationalizes the ideologies and practices of synergistic political and corporate elites. Concern focuses on the marginalization of localized interests within a dominant Olympic discourse that invokes notions of global harmony and promises community health and prosperity at the same time as it ignores legitimate community issues and anxieties. While on the one hand the appropriation and cooptation of Canadian Indian artifacts and histories served to bolster and distinguish the Calgary Olympic bid campaign, on the other hand the packaging and celebration of indigenous cultures as a show of Canadian multiculturalism concealed a history of injustice and systematic oppression and discrimination. Spearheaded by the Lubicon Lake Band of Cree, the Indian boycott of "The Spirit Sings," the signature show at the Calgary Olympic Arts Festival and a prominent display of Indian and Inuit artifacts at Calgary's Glenbow Museum, became an occasion for the Cree to protest the hypocritical stance of Calgary's wealthy and powerful interests (Feest 1987; Myers 1988).

The most publicized moments of resistance, however, have emerged as a result of the impact of the Winter Games on the environment (Chernushenko 1994). Precisely because the Winter Olympics are invariably held beyond the pale of civilization, amid pristine landscapes and unsullied natural vistas, organizing committees have inevitably clashed with ecologically conscious groups. As early as 1932, legal action brought by the Association for the Protection of the Adirondacks forced Lake Placid organizers to relocate the site of the bobsled run from the preferred Wilmington Notch site to Mount Van Hoevenberg in order to protect the "Forever Wild" Forest Preserve in the Adirondack region (Ortleff and Ortleff 1976). And in 1974, as a result of a highly charged public referendum, Denver rejected the Winter Games due to burgeoning antigrowth sentiments and public fears of excessive habitat destruction. Symptomatic of a rationalized and quantifiable model of elite sport and predicated on tourist expansionism with its concomitant emphasis on real estate speculation and venue construction, the Winter Games have increasingly inspired the work of environmentally conscious groups whose grass-roots activism has precipitated the creation of global sports policies.

Even the notion of "Green Games" that emerged as a central feature of the Lillehammer Olympics was not the result of a prescient state agenda but rather the result of complex and protracted negotiations among competing groups and inspired by grass-roots activism; "an unanticipated conjuncture of symbolic politicals and realpolitik," as Jon Lesjo (2000: 293) puts it. Likewise, the IOC's initial response to the environmental issue was defined less by a proactive affinity to global environmentalism and more by a reaction to the threat to its philanthropic transnational image (Cantelon and Letters 2000).

Consequently, in response to both the environmental havoc caused by the decentralized Albertville Games and the success of the "Green Games" of Lillehammer, the Olympic Movement has, albeit reactively, more recently adopted clearly articulated environmental protection policies, which governed the conduct of a Winter Olympics for the first time in 1998 at Nagano. But even though the IOC has declared the environment, alongside sport and education, to be the third dimension of the Olympic Movement, the challenge is still how to balance the requirements of modern winter sport (especially with its totemistic valuation of space) as well as the economic and political aspirations of a community with the need to protect the beauty and health of the natural environment.

The emergence of the Winter Olympic Games as a truly global hallmark event has forced official Olympic bodies to confront a variety of other local political and politicized issues, which have more typically been associated with the Summer rather than Winter Games, including, for example, the privatization of public space and publicly subsidized facilities, the corporatization of universities, the prioritization of Olympic venues and infrastructure over public services, the use and abuse of volunteer labor, the criminalization of poverty, the displacement and forced eviction of tenants, and—especially in light of the September 11 terrorist assaults against New York City and Washington, D.C.—enhanced government, police, and surveillance efforts (Lenskyj 2000). Salt Lake City, confronted with the tightest security in the history of the Olympics, faces the daunting task of not only coordinating the ubiquitous efforts of law enforcement agencies as well as managing a military presence but also balancing the sensitive political challenge of determining in practice how to maximize spectator and athlete experience and protect the civil rights and liberties of a community preoccupied with issues of security and safety.

The greatest fear in all of these developments must be that the Winter Olympics have now become such a globalized mega-event that social-activist, minority, and specialized local interests are in danger of being summarily dismissed in the face of a nationalistic entertainment juggernaut that serves the conservative interests of the corporate, political Olympic establishment. From the most radical political perspective, the Winter Games have emerged as yet another ineffaceable element of a globalized Olympic industry that stands as a threat to the values rooted in democracy and social justice (Lenskyj 2000).

It could certainly be argued that the global ambitions of the Olympic Movement affirm a fundamental disjuncture between the local and the global. There is also no doubt that the emergent monoculture of winter sport—itself yet another expression of the homogenization of the global sports culture—heightens the fear that the local is likely to be superseded by the global. As D. L. Andrews (1997: 78) argues, however, "there is a need to understand and hopefully transcend the politics of *fetishizing* the local and *fearing* the global." And as John Tomlinson (1999) points out, the local and global do not have to exist as cultural polarities and can exist instead as mutually interpenetrating principles—a position more clearly in accord with cosmopolitanism. Pushing the idea a little further, Tomlinson argues that we should think about cosmopolitanism as "ethical glocalism" (1999: 196), a cultural disposition that specifically does not exclude the perspective of the local. Clearly the debate over the environment more than amply demonstrates that the local periphery can indeed have an impact on the global in mutually beneficial ways. If, in fact, the Olympic Movement is to succeed in its ideological humanitarian and educational mission, it must continue to strive to be simultaneously universalist and pluralist; proactive and not just reactive, especially in response to local exigencies and agendas.

Domestic Politics

By "domestic politics" I mean the internal politics of the bodies, procedures, and relations that govern the Winter Olympics and that determine the role and status of the Winter Games within the broader panoply of Olympic political operations. No longer the "Frostbite Follies" as Avery Brundage (quoted in Daley 1977: 31) pejoratively labeled them, or merely an "appendage" as Coubertin (1979: 128) once described them, the Winter Olympics are now firmly ensconced in the vortex of Olympic political intrigue. In fact, the emergence of the Winter Games as an increasingly viable economic, media, nationalist, spectator, and public relations bonanza—a viability predicated in no small measure on the separation of the Summer and Winter Games—has thrown the Winter Games more than ever before into the constant welter of political campaigning, lobbying, and maneuvering that constitutes the inner workings of the entire Olympic bureaucracy.

The selection of the site for successive Winter Games offers a case in point. Once at the pleasure of the host NOC, site selection for the Winter Games quickly became subordinate to a broader, more complex and sensitive IOC political agenda. Consequently, even though the 1925 Prague Congress determined that the Summer and Winter Games should be held in the same year and in the same country and even though Coubertin (1979) argued that the Games should not be split under any pretext, the Games at Garmisch-Partenkirchen and Berlin were in fact the last Games to be held in the same country. Whether seeking to guarantee the very survival of the Games or driven to protect its image, whether reacting to geo-global politics or propagating Olympism, the IOC's selection of Winter Olympic hosts has become a part of the rarified atmosphere of high-octane Olympic political strategizing. In 1928, for example, St. Moritz was specifically chosen to mitigate the political climate surrounding the return of Germany to the Olympic fold; the 1984 Games in Sarajevo, to infuse the spirit of the Olympics to a new territory. There is still widespread speculation that the selection of Innsbruck in 1976 rested on an image badly tarnished by the disqualification of Austrian skier Karl Schranz, "as recompense for the affront" as John Kennedy (1996: 290) put it. Even the politics of snow has informed the bid procedure. During Lake Placid's bid for the 1980 Games, one IOC member inquired: "Aren't you going to have to haul snow in for the games?" To which the reply came: "Lake Placid is where they haul the snow from!" (quoted in Ortleff and Ortleff 1976: 91).

In the most recent years, the fortunes of both Summer and Winter Games sites have become inextricably entwined in a far-reaching, high-stakes game of clandestine political maneuvering, a development compounded by the alternating celebrations of Winter and Summer Games and predicated on the political and economic ramifications of geographical distribution. In a classic example that demonstrates the emergent power and currency of the Winter Games, the selection of Barcelona, the favored site and home city of the IOC president at the time, Juan Antonio Samaranch, was dependent on the selection of Albertville first, a vote that would invariably preclude the subsequent selection of Paris and hence protect the viability of the Barcelona bid. Similar political machinations drive nominations of host cities at the national and even localized level as organizers seek to maximize the odds of selection. In order to establish a credible bid from the Savoie, Albertville was chosen as the lead city not because of its charm and beauty—William O. Johnson (1991: 90) described the city as a "numbingly drab *dépotoir*"—or even on the basis of name recognition—few French people even knew the location of Albertville—but because it was larger and more accessible than many of the isolated resort villages scattered throughout the region and because the nomination of Albertville would likely defuse "the flaming jealousy that would breeze up and down the Tarentaise if they chose one of the more attractive resorts in the valley over the others" (1991: 94).

Inspired and empowered by the promise of handsome rewards, bid and organizing committees have become highly political bodies. No longer the purview of individual visionaries like Godfrey Dewey, who engineered the 1932 Lake Placid bid, or maverick speculators and entrepreneurs like Alexander Cushing, who pioneered the 1960 Squaw Valley bid, bids are now assembled and negotiated by teams constituted of local power elites and financed by million-dollar budgets. Like their summer counterparts, winter organizing committees are obliged to coordinate the work and specialized professional agendas of a wide variety of technospecialists from image makers to promotional wizards, from transportation experts to media gurus. Acknowledging the potentially self-serving and self-aggrandizing proclivities that can overrun organizing bodies, Kevin Wamsley (1996: 310) has shown how the enlightened and broad-based rhetoric of the Calgary bid committee quickly gave way to the practices of an organizing committee that adopted an impersonal corporate business strategy that quashed "any resistance to hosting the festival." Revelations of corruption among Nagano organizers spawned widespread cynicism and indifference, and the male-dominated make-up of the Calgary Board of Directors left the Calgary Organizing Committee wide open to charges of corporate chauvinism.

Manifestations of scandal, fraud, and graft have in fact long been a part of the politics of the Winter Olympics. As long ago as 1960, the chair of the Squaw Valley Organizing Committee, Alexander Cushing, resigned as a result of a conflict of interest engendered by his ownership of real estate in the valley. But nowhere have the egregious excesses of the Olympic Movement been more on display than during the still-evolving scandal surrounding the Salt Lake City bid procedures (Jennings 2000). At no other time have the recent politics of the Winter Olympics so overshadowed the politics of the Summer Games and at no other time have the politics of the Winter Games had such an impact on the image, operations, and relations of the Olympic Movement. Not that the Summer Games have not been implicated in the bid scandal—both Sydney and Atlanta officials admitted complicity in what the USOC (1999: 27) later called a "broader culture of improper gift-giving"—but it was specifically the improprieties surrounding the Salt Lake City bid procedure that finally exposed the seamy underbelly of the entire Olympic bidding process.

Although the Salt Lake City debacle imperiled the future of the Olympic Movement, the political salience of the scandal is that it forced the enactment of ethical reforms and practices intended to democratize the IOC and make its operations more accountable and transparent; laid bare the political power of corporate sponsors within the Olympic Movement; revealed the political culture within the IOC itself and the political modus operandi of the past president, Juan Antonio Samaranch; influenced the election of the new IOC president, Jacques Rogge; caused the IOC to embark on a global publicity campaign to repair its tarnished image; potentially influenced the selection of Turin as host of the 2006 Winter Games; and further strained USOC and IOC relations, thereby increasingly marginalizing the role of the United States in the ongoing politics of the Olympic Movement. In an ironic twist of fate, the post-9/11 zeitgeist may have actually served to strengthen the Olympics at a time when they appeared most vulnerable and most duplicitous by distracting attention away from the ongoing stream of embarrassing disclosures and soap-opera developments and by lending a renewed air of credibility and validity to the humanitarian and pacifist claims of the Olympic Movement in a time of deep global angst.

As the Salt Lake City scandal suggests, Winter Olympic issues have frequently played a role in the ongoing relations and operations of the USOC. Although it was thrust into strained relations with its own government during the 1980 boycott negotiations and even with U.S. Organizing Committees, including most obviously the Salt Lake City Organizing Committee, the USOC's most enduring and petulant relationship has been with the IOC. Fueled by a historical amalgam of frustration, distrust, and distinctly different styles of doing business, the confrontational and turbulent relations between the IOC and the USOC have devolved of late due to a variety of well-publicized issues, including what the IOC views as the patronizing attitude of the United States with regard to the IOC's efforts to combat drug abuse; negotiations over the disbursement of lucrative television rights, licensing, and the right to use Olympic symbols; and the political fallout from the Salt Lake City disclosures.

While the disposition of revenues generated from American business and television companies has inevitably created the most tension—including the sale of the television rights for the Calgary Games for $309 million, which empowered the USOC to press its claims for a greater share of the revenue—relations have most recently soured under the duress of Salt Lake City developments. From the IOC's position, the Salt Lake City incident demonstrated a distinct lack of oversight by the USOC; compromised the global aspirations and integrity of the entire Olympic Movement; imputed the IOC as being ethically culpable in the perpetuation of a gift giving/

receiving culture; subjected Samaranch to the vagaries of U.S. governmental interrogation; and contributed to the destabilization of the USOC itself. Despite recent efforts by both parties to ameliorate the tensions, the "family feud" continues (Barney, Wenn, and Martyn 2000).

Despite the political machinations that constitute the quotidian operations of Olympic bodies, the Olympic Movement must nonetheless be counted as one of the most optimistic aspects of the globalization process. In its most recent history, the IOC has embraced numerous initiatives that speak to a broadly conceived cosmopolitan cultural disposition. Regional, national, and international conferences and seminars on a wide variety of salient global issues, including tourism, the environment, and human rights; associations with humanitarian organizations such as the United Nations High Commissioner for Refugees; bureaucratic efforts like the integration of Olympic and Paralympic Games; and satellite association with sports events like the African-Asian Games as well as the more traditional Olympic Day Run, the European Youth Olympic Development, and the Fine Arts Festivals all bring issues of universal concern to localized lifeworlds and promote what Ulf Hannerz (1990: 239) calls "an intellectual and aesthetic stance of openness toward divergent cultural experiences." While prospects for broad cultural change may well be limited, it is clear that the efforts of international nongovernmental organizations like the Olympic Movement are far more likely to be successful than the efforts of both international and nation-state government institutions (Tomlinson 1999).

CONCLUSION: TOWARD A COSMOPOLITICS

From the very beginning two broad, largely congruent and ultimately conflated dimensions have underscored the politics of the Winter Olympic Games: nationalism and commercialism. As a vehicle for promoting nationalist sentiment, the Winter Games have functioned as an effective performative and discursive field for the establishment of what Benedict Anderson (1983) calls the "imagined community" of the nation-state, for the construction and production of historical nostalgia to both "invent" and signify "tradition," to both invoke and inculcate ideological and patriotic allegiance, and to impel athletes and coaches to victory. As Hoberman (1993) rightly points out, however, sportive nationalism is not a single generic phenomenon but a complex and convoluted sociopolitical response to broader sociopolitical exigencies and sportive nationalism to be understood in terms of the varying historical contexts in which it appears. The paroxysms of nationalism that gripped Americans in the wake of the 1980 "Miracle on Ice" were precipitated by very different circumstances than the national jubilation that accompanied the feats of Alberto Tomba, or the Jamaican bobsled team, or even Michael "Eddie the Eagle" Edwards.

In each case, though, and in keeping with the history of the Winter Games, the political capital to be gained has accrued mainly to the already powerful voices of Western and Northern Europe and North America. It is the same geographical isolation and limitations imposed by winter sport that caused Coubertin to rue that the separation of winter from summer sports would undermine the unity of the Olympics; that animated Avery Brundage to rail against the Winter Games as "grossly parochial," "a refrigerated appendage of the real thing" (Daley 1977: 31); and that energized IOC member Ashwini Kumar to worry that the North/South imbalance "may soon enlarge itself to such proportions that it may impair the global aspects of the Olympic Movement" and Alpha Diallo to ask rhetorically if the Third World athlete was merely "a supernumerary, a curiosity, or simply an added recruit for the opening parade?" (quoted in Hill 1996: 256). Such voices have also at various times located the Winter Games in the forefront of debates about the escalating size of the Olympics and the reconstruction or even elimination of winter sports as a legitimate political consideration in the effort to combat gigantism.

But if the politics of nationalism generated and sustained the Winter Olympics, the politics of commercialism have transformed them. No longer what Coubertin (1979: 107) called "so truly amateur, so frank, and so pure in their sporting dignity," the Winter Games have been fully absorbed into capitalism's universal market. It was clear that calling winter sports Olympic and placing them within the ancient Greek tradition was from the beginning good business and that neither Coubertin nor any other traditionalists in the IOC could eventually resist. Throughout the course of the twentieth century the Winter Games were blatantly used as a way to promote tourism, encourage economic development, and produce a winter sport culture for both domestic and foreign consumption. Increasingly intertwined with a powerful transnational bloc of financial, retail, travel, and media interests, and advanced by the fusion of state and private capital, the Winter Games have emerged as a highly visible and marketable component of the winter sports industry. Alternating Winter and Summer Games has further maximized revenue and exposure for the corporate Olympic complex. Like the Winter X Games and the Winter Goodwill Games, the Winter Olympics often seem like another made-for-TV spectacle that feeds into a nation's political economy and further expands consumer sport's global reach—developments that promise profound new dimensions for the politics of the Games.

The question is: which political dimensions do the Games need to emphasize? And to what ends? I would like to answer that the Olympic Movement needs to acknowledge its cosmopolitan roots and embrace a timely cosmopolitics that cultivates what Anthony Giddens (1994: 130) calls a "civil association" based on an "intelligent relationship between equals which respects the autonomy of the other." And as Tomlinson (1999: 190) notes, such a perspective needs to be "non-elitist, non-ethnocentric, non-patriarchal—and non-'globalist.'"

Given the current circumstances, it is hard not to agree with H. Berking (1996: 192) that we live in a world characterized by the "re-emergence of bloodthirsty xenophobic incendiaries" and "a corruption-prone political personnel that daily demonstrates to its astonished public the reprivatisation of opportunities of political power in the form of a blithe maximisation of its self-interest"; or with John Mearsheimer (2001) that we inhabit a grim universe where politics simply boils down to a relentless drive for power and hegemony; or with Hoberman (1993) that bioethical issues are likely to be the most significant ideological variables of the coming age; or with Herbert Schiller (1985: 19) that we live in a "homogenized North Atlantic cultural shop."

But, as Rob Wilson (1998: 360) argues, "the global terrain of the cosmopolitan does not belong only to transnational capital, imperial power, and jeremiad despair" but to cultures, political initiatives, and international organizations of global/local mixture "whose hope-generating resources can be marshaled to serve better ends than the xenophobic hegemony of mononations, monoraces, and monocreeds." The Olympic Movement has certainly made a celebratory contribution to the excesses of the late twentieth century; but it also represents the doggedly repeated triumph of hope over experience. Maybe the best we can hope for is what François Bourricaud (1987: 21) once recognized, that "modern societies are characterized less by what they have in common or by their structure with regard to well-defined universal exigencies than by the fact of their involvement in the *issue* of universalism." What might be possible, then, under the neomodern zeitgeist is a return to and a reaffirmation of the grand sport theory of internationalism that Coubertin (1898: 434) once adumbrated at the turn of the nineteenth century, a "true" and "sincere" internationalism as he called it, one grounded in a no less "true" and "sincere" nationalism: "Internationalism should be the state of mind of those who love their country above all, who seek to draw to it the friendship of foreigners by professing for the countries of those foreigners an intelligent and enlightened sympathy." This injunction remains today, as it always has been, the wellspring of the Olympic Movement and the ideological basis and promise for a future cosmopolitics of the Olympic Games.

References

Alexander, J. C. 1994. "Modern, Anti, Post, and Neo: How Social Theories Have Tried to Understand the 'New World' of 'Our Time.'" *Zeitschrift für Soziologie* 3: 165–197.

Anderson, B. 1983. *Imagined Communities: Reflections on the Origin and Spread of Nationalism*. London: Verso.

Andrews, D. L. 1997. "The (Trans)National Basketball Association: America's Commodity Sign Culture and Global Localization." In A. Cvetovitch and D. Kellner (eds.), *Articulating the Global and the Local: Globalization and Cultural Studies,* pp. 72–101. Boulder: Westview Press.

Barney, R. K., S. Wenn, and S. G. Martyn. 2000. "Family Feud: Olympic Revenue and IOC/OSOC Relations." *Olympika* 9: 49–90.

Berking, H. 1996. "Solidary Individualism: The Moral Impact of Cultural Modernisation in Late Modernity." In S. Lash, B. Szerszynski, and B. Wynne (eds.), *Risk, Environment, and Modernity: Toward a New Ecology,* pp. 189–202. Thousand Oaks, Calif.: Sage.

Bhabha, H. K. 1994. *The Location of Culture*. New York: Routledge.

Billig, M. 1995. *Banal Nationalism*. Thousand Oaks, Calif.: Sage.

Bourricaud, F. 1987. "Universal Reference and the Process of Modernization." In S. N. Eisenstadt (ed.), *Patterns of Modernity, Volume I,* pp. 12–21. London: Frances Pinter.

Cantelon, H., and M. Letters. 2000. "The Making of the IOC Environmental Policy as the Third Dimension of the Olympic Movement." *International Review for the Sociology of Sport* 35: 294–308.

Cheah, P., and B. Robbins (eds.). 1998. *Cosmopolitics: Thinking and Feeling beyond the Nation*. Minneapolis: University of Minnesota Press.

Chernushenko, D. 1994. *Greening Our Games: Running Sports Events and Facilities That Won't Cost the Earth*. Ottawa: Cenburion Publishing & Marketing.

Chiba, N., O. Ebihara, and S. Morino. 2001. "Globalization, Naturalization, and Identity: The Case of Borderless Elite Athletes in Japan." *International Review for the Sociology of Sport* 36: 203–222.

Cohen, S. 1996. *The Games of '36: A Pictorial History of the '36 Olympics in Germany*. Missoula: Pictorial Histories Publishing.

Coubertin, P. de. 1898. "Does Cosmopolitan Life Lead to International Friendliness?" *American Monthly Review of Reviews* 17: 429–434.

———. 1979. *Olympic Mémoires*. Lausanne: IOC.

Daley, A. 1977. "Once Again the Iceman Cometh." *New York Times,* February 6, p. 31.

Dayan, D., and E. Katz. 1992. *Media Events: The Live Broadcasting of History*. Cambridge, Mass.: Harvard University Press.

Druzin, R. 1998. "A Heroes' Welcome from 130,000." *New York Times,* February 24, p. C2.

Farrell, T. B. 1987. "The 1984 Winter Olympics as an American Event: An 'Official' Rhetorical Criticism." In R. Jackson and T. McPhail (eds.), *The Olympic Movement and the Mass Media: Past, Present and Future Issues,* pp. 63–65. Calgary: Hurford Enterprises.

Feest, C. 1987. "The Glenbow Incident: The Spirit Sinks." *Native American Studies* 1: 61–63.

Giddens, A. 1994. *Beyond Left and Right.* Cambridge: Polity Press.

Goksøyr, M., G. von der Lippe, and K. Mo (eds.). 1996. *Winter Games, Warm Traditions.* Second international International Society for the History of Physical Education and Sport (ISHPES) seminar, Lillehammer, 1994. Lillehammer: Norwegian Society of Sports History.

Gong, G. 1984. *The Standard of "Civilization" in International Society.* Oxford: Clarendon Press.

Hannerz, U. 1990. "Cosmopolitans and Locals in World Culture." In M. Featherstone (ed.), *Global Culture: Nationalism, Globalization, and Modernity,* pp. 237–251. London: Sage.

Hill, C. R. 1996. *Olympic Politics: Athens to Atlanta 1896–1996.* Manchester: Manchester University Press.

Hoberman, J. 1993. "Sport and Ideology in the Post-Communist Age." In L. Allison (ed.), *The Changing Politics of Sport,* pp. 15–36. Manchester: Manchester University Press.

Houlihan, B. 1994. *Sport and International Politics.* London: Harvester Wheatsheaf.

Jennings, A. 2000. *The Great Olympic Swindle: When the World Wanted Its Games Back.* London: Simon & Schuster.

Johnson, W. O. 1991. "Stompin' in the Savoie: A Pre-Olympic Tour of the French Alps Was No Waltz." *Sports Illustrated,* February 13, pp. 89–102.

Johnson, W. O., and A. Verschoth. 1986. "Olympic Circus Maximus." *Sports Illustrated,* October 27, pp. 39–43.

Kennedy, J. J. 1996. "Innsbruck 1976." In J. E. Findling and K. D. Pelle (eds.), *Historical Dictionary of the Modern Olympic Movement,* pp. 289–294. Westport, Conn.: Greenwood Press.

Kirsch, B. 1973. "Innsbruck, '64 Site, Gets '76 Olympics." *New York Times,* February 5, p. 35.

Klausen, A. M. (ed.). 1999. *Olympic Games as Performance and Public Event: The Case of the XVII Winter Olympic Games in Norway.* New York: Berghahn Books.

Koenig, H. 1983. "Sarajevo: A Miracle in the Balkans." *Physician and Sportsmedicine* 11: 146–153.

Kramer-Mandeau, W. 1996. "Latin America and the Winter Olympics—A 'Blank Spot' in Sports History." In Goksøyr, von der Lippe, and Mo (eds.), *Winter Games, Warm Traditions,* pp. 154–164.

Leftwich, A. 1984. *What Is Politics?: The Activity and Its Study.* Oxford: Blackwell.

Lenskyj, H. J. 2000. *Inside the Olympic Industry: Power, Politics, and Activism.* Albany: State University of New York Press.

Lesjo, J. H. 2000. "Lillehammer 1994: Planning, Figurations and the 'Green' Winter Games." *International Review for the Sociology of Sport* 35: 282–293.

Longman, J. 1998. "Cold Shoulder Turns into Warm Embrace." *New York Times,* February 6, p. C1.

MacAloon, J. J. 1991. "The Turn of Two Centuries: Sport and the Politics of Intercultural Relations." In F. Landry, M. Landry, and M. Yerles (eds.), *Sport— The Third Millennium,* pp. 31–44. Proceedings of the International Symposium, Quebec City, Canada, May 21–25, 1990. Sainte-Foy: Les Presses de l'Université Laval.

Maguire, J. 1999. *Global Sport: Identities, Societies, Civilizations.* Cambridge: Polity Press.

Mandell, R. D. 1971. *The Nazi Olympics.* New York: Macmillan.

McNeill, M. 1996. "Networks: Producing Olympic Ice Hockey for a National TV Audience." *Sociology of Sport Journal* 13: 103–124.

Mearsheimer, J. J. 2001. *The Tragedy of Great Power Politics.* New York: W. W. Norton.

Miller, G. 1979. *Behind the Olympic Rings.* Lynn, Mass.: H. O. Zimman.

Myers, M. 1988. "The Glenbow Affair." *Inuit Art Quarterly* (Winter): 12–16.

Niketic, M. 1984. "XIV Olympic Winter Games: Sarajevo 1984." *Yugoslav Survey* 25: 3–22.

Ortleff, G. C., and S. C. Ortleff. 1976. *Lake Placid, the Olympic Years, 1932–1980: A Portrait of America's Premier Winter Resort.* Lake Placid: Macromedia.

Pope, S. W. 1997. *Patriotic Games: Sporting Traditions in the American Imagination, 1876–1926.* New York: Oxford University Press.

Puijk, R. 2000. "A Global Media Event?: Coverage of the 1994 Lillehammer Olympic Games." *International Review of the Sociology of Sport* 35: 309–330.

Riggs, K. E., S. Eastman, and T. Golobic. 1993. "Manufactured Conflict in the 1992 Olympics: The Discourse of TV and Politics." *Critical Studies in Mass Communication* 10: 253–272.

Rinehart, R. E. 1998. *Players All: Performances in Contemporary Sport.* Bloomington: Indiana University Press.

Robbins, B. 1998. "Actually Existing Cosmopolitanism." In P. Cheah and B. Robbins (eds.), *Cosmopolitics: Thinking and Feeling beyond the Nation,* pp. 1–19. Minneapolis: University of Minnesota Press.

Robertson, R. 1995. "Glocalization: Time-Space Homogeneity-Heterogeneity." In S. Lash and R. Robertson (eds.), *Global Modernities,* pp. 23–44. London: Sage.

Roche, M. 2000. *Mega-Events and Modernity: Olympics and Expos in the Growth of Global Culture.* London: Routledge.

Schaffer, K., and S. Smith. 2000. "Introduction: The Games at the Millennium." In K. Schaffer and S. Smith (eds.), *The Olympics at the Millennium: Power, Politics and the Games,* pp. 1–18. New Brunswick, N.J.: Rutgers University Press.

Schiller, H. I. 1985. "Electronic Information Flows: New Basis for Global Domination." In P. Drummond and R. Patterson (eds.), *Television in Transition*, pp. 11–20. London: BFI Publishing.

Tomlinson, J. 1999. *Globalization and Culture.* Chicago: University of Chicago Press.

United States Olympic Committee (USOC). 1999. *Report of the Special Bid Oversight Commission.* March 1. Colorado Springs: USOC.

Wamsley, K. B. 1996. "Calgary 1988." In J. E. Findling and K. D. Pelle (eds.), *Historical Dictionary of the Modern Olympic Movement,* pp. 310–317. Westport, Conn.: Greenwood Press.

Wilson, R. 1998. "A New Cosmopolitanism Is in the Air: Some Dialectical Twists and Turns." In P. Cheah and B. Robbins (eds.), *Cosmopolitics: Thinking and Feeling beyond the Nation,* pp. 351–361. Minneapolis: University of Minnesota Press.

9

FLAME AND FANFARE

Victory Award Ceremonies and the Olympic Torch Relay

Robert K. Barney

In the striking world of modern sport, one can hardly dispute that the Olympic Games present the most elaborate and glorious sport spectacle known to us in modern times, indeed, as the erudite Olympic anthropologist John MacAloon tells us, a spectacle *par excellence*.[1] Think for a moment on things reflective of the Olympic Games experience: huge crowds streaming en masse toward stadium and course venues, hawkers of Olympic memorabilia, scalpers of events tickets, thousands of volunteers, masses of humanity clothed in costumes of every imaginable fashion and conversing in dozens of different languages, multitudes of pennants, banners, and trappings of every hue and design. Watching all this on television from the near and far corners of the global village are some 3.5 to 4 billion viewers. Exciting? You bet, as anyone who has ever attended an Olympic Games, Winter or Summer, will tell you—a once in a lifetime experience.

More solemn but nevertheless just as spectacular are the celebratory Olympic rituals and institutions that normally unfold: the climax of the torch relay and lighting of the stadium fire, the marching in of nations, raising the Olympic flag, the victory medal ceremonies, hymns and anthems, lofty proclamations, displays of national flags—all these and more, some flamboyantly overt, others tacit but nevertheless evident to viewers of the scenes. Among the more flamboyant, of course, are the literally thousands of striking expressions surrounding the Olympic atmosphere, featuring commercial advertising blurbs and signatures, both authorized and unauthorized in nature. In some cases, too, the penetrating forces of commercialism have been wedded to Olympic rite and ceremony. None started out that way in their infant evolutionary history, but some eventually succumbed to exploitative commercial forces. Some, despite their high-profile status in the galaxy of Olympic celebrations, continue to withstand the encroaching world of expanding Olympic commercialism—but for how long? one might ask. This essay examines two Olympic ceremonial affairs: the victory medal ceremony stands as almost the last bastion of commercial rebuff, while the torch relay exists at the other extreme, a transformation to business enterprise. Before treating the commodification issue, each celebration's ritualization and institutionalization process in the Olympic context is examined.

THE VICTORY MEDAL CEREMONIES

Though there are many parallels between the ancient and modern Olympic Games, there is little in the way of a message from the past that might provide clues as to how athletes' victory celebrations evolved in the modern Games. Three of the best works dealing with antiquity offer little beyond what awaited the victorious Greek when he returned in triumph to his city-state after a victory at Olympia.[2] For instance, we hear of winning athletes being borne through the crowd of spectators on the shoulders of compatriots, of a simple olive wreath placed on his head, of statues commemorating these victories erected in the sacred *altis* adjacent to the stadium. The Olympic Games of the modern era present a more indelible record of on-site athletic victory celebrations.

In the vast world of modern global elite sport, scarcely an athletic meeting is conducted without victory celebrations. And these celebrations are most glorified in the Olympic Games. Fanfares, public announcements, appearance of dignitaries, presentation of athletes, bestowing of awards, and, finally, display of national flags and rendering of anthems all make victory ceremonies climactic events. Indeed, the victory celebrations of some Olympic events are seen by many as nearly equal in drama to the competitions themselves.

A familiar aspect of these ceremonies is the victory podium, upon which the winners of the top three places stand and are presented with prizes. Given the victory podium's symbolic representation, is it any wonder that the verb "to podium" has become a cliché incessantly used by athletes readying themselves with hopes of victory in elite competition as well as by thousands of world journalists speculating on who tomorrow's champions might be? This is true for Olympic and non-Olympic sports, for summer as well as winter sports, for men as well as women, indeed, for sports played on each of the world's Olympic continents: Asia, Oceania, Africa, Europe, and the Americas.

Historians and anthropologists who have studied the ritual celebration of victory in modern sport culture point to the Olympic Games as the creator of victory ceremonies. From their glorious beginning in Athens in

1896, where the king of Greece presented Olympic winners with their awards during the closing ceremonies of the first Games, to Amsterdam in 1928, where Queen Wilhelmina and her husband, Prince Hendrik, did the honors, Olympic award ceremonies were constructed to intensify the general ritual aura exuded by the Games. From Athens to Amsterdam, too, Olympic athletes received their victory awards in a physical setting below the dignitaries and heads-of-state who bestowed their medals, or, as theorists might argue, in an inferior position. Did differences in rank and station in life between athlete and dignitary prescribe these conditions? We shall turn to that question later. One thing is certain, however. With the evolution of the victory podium a new order of victory celebration evolved, reversing the role and distinction of the Olympic medal recipient and dignitary medal bestower: winning athletes ascended, dignitaries assumed a less lofty position.

It is not the purpose of this essay to elaborate too deeply on the theoretical dimensions of athletic prize giving. I leave that pursuit for others more qualified. Rather, because the podium has played a central role in Olympic Games victory protocol for exactly seven decades and because the circumstances of its origin have defied discovery (reaching back into history to a time before the podium's first appearance in an Olympic context), it is part of my intent in this essay to examine the events that gave birth to what has become statutory Olympic victory ceremonial ritual.

Establishment of Ritual

In early May 1931 officials of the Organizing Committees of the Lake Placid Winter and Los Angeles Summer Olympic Games (scheduled to be celebrated in February and July 1932, respectively) received directives from the headquarters office of the International Olympic Committee (IOC) in Lausanne. Entitled *Presentation of Medals, Victory Flag Ceremonies, Loud Speaker Announcements,* the directive contained a subsection labeled "Ceremonies Occurring in the Olympic Stadium," the last paragraph of which stated: "Medals will be awarded by the President, Count de Baillet-Latour, or his appointee, from three pedestals, the center one higher than the other two, the first place winner standing on the center pedestal, the second on his right, the third on his left."[3] Lake Placid and Los Angeles Olympic Games organizers were nonplussed. This procedure was altogether different from past Olympic protocol: the consistent practice had been to award medals to athletes as they paraded before dignitaries and officials positioned on elevated platforms where they sat behind specially arranged tables or stood in official or royal boxes. Of some interest to Olympic historians and ritual anthropologists is the question: what are the events behind the origin of such a transformation in Olympic medal-awarding protocol?

Lake Placid, February 1932

On the morning of February 4, 1932, the third edition of the Olympic Winter Games opened in Lake Placid, New York. It was cold and clear, a relief to the anxieties of local organizers who had bemoaned sparse snowfalls and warm temperatures experienced in January during the days leading up to the Games. Present were 364 athletes from 17 countries. The number was disappointing; more had been expected. But these were the early years of a great world depression. In the face of vast economic woes, national states and Olympic committees found it difficult to raise the funds necessary to send athletes to international sports festivals. At 10:00 o'clock on that February 4 morning the assembled athletes commenced their traditional parade into the speed-skating venue. As they solemnly approached dignitaries arranged in the reviewing stand (among them New York governor Franklin Delano Roosevelt, invited to open the Games), a completely unfamiliar object stationed on the ice greeted their arrival: a small bi-level platform, with the middle level raised above two adjoining lower levels.[4] It stood there, stark and unadorned, a skeleton-like structure seemingly left in an unfinished state, as if its builder intended to return and complete the job at some later time.

As the Games unfolded during the following nine days, the structure performed two functions: it provided a raised platform on which dignitaries stood to deliver the usual hallowed messages of Olympic ceremony, including the rendering of the Olympic Oath and the closing remarks of Baillet-Latour; and it served as a stage for the presentation of the gold, silver, and bronze medals to Olympic winners. Thus the Olympic victory podium—that cherished and sanctified convening place for the most elite of Olympians, the medal winners—made its debut and became etched in IOC ceremonial protocol.

Los Angeles, July 1932

When the Los Angeles Summer Olympic Games opened some five months after the Lake Placid spectacle, the largest opening ceremony crowd in Olympic history (at least until Sydney's Summer Games in 2000) thronged into the Memorial Coliseum to witness the festivities.[5] Over a two-week period Los Angeles spectators, like those in Lake Placid, observed a new phenomenon in Olympic victory ceremony protocol. A sturdy but plain bi-level podium had been constructed for the occasion. Unlike the Lake Placid version of the podium, Los Angeles officials had emblazoned the number "1" on the top level. The two lower levels were marked "2" and "3." Still wearing sport uniforms, medal winners in the track-and-field events held in the coliseum mounted the victory podium to receive their awards shortly after their events had been concluded. On the day following the completion of specific individual and team events held in venues other than the Memorial Coliseum, victorious athletes convened in the huge stadium to receive their medals on the victory podium.[6]

The Scholars' Challenge

Jurgen Buschmann and Karl Lennartz, noted historians of the history of Olympic ceremonies, hypothesized that because Lake Placid's Olympic Games were the first to utilize a bi-level victory podium, the evidence for its creation must be buried in the records of the Organizing Committee of the IIIrd Winter Olympic Games. Los Angeles, conjectured Buschmann and Lennartz, simply followed Lake Placid's model.[7] Anthropologist John MacAloon also pinpoints the Lake Placid episode as the starting place of the victory podium's evolution, which ushered in a distinct transformation of athlete recognition in the Olympic context. Concerned that there has never been a sustained historical study of the Olympic victory ceremony in any academic discipline in any language, MacAloon challenged historians to discover the originator of the podium's sudden appearance in Olympic ceremonial protocol:

> Who then, gets the credit for such perspicacity, creativity, effort, and achievement? When the great transformation of the victory ceremony came about, Coubertin was retired, Baillet-Latour played no known role, and there is no clear evidence that the IOC as a whole did anything more than acknowledge and approve after the fact the whole complex innovations created in the victory ceremonies of Lake Placid and Los Angeles.[8]

GENESIS OF THE OLYMPIC VICTORY PODIUM IDEA

Some of the historic events narrated above are known to Olympic historians and ritual anthropologists. Yes, the victory podium did suddenly appear for the first time in the Olympic Games of the Lake Placid and Los Angeles festivals in 1932. Yes, a revolutionary transformation had occurred. But whose ideas were at play to produce the victory ceremonies at Lake Placid? What stimulation gave direction to Godfrey Dewey and Ernest

Gamache, the highest executive officials of the Lake Placid committee, to construct the first podium used at an Olympic Games? Further, what prompted William May Garland, president of the Los Angeles Organizing Committee, and his top aide, Zack Farmer, executive secretary of the committee, to provide similar circumstances some five months later, in July 1932? The evidence to answer such questions has long eluded scholars of Olympic history. The pieces of the puzzle reside in repositories located in separated world centers of research—that is, in Lausanne, Switzerland; Lake Placid, New York; Los Angeles, California; and, interestingly, in the holdings of a Canadian archive located in Hamilton, Canada. Without examination of materials in each location, the puzzle could not have been solved. And even then, had it not been for a chance remark in an obscure letter written by Baillet-Latour, the critical key to unlocking the mystery might never have been detected. These are the reasons why the evolutionary history of the Olympic victory podium has resisted decoding.

Lake Placid and Los Angeles records both reveal that one person, and one person only, dictated the organizer's efforts at creating a victory podium, thereby initiating "the great transformation." And, contrary to MacAloon's opinion that Baillet-Latour "played no known role," the successor to Coubertin as IOC president most assuredly was the visionary instructor of Lake Placid and Los Angeles officials. Found in the Godfrey Dewey Papers in Lake Placid and the William May Garland Papers in Los Angeles are almost identical letters of instruction from Baillet-Latour to the secretaries of the two organizing committees, Ernest Gamache of Lake Placid and Zack Farmer of Los Angeles. The now historic letters of instruction from Baillet-Latour were written in Europe on the same day, May 8, 1931. Other than personal greetings directed individually to Gamache and Farmer, the text instructions expressed in the two letters are identical. With regard to the "awarding of prizes," the Belgian count informed the two executive secretaries, "the three winners will have to take [their] place on three pedestals (similar to the one which is used for the athlete who takes the oath on opening day) which will be placed in front of the presidential box. The prizes will be given by myself or [a] substitute."[9] The taking of the oath is discussed later in this essay.

Upon receiving the IOC president's instructions for awarding the prizes, Gamache, the record indicates, sought no further elaboration from Baillet-Latour on what he had meant by "three pedestals." Instead, the energetic New Englander, one of the few non–New Yorkers engaged by the Organizing Committee to help in carrying out the Olympic project, set about at once to have his own conception of "three pedestals" constructed.[10] In general, it was an admirable effort, with individual steps leading to each level and a sturdy superstructure; the only deficiency, of course, was the podium's unadorned, almost skeletal look.

The first Olympian to take his place on the "victor's stand," as it was called by New York newspapers,[11] was Jack Shea, a 21-year-old Dartmouth College sophomore who reigned as America's national amateur speed-skating champion at distances from 500 to 1,500 meters. As a national champion and a Lake Placid native, Shea was selected by American Olympic officials to recite the Olympic Oath, which he did while standing on the lower left level of the podium. On the afternoon of February 4, as winner of the first speed-skating event, the 500 meters, Shea became the first athlete in Olympic history to receive his gold medal atop what Olympic protocol today defines as the victory podium. IOC president Baillet-Latour presented Shea with his medal. Bernt Evensen of Norway and Alexander Hurd of Canada stood on the two lower levels to receive their silver and bronze medals, presented respectively by Godfrey Dewey, president of the Lake Placid Organizing Committee, and Avery Brundage, president of the American Olympic Association. As Shea stepped down from the podium, still wearing his speed skates, he was congratulated by Brundage, the 45-year-old American Olympic boss, destined to become president of the IOC exactly two decades later.[12]

The next afternoon, February 5, Shea competed in the finals of the 1,500-meter race. Once again, he finished first. Two Canadian skaters, Alex Hurd (the 500-meters bronze-medal winner) and Willy Logan, finished second and third, respectively. Again Shea mounted the victor's stand to receive his medal from Baillet-Latour. But the podium's appearance on February 5 differed from that skeletal structure witnessed on the preceding day. Organizing Committee members, apparently embarrassed by the podium's obviously crude, unfinished appearance, had directed that the structure be draped with decorative bunting to disguise its stark features and better lend itself to the otherwise festive atmosphere.[13] On February 6 and 7 winners, runners-up, and third-place finishers in the two remaining speed-skating events, the 5,000- and 10,000-meter races, received their medals directly following their events, standing atop the bunting-draped podium.[14]

Each medal winner at Lake Placid—bob sledders, ski jumpers, figure skaters, Nordic skiers, even hockey players—eventually mounted the first victory podium in Olympic history. The awards for all events (except for speed-skating awards, which, as noted, were presented directly following the completion of the event) were made on the evening of February 13 during the closing ceremonies. Olympic figure-skating "queen" Sonja Henie was among the more notable of these medal recipients. Standing atop the podium, clad in an enveloping luxurious fur coat, the Norwegian darling of the winter sports world was presented her medal by Baillet-Latour. A blustering snowstorm swept through the stadium, dampening the proceedings and diminishing the crowd in attendance. At the end of the medal award ceremonies, Baillet-Latour himself mounted the podium to proclaim a final message of goodwill in closing the Games. Thus the 1932 Lake Placid Olympic Winter Games ended. Among other considerations, they had included a watershed event in Olympic victory ceremony ritual. Lake Placid officials probably never realized that they had created something that was shortly to become a centerpiece in Olympic ritual celebration. Indeed, when Jack Shea, the 500-meters speed-skating champion, mounted the victory podium on the afternoon of February 4, 1932, to receive his gold medal from Baillet-Latour, he was oblivious to the fact that he was the first Olympic champion to demonstrate "the great transformation." His only recollection is that by the time the medals were presented in the late afternoon following the conclusion of the event hardly a soul remained in the stadium.[15]

In Los Angeles Baillet-Latour's instructional letter of May 8 elicited a different response from Farmer. The Los Angeles Games, of course, were several times larger and exceedingly more complex to organize.[16] Zack Farmer needed elaboration from Baillet-Latour not only on the matter of the victory podium but on other arrangements as well. It is fortunate for the historical record of Olympic victory ceremonies that the perfectionist Farmer did indeed approach the IOC president for further counsel. Otherwise, Baillet-Latour's own inspiration for the victory pedestal might never have become known. On June 8, 1931, after receiving the IOC president's letter of May 8, Farmer responded to Baillet-Latour:

> My dear Mr. President . . . You refer to the requirement of three pedestals to be used in awarding the medals, and then you say that "the prizes will be given away by myself or [a] substitute." Do I understand it correctly that you, or your substitute, (in any event, one person) will award all the medals, first, second and third? In this event the three pedestals, or platforms, might be difficult for you. If you are awarding the medals, I would suggest a nice platform on which you would stand, and upon which would be a table with the first, second and third medals properly arranged, and the first, second and third winners would either just pass by and receive their medal from you, or we could have three elevations or three steps attached to this single platform, and this would differentiate the position of the first, second and third, one against the other, and at the same time place them all in front of you where you could conveniently make the award. On the other hand, if you, and two others, or substitutes, are to

award the medals, one person awarding exclusively each of the three classes, first, second and third, then three platforms and three pedestals could be arranged . . .[17]

Clearly, Farmer, unlike Gamache, was confused. Sensing this, Baillet-Latour wrote back without delay. In his letter of July 8, the Belgian count responded to a number of Farmer's queries, including the subject of prize-giving. "I will give all the prizes myself," wrote Baillet-Latour, "and will designate a substitute if I am prevented of being present. Three pedestals will have to be made, one higher than the two others. The first prize winner standing on the pedestal in the middle—the second on his right; the third on his left." At that moment in his instructions, Baillet-Latour added a crucial aside—the key, really, that unlocked his inspiration for the idea of a victory podium: "it worked very well that way last year at the Empire Games," he wrote.[18]

Zack Farmer knew little of what had transpired at the First British Empire Games staged in Hamilton, Canada, in 1930. He had not been there. But one member of the Los Angeles Organizing Committee had been present: sports technical director William Henry. Surely Henry must have observed the victory pedestal scenes to which Baillet-Latour referred. Be that as it may, there is absolutely no record in Los Angeles bearing a clue that Farmer received any inspiration or direction on the matter from Henry.[19] What Farmer finally ordered constructed as the victory podium for the Los Angeles Games was a plain wooden two-level arrangement with the numbers "1," "2," and "3" painted atop the appropriate levels on which the first-, second-, and third-place finishers were featured.

Baillet-Latour's Inspiration: Hamilton, Ontario's British Empire Games, August 1930

In August 1930 the First British Empire Games opened in Hamilton, Ontario, a bustling steel-manufacturing city of some 150,000 people located on the far western shore of Lake Ontario. The Empire Games were the result of the feverish energy of Melville Marks "Bobby" Robinson, a dedicated volunteer administrator of amateur sport in Canada who had served as honorary manager of the Canadian track-and-field team at the 1928 Amsterdam Olympic Games. While Robinson was on site in Amsterdam, surrounded by the glamorous Olympic setting, he first conceived the idea of staging British Empire Games in his own hometown of Hamilton, Ontario.[20] The concept of "Empire Games" had been around for almost a half-century; the idea dated back at least to a time in the late nineteenth century parallel to Pierre de Coubertin's vision of Modern Olympic Games.[21] In scarcely two years' time, after returning home from Amsterdam, Robinson mustered local Hamilton financial and logistical efforts to organize and stage an initial Empire Games festival that modestly approached the magnificence of Olympic Games celebrated up to that time. Hamilton newspapers trumpeted the fact that prospective Empire Games spectators, in effect, would view an exact replica of the Olympic Games themselves.[22] In fact, the Empire Games often were referred to in Hamilton and Toronto newspapers as "The Empire Olympiad."[23]

In mid-August athletes, sports officials, dignitaries, and spectators from the far corners of the British Empire gathered in Hamilton to experience the inauguration of the Empire Games, celebrated in modern times as the Commonwealth Games. Present among the dignitaries was one European visitor who had little to do with the "Empire": IOC president Henri de Baillet-Latour.[24] Extended a special invitation and assigned a seat in the front row of dignitaries and honored guests, he viewed at close range the sport delegations from throughout the British Empire as they marched into the stadium for the opening ceremonies on August 16, 1930.[25]

It was during those opening ceremonies that Baillet-Latour noted a phenomenon that in a short time was to transform Olympic ceremony protocol. Near the running track in front of the "Tribune of Honor" seating area stood a bi-level podium featuring a vertical rectangular frame extending upward at the front of the topmost platform. After the national delegations had marched into the stadium and were arranged on the infield and Governor-General Viscount Willingdon had formally opened the Games, the celebrated Canadian sprinter Percy Williams, winner of both the 100- and 200-meter races at the 1928 Olympic Games in Amsterdam, mounted the topmost level of the podium and rendered the Empire Games' version of the athlete's oath: "From many parts of the British Empire, we have assembled as amateur athletes to compete in friendly competition. We pledge our best endeavours to uphold the honour of our country and the glorious traditions of British sportsmanship."[26] In front of him, extending upward from a base set on the ground, was a microphone for the stadium's public address system. Also facing him, balanced on top of the rectangular frame, was a radio microphone, the property of CFCA, a popular Toronto radio station. The Empire Games' organizers had arranged for CFCA to present a moment-by-moment description of the opening ceremonies—as well as many of the sporting events—narrated by Canada's celebrated ice hockey broadcaster Foster Hewitt.[27] Thus Baillet-Latour's first impression of the

Empire Games podium was its use as the focal point for the oath-taker. The count was impressed. His one-line remark to Zack Farmer in his letter of July 8, 1931, confirms that fact.

But Hamilton authorities had other plans for the podium beyond its service in the oath-taking episode. When the athletic events began, the bi-level podium was removed from its opening ceremonies position to the middle of the stadium's infield. There it became the pedestal on which the winning athletes of the track and field events were presented to the assembled crowd of spectators. As their names were announced over the stadium's public address system, each mounted the podium: the winner on the top-most level, the second- and third-place finishers on the two lower sides. Standing in those positions, they greeted the spectators and dignitaries assembled with the Olympic salute—right arm held aloft, outstretched.[28] As these acts unfolded, an orchestra played an abbreviated national anthem of the winning athlete's country, and the national flags of all three athletes on the podium were raised above the scoreboard at one end of the stadium. The flag-raising and the playing of national anthems replicated ceremonial details that had begun to evolve in the very beginning of Olympic Games history, that is, at the Games in Athens in 1896.[29] By the time of the 1928 Games in Amsterdam, the anthem and flag-raising had become ritual. It is important to note that none of the track-and-field medal winners at the First Empire Games in Hamilton received their medals while standing on the podium. Instead, medals awarded to winning athletes in all events were presented as they had been in Olympic Games before 1932: at the closing ceremonies. In the case of Hamilton's Empire Games, they were presented at the festival's final banquet on the evening of August 23.[30]

Formalization of the Ritual

Sitting in his place of honor in the front row of these proceedings, Baillet-Latour was witness to a protocol that with his own inspirational modifications added would become part of the Modern Olympic Games celebratory ritual honoring athletic achievement. Drawing from victory ceremony events at Lake Placid and Los Angeles four years earlier, organizers at both Garmisch-Partenkirchen and Berlin in 1936 showcased medal award ceremonies featuring the "new" concept of an Olympic victory podium. The podium reappeared at the first post–World War II Olympic Games in St. Moritz and London. Following the 1948 Olympic festivals, the Olympic victory podium ceremony was transformed from "prescribed practice" to "Olympic Law."[31] It is worth noting, too, that British Empire Games festivals subsequent to the Hamilton experience retained and embellished on the idea of the victory podium.[32]

One looks in vain for newspaper awareness of or reaction to the Empire Games podium innovation, a strikingly new model for presenting winning athletes and a revolutionary change from various versions of awards ceremonies at Olympic Games celebrated prior to 1932—including, of course, the Olympic festival that "Robbie" Robinson himself had witnessed in Amsterdam, where winning athletes paraded by Queen Wilhelmina's royal box to receive their medals. As noted, the newspaper commentary had informed Empire Games spectators that they would be viewing an exact replica of the Olympic Games. It may well have been a widely held perception among onlookers at the First Empire Games that the presentation of winning athletes was no different from standard Olympic Games practice. Only one newspaper seems to have commented on the podium phenomenon: the *Times,* England's most prestigious daily. In a commentary written by the *Times'* special correspondent sent to Hamilton to report events, the following description appeared on August 18: "The ceremony of proclaiming the winner was a fine sight. The winner stood in the centre of the highest step of the dais, the second lower on the right, and the third still lower on the left."[33] Here the special correspondent reported incorrectly. The second- and third-place winners stood on exactly the same level, below and to either side of the winner, as the Games' photographs clearly show.[34] The *Times* commentary continued: "As the band played the national air, each of the three raised his outstretched right arm slowly. Fittingly, Canada had the first victory in the first Empire Games, and, as the band played, the three flags of the winners rose slowly over the score board at the end of the ground."[35]

In the final analysis, Baillet-Latour's inspiration for a new order in Olympic victory protocol came from the events he witnessed firsthand in Hamilton. His initial impression of the podium had been its use as a stage for the "oath-taker." His second impression was its use as a platform for the presentation of victorious athletes. There seems little doubt that Baillet-Latour—the chief organizer of the Antwerp Games in 1920, at which Olympic history's first rendering of the Olympic Oath took place—perceived a relationship between the oath-taker (a celebratory figure) and victorious athletes (equally celebrated). The pioneer oath-taker in Antwerp mounted a single pedestal to proclaim the oath: he could be viewed by athlete and spectator alike. At both Winter and Summer Olympic Games following Antwerp—Chamonix and Paris in 1924 and St. Moritz and Amsterdam in 1928—the Olympic oath-taker mounted an impressive dais to say the sacred words of the oath.

Victorious athletes, however, continued to be honored in those less-than-illustrious modes outlined at the beginning of this essay. It was not until Baillet-Latour witnessed the graphic relationship between oath-taking and victory presentation represented in Hamilton that the germination for a new order of Olympic victory protocol took place in his mind. Baillet-Latour's idea was, I believe, stimulated by a practical consideration: to elevate winning athletes so that they might stand out from all others assembled, like the oath-taker. To Baillet-Latour, the podium provided a mechanical means of presenting winning athletes: "it *worked* well in Hamilton last year" (emphasis added). It does not appear that he was guided by considerations of elevating the status of winning athletes above that of aristocratic medal bestowers, but he may well have been inspired to pay special distinction to the gold-medal athlete.

Baillet-Latour himself conceived the idea of actually presenting medals to athletes while they were arranged on the victory podium. This had not been done in Hamilton.[36] Baillet-Latour may have been guided by medal-presentation ceremonies in Antwerp in 1920, during which King Albert and Pierre de Coubertin sat behind an elevated cloth-draped table and presented awards to the gold-, silver-, and bronze-medal recipients, who stood on small, rudely fashioned platforms of equal dimensions. The numbers "1," "2," and "3" appeared on the standing surface of the individual platforms to distinguish the place winner. We shall probably never know precisely what went through Baillet-Latour's mind as the mechanics of oath-giving and victory rite ceremonies in Antwerp in 1920 crystallized with those of the Hamilton Games exactly one decade later. But the linkage between the two festivals presented the Modern Olympic Movement with a new method for honoring its most distinguished athletes.

THE TORCH RELAY

Of all the ceremonial rites surrounding an Olympic festival, the lighting of the sacred flame that consecrates all the events that will unfold over the following two weeks is perhaps the epitome. The torch relay from Olympia in Greece to the cauldron high above the central venue of the Games is, of course, the longest scenario of all those associated with presenting the Games to the world. The torch relay has an evolutionary history in the modern Olympic context almost as long as that of the victory podium. But its inspiration from antiquity is more indelible. Classical scholars of ancient Greek sports history are familiar with the vase painting scenes of naked runners handing a flaming torch to a running colleague. This epi-

sode in antiquity may have been associated with relay running contests with
team-members passing lighted torches to each other, the final aim being to
reach the sacred altar first and hence light the heavenly flame.[37] Better known,
of course, is the ancient Greek myth of how Prometheus brought a spark of
heavenly fire to earth as a symbol of reason and enlightenment, of freedom
and creativity, of progress and advancement of humankind. With respect to
the meaning of the flame's presence at ancient Olympia, one author, writing
romantically, stated:

> During the quadrennial festival of Zeus when all of Greece gathered at the
> altis, competitors and spectators alike were drawn to the Olympic flame.
> It served as an unequivocal touchstone of their civilization's and their gods'
> permanence. It represented generation after generation of Greek youth in
> their athletic prime, an unbroken line stretching back into the mists of time
> to the semidivine heroes from those who now stood before the flame drew
> their inspiration. Gallant champions came and went, city states rose and
> fell, and even the stoutest buildings crumbled to dust, but the flame burned
> on, providing hopes in times of hardship or hostilities that the spirit and
> ideals symbolized by the Olympics would never be extinguished.[38]

MacAloon reflects on the context of "heavenly fire" in Modern Olympic
Games ritual: "the lighting of the sacred flame at Achaia Olympia and its
relay to the 'New Olympia' are rites of separation from ordinary life, initiating a period of public liminality."[39]

A Ritual Is Born

It appears that Pierre de Coubertin himself was the first to express
the thought of linking an Olympic flame with the Modern Olympic Games.
In his speech closing the Stockholm Games of the Vth Olympiad in 1912,
the baron opened his remarks with the following: "And now, gentlemen,
see how a great people [the Swedish nation] has, by our arrangement,
received from your hands the Olympic flame and has undertaken to protect
it and, if possible, enhance the radiance of the precious flame. A custom has
been established that the last word spoken in the evening of the Olympic
Games is to greet the dawn of the next Games."[40] From this one might
grasp the concept of a flame lit to open Games and extinguished to close
them, exactly as in contemporary circumstances. Despite Coubertin's
remark, it took more than three decades of modern Olympic history for
the Games to establish a link with fire in a sacred context. Even then, the
origin was an event of modest consequence—no rite, no ritual, no ceremony.

The first Olympic Games in modern times to witness a flaming cauldron were those celebrated in Amsterdam in 1928. The Dutch architect Jan Wils designed an impressive Olympic stadium featuring a majestic "marathon" tower capped by a flame cauldron. Wils's original design featured a searchlight atop the tower. Sometime between March and June 1926 he altered his scheme to replace the searchlight with a cauldron, in which a flame would burn throughout Holland's Olympic Games. When the Games commenced in the summer of 1928, Dutch organizers simply ignited the flame and distinguished it afterward. No formal ceremonies surrounded the flame's presence. The original Amsterdam torch act was repeated four years later in Los Angeles; the flame was present, but no associated rites took place.

It fell to the noted sport historian and longtime German Olympic observer and sports functionary Carl Diem to arrive at the idea of establishing a torch relay in the modern Olympic context. Diem was born in Germany in 1882. Athlete, educator, scholar, and sport administrator in the Olympic affairs of both the Weimar Republic and Nazi Germany, he was ultimately appointed secretary-general of the Berlin Organizing Committee for the Games of the XIth Olympiad in 1936. Diem founded the Deutsche Hochschule für Leibesübungen (German National Sports University) in 1915 in Berlin.

Berlin, 1936

There is little doubt that Diem was inspired to institute a torch relay in an Olympic contest by dint of Berlin's award of the 1936 Olympic Games. But Diem knew about torch relays before 1936; he had long been fascinated by the history of sport worldwide, including, most importantly, the saga of ancient Greece. He eventually wrote one of the first and most authoritative world histories of sport. Even today, that mammoth work remains a classic.[41] There can be little doubt that Diem was familiar with the torch relay scenes on vase paintings of the ancient Greeks.[42] As Walter Borgers, the definitive historian of the torch relay, tells us, Diem witnessed a torch relay staged by students at the Deutsche Hochschule für Leibesübungen as part of the ceremonies celebrating the opening of the first Kampfspiele in 1922 (a kind of national Olympics) as well as the commemoration of Diem's fortieth birthday.[43]

Almost a decade passed before Carl Diem pondered the possibility of incorporating a torch relay into Modern Olympic ritual. There is no evidence to suggest that he was inspired by observing the venerated flame that burned throughout the Amsterdam Games, even though he was present there as an official of German's first post–World War I Olympic team.

The first concrete evidence of Diem's conceptualization of a torch relay is gleaned from an entry of August 25, 1931, some three months after the IOC's decision to award the 1936 Games to Berlin. In the guest-book of Diem's friend Walther F. Kleffel, discussion between the two old friends on the subject of a torch relay prompted Kleffel to write a single notation next to the place where Carl Diem had signed his name: "On the birthday of a new plan."[44]

In May 1931 Germany was awarded the Games of the XIth Olympiad, to be celebrated in the summer of 1936. Carl Diem was named to the most critical position in their organization: secretary-general of the Organizing Committee, serving under Germany's IOC member Theodore Lewald, who was named president of the committee. Reminiscing years later (1956), Diem related that his first thoughts were to connect the idea for a torch relay with the Los Angeles Games in 1932. Such an elaborate exercise, however, particularly organizing a torch relay to cover a distance between the ancient site of Olympia and Los Angeles, was beyond Diem's influence at that time, even if the organizers in Los Angeles had been amenable to the idea. Nevertheless, his position as secretary of the Organizing Committee for the 1936 Games gave him the necessary platform for transferring his torch relay vision from ethereal idea into glorious reality. Diem's reminiscence of 1956 also informs us that during the summer of 1933 he told Pierre de Coubertin of his plan, gaining the aging baron's "full approval." Still another "approval" was forthcoming in the summer of 1933, this time, as Diem stated, from the president of the IOC himself, Count Henri Baillet-Latour. On behalf of Berlin's Organizing Committee, Lewald presented "Diem's torch relay plan" to the IOC Session,[45] convened in Athens in May 1934.[46] The membership gave its full endorsement of the plan. After the close of the IOC Athens Session, IOC members journeyed to Olympia, stopping at Tegea for lunch. Luncheon discussion among the members on torch relay matters gave the impression to Greek listeners that "the grand idea" was born "then and there," in Tegea on May 22, 1934. After the Berlin Games a plaque was dedicated in Tegea, falsely commemorating the birth of the torch relay idea as having occurred in that precise spot two years earlier. Diem visited Tegea in early October 1936 and took a photograph of the "mistake."[47]

Conrado Durantez provides a graphic description of Olympic history's first torch relay: on the morning of July 21, 1936, thirteen Greek maidens attired in "the fashion of their day" lit the sacred torch in Olympia's excavated ancient stadium by reflecting rays of the sun in a parabolic mirror to "ignite the fuel, then to be borne by a relay series of 3075 runners threading their way across seven countries in eleven days and twelve nights before arriving at the great Olympic stadium in Berlin to finally ignite the sacred cauldron resplendent above the vast throng assembled for the opening ceremonies."[48] An Olympian ritual had been established.

There were no Olympic Games in 1940 and 1944. As in the case of the Games in 1916 in the middle of World War I, the Games of the XIIth and XIIIth Olympiads were canceled too—much of the world was once again at war. In September 1946 the IOC held its first session since 1939. Sixteen members had died since the start of the war in September 1939, among them Baillet-Latour, who passed away in 1942. When London was awarded the first post–World War II Games scheduled for 1948, the subject of organizing a torch relay was placed on the session's agenda. The entire Berlin Games torch relay episode in 1936 had been greeted by the public with great acclaim at the time. The Executive Committee recommended that the torch relay be repeated in 1948, because, as they exclaimed, it provided "fantastic publicity for the Olympic Movement."[49] As Borgers describes, the 1948 rendition of the torch relay from Olympia to London, via Italy, Switzerland, France, Luxembourg, and Belgium, enlisted a total of 1,416 torch bearers over a 12-day period and covered some 2,665 kilometers on land and about 700 kilometers by ship from Greece to Italy across the Ionian Sea and from Belgium to England across the English Channel.[50] And so a ritual became entrenched. Formalization was quick to follow.

Formalizing a Ritual

The initial step in the institutionalization of the torch relay occurred in April 1949 when the IOC met for its 43rd General Session in Rome. After discussion, it was agreed to add an addendum to Rule 33 of the *Olympic Charter* concerning the torch relay in Olympic Games protocol. Focusing on the final act in the relay scenario, a simple sentence culminated the new dictum: "The Olympic Flame arrives by a courier and after circling the track the Sacred Fire is lit."[51] As Olympic festivals unfolded after 1948 the torch relay became a systematic theme, including its implementation at Olympic Winter Games beginning in Oslo in 1952. Even though the Olympic Games started to be celebrated in areas of the world other than Europe and North America (Australasia/Oceania and Asia), the torch relay phenomenon continued. The flame was lit at Olympia and sent on its way by almost every conveyance imaginable—human runners, automobile, boat, airplane, bicycle, even electronic beam. In fact, only in association with the Munich Games in 1972 has the feat ever been duplicated of traversing the complete route from Olympia to the Olympic stadium entirely by runners on foot. The most up-to-date version of the *Olympic Charter* has little to say about the Olympic Flame and torch relay, except to state that the flame must be "kindled in Olympia under the authority of the IOC," that an "Olympic torch is a torch or replica thereof on which the Olympic flame burns," and that "the IOC holds all the rights of any kind relating to the use of the Olympic flame and Olympic torches."[52] Further, the *Charter* makes the relevant National Olympic Committee (NOC) "responsible for organizing all plans involving celebrations to which the crossing and arrival of the Olympic flame gives rise...the IOC Executive Board shall approve all arrangements."[53]

THE COMMODIFICATION ISSUE

Obviously, Olympic ceremonial episodes with such brilliant images and worldwide viewer focus as the Olympic victory ceremonies and torch relay present commercial enterprise with magnificent potential opportunities for advertising in the global marketplace, particularly in relationship to television. Both the victory ceremonies and the torch relay engender almost as much viewer attention on television broadcasts as do the athletic struggles in the stadium and other Olympic competition venues. For those critically important reasons—*image* and *exposure*—both formal events are ripe plums to be plucked by the influential and powerful forces of commercialism.

Thus far, the Olympic victory ceremonies have remained isolated from the grasp of commercialization. This is largely due to the fact that the IOC has hard and fast policies on advertising inside Olympic competition venues. Only once in the over-100-year history of the Games has this rule been relaxed. In 1924, amid the splendor of the Games of the VIIIth Olympiad celebrated in Paris, organizers, including Pierre de Coubertin himself, granted permission to various French commercial firms to advertise their products on the interior facades and high towers of the Colombes Stadium. Dubonnet, Cinzano, Ovalmaltine, and the elegant perfume Chevine Niger, among other commercial images, appeared amidst athletes performing their disciplines.[54] The appeal of victory ceremonies to commercial firms is evident in viewing the bestowing of awards at various international athletic meetings around the world (car-racing and bicycle-racing, for example), where the brand logos of various business entities proliferate on the camera-visible surfaces of the victory podium.

There has long been a tacit link between the torch relay and business commercialism. The well-known German steel manufacturer Krupp A.G.–Essen, for example, produced the torches for the original Berlin Games relay in 1936. Krupp branded each torch with its manufacturing identification. And Krupp was not the only firm that Diem pursued to help underwrite the expenses of the support system needed for the relay. Daimler-Benz provided the necessary automobile support; Carl Zeiss-Jena, the elaborate mirror apparatus for lighting the flame in Olympia; Erdölwerke, the propane gas for the torch flame itself.[55] As various Winter and Summer Olympic Games unfolded over time, host city Organizing Committees pursued business firms to donate goods, services, and the apparatus and support infrastructure needed to carry out the relay project. And why not? It was good business: good for Organizing Committees consistently in dire need of financial help and good for business too—the advertising exposure was well worth the expense. As the identification and popularity of the torch relay grew, so, too, did the quest of business enterprise to be associated with it. The report of the Melbourne Games in 1956, for instance, contains a full-page advertisement linking the "cauldron flame" and "torch runner" with Ovaltine, "the Vitamin-fortified Food Beverage."[56] Despite the usual donation of such items as runners' uniforms, the torches themselves, the fuel to light them, and occasionally some support vehicles, the link between commercialism and the Olympic torch relay remained quite modest until 1984 and the organization of the Los Angeles Games under the direction of Peter Ueberroth. Then again, quite a few things relative to Olympic matters changed drastically after 1984.

Los Angeles, 1984

In the wake of public refusal by Los Angelenos to allow public tax monies to underwrite deficits that might be incurred in the organization and execution of the Games of the XXIIIrd Olympiad, the IOC, in an unprecedented decision, agreed to allow a private group headed by Peter Ueberroth to stage the festival. Ueberroth used the vehicle of private enterprise to fund the Games. A number of corporations paid substantial sums in return for the exclusive privilege of advertising their products and services as "Official Olympic goods." Ueberroth's operations were undergirded by tight budget restrictions. His conservative approach paid off handsomely. After the dust had settled and the Games were history, accountants announced a $215 million profit, shared on a 60 percent–40 percent basis for the USOC and the development of amateur sport in the City of Los Angeles and state of California, respectively. Ueberroth, of course, was accountable for mounting a torch relay. Was it not "Olympic Law"? It would be done at minimum expense to Ueberroth and his associates.

To the rescue came a noted corporate giant: AT&T (American Telephone and Telegraph). In return for its official sponsorship of the entire torch relay, it agreed to pay all logistical costs of the venture—vehicles, maintenance, personnel, communications, and the conscription and support of runners in rural areas of the country where local runners could not be engaged. AT&T's costs amounted to hundreds of thousands of dollars. But it was good business. The dividends were well worth it. During the period when AT&T was considering the torch relay sponsorship question, a federal ruling on an antitrust lawsuit against the giant telecommunications firm was upheld and the company was ordered to deregulate. AT&T used its torch relay sponsorship to retain its national "united" image and profile during the restructuring process that followed on the heels of the company's ordered deregulation.[57]

There was another twist to history's first energetic attempt to profit commercially from the torch relay. In order to muster the more than 3,500 runners necessary to convey the torch along its ultimate route of over 9,000 miles from New York to Los Angeles,[58] through thirty-three states and the District of Columbia, a plan was put in place whereby any individual, community organization, or business might sponsor a runner to run a one-kilometer leg of the relay. The sponsorship cost was $3,000 per runner. The money accrued was to help finance local amateur sport or charitable initiatives. In this way, Ueberroth would get his much needed relay runners, and worthy community projects might benefit. The Greeks, the self-appointed "guardians" of the sacred flame, were incensed. Crass "commercialism of the flame," cried the two Greek IOC members at the 86th IOC Session in New Delhi in March 1983. A scathing letter followed. According to Ueberroth, the Hellenic Olympic Committee accused Los Angeles of using the Olympic torch relay "as a tool for collection of money for athletic resources." Furthermore, "our protest reflects also the entire Greek public opinion which has the unshaken belief that a 'sacrilege' is attempted against an institution which Greece considers sacred and is determined to protect by all possible means."[59]

Despite Greek disgust, Ueberroth's torch relay scheme was carried out. AT&T received what it desired from its official sponsorship—brand name and company advertising exposure to combat newly formed market competitors spawned as a result of the deregulation process. "The largest fundraiser of its kind ever held" generated approximately $11 million, the biggest beneficiaries being Young Men's Christian Associations, Boys and Girls

Clubs of America, and Special Olympics programs.[60] And so it was that the Olympic torch relay began to become "big business." The sponsors were happy about this; the Greeks, of course, were not.

Sydney, 2000

Fast-forward past the immense Petro-Canada and Coca-Cola investments in sponsorship of the "trans-Canada" and "across-America" torch relays associated with Calgary's Olympic Winter Games in 1988 and the Centennial Olympic Games in Atlanta in 1996 to the first Olympic festival in the new millennium, Sydney 2000. Australian Mutual Provident (AMP), the insurance and securities colossus, spent more than $100 million to secure exclusive sponsorship and execute the torch relay associated with Sydney's Olympic Games. It entered the Olympic sponsorship field for the same reasons that prompt most commercial enterprises to do likewise: (1) to generate new business (market exploitation), (2) to cultivate loyalty and retain existing customers (market protection), (3) to improve employee morale and productivity, and (4) to enhance brand awareness.[61]

The torch relay, an emotion-filled, people-oriented ritual, was a fundamental factor in the eventual popular success of the Sydney Games, just as the relay was for Salt Lake City's Olympic Winter Games in 2002.[62] In fact, the torch relay is sometimes referred to as "the people's event," evoking celebration and goodwill—exactly the qualities that AMP executives hoped would be associated with their company. The relay wound its way across each of Australia's six states and two territories, through 187 communities from the Indian Ocean coast of Western Australia to the nation's eastern Pacific Ocean shore, from Darwin in the far north to the island state of Tasmania, some 500 kilometers off the mainland's southern coast, finally arriving in Sydney on the day of the opening of the Games, greeted by a tumultuous welcome.[63]

When the Games were over, AMP claimed a 40 percent increase in several of its business areas and an increase in its number of clients from 230,000 to over 300,000. There were also less obvious benefits, such as the development and testing of improved marketing methods as well as experimenting with new customer relationships management programs. But, in the end, building goodwill between the company and its current and prospective clients remained AMP's primary motivation for its association with the torch relay. After it was all over, AMP glowed with satisfaction. Stated a company spokesman: "We wanted to bring the excitement of the Olympics to as many Australians as we could, and it has all come together and we have done it. We wanted people to thank AMP for helping them to be a part of the Games and they are. We have hundreds of thank you letters—how do you put a dollar value on that?"[64] How, indeed?

A FINAL THOUGHT

What is it about the torch relay, a prominent episode of ritualized and institutionalized Olympic tradition, that presents the danger of increasing exploitation by the forces of commercialism? Even though most of the torch relay takes place largely away from the stadium and other Olympic competition venues and precincts, the final and most climactic episodes are carried out inside the major Olympic stadium, the primary focus of the television camera. To date, of course, the Olympic guardian (the IOC) has held fast (with, of course, one exception) against allowing commercial advertising to penetrate the hallowed grounds of competition. Despite the IOC's entrenched position on commercial matters in the stadium, the Olympic torch and flame are not protected from commercial exploitation by IOC statute in the same manner in which the IOC has attempted to protect the Olympic five-ring symbol, the Olympic flag, the Olympic anthem, and the Olympic motto, "Citius, Altius, Fortius."[65]

The question must be asked: in an age when much about the Olympic Games is being reduced to the importance of the marriage between the Olympic Movement and commercial enterprise, can the present state of affairs remain secure with regard to the final acts of the torch relay saga in the stadium? The pressure for advertising in the stadium is certainly growing. In non-Olympic sports events—world championships of all sorts, for example—commercial advertising motifs engulf the competition venues; indeed they often surround some of the most important associated proceedings, such as victory award ceremonies. How long will resistance be maintained against such an atmosphere occurring in the Olympic Games, given the exposure that stadium events offer to business firms with zealous desires and rich treasuries to muster in an attempt to link brand logos and advertising messages with the image and exposure possibilities of the great festival? We have seen how events concerning commercialization of the torch relay have advanced to an alarming state. In fact, torch relay commercial trappings have literally reached the gates and walls of the stadium, the last barrier of separation preventing total immersion by business forces. If the gates and walls are breached by even the most tacit commercial initiative, it would be but a fleeting moment before one of the Modern Olympic Movement's most cherished and enduring institutionalized rituals bows to commodification. If that happens, perhaps the Greeks would be right: "it would be sacrilege."

Notes

1. John J. MacAloon, "Olympic Games and the Theory of Spectacle in Modern Societies," in *Rite, Drama, Festival: Rehearsals Toward a Theory of Cultural Performance* (Philadelphia: Institute for the Study of Human Issues, 1984), p. 252.

2. See Ludwig Drees, *Olympia: Gods, Artists, and Athletes* (New York: Frederick A. Praeger, Publishers, 1968); David C. Young, *The Olympic Myth of Greek Amateur Athletics* (Chicago: Ares Publishers, 1984); and H. W. Pleket, "Games, Prizes, Athletes and Ideology," *Stadion* 1, no. 1: 49–89.

3. These two identical protocol documents can be viewed in the Godfrey Dewey Papers, Dewey File, IOC Folder, Lake Placid Museum Archives, Lake Placid, New York; and the William May Garland Papers, Los Angeles Amateur Athletic Foundation-Ziffren Library, Los Angeles, California.

4. In his essay "On the Structural Origins of Olympic Individuality" (*Research Quarterly for Exercise and Sport* 67, no. 2 [June 1996]), John J. MacAloon refers to the Olympic victor's podium as a "tri-level" structure (see p. 137). But the podium in effect exhibits only two levels, not three: one distinct level for the winning athlete and two places of equal height for the runner-up and third-place athlete. Thus my reference throughout to a "bi-level" podium.

5. Prior to Sydney's 2000 Games opening ceremonies, the slightly more than 101,000 spectators present at the 1932 Summer Games opening ceremonies constituted the largest single-event audience in Olympic history. For more on this, see Robert K. Barney, "Resistance, Persistence, Providence: The 1932 Olympic Games in Perspective," *Research Quarterly for Exercise and Sport* 67, no. 2 (September 1996): 158, note 1.

6. IOC, *Presentation of Medals, Victory Flag Ceremonies, Loud Speaker Announcements* (Lausanne: IOC, 1931). This new method of medal presentation for events held in venues located away from the main stadium was outlined in two subsections of the document: (1) Ceremonies Occurring in the Olympic Stadium and (2) For Competitions Occurring Outside the Olympic Stadium.

7. Jurgen Buschmann and Karl L. Lennartz, "From Los Angeles (1932) to Melbourne (1956): The Olympic Torch's Protagonism in Ceremonies," in M. de Moragas, J. MacAloon, and M. Llines (eds.), *Olympic Ceremonies: Historical Continuity and Cultural Exchange* (Lausanne: International Olympic Committee, 1996), p. 124.

8. MacAloon, "On the Structural Origins of Olympic Individuality," p. 144.

9. Henri Baillet-Latour, President of the International Olympic Committee, to Ernest Gamache, Executive Secretary of the Lake Placid Organizing Committee, May 8, 1931, Dewey File, IOC Folder, Lake Placid Olympic Museum Archives, Lake Placid, New York; and Baillet-Latour to Zack Farmer, Executive Secretary of the Los Angeles Organizing Committee, May 8, 1931, Garland Papers, Los Angeles Amateur Athletic Foundation-Ziffren Library, Los Angeles, California.

10. Ernest Gamache was a native of Leominster, Massachusetts, a suburb of Boston.

11. A survey of the *New York Times* during the period of the Games confirms this fact.

12. In the summer of 1999, sixty-seven years after the occurrence of the event, 88-year-old Jack Shea saw for the first time ever the only known surviving newsphoto (*Albany Evening News,* February 4, 1932) of the first victory podium circumstance in Olympic history. He noted at that time (1999) that—despite Baillet-Latour's careful instructions regarding where the silver and bronze medal-ists should stand relative to the gold medalist—Evensen and Hurd mounted the podium in the wrong places, as the picture clearly showed. Hurd (the bronze medal winner) stood on the silver-medal platform; Evensen (the silver medal win-ner), on the bronze-medal platform.

13. A survey of the type of decorative bunting used by Lake Placid officials in their decoration schemes for both the stadium and other venues suggests that the bunting applied to the podium came from the supply bunting in general Olympic facility use. How the transformation from "bare skeleton" circumstance to "bunting-draped" podium occurred, and at whose suggestion, continues to remain a mystery. Ernest Gamache's personal secretary for Organizing Committee mat-ters, Mrs. Seymour (Mary) McKenzie, remembers nothing about "podium mat-ters" (telephone interviews with Mrs. McKenzie of Lake Placid, New York, June 24 and August 18, 1998). McKenzie does remember the extent of the village's decoration during the Olympic Games, which is supported by descriptions in the Organizing Committee's official report (*Official Report: III Olympic Winter Games* [Lake Placid: Lake Placid Olympic Publicity Committee, 1932], p. 167), noting that "great hotels and clubs, cottages, private homes and business houses were brave with bunting." On the eve of the opening of the Games, the decoration budget stood at $5,000. See Dewey File, III Olympic Winter Games Budget, Lake Placid Olympic Museum Archives, Lake Placid, New York.

14. In the case of the 5,000 meters, Irving Jaffee of the United States won gold, followed by his American teammate, Edward Murphy (silver), and Canada's Willy Logan (bronze). In the concluding speed-skating event, the 10,000 meters, Jaffee won again. On the victory podium with Jaffee were Norway's Ivar Ballan-grud (silver) and Canada's Frank Stack (bronze).

15. This reminiscence was recounted to me by Jack Shea in personal conver-sations occurring on June 24, 1998.

16. Well over one million people attended the Los Angeles Games. Forty na-tions and almost two thousand athletes were present. These logistics alone demanded much more planning and organization than that faced by Lake Placid organizers.

17. Zack Farmer to Baillet-Latour, June 8, 1931, Lausanne, IOC Archives, Baillet-Latour Correspondence File.

18. Baillet-Latour to Zack Farmer, July 8, 1931, *Garland Papers,* Los Angeles Amateur Athletic Foundation-Ziffren Library, Los Angeles, California.

19. For a brief notation of Henry's visit to Hamilton, see *Olympic: Official Publication of the Organizing Committee, Games of the X Olympiad* 2 (September 30, 1932): 4.

20. As part of his Amsterdam mission, Canadian Olympic Committee authorities delegated Robinson to "feel out" various sport representatives of commonwealth countries for a commitment to send athletes to Empire Games in Canada if indeed they could be organized. European feelings on the subject were "lukewarm." But Robinson persisted after returning home. Capitalizing on the fact that he was the sports editor of the *Hamilton Spectator,* he launched a vigorous local campaign to organize history's first British Empire Games in his own city. For more on Robinson's quest to bring Empire Games to Hamilton, see, for instance, the city of Hamilton's "other" daily newspaper, the *Hamilton Herald,* July 8, 1930, and August 8, 1930.

21. Several authors have highlighted this fact. For a condensed survey, see Glynn A. Leyshon, "The First British Empire Games, Hamilton, Ontario, Canada, 1930," in Roland Naul (ed.), *Contemporary Studies in the National Olympic Games Movement* (Frankfurt am Main: Peter Lang, 1997), pp. 205–206.

22. The First Empire Games recorded eleven countries and some four hundred athletes as participants. With elaborate opening ceremonies, release of carrier pigeons, the oath-taking ritual, victory ceremonies, banquets, parades, and so forth, the Empire Games embraced all the usual trappings of an Olympic Games celebration.

23. See, for instance, *Hamilton Herald,* August 15 and 16, 1930; and *Hamilton Spectator,* August 18, 1930.

24. The *Toronto Daily Star,* August 11, 1930, announced the arrival of Baillet-Latour in Montreal on his way to Hamilton. Newspaper reporters queried the IOC president on the question of where the 1936 Olympic Games would be held (a host city had not yet been designated). "Not in Canada," proclaimed Baillet-Latour. "North America will have to wait its turn since Los Angeles will stage the Games two years from now." The front page of the August 16 issue of the *Star* featured a picture of Baillet-Latour.

25. See *Hamilton Spectator,* August 18, 1930. The *Spectator* related that Baillet-Latour joined other dignitaries in a special "guest enclosure" located beside the governor-general's box. Pictures of the assembly of dignitaries standing as the various teams entered the stadium show Baillet-Latour in the front row, several seats removed from Viscount Willingdon's left.

26. Among other sources, the oath enunciated by Percy Williams is cited in Leyshon, "The First British Empire Games," p. 205; and *Hamilton Spectator,* August 18, 1930.

27. For CFCA's announcement that Percy Williams's "oath taking" would be broadcast, along with descriptions of other aspects of the opening ceremonies and following athletic events, see *Toronto Daily Star,* August 16, 1930. For a sample daily schedule of CFCA's Empire Games broadcast, see *Toronto Daily Star,* August 20, 1930.

28. The "Olympic salute" first appeared in the 1920 Games in Antwerp when French athletes greeted officials and spectators in this manner as they marched into the stadium for the opening ceremonies and the following athletic events.

The salute was copied by the Olympic teams of other countries at Games held in the 1920s and 1930s. With the rise of National Socialism in Germany and fascism in Italy in the 1930s, each of which adopted a salute similar to the Olympic greeting, the salute in the Olympic context disappeared, for obvious reasons.

29. Though it is well established that the national flags of winning athletes were "run up the masthead" in the stadium and at other Olympic venues in Athens in 1896, it is less well known that the first instance of a winner's national anthem being played in concert with the raising of the national flag also occurred in Athens. For instance, Charalambos Anninos gave an eyewitness account of events surrounding the immediate aftermath of Spiridon Louis's victorious finish in the marathon: following the raising of the Greek flag to the masthead, "the first chords of the National Anthem struck up and its strains found an echo in the heart of every true Hellene" (Pierre de Coubertin, Timoleon J. Philemon, N. G. Politis, and Charalambos Anninos, *The Olympic Games: B.C. 776–A.D. 1896—Second Part, The Olympic Games in 1896* [English translation by A. V. K.; Athens: Charles Beck Publisher, 1897], p. 89). Following Hungarian swimmer Alfred Hajo's victory in the 100-meter freestyle, Prince George of Greece himself hoisted the Hungarian flag while the orchestra mistakenly began to play the national anthem of Austria. The anthem-playing stopped abruptly when the Hungarian contingent present joined voices in singing the Hungarian national anthem (Bill Mallon and Ture Widlund, *The 1896 Olympic Games: Results for All Competitors in All Events, with Commentary* [Jefferson, N.C.: McFarland & Company Publishers, 1998], p. 104).

30. For details of this, see *Hamilton Spectator,* August 22, 1940.

31. Buschmann and Lennartz, "From Los Angeles (1932) to Melbourne," p. 126.

32. For a graphic picture of the combination oath-taking and victory stand podium used in the 1934 British Empire Games in London, see Stan Tomlin, *Empire Games—Athletics* (Surrey, England: Modern Athlete Publications, Ltd., 1958), p. 14. I am grateful to Torontonians Birgitte Worrall and Jim Worrall (who was himself a medal winner at London's Empire Games) for bringing this source to my attention.

33. *Times* (London, England), August 18, 1930.

34. Toronto and Hamilton newspapers of the period August 17 to 24, 1930, are replete with pictures of winning athletes on the "victory dais."

35. The *Times* (London, England), August 18, 1930.

36. The entire Hamilton scenario deserves a brief postscript. It is unfortunate that the original minutes of the Hamilton Organizing Committee for the First British Empire Games have not survived. They are not in any of several Hamilton archives; in fact, we hear of a fire that ravaged and ultimately destroyed the building in which the records were stored. A pity! If they had survived they might allow us to add to the extant record, that is, that the oath/victory podium idea was the collective inspiration of the Empire Games Organizing Committee. Was there a singular author within the committee responsible for the innovation? We shall probably never know the answer. As in Lake Placid, Los Angeles, Hamilton,

and indeed scores of other Olympic and international sport festival host cities, much of the record of some of history's most important sport moments has been destroyed or lost (witness Nagano, Japan, host city of the 1998 Olympic Winter Games, for instance) due to the human penchant for ignoring all too readily the need to preserve an indelible record of the past.

37. Philostratus (as translated and recounted by Rachel Robinson) refers to the origin of the stade race in the ancient Olympic Games. "The one stade race was invented thus: when the people of Elis were making the appointed sacrifice the offering was laid upon the sacred altar but fire was not for the moment applied to it. Runners were lined up a sated away from the altar and a priest, torch in hand, took his stand in front of it as umpire; the one who ran to the altar first lighted the fire, and departed as an Olympic victor" (Rachel Sargent Robinson, *Sources for the History of Greek Athletics* [Cincinnati: Published by the author, 1955], p. 214).

38. James M. Lynch, *The Ancient Olympiads and Bridges to the Modern Era,* The Olympic Century, vol. 1 (Los Angeles: World Sport Research & Publications, 2000), p. 58.

39. MacAloon, "Olympic Games and the Theory of Spectacle in Modern Societies," p. 252.

40. In its original French: "Et maintenant, Messieurs, voici qu'un grand peuple a, par notre entremise, reçu de vos mains *le flambeau des Olympiades* et s'est engagé par là à en préserver et, si possible, à en aviver la flamme précieuse. Une contume s'est établie que la dernière parole dite au soir des Jeux Olympiques fut pour saleur *l'aurore de Jeux suivants*" (as cited by Bill Mallon and Ture Widlund, *The 1912 Olympic Games* [Jefferson, N.C.: McFarland & Company Publishers, 2002], p. 25; emphasis added).

41. Carl Diem, *Weltgeschichte des Sports und der Leibeserziehung* (Stuttgart: Cotta Verlag, 1960).

42. Ibid. In fact, plate 133 (Fackel Staffellauf) of Diem's book displays one of the more familiar vase-painting scenes of naked Greek runners of antiquity passing the torch (p. 167). Diem's book also shows a group of youthful runners seemingly being counseled by an official who is himself holding a torch aloft (plate 134, p. 168).

43. Walter Borgers, *Olympic Torch Relays* (Kassel: Agon-Sport, 1996), p. 16. These "national games" were designed to fill the void caused by Germany's disqualification from participating in Olympic Games following its defeat in the Great War. Excluded from the 1920 Games in Antwerp and the 1924 Games in Paris, Germany returned to Olympic participation in 1928 at the Games of the IXth Olympiad in Amsterdam.

44. *Walther Kleffel's Guestbook,* August 25, 1931, Carl Diem Archives, Cologne. As cited by Borgers, *Olympic Torch Relays,* p. 16.

45. There have been some insinuations that it was not Diem but rather a functionary in Joseph Goebbels's Ministry of Propaganda for Hitler's Third Reich government that first conceptualized an Olympic torch relay for Germany's

Games. A statement (drawn from the minutes of a Propaganda Committee meeting of February 8, 1934) appearing in the *Official Report* for the Games of the XIth Olympiad asserted: "From Minister Haegert's proposal to organize an Olympic Relay, the secretary-general's [Diem's] plan to have a torch relay from Olympia to Berlin was developed, based on the recollection of an ancient relief in the Palazzo Colonna in Rome which shows the torch relay of Eros figures" (*XI Olympiade Berlin 1936, Amtlicher Bericht,* vol. 1, ed. by Organisationskomite für die XI. Olympiade Berlin 1936 [Berlin: W. Limpert, 1937], p. 58; as cited by Borger, *Olympic Torch Relays,* p. 18). See also Karl Lennartz, "The Genesis of Legend," *Journal of Olympic History* 5, no. 1 (Spring 1997): 8–9. It is obvious from the quoted passage above that it was "the secretary-general's [Diem's] plan to have a torch relay" and that Haegert's action was aimed at formally proposing this to the committee.

46. See "Minutes of the 33rd IOC Session—Athens, 16–19 May 1934," in Wolf Lyberg, *The IOC Sessions, 1894–1955,* vol. 1 (Lausanne: IOC, n.d.), p. 182.

47. These events are cited in Borgers, *Olympic Torch Relays,* p. 19. See also Lennartz, "The Genesis of Legends," pp. 8–9.

48. Conrado Durantez, *The Olympic Flame* (translated from the original Spanish by Garry Serafin; Lausanne: International Olympic Committee, 1988), pp. 49–50.

49. "Minutes of the 39th IOC Session—Lausanne, 4–6 September 1946," in Lyberg, *The IOC Sessions, 1894–1955,* p. 231.

50. See Borgers, *Olympic Torch Relays,* pp. 58–59. To date there is no substantive evidence (pictorial or literary) that a torch relay was organized for the 1948 Olympic Winter Games in St. Moritz, Switzerland.

51. *Olympic Charter* (Lausanne: IOC, 1949), p. 15; as cited by Borgers, *Olympic Torch Relays,* p. 29.

52. *Olympic Charter—2000* (Lausanne: IOC, 2000), p. 23.

53. Ibid., pp. 91–92.

54. See Robert K. Barney, Stephen R. Wenn, and Scott G. Martyn, *Selling the Five Rings: The International Olympic Committee and the Rise of Olympic Commercialism* (Salt Lake City: University of Utah Press, 2002), p. 27.

55. Borgers, *Olympic Torch Relays,* p. 51.

56. *Official Report XVIth Olympiad—Melbourne 1956* (Melbourne: Croydon, 1956), p. 6.

57. For more on this, see Peter Ueberroth, *Made in America* (New York: William Morrow & Company, 1985), pp. 188–191.

58. After being lit in traditional fashion in Olympia, the flame was flown to Athens by helicopter then conveyed to New York by a special plane commissioned by the White House.

59. Ueberroth, *Made in America,* pp. 192–195.

60. Ibid., p. 369.

61. For a larger discussion of corporate sponsorship in the Olympic Games, see Barney, Wenn, and Martyn, *Selling the Five Rings.*

62. The torch relay at the Salt Lake City Olympic festival was jointly sponsored by Chevrolet and the longstanding "king" of Olympic sponsorship initiatives, Coca-Cola.

63. As the flame was conveyed throughout Sydney and its environs, an estimated almost one million people witnessed the event. At Coogee Beach, where the flame was transferred to a boat for the two-mile ocean passage to Bondi Beach, some twenty thousand people congregated. More than thirty thousand were present at Bondi for the flame's arrival.

64. Philippa Walsh, "AMP Torch Ignites Emotion and Profit," *Sydney Daily Telegraph,* September 30, 2000.

65. *Olympic Charter—2000,* p. 21.

10

THE WINTER PARALYMPICS

Past, Present, and Future

Gudrun Doll-Tepper

"Who says you need arms and legs to be able to ski?" began a newspaper report entitled "The 'Nevertheless' Athletes" written on the occasion of the 4th Paralympic Winter Games 1988 in Innsbruck, Austria (Kunkel 1988). Almost four years later the *National Enquirer* (November 1991) reported on the famous "one-legged wonder woman" Diana Golden, who skied, climbed mountains, went backpacking, and was a true pacesetter who progressed from recreational sport to Olympic gold. Are there now sports, and more specifically winter sports, for individuals with disabilities without any limits?

When we look back through history, we find different approaches and motives for the participation in winter sports activities. Although the general trend in sports for individuals with disabilities is to advance from rehabilitation and therapy exercise (Schmidt 1943; Guttmann 1976; Doll-Tepper 1999) to recreational sport and even competition and high-performance athletics is applicable to winter sports, there is clear evidence that the roots of physical activities in winter differ in some ways from summer sports (Yabe 1998).

Almost all developments in sport for the disabled are connected with enthusiastic, creative, and courageous persons who were disabled themselves. This is especially true for those men who were wounded during World War II, returned to their home country, and tried immediately to continue with normal activities, such as skiing. Nevertheless, in these years very few individuals experimented with equipment and technique. One of the pioneers of skiing for persons with physical disabilities was Austrian Sepp Zwicknagl, who, after losing both legs, started skiing again using his prostheses. Others used crutches, which they adapted for skiing, and thus the so-called three-track skiing was born.

It was not before the 1960s and 1970s that various winter sports were open to persons with different disabilities. These developments are described in more detail below, focusing on the specific disability groups and on international competitions. With regard to the slow development of winter sports activities, especially for wheelchair users, there was in the beginning a lack of encouragement and self-confidence among the disabled community (Kuhn and Deville 1990). There was also a lack of basic research with regard to physiological capacities and physical limitations, an organizational structure to provide direction, financial support to allow the development of equipment including specific adaptations, and the broad distribution of equipment.

Disability sport has changed tremendously, not only with regard to different disability groups that are now involved in physical activities but also with regard to the different types of winter sports that are practiced by individuals with disabilities, be it for recreational or competitive pursuits. More specifically, Paralympic sport has made tremendous developments over the past years. There is remarkable interest by the media and the public in Paralympic Games; and the relationship between the International Olympic Committee (IOC) and the International Paralympic Committee (IPC) is now based on formal contracts.

Although traditionally the Paralympic Summer Games have received a lot more attention, it is important to note that the Winter Paralympic Games have reached new heights in terms of performance of the athletes and public recognition. In this essay I focus on past, present, and future developments of the Winter Paralympics but also discuss different disability groups and sport events for those who are not part of the Paralympic Movement.

HISTORICAL DEVELOPMENTS: WINTER PARALYMPIC GAMES

The Paralympic Movement was initiated by and strongly influenced after World War II by Sir Ludwig Guttmann, a medical doctor working at the Stoke Mandeville Hospital in England who introduced sport to persons with spinal cord injury as part of the rehabilitation process (Scruton 1998a, 1998b). In 1948 Guttmann began the Stoke Mandeville Games, the precursor of the Paralympics. The first Summer Paralympic Games date back to 1960, when competitions for athletes with physical disabilities were held in Rome, Italy.

The Winter Paralympic Games have a much shorter history than those held in summer, with the first Winter Games being held in 1976 in Ornskoldsvik, Sweden. It is interesting to highlight the development of winter

Table 10.1. Nations and Athletes Participating in the Paralympic Games

Year	Venue	NPCs*	Participants
1976	Ornskoldsvik, Sweden	15	250+
1980	Geilo, Norway	18	350+
1984	Innsbruck, Austria	22	500
1988	Innsbruck, Austria	22	700
1992	Tignes, France	24	600+
1994	Lillehammer, Norway	31	950+
1998	Nagano, Japan	32	1,000+
2002	Salt Lake City, USA	40	1,100

*NPC = National Paralympic Committee.

sports for persons with a disability from different perspectives, however. The first Winter Paralympic Games offered competitions only in Alpine skiing and Nordic skiing. Over the years competition events in biathlon and ice-sledge hockey were added. Table 10.1 shows the increase in participating nations and participating athletes.

When considering documents from the various organizing committees and historical reports concerning the number of participating nations and athletes, one notices differences in reported figures (see Jahnke 2001). The relevant documents do not always clearly specify how many athletes, coaches and officials, and support personnel were part of each team. Nevertheless, there has been a definite increase in the number of nations and athletes with each successive Games.

The different names, logos, and sites that were chosen for the Winter Paralympics also illustrate the development of the Games.

The evolution of the names used for the Winter Paralympic Games reveals the evolution of concepts about the Games and the search for the most appropriate terminology to identify them. The first two Games used the term "Olympic" and "Disabled," the former term conflicting with the Olympic Games themselves. The two Innsbruck games were termed "World Winter Sports for the Disabled." In 1992 "Winter Paralympics" first appears; then, after the absence of seasonal designation in 1994 and 1998, the Salt Lake Games carried the now official title "Winter Paralympic Games," which closely parallels "Winter Olympic Games."

After the 1994 Winter Paralympics the logo of the IPC had to be changed from five drops to three drops based on a formal request from the IOC. Elizabeth Dendy (1994: 362) reports: "We have an example of their [IOC]

Table 10.2. Sites of Paralympic Winter Games

1976 Ornskoldsvik, Sweden: ISOD Winter Olympic Games for the Disabled

1980 Geilo, Norway: 2nd Olympic Winter Games for Disabled

1984 Innsbruck, Austria: III. Weltwinterspiele für Korperbehinderte

1988 Innsbruck, Austria: IV. Weltwinterspiele für Korperbehinderte

1992 Tignes-Albertville, France: V. Jeux Paralympiques

1994 Lillehammer, Norway: Paralympics

1998 Nagano, Japan: Paralympics

2002 Salt Lake City, USA: VIIIth Winter Paralympic Games

power in relation to our logo; the IPC General Assembly agreed by a large majority to retain the Seoul logo, yet pressure from the IOC forced us to change."

Another important issue relates to the sites of the Winter Paralympic Games compared to the Winter Olympic Games. During the first period of the Winter Paralympic Games, as with the Summer Olympic Games, the Paralympic and the Olympic Games of the same year were held at different sites. An indication of closer cooperation between the Olympic and the Paralympic Games was seen in 1984 at the Sarajevo Olympic Winter Games, where for the first time in history a demonstration event for athletes with a disability was included in the Olympic program (Princivalle 1984). Since the 1988 Summer Olympic Games in Seoul, Korea, and the 1992 Barcelona and Tignes-Albertville Games, the Winter and Summer Olympics and Paralympics have been held at the same site.

How did all of this happen? Where did it start? And who were the pioneers in this development? To place the Paralympic Winter Games in proper perspective, it is necessary to survey the development of sport for the disabled.

PERSONS WITH A DISABILITY IN WINTER SPORTS: A HISTORICAL PERSPECTIVE

Although the focus of my presentation is specifically the Winter Paralympics, it needs to be emphasized that persons with different disabilities have actively participated in various kinds of winter sports for many decades. Here I highlight some of the developments that resulted in our current situation. The most popular winter sports for persons with disabilities (depending, of course, on the specific disability) are Alpine skiing (slalom, super G, giant slalom, and downhill), Nordic skiing (races from 2.5 kilo-

Table 10.3. Olympic and Paralympic Winter Game Sites

Year	Site of Winter Olympic Games	Site of Winter Paralympic Games
1976	Innsbruck, Austria	Ornskoldsvik, Sweden
1980	Lake Placid, USA	Geilo, Norway
1984	Sarajevo, Yugoslavia	Innsbruck, Austria
1988	Calgary, Canada	Innsbruck, Austria
1992	Tignes-Albertville, France	Tignes-Albertville, France
1994	Lillehammer, Norway	Lillehammer, Norway
1998	Nagano, Japan	Nagano, Japan
2002	Salt Lake City, USA	Salt Lake City, USA
2006	Torino, Italy	Torino, Italy

meters to 30 kilometers, relays, and biathlon), ice skating and speed skating, ice hockey (sledge hockey), and tobogganing and ice-picking (ice-sledding) (Paciorek and Jones 1989).

Almost all of the initial progress in winter sports opportunities for persons with a disability—at least after World War II—was based on initiatives of individuals and later sport organizations for specific disability groups. Therefore, the following description of these historical developments initially had a disability-oriented structure, although most current developments are directed toward sport-oriented approaches.

Winter Sports for Deaf and Hearing-Impaired Persons

Despite a very long tradition of physical activity and international competitions, winter sports events for deaf persons did not start until 1949. Since that time deaf athletes have participated in World Winter Games for the Deaf (Winter Deaflympics) under the auspices of the Comité International des Sports des Sourds (CISS); these competitions are always separate from the Paralympic Games.

In the World Winter Games for the Deaf athletes compete in Alpine skiing, cross-country skiing, and ice hockey. Curling and snowboarding were introduced as demonstration events in Banff in 1991 and Davos in 1999, respectively.

The sport activities and events in which deaf athletes participate inevitably raise the issue of "integration versus segregation." In this context David Stewart's observation is most revealing: "Deaf athletes competing in the

Table 10.4. World Winter Games for the Deaf

1949	Seefeld, Austria
1953	Oslo, Norway
1955	Oberammergau, West Germany
1959	Montana-Vermala, Switzerland
1963	Are, Sweden
1967	Berchtesgaden, West Germany
1971	Adelboden, Switzerland
1975	Lake Placid, United States
1979	Meribel, France
1983	Madonna di Campiglio, Italy
1987	Oslo, Norway
1991	Banff, Canada
1995	Yllas, Finland
1999	Davos, Switzerland

WWGD [World Winter Games for the Deaf] and other deaf games come in contact with a sizeable number of other athletes who share the experience of deafness, most of whom use sign language as their preferred means of communication. This communality, peculiar to the deaf community, is the primary reason deaf games were established and will continue to exist" (Stewart 1991: 19). Despite the fact that all international sport events share a common goal of "including as many countries and athletes as possible, increasing the number of sports and sports events each quadrennium, and continuing to upgrade the quality of individual and team performance" (Sherrill 1988: 19) and despite national and international trends toward setting up umbrella organizations for sport for individuals with disabilities, Stewart (1991: 23) states that "there appears to be no movement within the international deaf sport community to merge World Games for the Deaf with the Paralympic Games or other international games for the disabled." He summarizes the current state of deaf sports as related to the hearing community thus: "World Games for the Deaf in their isolation from non-deaf sport organisations should be treasured for what they are."

In the early years of the International Paralympic Committee (IPC), the international deaf sport organization Comité International des Sports des Sourds (CISS) was a member of the IPC. In 1990 the CISS and the IPC signed an agreement (*IPC Newsletter* 1991: 8–9) in which the IPC granted full recognition to CISS as the supreme authority for sports for and by deaf people and acknowledged the CISS World Games for the Deaf (both summer and winter) as international events of status equal to the Paralympic Games. CISS left the IPC in 1995, however, and currently organizes its own World Games for the Deaf both in summer and in winter (Stewart 1991; Stewart and Ojalas 1995; Stewart and Ammons 1999).

Winter Sports for Individuals with Mental Retardation or Intellectual Disability

Winter sports activities are increasingly offered in many countries to individuals with mental retardation or intellectual disability. Many programs stress the noncompetitive character of their activities. The largest of these programs is the Special Olympics, founded in 1968 by Eunice Kennedy Shriver, sister of U.S. president John F. Kennedy, which has organized international winter sport events in different areas since 1977. Special Olympics World Winter Games include the following events: Alpine skiing (downhill), Nordic skiing (cross-country), figure skating, floor hockey, and snowshoeing and snowboarding. Kennedy Shriver (1985) traced the growth of the Special Olympics Winter Sports Program and reported on the different sports as well as important aspects of these games such as the training of coaches, media interest, individual and corporate involvement, and the so-called unified sports programs that bring persons with and without disabilities together.

International Special Olympic Games are held every four years and are separate from the Paralympic Games. Athletes with an intellectual disability have been involved in Paralympic Games since 1994, however, under the leadership of INAS-FMH (International Sport Association for Persons with a Mental Handicap), later INAS-FID (International Sport Association for Persons with an Intellectual Disability). Due to unsolved problems of determining eligibility with diagnostic accuracy and a scandal at the Sydney 2000 Summer Paralympic Games (INAS-FID disqualified the gold-medal-winning Spanish basketball team after discovering that none of the athletes had a disability), no athlete with an intellectual disability participated in the 2002 Winter Paralympic Games in Salt Lake City.

Winter Sports for Blind and Visually Impaired Persons

Sport for blind people has made great progress over the past years, with new sporting opportunities being offered especially in winter sports. Besides recreational and competitive winter sports activities, particularly in Alpine and Nordic skiing, athletes with visual impairments participate in international ski events. One of the pioneers was Erling Stordahl, "a blind visionary, 'founder' of modern XC-skiing for persons with visual impairments and other disabilities" (Morisbak 1998: 3). He established the famous winter sports event the Ridder-week and Beitostølen Healthsports Center (BHC), which he headed as director for more than twenty years until his death in October 1994 (Morisbak 1998: 3).

Another key figure is Willi Hohm of Vienna, the founder of skiing for the blind in Austria. He and a small number of blind skiers began their first attempts in winter 1946–1947. Despite these encouraging experiences it was not before winter 1971–1972 that skiing for the blind was officially introduced as a section of the Austrian Sports Federation for War Veterans. In the middle of the 1980s cooperation started between this organization and the Austria Ski Federation/Section of Skiing for the Disabled.

At the World Games in Switzerland in 1982 for the first time new categories of disabled skiing were opened to competitors, including blind athletes. In his report about this international event Willi Hohm, chairman of the Sports for the Blind section of the Austrian Sport Federation for the Disabled, fully supported the introduction of giant slalom and downhill races for skiers with all kinds of visual impairments. He not only advocated these events but pleaded for an inclusion of visually impaired and blind skiers in the decisionmaking processes with regard to competitive ski events. Hohm strongly criticized the courses for the races as well as the rules, which forced blind skiers who had lost one or two skis due to falling, for example, to crawl on all fours, fumbling to find their skis. These first experiences led to major changes in the regulations for competitive skiing, but there are still a lot of problems that need to be solved, especially concerning downhill races for the blind. In addition to Alpine skiing, different kinds of Nordic skiing (2.5-kilometer, 5-kilometer, 10-kilometer) are open to individuals with visual impairments.

Some national games for blind athletes also include speed skating events (Miller and Duffield 1986). In a report on the United States Association of Blind Athletes (USABA) Games 1987 in Albuquerque, New Mexico, Gay Clement described this event: "In speed skating, the guide may skate behind the competitor and verbally lead the skater through the course or the guide may lead (skating backwards). The former method was most often used in speed skating. NO physical contact may be made between guide and competitor" (Clement 1987: 44).

Winter Sports for Persons with a Physical Disability

Historically, "handicap skiing" seems to have its roots in two forces: accidental injury and war. According to oral accounts, the concept of "crutch skiing" originated in Switzerland but was developed almost at the same time—during World War II—in Germany and Austria (O'Leary 1994). In 1942–1943 skiing for individuals with disabilities started as three-track skiing introduced by Franz Wendl of Berchtesgaden, Germany, a true pioneer of skiing for individuals with disabilities. He had been a passionate skier and alpinist (mountain climber) before the war but was wounded in March 1941 in Russia. Wendl and a friend, Friedl Tauber, a locksmith and a skier too, continuously developed adaptations to the equipment until they were satisfied with the results.

Herbert Zimmermann and Karl Winter, two above-knee amputees, started three-track skiing in Austria. Zimmermann had been wounded in early 1943 in Africa. When he returned to Salzburg, he immediately tried to ski using his prosthesis, but it did not work. After this disappointing first attempt, he received information about the successful experiences of Wendl. By August 1944 Zimmermann and Winter had successfully developed adapted equipment for mountaineering, enabling them to reach the top of the famous Grossvenediger mountain (3,660 m). During the last months of the war, contacts between the war veterans diminished; and it was not until February 1948 that Herbert Matz of Vienna created a three-track-skiing course with seventeen participants from all over Austria. The next year the first Austrian championships for three-track skiing took place in Badgastein, Austria, from February 17 to 22, 1949.

At the same time, below-knee amputees started skiing using their prostheses. Rudi Scholz from Innsbruck, one of the most well-known and popular Austrian skiers who used his prosthesis, started skiing on January 1, 1944, after being wounded in May 1943. Arm-amputees had fewer problems than the leg-amputees in returning to their sporting activity.

Another outstanding personality in the pioneer years of skiing for physically disabled individuals was Sepp Zwicknagl. He was wounded in April 1942. He lost both lower legs and first attempted to walk and then to ski by using his prosthesis in 1943. In a report given on the occasion of the fiftieth anniversary of the Hahnenkamm ski race in Kitzbuhel, Austria, he describes his initially disappointing but overall challenging and finally successful attempts to ski again (Zwicknagl 1990). His efforts were publicized in a newspaper article titled "Sepp is skiing again." He, like the rest of the pioneers in skiing for persons with a disability, became a role model for other war veterans and persons with disabilities.

But Sepp Zwicknagl achieved more than being a skier again. In fall 1945 he read about the possibility of becoming a ski instructor and physical education teacher by completing a four-semester-course at the Austrian Federal Institute of Physical Education in Innsbruck. Despite his handicap he successfully passed all examinations and became a certified ski instructor at the ski school at Kitzbuhel. In addition to these professional activities Zwicknagl successfully established a section of Skiing for the Disabled aimed at disseminating information, publishing articles, introducing programs and regional and national events for disabled skiers by using a classification system, and offering courses for instructors.

On October 31, 1947, Sepp Zwicknagl wrote a letter to Professor Frank Ritschel, ski instructor and member of the Austrian Ski Federation, in which he suggested a demonstration event of five disabled skiers to participate in the Winter Olympic Games of 1948 in St. Moritz, Switzerland. The Austrian Ski Federation as well as the Austrian Ministry of Education reacted positively, but the Austrian Olympic Committee, the International Ski Federation, the Swiss Ski Federation, and the ski club of St. Moritz refused to introduce this event by stating that the public would not like to be reminded of war on the occasion of Olympic Games. During the following years, skiing activities for persons with a disability expanded, but ski races were not promoted. "Competitive" skiing was not seen as a goal; therefore, no downhill races were allowed. In order to make comparisons between participants possible but to avoid an increase of competitive activities, even the word "championships" was not used anymore for a number of years.

In 1949 a film about Zwicknagel's skiing experiences titled *Ten Years Later,* directed by Dr. Harald Reindl, premiered and did much to promote disabled skiing. An English version was also made; the German airline Lufthansa showed this film on transatlantic flights for many years.

In the late 1940s many Europeans and Americans were involved in rehabilitation programs at army hospitals, rehabilitation centers, and similar facilities. Various attempts were undertaken to develop adaptive skiing techniques and equipment. In the early 1960s pairs of outriggers from Austria had been acquired by American amputees; and in the 1962–1963 ski season America had its first certified disabled ski instructor, from the United States Ski Association's Northwestern Division in Oregon.

Three-track skiing also improved remarkably during the late 1960s, when Vietnam War Veterans got involved in rehabilitation and recreation programs. A most remarkable winter sports program was developed in the late 1960s in Winter Park, Colorado, which is described later.

Disabled skiing advanced in other areas as well. In Switzerland by 1965–1966 ski instruction was offered to children with cerebral palsy. This first group was instructed by Elsbeth Köng. Later on children with cerebral palsy were taught by Anne-Marie Ducommun (1977), who wrote one of the first instruction books on skiing for individuals with disabilities, in particular for those with cerebral palsy, entitled *We Too Can Ski.*

Winter sports for wheelchair users developed in Switzerland (Kuhn and Deville 1990), and major contributions to winter sports and skiing in particular were made by Norwegians practicing the sport in the Beitostølen Healthsports Center (BHC) (Morisbak 1998). In 1970 Widar Jonson, a Norwegian paraplegic, began using a plastic seatshell for excursions as well as ice-hockey and cross-country skiing. Inspired by Jonson, the Swiss paraplegic Peter Gilomen constructed a "cross-country sledge by adding two ordinary cross-country-skis to the seat shell. Thus the cross-country sledge for wheelchair users was born" (Kuhn and Deville 1990: 115).

The beginning of skiing for persons with a disability in the United States is closely linked to the foundation of the National Amputees Skier's Association in 1962, which changed its name to the National Inconvenienced Sportsman's Association in 1972. The regrettable casualties of the Vietnam War provided an impetus to the development of three-track skiing in the United States: "At Fitzsimons General Hospital in Denver, the need for rehabilitation of amputees, support of their morale and the presence of nearby magnificent skiing in the Colorado Rockies combined to move three-track skiing to the forefront" (O'Leary 1994: 12). In 1968 the Children's Amputee Clinic at Denver's Children's Hospital initiated a ski program for people with disabilities, the National Sports Center for the Disabled (NSCD). In the 1968–1969 ski season the first courses started at Arapahoe Basin but soon moved to Winter Park, Colorado.

Hal O'Leary is considered one of the "founding fathers" of adapted skiing in the United States. In 1970 O'Leary, who entered the program as the first NSCD amputee ski instructor, became the director of the program. Three years later he wrote the first manual on skiing for persons with a disability, *The Winter Park Amputee Ski Teaching System;* and in 1987 he published his outstanding experiences in adaptive skiing, *Bold Tracks— Teaching Adaptive Skiing,* which was updated in 1989 and 1994. Under his leadership the National Sports Center for the Disabled soon grew into a serious educational enterprise.

The Handicap Nationals, begun at Winter Park in 1972, marked the growth of adaptive skiing in the United States. A freestyle event was added in 1978, and the next year blind skiers participated in Alpine racing (O'Leary 1994: 14). Thereafter many other national and international events were hosted (Abood 1990); and people with disabilities represented the United States at many international winter sports competitions throughout the world. Media coverage helped the program to become well-known around the world, and it quickly spread across the United States and Canada as well as South America, Europe, Australia, and New Zealand.

Another remarkable program is administered by the National Ability

Center, located in Park City, Utah, which started with ski lessons in the winter season of 1985. Under the slogan "If I Can Do This, I Can Do Anything!" the National Ability Center "offers a wide variety of year-round recreational activities for individuals of all ages and abilities. Participants include families, friends, and groups, and are designed to include those with orthopedic, spinal cord, neuromuscular, visual and hearing impairments, as well as those with cognitive and developmental disabilities" (http:// www.nationalabilitycenter.org on the Internet).

Another pioneer in skiing for persons with a disability is Jack Benedick, founder of the National Handicapped Sports and Recreation Association. Benedick served as its president from 1979 to 1983 and currently is the chairperson of the Alpine Technical Committee for the IPC. He has made a remarkable contribution to the development of Paralympic winter sports and has shared his experiences and visions in many articles (see, for example, Benedick 1998, 2001).

Skiing for individuals with disabilities in Canada began in Ontario in the early 1960s. Persons with different (mainly visual and physical) disabilities started skiing as a recreational activity, which gradually became competitive. In 1969 Jerry Johnston initiated a recreational club for amputee skiers in Banff, which later became known as the Alberta Amputee Ski Association. In 1974 the first competitive event for amputee skiers in Canada took place at the Sunshine Ski Resort in Banff National Park. With Johnston as the founding president, the Canadian Association for Disabled Skiers (CADS) was established in 1976. The Canadian International Disabled Ski Meet in Sunshine Village, Banff, was held in conjunction with the establishment of this organization in April 1976. This meet became an annual event with international participation. Its purpose is to further the advancement of skiing on both a competitive and recreational level.

In many other parts of the world, similar efforts were made to introduce persons with a disability to winter sports.

CURRENT DEVELOPMENTS AND ISSUES

The IPC and Its Relations with CISS, the Special Olympics, and the IOC

The International Paralympic Committee was founded in 1989 in Dusseldorf, Germany, as the umbrella organization to host Paralympic Games and multi-disability world championships. The International Sport Association for Persons with a Mental Handicap (INAS-FMH) became a member of the IPC in 1989, and the International Sport Association for Persons with an Intellectual Disability (INAS-FID) joined in 1997. As a result, athletes with an intellectual disability took part in the 1992, 1994, and 1998 Winter Paralympic Games. After the above-mentioned scandal at the Sydney 2000 Summer Paralympic Games, however, the IPC suspended INAS-FID from competition; thus athletes with an intellectual disability did not compete in the 2002 Salt Lake City Winter Paralympic Games. Therefore, at present, athletes from National Paralympic Committees and the following four international sport organizations are competing in the Games: the International Stoke Mandeville Wheelchair Sports Federation (ISMWSF), the International Sports Organisation for the Disabled (ISOD), the Cerebral Palsy International Sport and Recreation Association (CP-ISRA), and the International Blind Sports Association (IBSA). As no official relation exists between the IPC and Special Olympics International (SOI), international Summer and Winter Special Olympics Games are held separately from the Paralympic Games (Kennedy Shriver 1985).

Since the establishment of an International Co-ordinating Committee in 1982 (Scruton 1998a), joint efforts of the different sport organizations for persons with a disability have been made toward improved cooperation with the International Olympic Committee. As a result, despite several points of disagreement, such as the logo issue, the relations today between the IOC and the IPC are excellent. This is reflected in agreements of cooperation signed in 2000 and 2001 by both presidents, Dr. Robert Steadward (IPC) and Juan Antonio Samaranch (IOC).

Classification

As previously indicated, the athletes participating in the 2002 Winter Paralympic Games in Salt Lake City came from a population with a variety of physical disabilities and visual impairments. As a result, each sport has a number of competition categories, depending on an evaluation of the functional abilities of each athlete. Consequently, not one but several gold medals are awarded in each discipline, according to the number of categories in the competition. Moreover, in both Alpine and Nordic events, "if a category has an 'entry by number' that is below a specified threshold, the collocated categories are combined and a factor built into the system to ensure that the more severely disabled participants in such a combined event are not disadvantaged" (Sainsbury 2002: 31–32). Within the Paralympic movement, classification is an ongoing issue with regard to athletes with a physical disability and visual impairment/blindness and, in particular, athletes with an intellectual disability (Natvig 1980; Vanlandewijck and

Chappel 1996). Although progress has been made, the process of refinement will go on to ensure the utmost fairness of competition (an excellent
overview of classification is Blomqwist and Kipfer 1998).

Equipment and Prostheses

Since the beginning of disability sport, the development of specific
equipment adapted to special needs has played an important role. This is
also true for the development of specific prostheses to be used in competitive sports. A lot of changes in that area have occurred during past years, as
technological advancements have had an enormous impact on the practice
of winter sport.

Doping

Dr. Michael Riding, the former IPC medical officer, was involved in
doping control for many years. Under his direction the first doping tests in
the Paralympic Games were administered at the wheelchair segment at Stoke
Mandeville in 1984. None of the eight tests were positive (Riding 2001:
273). The list of banned substances is almost the same for the IOC and the
IPC, including anabolic steroids and masking agents. Blood doping and
erythropoetin (EPO) are also banned. There are some differences, however, in allowable performance-enhancing substances between Olympic and
Paralympic athletes. Since many of the disabled athletes take medications
that appeared on the banned list, steps were taken prior to the 1996 Summer Paralympics in Atlanta to allow such athletes to compete. A process of
identifying and registering medicinal substances has been formalized so
that competitors know they are eligible to represent their country despite
using otherwise banned substances (Riding 2001: 274). Riding refers to
the so-called recreational drugs such as cocaine, to be more controversial,
but emphasizes the ethical responsibility that needs to be taken in consideration. He clearly states: "We must demand of our IPC members proof of
out-of-competition testing and aim for a time when those aspiring to Paralympic competition carry passports confirming their dope-free status" (Riding 2001: 277).

Participation Opportunities for All?

During the past decades there has been a growing interest in sport
for persons with a disability in various settings, including physical education
in schools, recreational activities, and high-performance sport in clubs,

sport organizations, and community-based programs. Equity and equality issues remain unsolved, however, when it comes to participation of girls and women with disabilities, persons with severe disabilities, and athletes with disabilities from less developed countries. Many efforts are being made in countries around the world to offer more sporting opportunities to persons with a disability. This is closely linked to the introduction of new training opportunities for athletes with a disability (e.g., in Germany Paralympic athletes train alongside Olympic athletes in Olympic training centers), improved education, and professional training for volunteers, coaches, and others (DePaepe and Roswal 1987; O'Leary 1994; Pringle 1999; Gillwald 2000; Whitney 2000). Many of the existing programs emphasize an inclusive approach (Benedick 2001).

Media and Public Interest

Media and public interest in disability sport and, in particular, in the Paralympic Games has steadily grown. Especially since the 1988 Seoul Summer Paralympics and the 1992 Barcelona Summer Paralympics there has been a growing media interest in the performances of Paralympic athletes in many countries worldwide. The Winter Paralympic Games have also reached higher levels of media interest in recent years, mainly in those countries where winter sports play an important role with the public. Many Paralympic athletes are well known in their own country and beyond and have signed contracts with major sponsors. They are among those being awarded "sportsman or sportswoman of the year" honors and compete in this respect with their able-bodied counterparts. Media interest, sponsoring, and marketing issues are becoming increasingly important in Paralympic sport. The 2002 Winter Paralympics in Salt Lake City set new standards in terms of public interest, with television broadcasting (for the first time the Salt Lake Games enjoyed daily one-hour coverage on cable television) and newspaper reports not only within the United States but in many countries around the globe.

Paralympic Winter Sports

At the first Winter Paralympic Games in Ornskoldsvik in 1976 there were competitions in Alpine and Nordic skiing for amputee and visually impaired athletes, and a demonstration event in sledge racing. At the games in Geilo athletes with locomotor disabilities participated; a demonstration event was held in sledge downhill racing. In both 1984 and 1988 in Innsbruck athletes with locomotor disabilities participated in the Winter

Paralympic Games, and sit-skiing was introduced as another event in both Alpine and Nordic competitions. In 1992 no facilities for ice-sport existed; therefore, only Alpine and Nordic events were held. Athletes with mental disabilities took part in demonstration events in Alpine and cross-country skiing. In Lillehammer ice-sledge hockey appeared for the first time on the Paralympic program. Other competitions included Nordic skiing and biathlon events as well as Alpine skiing and sledge-racing. In Nagano five events were part of the Winter Paralympics: Alpine skiing, cross-country skiing, biathlon, ice-sledge racing, and ice-sledge hockey. The Salt Lake City Winter Paralympic Games had events in Alpine and Nordic skiing, biathlon, and ice-sledge hockey.

Injuries and Sport Medical Issues

In 1980 the First International Medical Congress on Sports for the Disabled was held in conjunction with the Winter Paralympic Games in Geilo. Scientific papers on various medical issues, including doping, in sport for athletes with a disability were presented. Since then medical research focused increasingly on sport performance of athletes with different disabilities. Mike Ferrara (2001) on the occasion of the VISTA '99 conference presented a paper on "Injuries to Athletes with a Disability: The State of the Art," which discussed the definition of the population and the definition of injury and included "The Athletes with Disability Injury Registry." Specific information about injuries of athletes with disabilities in winter sport was provided. Others have reported on physiological parameters in athletes with disabilities (Schmid 2001; Bhambhani 2001).

THE IMPORTANCE OF RESEARCH, SPORT SCIENCE, AND EDUCATION

After the establishment of the IPC in 1989, strong efforts were made to assist the Paralympic Movement from a scientific and educational perspective (Doll-Tepper et al. 1994). Several scientific events highlighted the importance of research and education with regard to Paralympic sport, including the Seventh International Symposium on Adapted Physical Activity in Berlin, Germany (1989); the First Paralympic Congress in Barcelona, Spain (1992); VISTA '93: The Outlook Conference in Jasper, Canada (1993); and VISTA '99: New Horizons in Sport for Athletes with a Disability Conference in Cologne, Germany (1999). On the occasion of VISTA '93, the IPC Sport Science Committee was formed, which has made a major contribution to identifying and addressing issues in Paralympic sport.

The VISTA '99 conference identified the following key areas and issues in Paralympic sport: Exercise Physiology, Advances in Training Techniques, Technical Developments/Equipment, Sports Medicine, Classification, Ethics, Integration/Development/ Recruitment, Organization/Administration, and Media/Marketing/Sponsoring (Doll-Tepper, Kröner, and Sonnenschein 2001).

The committee aims to enhance the knowledge about Paralympic sport by intensifying cooperation and communication among athletes, coaches, and sport administrators on one side and medical personnel and researchers on the other. The committee's tasks include needs assessment and the development, evaluation, dissemination, and application of a body of knowledge about Paralympic sport relevant to the initiation and continuation of sport participation, sport performance, and retirement from sport. This mission is achieved through activities directed toward the integration of theory and practice and the promotion of sport science education.

In addition, research projects and guidelines for research at Paralympic Games and for hosting Paralympic congresses were developed, and ethical guidelines for coaches were formulated. Since 1994 the Paralympic Congress has been held in conjunction with the Winter Paralympic Games (Royal Norwegian Ministry of Cultural Affairs 1994).

Unfortunately, due to decisions of the Salt Lake Organizing Committee and the IPC following the tragic events of September 11, 2001, the Winter Paralympic Congress in Salt Lake City was canceled. In April 2001 the IPC Executive approved the change of the name of the committee, which is now called the IPC Sport Science, Research, and Education Committee.

Major efforts are currently being made to offer opportunities for the exchange of scientific findings and experiences between athletes, coaches, administrators, and researchers on the occasion of VISTA Conferences, following the example of Jasper in 1993 and Cologne in 1999 and during Paralympic Congresses, Pre-Olympic Congresses, and other scientific world events (Steadward, Nelson, and Wheeler 1994; Doll-Tepper, Kröner, and Sonnenschein 2001). Future developments need to be based on the identification and analysis of research priorities in disability sport (Reid and Prupas 1998). International communication and cooperation in Paralympic sport with all relevant partners in the professional field are given highest priority. Within the professional network of the International Council of Sport Science and Physical Education (ICSSPE) emphasis is placed on partnerships: for example, with the IPC, the International Sport Federations, the International Federation of Adapted Physical Activity (IFAPA), and the International Committee of Sport Pedagogy and with ICSSPE's partners, such as the IOC, United Nations Educational, Scientific and Cultural Organization

Table 10.5. Paralympic Congress Meetings

1992	Barcelona	1st Paralympic Congress
1994	Lillehammer	2nd Paralympic Congress
1996	Atlanta	3rd Paralympic Congress
1998	Nagano	4th Paralympic Congress
2000	Sydney	5th Paralympic Congress

(UNESCO), World Health Organization (WHO), and Fédération Internationale de Médecine Sportive (FIMS). This offers excellent networking opportunities for professionals worldwide.

CHALLENGES FOR THE FUTURE

Without any doubt, the Paralympic Movement has made remarkable progress. The Summer and Winter Paralympic Games are significant world events on the international calendar (Steadward and Peterson 1997). The IPC and the IOC have reached important agreements with regard to financial support and the bidding and selection procedures for future hosts of Olympic and Paralympic Games. In my summary, I highlight some selected issues related to Paralympics and in particular Winter Paralympics.

Among the various challenges is the issue of integration or inclusion (DePauw 1986; DePauw and Gavron 1995; Steadward 1996; DePauw and Doll-Tepper 2000). Many experts have reflected upon the future of the Paralympic Games as it relates to the Olympic Games (Lindstrom 1992; Price 1994; Doll-Tepper and Von Selzam 1994; Von Selzam 2001). Since 1988 we have witnessed closer cooperation with regard to IOC and IPC as well as with regard to the organizing committees. In 2002, for the first time in history, there is only one organizing committee for both the Olympic and the Paralympic Games, the Salt Lake Organizing Committee. This is an important step forward for the future of Paralympic Games. Controversial positions still exist with regard to partial or full inclusion of Paralympic athletes in the Olympic Games. Although attempts were made toward inclusion (Steadward 1996), many athletes, coaches, sport representatives, administrators, and others within the Paralympic Movement are advocates for preserving the identity of Paralympic sport and the Paralympic Games. It remains to be seen what will happen at the international level. This also depends to a large extent on developments with regard to cooperation with the International Sport Federations and on developments at the national level. Over the past decades new sports have been included in the Paralympic program. This trend will continue, as new winter sport activities will be practiced more frequently and intensely by athletes with a disability in various countries.

Bridging the gap between sport opportunities for athletes with a disability from so-called developed countries with those from less developed/developing countries is a great challenge for the future. Paralympic solidarity programs need to be formulated and implemented. This includes not only training and competition opportunities but also access to adapted equipment and the appropriate material, such as prostheses, wheelchairs, etc. Increased efforts are necessary to include girls and women with a disability into sport at all levels and to qualify and empower them to take over leadership positions (DePauw and Gavron 1995; DePauw 2001; Hums and Moorman 2001; Sherrill 2001). The issue of athletes with severe disabilities and with intellectual disabilities needs to be addressed as well, so that an inclusive approach is being practiced. Doping and other forms of prohibited performance enhancement are challenges to Paralympic sport and require not only clear rules but also a worldwide fight for dope-free sports based on ethical consideration and values (Riding 2001; Chow 2001; Wheeler 2001). Various issues of athletes with a disability have to be addressed: for example, how to recruit them, how to offer them the appropriate training and competition opportunities, and how to assist them in the process of retirement (Wheeler, Malone, Van Vlack, Nelson, and Steadward 1996). We all have to contribute to a better linking of theory and practice (Fay 1994). We have to increase our efforts both in education and in research in order to provide scientifically based information to athletes, coaches, administrators, and others. We have to use existing networks, build up new ones, and cooperate wherever we can—for the benefit of the athletes.

Since the first Winter Paralympic Games in 1976 in Ornskoldsvik, Sweden, this event has grown in quantity and quality. It has become an important part of the world of sport, and it reaches out to all societies around the world with a message that goes beyond sport. The 2002 Paralympic Games in Salt Lake City were a celebration of the human spirit and will leave an important legacy for the future of sport and society in general.

References

Abood, Thomas J. 1990. "Winter Park—Jackson Village: The Two World Championships—Alpine and Nordic Skiing." *Palaestra* 6: 34–41.

Benedick, Jack. 1998. "Nagano: My View." *Palaestra* 14: 43–47.

————. 2001. "Integration of Athletes with a Disability: The Alpine Skiing Model." In Doll-Tepper, Kröner, and Sonnenschein, (eds.), *New Horizons in Sport for Athletes with a Disability,* pp. 599–602.

Bhambhani, Yagesh. 2001. "Bridging the Gap between Research and Practice in Paralympic Sport." In Doll-Tepper, Kröner, and Sonnenschein, (eds.), *New Horizons in Sport for Athletes with a Disability,* pp. 5–25.

Blomqwist, Birgitta, and Mirre Kipfer. 1998. "Classification." In Yabe (ed.), *Trends and Issues in Winter Paralympic Sport,* pp. 63–66.

Chow, York. 2001. "Ethical Issues in the Paralympics: What Is Right and What Is Fair?" In Doll-Tepper, Kröner, and Sonnenschein (eds.), *New Horizons in Sport for Athletes with a Disability,* pp. 401–433.

Clement, Gay. 1987. "USABA Winter Games." *Palaestra* 3: 43–44.

Dendy, Elizabeth. 1994. "Integration Issues in Sport for People with Disabilities: An Overview." In Steadward, Nelson, and Wheeler (eds.), *VISTA '93—The Outlook,* pp. 359–366.

DePaepe, James, and Glen M. Roswal. 1987. "Increasing Instructor Sensitivity for Teaching Skiing to the Disabled." *Palaestra* 3: 8–10.

DePauw, Karen P. 1986. "Toward Progressive Inclusion and Acceptance: Implications for Physical Education." *Applied Physical Activity Quarterly* 3: 1–5.

————. 2001. "Equity Issues in Disability Sport." In Doll-Tepper, Kröner, and Sonnenschein (eds.), *New Horizons in Sport for Athletes with a Disability,* pp. 619–629.

DePauw, Karen P., and Gudrun Doll-Tepper. 2000. "Toward Progressive Inclusion and Acceptance: Myth or Reality?: The Inclusion Debate and Bandwagon Discourse." *Applied Physical Activity Quarterly* 17: 135–143.

DePauw, Karen P., and Sue Gavron. 1995. *Disability and Sport.* Champaign, Ill.: Human Kinetics.

Doll-Tepper, Gudrun. 1999. "Disability Sport." In James Riordan and Arnd Kruger (eds.), *The International Politics of Sport in the 20th Century,* pp. 177–190. New York: Routledge.

Doll-Tepper, Gudrun, et al. (eds.). 1990. *Adapted Physical Activity—An Interdisciplinary Approach.* Berlin: Springer-Verlag.

Doll-Tepper, Gudrun, et al. 1994. *The Future of Sport Science in the Paralympic Movement.* Berlin: n.p.

Doll-Tepper, Gudrun, Michael Kröner, and Werner Sonnenschein (eds.). 2001. *New Horizons in Sport for Athletes With a Disability.* 2 vols. Aachen: Meyer & Meyer Sport.

Doll-Tepper, Gudrun, and Harald Von Selzam. 1994. "Towards 2000: The Paralympics." In Steadward, Nelson, and Wheeler (eds.), *VISTA '93: The Outlook,* pp. 478–487.

Ducommun, Anne-Marie. 1977. *Auch Wir Fahren Ski: Skifahren Lernen Trotz Cerebraler Bewegungsstörung.* Bern: H. Huber.

Fay, Ted. 1994. "Technical Developments for Winter Sports Athletes: An Interrelationship of Research and Practice." In Steadward, Nelson, and Wheeler (eds.), *VISTA '93: The Outlook*, p. 145.

Ferrara, Mike. 2001. "Injuries to Athletes with a Disability: The State of the Art." In Doll-Tepper, Kröner, and Sonnenschein (eds.), *New Horizons in Sport for Athletes with a Disability*, pp. 257–265.

Gillwald, Shelley. 2000. "National Ability Center." *Palaestra* 16: 32–39.

Guttmann, Ludwig. 1976. *Textbook of Sport for the Disabled*. Aylesbury: HM & M.

Hums, Mary A., and Anita M. Moorman. 2001. "Women Working in Sport for People with Disabilities: Career Paths and Challenge." In Doll-Tepper, Kröner, and Sonnenschein (eds.), *New Horizons in Sport for Athletes with a Disability*, pp. 655–666.

IPC (International Paralympic Committee). 1991. *Newsletter* 2, no. 1.

Jahnke, Britta. 2001. "Entstehung und Entwicklung der Paralympischen Winterspiele von 1976 bis 1998." Diplom-Arbeit, Deutsche Sporthochschule Köln.

Kennedy Shriver, Eunice. 1985. "Tracing the Growth of the Special Olympics Winter Sports Program." *Palaestra* 1: 15–18.

Kuhn, Werner, and Andre Deville. 1990. "Winter Sports for Wheelchair Users." In Gudrun Doll-Tepper et al. (eds.), *Adapted Physical Activity—An Interdisciplinary Approach*, pp. 115–118.

Kunkel, R. 1988. "Die Trotzdem-Athleten." *Die Zeit* 6: 70.

Lindstrom, Hans. 1992. "Integration of Sport for Athletes with Disabilities into Sport Programmes for Able-Bodied Athletes." *Palaestra* 8: 28–32, 58–59.

Miller, Oral, and James Duffield. 1986. "Speed Skating for the Blind." *Palaestra* 3: 14–15.

Morisbak, Imge. 1998. "Winter Sports." In Yabe (ed.), *Trends and Issues in Winter Paralympic Sport*, pp. 3–10.

Natvig, Harald (ed.). 1980. *The First International Medical Congress on Sports for the Disabled*. Oslo: n.p.

O'Leary, Hal. 1994. *Bold Tracks—Teaching Adaptive Skiing*. 3rd ed. Boulder: Johnson Books.

Paciorek, Michael J., and Jeffrey A. Jones. 1989. *Sports and Recreation for the Disabled: A Resource Handbook*. Indianapolis: Benchmark Press.

Price, Robert. 1994. "Future Directions for the International Olympic Committee and the Paralympic Committee." In Steadward, Nelson, and Wheeler (eds.), *VISTA '93: The Outlook*, pp. 452–466.

Princivalle, Guy. 1984. "Sarajevo 1984 or the Game of Hope." *Palaestra* 1: 34.

Pringle, Doug. 1999. "Skiing for Individuals with Disabilities: A Beginning." *Palaestra* 15: 44–45.

Reid, Greg, and Andrea Prupas. 1998. "A Documentary Analysis of Research Priorities in Disability Sport." *Adapted Physical Activity Quarterly* 15: 168–178.

Riding, Michael. 2001. "Doping—A Paralympic Perspective." In Doll-Tepper, Kröner, and Sonnenschein (eds.), *New Horizons in Sport for Athletes with a Disability*, pp. 273–277.

Royal Norwegian Ministry of Cultural Affairs. 1994. *Second Paralympic Congress-Report*. Lillehammer: Royal Norwegian Ministry of Cultural Affairs.

Sainsbury, Tony. 2002. "The VIII Winter Paralympic Games." *Olympic Review* 28: 31–35.

Schmid, Andreas. 2001. "Glucose, Insulin, Cortisol and Catecholamines in Trained and Untrained Spinal Cord Injured Persons at Rest and during Exercise." In Doll-Tepper, Kröner, and Sonnenschein (eds.), *New Horizons in Sport for Athletes with a Disability*, pp. 27–38.

Schmidt, V. 1943. "Ueber Skilauf als Sporttherapie bei Beinamputierten." *Schriftenreihe ueber Aerztliche Sonderfuersorge fuer Schwerverwundete* 3 (Stuttgart): 51–52.

Scruton, Joan. 1998a. "The Legacy of Sir Ludwig Guttmann." *Palaestra* 14: 24–27, 44–47.

———. 1998b. *Stoke Mandeville: Road to the Paralympics*. Brill-Aylesbury: Peterhouse.

Sherrill, Claudine. 1988. *Leadership Training in Adapted Physical Education*. Champaign, Ill.: Human Kinetics.

———. 2001. "Gender Concerns in Integration, Development and Recruitment of Female Athletes with a Disability." In Doll-Tepper, Kröner, and Sonnenschein (eds.), *New Horizons in Sport for Athletes with a Disability*, pp. 631–641.

Steadward, Robert. 1996. "Integration and Sport in the Paralympic Movement." *Sport Science Review, Adapted Physical Activity* 5: 26–41.

Steadward, Robert, Ewin R. Nelson, and Garry D. Wheeler (eds.). 1994. *VISTA '93: The Outlook*. Edmonton: Rick Hansen Centre.

Steadward, Robert, and Cynthia Peterson. 1997. *Paralympics—Where Heroes Come*. Edmonton: One Shot Holdings Publisher.

Stewart, David A. 1991. "Reflections on the 1991 World Winter Games for the Deaf." *Palaestra* 8: 18–23.

Stewart, David A., and Donalda K. Ammons. 1999. "Contrasts: The 14th Deaf World Winter Games." *Palaestra* 15: 38–43.

Stewart, David A., and Risto Ojalas. 1995. "The XIII World Winter Games for the Deaf." *Palaestra* 11: 35–38.

Vanlandewijck, Yves, and Rudy Chappel. 1996. "Integration and Classification Issues in Competitive Sports for Athletes with Disabilities." *Sport Science Review, Adapted Physical Activity* 5: 65–88.

Von Selzam, Harald. 2001. "Paralympic and Olympic Games—Separate or Together." In Doll-Tepper, Kröner, and Sonnenschein (eds.), *New Horizons in Sport for Athletes with a Disability*, pp. 583–597.

Wheeler, Garry D. 2001. "Institutional Responsibilities and the Athlete in Transition: What Happens to Athletes with a Disability When They Retire and What Responsibilities Do We Have with Regard to the Athlete during and after Transition from Elite Sport." In Doll-Tepper, Kröner, and Sonnenschein (eds.), *New Horizons in Sport for Athletes with a Disability*, pp. 435–463.

Wheeler, Garry D., Laurie A. Malone, Sandy Van Vlack, Ewin R. Nelson, and Robert Steadward. 1996. "Retirement from Disability Sport: A Pilot Study." *Adapted Physical Activity Quarterly* 13: 382–399.

Whitney, Mary Ellen. 2000. "Project Stride—Sliding Successfully for 15 Years!" *Palaestra* 16: 29.

Yabe, Kyonosuke. 1998. *Trends and Issues in Winter Paralympic Sport*. Nagano: Nagano Paralympic Organizing Committee.

Zwicknagl, Sepp. 1990. "Rueckblick ueber den Anfang des Versehrten-Skilaufs in Oesterreich und ueber Seine Entwicklung innerhalb des OSV bis 1955." Presentation, Kitzbuehel.

11

SALT LAKE CITY 2002

XIXth Olympic Winter Games

Lex Hemphill

Salt Lake City's engagement with the Winter Olympics provides persuasive evidence of the redemptive power of the Games, for no city required more redemption than did the capital city of the state of Utah. After pursuing the Winter Olympics for thirty years, Salt Lake City finally won the right to stage the 2002 Games in 1995, whereupon it embarked on what was surely the most tumultuous seven-year preparation period ever endured by an Olympic host city. During that time, the city that is headquarters to the Church of Jesus Christ of Latter-day Saints (Mormon) had its name permanently affixed to the most damaging scandal in the history of the International Olympic Committee. But after that painfully bumpy ride, Utahns finally got their fortnight in the sun, literally and figuratively, when they presented a superb Olympics in February 2002. For them, those two weeks counterbalanced the scandal-filled, seven-year run-up to the Games. And they left Salt Lake City with a unique—and, yes, redemptive—story to tell about the ups and downs of hosting the Winter Olympics.

Salt Lake City's unmatched geographical asset as a potential Olympic host city—the close proximity of a major urban center to the magnificent Wasatch Mountains—was remarked upon as early as 1928, when Amateur Athletic Union officials idly mused upon Utah as a site for the 1932 Winter Games. But it was not until the mid-1960s that the city formally pursued the Olympics. In 1965, at the behest of Utah governor Calvin Rampton, civic leaders formed a committee to seek the 1972 Winter Olympics. The goal was not so much to win the Games as to generate free publicity for

Originally published in *Historical Dictionary of the Modern Olympic Movement*, eds. John E. Findling and Kimberly D. Pelle. 2nd ed. Praeger Publishing, 2003. Reprinted by permission of Greenwood Publishing Group, Inc.

Utah's ski industry, and the campaign succeeded on that count. In January 1966 Salt Lake City won the U.S. Olympic Committee's nod as America's candidate city for 1972 but lost the IOC balloting to Sapporo, Japan. The same group of bidders stayed in the hunt for the 1976 Games but lost the USOC candidature to Denver. When Denver and Colorado voters rejected the 1976 Olympics, the USOC turned to Salt Lake City in early 1973 to try to keep the '76 Games in the United States. But the IOC, spurned already by the Americans, opted for Innsbruck, Austria.

Olympic talk in Utah quieted for a decade until a new group of bidders, led by corporate attorney Tom Welch, came on the scene in 1985 to seek the USOC candidature for the 1992 Winter Games, a contest that late-entering Salt Lake City lost to Anchorage. But four years later, in June 1989, the Utah bidders came back and beat three other cities to become the USOC candidate for the 1998 Winter Games (and eventually 2002 as well). The American designation came with a unique requirement attached, however: the USOC, chastened by the weak showing of its winter athletes in Calgary in 1988, extracted a commitment from the winning city to build winter-sports facilities for its athletes, whether or not it eventually won the IOC bid.

Salt Lake City's bid leaders knew they needed popular backing to make such a commitment. So they put a measure on the statewide November ballot asking Utah taxpayers to dedicate a portion of their sales tax (1/32nd of a cent) to the construction of winter-sports facilities. On November 7, 1989, Utah citizens, aware they were risking the building of white elephants if the Olympics never came, approved the referendum, with 57 percent of the nearly 380,000 voters consenting. It would be the only statewide ballot ever held on the Olympic question in Utah, and voters were banking on the bidders' intent, as stated in the ballot question, to repay the state "if revenues generated by the Olympic Games are adequate." The dedicated sales tax over a 10-year period, eventually capped at $59 million, funded the construction of ski jumps and a bobsled-luge run at Utah Olympic Park, as well as the speed-skating oval (not including its roof) in Kearns.

A year and a half after the 1989 referendum, Welch and his righthand man, Dave Johnson, brought their bid to the IOC members in Birmingham, England. The prospects of Salt Lake City, already an underdog to Nagano, Japan, had been further diminished in September 1990, when the IOC awarded Atlanta the 1996 Summer Olympics; it was thought unlikely that the United States would win back-to-back Olympics. On June 15, 1991, Salt Lake City indeed lost to Nagano by a 46–42 vote in the final round of balloting, after needing to win a tiebreaker with Aosta, Italy, just to get past the first round. Salt Lake City's strong runner-up showing, despite the obstacles in its way, stamped it as the prohibitive favorite to win the bid for the 2002 Games.

Nine cities bid for the 2002 Winter Games; and for the first time the IOC used a preliminary round to winnow the candidates down to a workable number for the final vote. In January 1995 the IOC cut the field to four: Quebec, Canada; Ostersund, Sweden; Sion, Switzerland; and Salt Lake City. On June 15, 1995, in Budapest, Salt Lake City won on the first ballot with fifty-four votes, swamping Sion and Ostersund, which had fourteen votes each. The advantages of its geography, its advance venue construction, and its thirty-year effort were sufficient explanations for Utah's overwhelming victory. But events that would unfold three and a half years later revealed that something else had played into Salt Lake City's successful bid: excessive generosity toward IOC members by the Utah bidders.

The transition from the bid committee to the Salt Lake Organizing Committee (SLOC) was seamless enough. Welch remained the organization's president, although he expressed disappointment in late 1995 when he was given an annual salary of $315,000, after having worked on the bid effort for ten years on a mostly voluntary basis. At one point Welch proclaimed that he was "better" than his Atlanta counterpart, Billy Payne, who was making twice the salary. Johnson remained as SLOC's vice-president.

The ink was barely dry on the bid award when SLOC received its first piece of wondrous news. In August 1995 NBC announced a package deal to broadcast the Sydney and Salt Lake City Olympics, with the rights to the latter coming in at an unexpectedly high $545 million, a record for a Winter Olympics and even higher than the rights fee NBC paid for the 1996 Summer Olympics in Atlanta. SLOC's share of that total would be $327 million, more than one-third higher than it had budgeted in its revenue projections, offering a sense of temporary relief to those Utahns who feared that a budget shortfall might leave them with a hefty post-Olympics bill.

Much of SLOC's time during the first two years was spent on finalizing details for its sports venues. While the strength of Salt Lake City's bid was the advanced preparation of its venues, some of them changed sites after the bid. The most notable of these was the cross-country skiing and biathlon venue. The original site, Mountain Dell Golf Course, was deemed too flat and boring by international ski officials, and it did not hold snow well. After months of studying an alternate site in Salt Lake City's watershed area, the committee finally opted to go beyond Salt Lake County to Soldier Hollow, on the edge of Wasatch Mountain State Park, in late 1997.

Two other venue development plans on which SLOC worked feverishly in this period ultimately required action from the U.S. Congress for completion—the Olympic Village at the University of Utah and the downhill skiing venue at Snowbasin. To complete the Olympic Village, SLOC and the university sought the transfer of eleven acres from the adjoining Fort Douglas military base, a long and tangled process that did not become final until 1998. The development of Snowbasin entailed a land exchange that Congress finally approved in October 1996, but it was a deal that created the loudest environmentalist fury in the pre-Olympic preparation period.

Snowbasin owner Earl Holding, a SLOC board member and also the owner of the Sun Valley resort in Idaho, had long sought to acquire 1,320 acres of Forest Service land in order to transform the small ski area into a four-season destination resort. After Utah won the bid, the Snowbasin forces skirted the normal environmental review process and went straight to Congress with a land-exchange proposal, claiming a bit disingenuously that it was necessary for staging the Olympic downhill. Under the deal, Holding ultimately got 1,377 precious acres at Snowbasin from the Forest Service in exchange for 11,757 acres in various parcels he owned in northern Utah— equal value in the appraisers' estimation but certainly not to environmentalists. Critics were further irritated by the fact that Holding got a $15 million access road to Snowbasin paid for by the federal government.

SLOC's fairly routine existence dealing with these issues was shattered on July 17, 1997, when it was reported that Salt Lake City police were investigating a domestic dispute between Tom Welch and his wife, Alma. The incident had taken place in the garage of the family's Salt Lake City home on July 9, boiling over from a discussion of Welch's relationship with another woman, one that he would later describe as platonic. Police were summoned by a call from the couple's 11-year-old son and were told differing stories by Alma, who claimed she had been thrown into the garage wall, and by Tom, who claimed there was no struggle.

Welch, who had gone to Africa on a hunting trip shortly after the encounter and returned home early when news of the incident broke, faced a misdemeanor charge of domestic violence battery, to which he pleaded no contest (the charge was dismissed a year later after he completed family counseling). Also, after consulting with SLOC's executive board, he resigned as president of the organization. By the end of a dizzying July, Welch's 12-year Olympic adventure had skidded to an end, and SLOC sought to recover from its first real crisis.

But things got worse before they got better. SLOC was poised to offer Welch a $2 million severance package, but members of the public and the Salt Lake City Council were incensed at the proposal. Welch offered to forego recompense for his past bid committee service, and the package was eventually scaled down to $1.1 million. In addition, there was the matter of succession. Frank Joklik, chairman of the SLOC board and of the bid committee board before that, moved into Welch's position as president without a hiring search by the board, a quick coronation that some board members opposed. Robert Garff was subsequently appointed as board chairman.

The chief highlight of Joklik's reign, which would also prove to be brief, was the solidifying of SLOC's budget. It had been set at roughly $800 million during the bid days; but after winning the bid, SLOC began operating under the assumption of a $920 million cash budget, not including un-determined value-in-kind items. In the fall of 1998, after a nearly year-long process initiated by Joklik, SLOC presented an intricately detailed budget to local public officials. The grand total: $1.45 billion. And that did not in-clude expected federal dollars for transportation and security. The jittery part of the budget was that, with three and a half years to go before the Games, SLOC still had to generate $375 million from corporate sponsors in an uncertain economic climate—a task that would soon become even more difficult.

Just sixteen months after the Welch incident, the real seismic event hit. On November 24, 1998, Salt Lake City television reporter Chris Vanocur, of KTVX-TV, revealed the existence of a two-year-old draft letter from Johnson, SLOC's vice-president, to Sonia Essomba, the daughter of an IOC member from Cameroon. The letter stated that an enclosed check for more than $10,000 would be the last SLOC payment toward her education at American University. The implication of the letter was clear: SLOC had made education payments to the relative of an IOC member at a time when it was seeking IOC votes for its 2002 bid. Two weeks later, after a SLOC review of bid records, Joklik responded that the bid committee had made such payments to thirteen individuals, six of whom were relatives of IOC members, and that the payments totaled nearly $400,000. He insisted that these payments constituted humanitarian aid, in the spirit of the Olympic Solidarity program, and should not be construed as bribes.

But "bribes" is exactly what venerable IOC member Marc Hodler was calling them a few days later in Switzerland, where the IOC was preparing for a regularly scheduled meeting. Hodler then raised the rhetorical ante between sessions of the IOC meeting on December 12, when he claimed that the Olympics were for sale, that certain agents deliver bid-city votes in exchange for a fee, that a handful of IOC members can be bought, that the last four site-selection processes had been so tarnished, and that Salt Lake City was more victim than villain in the process. On that tumultuous week-end in Lausanne, the Salt Lake City scandal became an international cause célèbre. By Christmas no fewer than four investigations had been launched into the scandal—one each by the IOC, the USOC, and SLOC and a fourth by the U.S. Justice Department into possible unlawful activity by the Salt Lake bidders.

As the new year 1999 dawned, in a scandal-tinged America already consumed at the time by the impeachment of President Bill Clinton, the Olympic bribery story mushroomed. While the various investigators worked on their reports, news trickled out not only of scholarships for IOC relatives but of other favors, even including cash payments, given to IOC members by bidders (IOC rules had limited bid-city gifts to a value of $150). On January 8 the scandal claimed its first casualties, when Joklik and Johnson, the top two officers in SLOC's administration, submitted their resignations. Joklik, who had been chairman of the bid committee board in the early 1990s when the questionable activities occurred, said he did not know about the improper payments at the time but would step aside since the excessive gifting took place on his watch. Utah governor Mike Leavitt, expressing disgust at the bid revelations, stepped into the state's Olympic leadership vacuum, while Salt Lake City mayor Deedee Corradini announced that she would not seek another term in office; both had served on the bid committee and denied knowing of the improper activities.

The first of the scandal reports to be presented publicly was that of the IOC's ad hoc panel, headed by Canadian Richard Pound and focused primarily on the conduct of IOC members who "abused their positions." On January 24 in Lausanne, the IOC announced that its executive board, acting on the Pound report, was recommending the expulsion of six IOC members (three others had already resigned prior to the meeting) for accepting excessive favors from the Salt Lake City bidders. Two months later, on March 17, the whole IOC membership met to act on the recommendations and voted to expel six of its members and to issue warnings of varying degrees to nine others. Four had resigned by then, meaning that in all nineteen IOC members, more than 15 percent of the body, were disciplined in the Salt Lake City scandal. And that did not include Rene Essomba, whose daughter Sonia was the subject of the infamous leaked letter; he had died before the scandal broke.

But the IOC had to do more than police its guilty members. With sponsors becoming wary of continuing their financial support of the Olympic Movement and with American members of Congress threatening to impede the flow of U.S. corporate dollars to IOC coffers, the IOC also had to reform its process of selecting future Olympic host cities. IOC president Juan Antonio Samaranch, who received an overwhelming vote of confidence from IOC members at the March meeting, favored eliminating bid-city trips for IOC members, thus drying up the opportunities for gift-giving. He set up two commissions, one to examine bidding procedures and another to revamp the IOC's ethics code. After those panels completed their work and offered recommendations, the IOC met on the weekend of December 11–12, 1999, in Lausanne and passed fifty reform proposals, the most important of which was that site visits to Olympic bid cities were now prohibited. After getting his way, Samaranch declared the problem to be "solved" and then went to Washington, D.C., to subject himself to questioning by a U.S. House subcommittee, an unfriendly barrage that he weathered reasonably well.

While the IOC's process of internal reform took almost all of 1999, SLOC's did not take nearly that long. About two weeks after the release of the IOC's Pound report, SLOC's sitting ethics committee, charged with ferreting out the bid committee's activities, released its 300-page report on February 9, 1999. It was the most complete catalogue of the Salt Lake City bidders' gifting practices from 1991 to 1995 and placed most of the blame on Welch and Johnson—who simply became "Tom and Dave" in local lore—while only mildly chastising the bid committee's board for weak oversight. The Salt Lake bidders offered gifts, favors, and payments estimated at more than $1 million, including $70,000 in direct cash payments to Jean-Claude Ganga of the Republic of Congo, one of the IOC members eventually expelled. So eager was Welch to please fellow members of the "Olympic family" that in one instance he took $30,000 out of his own children's trust accounts to make a loan to the spouse of a Samoan IOC member. The revelations were still fresh when, two days after releasing the report, SLOC set itself on a new course and named Massachusetts venture capitalist Mitt Romney to succeed Joklik as the organization's president.

After the release of the IOC and SLOC reports, the USOC's specially created oversight commission, chaired by former U.S. senator George Mitchell, issued its report on March 1. It placed blame on the IOC for its "culture of improper gift-giving," on SLOC for its bid procedures, and on the USOC for failing to monitor the activities of American bid cities. The Mitchell report also noted that it "strains credulity" to think that Welch and Johnson engaged in their improprieties without the knowledge of the high-profile members of Salt Lake City's bid committee board, an opinion that was shared by many Utahns. As for direct USOC involvement, one of its officials, Alfredo La Mont, the director of international relations, resigned in January due to his undisclosed relationship with Welch in assisting the Salt Lake City bid. A year later, La Mont pleaded guilty to two federal tax fraud charges in regard to a fictitious company through which he had received payments from the Salt Lake City bidders.

The fourth investigation, by the U.S. Justice Department, was the one that could most imperil the Salt Lake City bidders. With the exception of a guilty plea obtained from a Salt Lake City businessman on a tax fraud charge in August 1999 and the two from La Mont in March 2000, the federal investigation yielded little for a year and a half. Then on July 20, 2000, the hammer dropped on Welch and Johnson in the form of a federal grand-jury indictment on fifteen felony counts of conspiracy, racketeering, and fraud, charges for which the two bid leaders could have received prison time. More ominously for SLOC, the prospect loomed of Utah civic leaders being called to the witness stand and questioned about their professed ignorance of the bid improprieties, all of it possibly happening in a Salt Lake City courtroom at or near the time of the Olympics themselves. A year later, on July 16, 2001, U.S. District Judge David Sam dismissed four counts against Welch and Johnson, arguing that Utah's commercial bribery statute upon which they were based was ill applied in this case. Finally, on November 15, 2001, less than three months before the Olympics, Sam threw out the rest of the case, much to the relief of all involved. The Justice Department filed an appeal to Sam's ruling on January 23, 2002, but at least the 2002 Olympics would now proceed without the concurrent distraction of a federal trial.

In the meantime, it was left to Romney, a Mormon and the son of a former Michigan governor, to pick up the pieces in Salt Lake City. His most critical task was to eliminate the huge budget gap of roughly $375 million between revenues and expenses; he did it by paring the budget to $1.3 billion and generating revenues by collecting commitments from previously wary sponsors. In the fall of 2000 SLOC launched its ticketing campaign and sold about $30 million worth of tickets on the first day, putting it well on its way to achieving its goal of $180 million in ticket sales. The 2000–2001 winter season featured a series of successful test events at SLOC's competition venues; the last site to be completed was the enclosed speed-skating oval, where cracks in the concrete forced a repouring of the surface in late 2000, prior to a record-setting debut in March 2001.

In two and a half years, the charismatic Romney had restored SLOC's equilibrium; but there would be one more crisis to face. On September 11, 2001, just five months before the start of the Olympics, terrorist attacks on the World Trade Center in New York and on the Pentagon in Washington stunned the nation and, as a footnote, called the 2002 Winter Olympics into question. Romney, who was in Washington at the time of the attacks to lobby Congress for more federal dollars for security, bravely stated that the Games would go on. Picking up that refrain in Lausanne was new IOC president Jacques Rogge, who had succeeded Samaranch just two months earlier. But the climate was too unsettled for such certainty; and when the United States began air attacks in Afghanistan in October, IOC member Gerhard Heiberg was quoted as saying that "a country at war can't organize the Olympic Games." Heiberg quickly apologized, contending that was not what he meant. And Romney and IOC officials asserted a more positive message: it was precisely in such difficult times that the Olympic dynamic of universality and friendship is most needed.

The events of September 11 naturally focused SLOC and the IOC on the issue of security. The federal government stepped up its investment in Games security, which SLOC ultimately reported to be $350 million. Athletes, media, and spectators would all be exposed to greater security measures at venue access points than at previous Olympics. And there would be no commercial or private access to the airspace over Salt Lake City for the duration of the opening and closing ceremonies at the open-air 50,000-seat Rice-Eccles Stadium on the University of Utah campus. But the most important security development was that there were no other terrorist attacks after September 11 to jeopardize the Games. And, as the Olympic torch relay made its way across the country over a two-month period, beginning on December 4, a spirit of renewed patriotism fused with the Olympic spirit to heighten anticipation of the Games.

Finally, on February 8, 2002, Salt Lake City's excruciating incubation period came to an end. The opening ceremonies that night, which featured the moving presentation of the tattered flag that had survived the World Trade Center attacks five months earlier, launched the largest-scale Winter Olympics ever—more than 2,500 athletes from 77 countries, competing in 78 events, a 70 percent increase in the program since the last time these Games had visited North America in 1988. The weather, so balky an element in previous Winter Olympics, cooperated not just for the opening but for most of the two weeks; there were a few wind-caused postponements on the first weekend, but sunny conditions prevailed. The logistical operation of the Games was nearly flawless, and for Americans there was the added bonus of the improbable success of the home team. Never a winter sports power, the United States won an astonishing thirty-four medals over the Olympic fortnight, one fewer than first-place Germany and twenty-one more than the United States had ever won before.

For all the inspirational moments, though, the event that overshadowed all others in the Olympics was the scandalous outcome of the pairs figure-skating competition. On the fourth night of the Games, reigning world champions Jamie Sale and David Pelletier of Canada skated a marvelous free program that the Delta Center crowd assumed was redeemable for a gold medal. But the judges delivered a 5–4 victory to Elena Berezhnaya and Anton Sikharulidze, the eleventh consecutive Olympic gold in pairs for Russian skaters. North American fans and media howled at the decision, but it might have stood as just another unpopular figure-skating result, were it not for the controversy that emerged around the pro-Russian vote of French judge Marie Reine Le Gougne. At a review meeting of the judges and the referee the morning after the pairs free skate, an emotional Le Gougne said she had cast her vote under pressure from Didier Gailhaguet, the president of France's ice sports federation, a tale she recanted before the week was out. Her story, accompanied by rumors that the French were vote-swapping with the Russians in order to get a favorable result for their ice-dance team, threatened to overtake the Games.

Rogge, the IOC president overseeing his first Olympics, prevailed upon Ottavio Cinquanta, president of the International Skating Union, to resolve the matter quickly. Cinquanta got his ISU board members together three nights after the pairs competition, and they decided to give gold medals to the jilted Canadian pair as well. The next morning the IOC approved the solution, and Sale and Pelletier, by then objects of international sympathy, were declared co-winners. The double-gold solution defused the tempest for the rest of the Olympic fortnight, but the "Skategate" mess continued long after the Games. On April 30 in Lausanne the ISU suspended both Le Gougne and Gailhaguet for three years (and for the 2006 Olympics). Then, in June at a meeting in Kyoto, Japan, the ISU voted to overhaul its scoring system over the next two years in an attempt to restore public confidence in the sport.

But the most stunning aftershock of Skategate came on July 31, when U.S. prosecutors charged Alimzhan Tokhtakhounov, a reputed Russian organized crime figure who was then living in Italy, with conspiring to fix the figure-skating results in Salt Lake City. His supposed scheme was to ensure a pairs gold for the Russian team and a gold in ice dancing for the French team of Gwendal Peizerat and Marina Anissina, a Russian native—both of which happened—in exchange for the personal procurement of a French visa. The allegations, which resulted in a five-count indictment handed down by a federal grand jury in New York on August 21, were based on Italian police wiretaps of Tokhtakhounov's phone conversations, including one in which he reportedly told Anissina's mother that even if the skater were to fall in her Olympic competition "we will make sure she is No. 1." The Russian connection in Skategate, which the ISU had ignored in its own investigation, cast a post–Salt Lake pall over the Winter Olympics' most popular sport.

In addition to the skating corruption at the Salt Lake City Games, there were the requisite Olympic doping stories. In the wake of a doping scandal at the 2001 Nordic ski championships in Finland, the IOC and SLOC focused on having a clean Games. To that end, 95 percent of the Olympic athletes underwent testing before coming to Salt Lake City. There was little doping news during the Olympic fortnight; but on the last day of the Games three

Nordic skiing medalists—triple gold medalist Johann Muehlegg of Spain and Russian stars Larissa Lazutina and Olga Danilova—were busted for using darbepoetin, a new stamina-boosting drug. Muehlegg and Lazutina each lost one gold medal; and much later, at an International Ski Federation meeting in June, the three skiers were each suspended for two years. In all, there were seven confirmed doping cases at the 2002 Games, more than in all previous Winter Olympics.

Still, these Olympics were distinguished more by positive stories than by positive drug tests. The stunning performance in the women's figure-skating competition by American Sarah Hughes washed out some of the bad taste left from the pairs controversy. Canada's hockey triumphs by both the men and women were notable, particularly that of the men, who ended a fifty-year Olympic gold drought by winning the second Olympic tournament that featured National Hockey League players. And a handful of athletes ruled their sports with multi-gold performances: Croatia's gritty Janica Kostelic, whose four medals (three of them gold) were the most by an Alpine skier in a single Olympics; Switzerland's boyish Simon Ammann, who won both ski-jumping events; Norway's Ole Einar Bjoerndalen, who won four gold medals in biathlon; and Finland's Samppa Lajunen, who won three golds in Nordic combined.

Perhaps the most moving story of these Games was written by American Jim Shea, who won gold in the men's skeleton, an event that was making its first appearance in the Olympics since 1948. Shea was a third-generation Winter Olympian, following his father (a 1964 Nordic skier) and his grandfather (a 1932 speed skater). The venerable Jack Shea, who won two gold medals in the 1932 Olympics in his hometown of Lake Placid, New York, had planned on being in Salt Lake City with his Olympian son and grandson; but less than a month before the Games, he died in a car accident near his home at the age of ninety-one. After his skeleton victory just a month later, Jim Shea pulled a picture of his late grandfather from his helmet and flashed it proudly to an emotional crowd.

The triumphs of Shea and Tristan Gale in skeleton signified American success in relatively new "X" sports that had gained Olympic acceptance in the previous decade, including short-track speed skating, freestyle skiing, and snowboarding. The emergence of these sports enabled a non–winter sports country like Australia to win Winter Games gold for the first time, by Steven Bradbury in short-track and Alisa Camplin in aerials. In addition, the growing ethnic diversity in the Winter Olympics was underscored by some of the Salt Lake City medal winners: bobsledder Vonetta Flowers, the first African-American gold medalist; bobsledders Garrett Hines and Randy Jones, the first African-American male medalists; speed skater Derek

Parra, the first Mexican-American gold medalist; and speed skater Jennifer Rodriguez, the first Cuban-American medalist (two bronzes).

The 2002 Olympics were an artistic and popular success, as were the Paralympics that followed in March, the first Winter Paralympics ever taken under the wing of an Olympic Organizing Committee. A few days after the Olympics ended, Romney went to the state capitol to pay Utahns their long-promised $99 million—the $59 million that they had committed to building Olympic facilities in the 1989 referendum and a $40 million legacy fund to operate them. Then, on April 24, Romney convened his last SLOC meeting and announced that his organization finished with a $56 million surplus. With that, Romney left Utah and returned to Massachusetts to run as the Republican candidate for governor (he won election in November), leaving SLOC's shutdown duties to his righthand man, Fraser Bullock. On September 18 Bullock conducted the last SLOC board meeting, at which he estimated SLOC's final profit to be $100 million. The Utah Athletic Foundation, the entity in charge of post-Olympic operation of the main sports venues (the Utah Olympic Park, the Olympic Oval, and the Soldier Hollow Nordic skiing site), would ultimately receive $76.5 million, almost double the budgeted $40 million legacy fund. Thus the Salt Lake City Olympics were a financial triumph, despite the stain of scandal that was attached to them.

CONTRIBUTORS

David C. Young, professor of classics at the University of Florida, has written and lectured extensively on both the ancient Greek poet Pindar and the ancient Olympics. In addition to numerous scholarly articles, he is the author of *Three Odes of Pindar: A Literary Study* (1968), *Pindar Isthmian 7, Myth, and Exempla* (1971), *The Olympic Myth of Greek Amateur Athletics* (1984), and *The Modern Olympics: A Struggle for Revival* (1996).

Professor Roland Renson is chairman of the Department of Sport and Movement Science and member of the Faculty of Physical Education and Physiotherapy at the Katholieke Universiteit Leuven, Leuven, Belgium, the oldest existing Catholic university in the world (established in 1425). Renson is the founding president of the International Society for the History of Physical Education and Sport (ISHPES). His publications include *The Games Reborn: The VIIth Olympiad, Antwerp 1920* (1996). He is also co-editor of *Annotated Bibliography of Traditional Play and Games in Africa* (1998).

Kari Fasting is a professor in the Department of Social Science in the Norwegian University of Sport and Physical Education in Oslo, Norway. She has written numerous scholarly articles, given many conference presentations and invited lectures, and taught as a visiting professor. Fasting is the former rector (vice-chancellor) of her university and has served as vice-president of Womensport International and as president of the International Sociology of Sport Association and the Norwegian Society for Research in Sport.

Kevin B. Wamsley is director of the International Centre for Olympic Studies and associate professor in the School of Kinesiology at the University of Western Ontario in London, Ontario, Canada. Co-editor of *Olympika: The International Journal of Olympic Studies,* he is the editor of *Method and Methodology in Sport and Cultural History* (1995) and co-editor of *Global and Cultural Critique: Problematizing the Olympic Games* (1998) and *Bridging Three Centuries: Intellectual Crossroads and the Modern Olympic Movement* (2000).

Richard Gruneau received a Ph.D. in sociology from the University of Massachusetts and is currently professor of communication at Simon Fraser

University in Burnaby, British Columbia, Canada, where he teaches in the areas of media and popular culture, cultural studies, and the political economy of communication. He has authored or co-authored three books, including *Class, Sports and Social Development* (1983) and *Hockey Night in Canada: Sport, Identities and Cultural Politics* (1993), and edited or co-edited four volumes, including *Canadian Sport: Sociological Perspectives* (1976) and *Sport, Culture and the Modern State* (1982).

Stephen R. Wenn is associate professor of kinesiology and physical education at Wilfrid Laurier University, Waterloo, Ontario, Canada. He is the author of numerous articles on the Olympic Movement and television and co-author of *Selling the Five Rings: The International Olympic Committee and the Rise of Olympic Commercialism* (2002).

Mark Dyreson, recipient of a Ph.D. in American cultural history, is assistant professor of kinesiology and affiliate assistant professor of history at Pennsylvania State University, University Park. He has written widely on the subject of sport and American culture and is the author of *Making the American Team: Sport, Culture and the Olympic Experience* (1998).

Jeffrey O. Segrave is varsity women's tennis coach as well as professor and chair of the Department of Exercise Science, Dance and Athletics at Skidmore College in Saratoga Springs, New York. He has published extensively on a wide variety of sport and physical education topics and has co-edited *Olympism* (1981), *Sport and Higher Education* (1985), and *The Olympic Games in Transition* (1988).

Robert K. Barney, professor emeritus in the School of Kinesiology at the University of Western Ontario, London, Ontario, Canada, is the founding director of the International Centre for Olympic Studies and the founding editor of *Olympika: The International Journal of Olympic Studies*. Former president of the North American Society for Sport History, he is co-editor of five volumes and co-author of *Selling the Five Rings: The International Olympic Committee and the Rise of Olympic Commercialism* (2002).

Gudrun Doll-Tepper is a professor in the Department of Sport Science of the Humboldt-Universität zu Berlin, Berlin, Germany. In recognition of more than 250 articles, books, and films in the area of disabled sport, she has received numerous honors, including election as president of the International Council of Sport Science and Physical Education and the International Federation of Adapted Physical Activity, chairperson of the International Paralympic Committee Sport Science Committee, and recipient of the Distinguished Service Cross of the Federal Republic of Germany. In Salt Lake City in 2002 she was named to the prestigious Paralympic Order, the highest honor accorded by the International Paralympic Committee.

Lex Hemphill is a former sports reporter and editorial and feature article writer for the *Salt Lake Tribune*. Prior to Salt Lake 2002 he wrote numerous articles on the history of the Winter Games.

Larry R. Gerlach is a professor of history and faculty athletics representative at the University of Utah. He has written extensively on early American history as well as American sport history.

INDEX

321